T0305703

Legal and Economic Principles of World Trade Law

The World Trade Organization (WTO) Agreement covers the vast majority of international commerce in goods and services. The Agreement covers not only measures that directly affect trade, such as import tariffs and import quotas, but potentially almost any type of internal measure with an impact on trade. Thus WTO legal texts are by necessity expressed in vague terms, and in need of continuous interpretation.

The overarching aim of the project *Legal and Economic Principles of World Trade Law*, led by the American Law Institute, is to contribute to the analysis of WTO law in not only law but also economics. This volume reports work done thus far to identify improvements to the interpretation of the Agreement. It starts with two background studies, the first of which summarizes the study *The Genesis of the GATT*, published by Cambridge University Press in 2008, which highlights the negotiating history of what became the GATT 1947–1948; the second study, coauthored by Gene M. Grossman and Henrik Horn, is an introduction to the economics of trade agreements. These are followed by two main studies. The first, authored by Kyle Bagwell, Robert W. Staiger, and Alan O. Sykes, discusses legal and economic aspects of the GATT regulation of border policy instruments, such as import tariffs and import quotas. The second, written by Gene M. Grossman, Henrik Horn, and Petros C. Mavroidis, focuses on the core provision for the regulation of domestic policy instruments – the National Treatment principles in Art. III GATT.

The American Law Institute is the leading independent organization in the United States producing scholarly work to clarify, modernize, and otherwise improve the law. The Institute (made up of 4,000 lawyers, judges, and law professors of the highest qualifications) drafts, discusses, revises, and publishes Restatements of the Law, model statutes, and principles of law that are enormously influential in the courts and legislatures, as well as in legal scholarship and education.

Legal and Economic Principles of World Trade Law

Edited by

Henrik Horn
Research Institute of Industrial Economics, Stockholm

Petros C. Mavroidis
European University Institute

THE AMERICAN LAW INSTITUTE

CAMBRIDGE
UNIVERSITY PRESS

CAMBRIDGE
UNIVERSITY PRESS

University Printing House, Cambridge CB2 8BS, United Kingdom

One Liberty Plaza, 20th Floor, New York, NY 10006, USA

477 Williamstown Road, Port Melbourne, VIC 3207, Australia

314-321, 3rd Floor, Plot 3, Splendor Forum, Jasola District Centre, New Delhi - 110025, India

103 Penang Road, #05-06/07, Visioncrest Commercial, Singapore 238467

Cambridge University Press is part of the University of Cambridge.

It furthers the University's mission by disseminating knowledge in the pursuit of
education, learning and research at the highest international levels of excellence.

www.cambridge.org
Information on this title: www.cambridge.org/9781107038615

First published 2013
First paperback edition 2014

A catalogue record for this publication is available from the British Library

Library of Congress Cataloging in Publication data
Horn, Henrik.
Legal and economic principles of world trade law / Henrik Horn, Research Institute of Industrial
Economics, Stockholm; Petros C. Mavroidis, European University Institute.
    pages cm. – (American Law Institute Reporters' Studies on WTO law)
Includes bibliographical references and index.
ISBN 978-1-107-03861-5 (hardback)
1. Foreign trade regulation.   2. Foreign trade regulation – Economic aspects.   3. World Trade
Organization.   4. General Agreement on Tariffs and Trade (Organization).   I. Mavroidis,
Petros C.   II. Title.
K4600.H67   2013
382´.92–dc23   2012049274

ISBN 978-1-107-03861-5 Hardback
ISBN 978-1-107-45964-9 Paperback

Contents

Foreword

In 2001, the American Law Institute (ALI) began work on the law of world trade. The project was different from all prior Institute work in two ways. First, the goal was to have every aspect of the work accomplished by economists and lawyers working together. Second, the Chief Reporters, Professors Henrik Horn of Stockholm and Petros C. Mavroidis of Columbia University and lately the European University Institute, were both Europeans. Principles of trade law require both legal and economic analysis, and the subject could not be satisfactorily understood without input from many continents.

We did not accomplish the drafting of principles appropriate for ALI debate and then Council and Annual Meeting approval. For that, this area of law requires more development, more evolution through decisions by the Appellate Body of the World Trade Organization (WTO), and more academic agreement. But we have accomplished a great deal in two directions. First, we have authored and Cambridge University Press has published volumes analyzing the important WTO decisions of the past decade. In each instance, the papers were written by economist–lawyer teams and then subjected to rigorous discussion and criticism from experts. Most of the discussion meetings were held in the WTO building in Geneva, allowing participation from top WTO officials. Second, our distinguished scholars have now completed a major volume that contains analysis of the most important issues in the law of world trade and makes policy recommendations for improving current law. This volume begins with a short summary of the origins of trade law in the General Agreement on Tariffs and Trade. (The full story of the post–World War II history is in *The Genesis of the GATT*, a product of the ALI's work that was published by Cambridge University Press in 2008.) Next in the new volume comes the economics of trade agreements: what the GATT framers had in mind, how today's economists think about trade liberalization, and how "non-discrimination" should be framed and applied as a legal obligation. Finally, the book asks whether law as interpreted in decided cases makes sense. Does the world now need new treaty language, or can the existing agreements be interpreted in the dispute-resolution process to achieve economically desirable results? The authors propose a series of legal principles that would bring case-law interpretation back to what they believe were the original intentions of the legal pioneers who created the current structure. The tremendous accomplishments in this new book are the work of Professors Kyle Bagwell, Gene Grossman, Bob Staiger, and Alan Sykes, as well as the Chief Reporters, Professors Horn and Mavroidis. Professor Doug Irwin played a major role as a coauthor of the earlier *The Genesis of the GATT* volume.

In addition to the authors mentioned above, we have had essential input from a substantial number of other academics, practicing lawyers, WTO Appellate Body members, and WTO leaders. Of course, our major debt is to Henrik Horn and Petros Mavroidis, who have recruited colleagues, made sure deadlines were achieved, and throughout maintained the highest standard for economic and legal thinking and collaboration and for policy recommendations based on economic validity, understanding of international politics, and awareness of the challenges facing the WTO dispute-resolution process, a new institutional setting for peaceful application of what are often immensely difficult international disputes.

The ALI also thanks The Jan Wallander and Tom Hedelius Research Foundation in Stockholm, the Milton and Miriam Handler Foundation, and all who have participated in the many meetings necessary to advance the publications already published and soon to be published.

Lance Liebman
Director
The American Law Institute
January 15, 2013

Preface

The World Trade Organization (WTO) Agreement covers the vast majority of international commerce in goods and services, and also contains an agreement on the protection of intellectual property. The Agreement covers not only measures that directly affect trade, such as import tariffs and import quotas, but potentially almost any type of internal measure with an impact on trade.

The WTO legal texts are by necessity expressed in vague terms, and in need of continuous interpretation. To this end, the WTO contains a rarity in international relations, a compulsory third-party adjudication system. While there is an expressed preference for bilateral resolutions of trade conflicts, the system embodies the idea that trade conflicts that cannot be resolved bilaterally should be resolved through multilateral adjudication rather than through unilateral actions. This two-level system of legal adjudication – the Dispute Settlement (DS) system – plays a core role in the WTO by determining the practical ambit of the legal obligations in the various agreements comprising the WTO Agreement.

The WTO Agreement, and its interpretation by WTO adjudicating bodies, is subject to intensive policy debate, conducted largely by politicians and non-governmental organizations. There is also an ongoing debate among mainly trade-law practitioners and legal scholars, concerning the appropriate interpretation of the law.

The overarching aim of the project *Legal and Economic Principles of World Trade Law* is to contribute to the analysis of WTO law. The distinguishing feature of the project is the aim to base the analysis not only in Law but also in Economics. Such an interdisciplinary approach is, in our view, necessitated by the fact that the WTO Agreement has inherently economic objectives. For instance, its Preamble states that the objectives of the Agreement are to contribute in:

> ...raising standards of living, ensuring full employment and a large and steadily growing volume of real income and effective demand, and expanding the production of and trade in goods and services, while allowing

for the optimal use of the world's resources in accordance with the objective of sustainable development, seeking both to protect and preserve the
environment and to enhance the means for doing so in a manner consistent with their respective needs and concerns at different levels of economic
development. . . .

A fundamental methodological problem facing a joint economic and legal
analysis of the WTO contract is that there is yet no field "The Economics of Trade
Law" that could be leaned against for such analysis. Instead, the relevant specialized fields, such as International Trade Law and International Economics, differ
widely, in terms of both aims and methods. Lawyers and economists are also typically too specialized in their respective fields to be able to undertake legal-*cum*-
economic analyses of the law alone. It is therefore necessary that an analysis of
the agreement is conducted jointly by economists and lawyers.

The project *Legal and Economic Principles of World Trade Law* proceeds
along two complementary paths. The first part analyzes regularly the emerging case law from the adjudicating bodies of the WTO. Each dispute is evaluated
jointly by an economist and a lawyer. To date, almost 70 reports have been written, covering all disputes that came to an end during the years 2001–2011. The
disputes have concerned all three major WTO agreements – the GATT and the
other Annexes forming the multilateral regulation of trade in goods, the services
agreement, the General Agreement on Trade in Services, as well as the Agreement on Trade-Related Aspects of Intellectual Property Rights. But reflecting the
use of the Dispute Settlement system, most analyzed cases have involved trade
in goods.

The second part of the project aims to identify improvements to the interpretation of the agreement. This volume reports work done thus far in this
leg of the project. It starts with two background studies. The first briefly summarizes the study *The Genesis of the GATT*, which highlights the negotiating
history of what became the GATT 1947–1948. This study was undertaken by
Douglas A. Irwin (Dartmouth College), Petros C. Mavroidis, and Alan O. Sykes,
and has been published by Cambridge University Press. The study argues that
the GATT was essentially an agreement about border barriers to trade, where the
two superpowers at the time (the UK and the United States) aimed at constraining each other's behavior. But in order to prevent members from circumventing
the commitments on border instruments by use of domestic policy measures,
two lines of defense were put in place: first, whatever policy was (unilaterally)
devised at home would be applied in even-handed manner (nondiscriminatory)
to domestic and imported goods – the National Treatment principle; second, if
concessions were eroded even though nondiscrimination had been observed,
trading nations could always invoke the so-called non-violation complaints, an

instrument meant to provide the ultimate defense for those whose expectations have been defied.

The second preparatory study – *Why the WTO? An Introduction to the Economics of Trade Agreements*, authored by Gene M. Grossman and Henrik Horn – lays out the perceptions by which most economists approach trade agreements, to readers with little or no training in economics. It follows most of the economic literature by viewing trade agreements as means for countries to address the negative international externalities that would result if governments were to set their trade policies unilaterally and without regard to their effects on actors in other countries. The study discusses economic aspects of a number of general features of trade agreements, such as their reciprocal nature, the need for agreements to be self-enforcing, the inevitable contractual incompleteness of trade agreements, and the fact that trade agreements are manifestly textual documents.

The volume contains two main studies. The first, *Legal and Economic Principles of World Trade Law: Border Instruments*, authored by Kyle Bagwell, Robert W. Staiger, and Alan O. Sykes, discusses legal and economic aspects of the GATT regulation of border policy instruments, such as import tariffs and import quotas. The goals of the study are both positive and normative. From a positive perspective, it draws on the economic theory of international trade and relevant aspects of economic history to explain the legal treatment of border instruments in the WTO/GATT system as it has evolved over time. From a normative perspective, the study builds on an economic understanding of the function of the various legal disciplines to critique elements of the treaty text and the case law. The study focuses on the core provisions regulating border instruments, such as tariff bindings, quantitative restrictions, and the "most-favored-nation" (MFN) obligation.

The final study, *Legal and Economic Principles of World Trade Law: National Treatment*, written by Gene M. Grossman, Henrik Horn, and Petros C. Mavroidis, focuses on the core provision for the regulation of domestic policy instruments – the National Treatment principles in Art. III GATT. The study first examines the negotiating record relevant to the rationale for the enactment of the National Treatment provision, the manner in which case law has understood it, and the economic rationale for the provision. The study also discusses the manner in which the provision has been implemented in case law. In light of the dissatisfaction with the case-law interpretations of some key terms, the study presents two possible interpretations of the National Treatment provision, one of which is argued to be preferable.

Finally, we would like to sincerely thank the ALI and its Director, Lance Liebman, for the support the project has received over the years, *sine qua non* the project would not have existed. We also want to express our sincere gratitude to The Jan Wallander and Tom Hedelius Research Foundation in Stockholm, and the Milton and Miriam Handler Foundation in New York, for financial support.

Henrik Horn
Petros C. Mavroidis

1 The Genesis of the GATT Summary

Our study on the negotiating record of the GATT[1] was meant to shed some light on the objectives that the framers of the GATT pursued through the establishment of the first genuine multilateral trade order in the 1940s: the quintessential element of the GATT was a tariff bargain supported by commitments on domestic instruments aimed at ensuring the value of tariff concessions entered by the negotiating partners. The whole enterprise was largely a trans-Atlantic negotiation between the UK (United Kingdom) and the U.S. (United States), where the former was requesting widespread MFN (most-favored nation) tariff cuts, and the latter, in return, the abolition of the UK imperial preferences.

1.1 The Years Before the Negotiation

The setup was a negotiation among like-minded countries (with very few exceptions), a ploy that was purposefully privileged in order to reduce negotiating costs: the idea was of course to extend the outcome to all nations, but it is of course one thing to negotiate a legal instrument of this scope, and a different thing to accede to it. The GATT was negotiated in three short (compared to today's trade negotiations) terms between 1946 and 1947, but the events that led to the negotiation predate this phase.

The outbreak of World War I in 1914 interrupted what had been a period of growing worldwide economic prosperity with moderate tariffs and expanding world trade supported by a well-functioning international monetary system (the gold standard). After the shock of World War I, the international trade and payments system recovered very slowly during the 1920s. Most countries only gradually phased out wartime controls on trade, while tariff levels remained higher than before the war. The UK did not return to the gold standard until 1925, and other countries waited even longer before restoring the convertibility of their

---

[1] Douglas A. Irwin, Petros C. Mavroidis, Alan O. Sykes, *The Genesis of the GATT*, Cambridge University Press: New York City, 2008.

currencies. Under the auspices of the League of Nations, the World Economic Conference of 1927 aimed to restore the world economy to its previous state of vigor. But the Conference started only an international discussion of matters such as tariff levels, MFN clauses, customs valuation, and the like.

The gradual restoration of the world economy was interrupted by a worldwide recession starting in 1929. This economic downturn was met by greater protectionism, which in turn further reduced world trade. Although monetary and financial factors were primarily responsible for allowing the recession to turn into the Great Depression of the early 1930s, the spread of trade restrictions aggravated the problem. The commercial policies of the 1930s became characterized as "beggar-thy-neighbor" policies because many countries sought to insulate their own economy from the economic downturn by raising trade barriers. Blocking imports proved to be a futile method of increasing domestic employment because one country's imports were another country's exports. The combined effect of this inward turn of policy was a collapse of international trade and a deepening of the slump in the world economy.

The U.S. bore some responsibility for this turn of events. What started out in 1929 as a legislative attempt to protect farmers from falling agricultural prices led to the enactment of higher import duties across the board in 1930. The Hawley-Smoot tariff of that year pushed already high protective tariffs much higher and triggered a similar response by other countries. According to the League of Nations (1933, 193),

> ...the Hawley-Smoot tariff in the United States was the signal for an outburst of tariff-making activity in other countries, partly at least by way of reprisals.

Canada, Spain, Italy, and Switzerland took direct retaliatory trade actions against the U.S., while other countries also adopted higher tariffs in an attempt to insulate themselves from the spreading economic decline. The UK made a sharp break from its traditional free-trade policies by imposing emergency tariffs in 1931 and enacting a more general Import Duties bill in 1932. France and other countries that remained on the gold standard long after others had abandoned it for more reflationary policies imposed import quotas and exchange restrictions in an attempt to safeguard their balance of payments and stimulate domestic economic activity.

Many countries also turned to discriminatory trade arrangements in the early 1930s, for both economic and political reasons. At a conference in Ottawa in 1932, the UK and its dominions (principally Australia, Canada, New Zealand, and South Africa) agreed to give preferential tariff treatment for one another's goods. This scheme of imperial preferences involved both higher duties on non-British Empire goods and lower duties on Dominion goods and drew the ire of excluded countries for discriminating against their trade. Meanwhile, under the guidance of Reichsbank President Hjalmar Schacht, Nazi Germany concluded a series of bilateral clearing arrangements with central European countries that effectively created a new trade bloc, orienting the trade of these countries toward Germany at the expense of others. In Asia, Japan created the Greater East Asia Co-Prosperity sphere to extend its political and economic influence throughout the region and siphon off trade for its own benefit.

The outcome of these protectionist and discriminatory trade policies was not just a contraction of world trade, but a severe breakdown in the multilateral trade and payments system that the world economy had previously enjoyed prior to World War I and had started to revive in the late 1920s. Official conferences and multilateral meetings, notably the World Economic Conference in 1933, offered pronouncements to resist protectionism, but failed to stem the spread of inward-looking anti-trade economic policies. The economic distress of the decade also had political consequences, undermining faith in democratic governments to manage their economies and hence abetting a turn to more authoritarian regimes in Germany and Italy.

1.2 The Negotiation

Following bilateral consultations between the UK and the U.S. that led to the drafting of the Suggested Charter (a document prepared by the U.S. delegation that reflected the bilateral negotiations with the UK), negotiations on the GATT were convened the last three months of 1946 and the first half of 1947 in three different places: London, Lake Success (New York), and Geneva. When the gavel went down in Geneva, a train consisting of hundreds of tariff concessions supported by commitments not to discriminate when recourse to domestic instruments was being made had left the station of protectionism.

The GATT was originally planned to be an agreement coming under the aegis of the ITO (International Trade Organization). Later on, when the ITO negotiation became increasingly difficult, it was decided that the GATT should enter into force only to be eventually superseded by the ITO, when the negotiation of the latter would eventually be completed. The ITO never saw the light of day; the GATT came into life with birth defects (since many of the terms, for example, were supposed to be further negotiated within the ITO) and lived on for close to 50 years: it became a *de facto* institution in order to fill the void left by the non-advent of the ITO. Contrary to the ambitious ITO project, the GATT is limited to regulating state behavior only, without touching upon trade impediments that are attributed to private behavior.

By accepting the GATT, trading nations signed up to a trade-liberalization model, whereby they accepted that they could, in principle, protect their domestic producer through tariffs only: QR are illegal, and domestic instruments should not operate so as to afford protection. Trading nations further accepted that tariffs would be negotiated down in successive rounds of trade liberalization and that, in principle again, all tariff advantages would be extended to all their trading partners that have signed up to the GATT. Nevertheless, the ambit of nondiscrimination was tempered essentially, by accepting that imperial (and other, following the insistence of Chile to this effect) preferences would remain in place, at least during a transitional phase. This bargain is very much the outcome of the negotiation between the two transatlantic partners, the UK and the U.S. An implicit *quid pro quo* between them was the reduction of imperial preferences for an extension of MFN.

Nondiscrimination was further tempered by accepting an explicit provision on preferential trade agreements which opened the door to dozens of similar arrangements that proliferated slowly in the first post-World War II years, and at a much faster pace later on.

The basic bargain of the GATT was, as briefly mentioned supra, the tariff bargain, whereby trading nations promised each other reductions of their pre-GATT levels that they would consolidate and apply on an MFN-basis. The GATT, however, could not have contained just a provision on tariff consolidation and the MFN. For one thing, negotiating history reveals that negotiators were quite aware of (at least some of) the equivalence propositions: an import tariff can be decomposed to a domestic tax on consumption and a domestic-production subsidy that would produce comparable effects to that of the import tariff. This is why negotiators felt that a provision disciplining domestic instruments was a necessary addition that would operate as an anti-circumvention provision that would insure trading nations who had to "pay" through their own tariff concessions, for the tariff concessions obtained by their trading partners against the risk of seeing the value of concessions obtained, diluted through recourse to domestic instruments. A similar function explains of provisions such as the disciplining of state trading, and the introduction of NVCs (non-violation complaints) in the GATT text.

The GATT text, nevertheless, contains many provisions additional to those necessary to ensure that the tariff bargain would not be undermined: antidumping, balance of payments, safeguards, institutional provisions, etc. In our view, at least the following important explanatory variables have determined what should be added in the GATT next to the basic tariff-bargain:

(a) the influence that the failure to conclude the ITO has had on the negotiation of the GATT;
(b) the leading nation at the time (U.S.) was unwilling to undo some key trade-related legislation of its own;
(c) the different perceptions of the UK and the U.S. delegations on the role of the state in the handling of international trade relations;

(d) the emergence of some developing countries that became serious negoti-
    ating partners over the years.

Some remarkable people participated in the negotiation of the GATT from James
Meade and Lionel Robbins (UK), to Cordell Hull and Will Clayton (U.S.) to
Alexandre Kojève (France). The post-World War II era was indeed a time for
statesmanship, as the participation of the leading economist of that era, John
Maynard Keynes, in the Bretton Woods negotiation (that led to the advent of the
World Bank and the International Monetary Fund) shows.

Finally, it bears mentioning (especially because of the law-and-economics
nature of our project) that the drafting of the GATT was entrusted to a U.S. delegate trained in economics, John Leddy.

1.3 Property Rights of the GATT

The U.S. government entered the negotiations with considerable contractual experience, since it had negotiated similar trade deals before. The experience of the UK government in international trade issues was quite substantial
as well. It was, thus, quite natural that the two transatlantic partners dominated
the negotiations on the GATT/ITO, as they had also dominated the negotiations
during the Bretton Woods conference a few years before. From a negotiating perspective, however, the UK was an ailing empire, while the U.S. emerged from
World War II as the undisputed hegemonic power. The GATT would not have
come into existence without the leadership of the UK and the U.S. However,
there were many junctures in which the U.S. and the UK could have destroyed
the plans for a multilateral commercial agreement.

In addition, other countries played an important role in shaping the GATT. It
is interesting to note that, despite its overwhelming economic strength in comparison to other countries, the U.S. could not dominate or dictate the outcome
to other countries. Rather, the U.S. often accommodated the demands for exceptions or weaker language at various points in the negotiations to ensure the continued participation of other countries. This is probably the influence of Cordell
Hull, who wanted a trade deal and believed that it was the duty of the U.S. as
a leader to enforce the deal, even if it meant concessions on its behalf. Chile
requested and obtained the extension of exceptions to MFN. A host of developing
countries should be credited with the inclusion of provisions on infant-industry
protection, and so on.

The input of the other (than the UK and the U.S.) players should not be
overestimated: the bulk of the negotiation was entrusted to the two transatlantic partners; UK and U.S. delegates participated in all committees, groups, etc.
established. As we unveil the negotiating history of the GATT, it becomes apparent that this observation holds true throughout all stages of the negotiations.

Although participation in the various committees is no perfect proxy to measure the influence that participating delegations have had on the final text, few would argue with the point that participation is a necessary (albeit, not sufficient) condition for influencing the eventual outcome. It bears repetition that UK and U.S. delegates are the only national delegates that participated in all committees, groups, etc. Their point of view on each and every provision that made it to the final GATT text has been consistently discussed (and often, retained). With one exception, they were simultaneously present in all committees during the London Conference, where the "heart and soul" of the GATT was constructed.

The transatlantic partners should be credited not only with the basic architecture of the GATT, but also with the shaping of technical provisions aimed to support the whole edifice. A good illustration is offered by the provisions regarding customs valuation, fees, and formalities. It is the UK and U.S. administrations that possessed the more sophisticated customs administration that were routinely dealing with thousands of customs-clearing transactions: it is, consequently, only natural that it is the UK and U.S. delegates that shaped Arts. II, V, VII, and VIII of the GATT.

A comparison, of the provisions retained, points to the same conclusion: most provisions agreed to in the London Conference are directly inspired from the corresponding provisions in the Suggested Charter, which had been negotiated only between the UK and the U.S. And the London text was only partially and marginally modified in the subsequent Lake Success and Geneva negotiations.

There is more evidence pointing to this conclusion: Johnson (1968) explains that the principal-supplier rule, followed in the original negotiation, effectively barred developing countries from effective participation, since no developing country was a principal supplier in any commodity. MFN somewhat diminished the effects of nonparticipation in the tariff negotiation, but is not a perfect substitute. In his words (p. 368):

> ... the real trouble with the GATT is not the institution of bargaining for tariff reductions, but the techniques for bargaining. ...

The negotiating rules changed only in the fourth round (Geneva), as reported in Kock (1969). Wilkinson and Scott (2008, 484ff.) point out that many developing countries were more active during the ITO negotiations, since they thought that the GATT would effectively come under the aegis of the ITO. Scarcity of negotiating resources among them meant the need to prioritize their efforts, and in their view, the ITO was priority. The failure of the ITO means, ipso facto, that their negotiating efforts were in vain. It also meant that their influence on the drafting of the GATT remained marginal.

Finally, one should not turn a blind eye to the "nucleus" approach advocated by Canada and accepted by all participants: the GATT was designed to become the vehicle for trade liberalization around the world; in Canada's view neverthe-less, the negotiation would suffer had it been open from day one to all trading nations. Rather, the whole endeavor would be greatly facilitated if the negotia-tion were to take place across like-minded countries. This is what largely hap-pened. The USSR (Union of Soviet Socialist Republics) was invited but declined the invitation; it is the nationalist China that participated in the negotiation, and Czechoslovakia entered the negotiation as a Western country (finished it as "socialist," but did not abandon the GATT). The only concession to the "nucleus" approach was the acceptance of developing countries in the negotiation. But at that point in time (1946), Australia would qualify as a developing country, as would many European countries devastated by World War II.

1.4 What Did The GATT Framers Have in Mind?

Economic theory has advanced two theories to rationalize why trade agree-ments occur: the commitment theory, and the terms-of-trade theory. The for-mer focuses on the relationship between government and its private sector: a government will choose its trade policy and will commit it in an international agreement signed to this effect; the private sector will act accordingly. The gain for the government is that investment decisions are forestalled; it will lose, how-ever, contributions by the various lobbies. The latter differs in that it traces the rationale for trade agreements not in domestic distortions but in international externalities (and in the manner in which they "travel"). The study of the negoti-ating record does not make a conclusive case for either. Indeed, this is one of the reasons why we decided to undertake a separate study on the economic ratio-nales for the GATT.

It definitely, though, rejects the commitment theory: as mentioned, domes-tic instruments are not disciplined by the GATT other than GATT through the principle of nondiscrimination. The GATT is a negative integration-contract, where domestic policies will be defined unilaterally and must only respect the obligation not to discriminate across domestic and foreign goods participating in the same product market.

Some elements of the GATT, like the principal-supplier rule, lend some sup-port to proponents of the terms-of-trade theory. At the same time, the extension of MFN to all (and future) participants underscores the idea that Cordell Hull's initial aspiration to conceive the establishment of a world-trade order as a con-tribution to world peace ultimately carried the day.

REFERENCES

Johnson, Harry G. 1968. "U.S. Economic Policy toward the Developing Countries." *Eco-nomic Development and Cultural Change* 16: 357–384.

Kock, Karin. 1969. *International Trade Policy and the GATT 1947–1967.* Stockholm: Almqvist & Wiksell.

League of Nations. 1933. *World Economic Survey.* Geneva: League of Nations.

Wilkinson, Rorden, and James Scott. 2008. "Developing Country Participation in the GATT: A reassessment." *World Trade Review* 7: 473–510.

2 Why the WTO? An Introduction to the Economics of Trade Agreements

2.1 Introduction

This study is part of The American Law Institute (ALI) project *Legal and Economic Principles of World Trade Law*. The project aims to analyze the central instrument in the *World Trade Organization* (WTO) Agreement for the regulation of trade in goods – *The General Agreement on Tariffs and Trade* (GATT). The present study is one of two background studies for this project.[1] The first study, *The Genesis of the GATT*, appraises the rationale for the creation of the GATT, and tracks its development from a historical and legal perspective. This second study provides an overview of the economics of trade agreements.

A distinguishing feature of this ALI project is the desire to base the analysis of the GATT firmly in both economics and law. The necessity of legal analysis needs no justification. But why also base the study in economics? Art. 31.1 of the *Vienna Convention of the Laws of Treaties* states that an international agreement should be interpreted "in the light of its object and purpose." There are fundamental reasons why the interpretation of the GATT therefore cannot be adequately addressed without economic analysis. First, we will discuss below the possible purposes of the agreement in much greater detail, but for now let us just quote the Preamble to the GATT, to show that the *objectives* of the GATT are expressed in inherently economic terms:

> ...Recognizing that their relations in the field of trade and economic endeavour should be conducted with a view to raising standards of living, ensuring full employment and a large and steadily growing volume of real income and effective demand, developing the full use of the resources of the world and expanding the production and exchange of goods,...

---

[1] There is a second leg to the ALI project, in which economists and lawyers jointly analyze the emerging case law from the WTO dispute-settlement mechanism.

This study builds on joint work, and many discussions, with Kyle Bagwell and Robert W. Staiger. We have also greatly benefited from many exchanges with Wilfred J. Ethier and Donald Regan. Don also provided very helpful comments on an earlier draft, as did Evan Wallach.

Furthermore, these objectives are linked to the policies that the GATT regulates through the *operation of markets*. It is clearly necessary to understand these mechanisms in order to appropriately interpret the agreement, and this in turn requires economic analysis. Hence, an appreciation of both the objectives of the GATT and the mechanisms by which its stipulations further those objectives requires that the analysis is based in economics. An analysis of the GATT that relied solely on a traditional legal perspective would be inadequate.

The need for a joint economic and legal analysis of the GATT implies that the analysis must be undertaken jointly by economists and lawyers. Such collaboration requires an understanding among economists of the law and of legal analysis, and a corresponding understanding among lawyers of fundamental economic concepts and reasoning. The purpose of this second background study is to lay out to readers with little or no training in economics (but with sufficient patience and intellectual curiosity), the perspective that most trade economists bring to the study of trade agreements, in general, and the GATT in particular. The aim is not to provide a comprehensive survey of the literature on trade agreements, nor to evaluate the relative importance of the contributions to the literature, but rather to sketch some of the basic underlying principles.[2] To this end, the study focuses on the main analytical approach to the study of trade agreements, largely putting other approaches aside, irrespective of their intellectual merits.

To illustrate the importance of understanding the purpose of the agreement when interpreting it, consider the role of a safeguard provision that allows a country to temporarily exceed its tariff binding for an industry, provided that the industry has suffered "serious injury" as a consequence of increased imports. How should the word "serious" be interpreted in this context? The answer depends on what the GATT Member governments are trying to achieve. If, with the creation of the GATT, governments hoped to achieve more liberal trade but needed assurances that they could "escape" from negotiated commitments if unanticipated events later occurred, then economic arguments would suggest caution in interpreting the serious-injury standard too stringently, lest governments, fearing the "straightjacket" that GATT commitments might then imply, would be hesitant to accept tariff commitments in the first place. If, instead, governments hoped to "tie their hands" with GATT commitments, so that when later faced with protectionist pressures they could resist offering palliatives, then a "straightjacket" would be exactly what the governments would have hoped

---

[2] Surveys of various strands of the literature can be found in, e.g., Bagwell and Staiger (2002), Ethier (2011), Hoekman and Kostecki (2009), Magee (1994), Nelson (1988), Schropp (2009), Rodrik (1995), Staiger (1995), and WTO (2008).

to achieve with their GATT commitments. In this case, economic arguments would counsel caution in interpreting the serious-injury standard too permissively. Consequently, we are led to very different conclusions depending on the assumed role of the agreement.

Finally, even if one accepts the importance of being clear about the purposes of the GATT, one might question the need for deep analysis of this matter. Is it not obvious that the purpose of the GATT simply is to facilitate maximal exploitation of the gains from international trade in their various forms? While it is certainly true that governments often are willing to liberalize trade in order to reap the benefits from international exchange, the matter must be more subtle than this. If governments cared only about reaping the efficiency gains from trade, there would be little need for an international agreement. Instead, the governments could practice unilateral free trade and otherwise let goods flow where they may. The fact that governments actively pursue a myriad of policies that alter the incentives to trade already suggests that their goals are more nuanced. The very complexity of the GATT suggests that multiple objectives are at play and that governments' motives are not obvious. This observation is compounded by the apparent incongruity between standard economic arguments in favor of completely free trade and the manner in which governments approach their negotiations under the umbrella of the GATT. Evidently, clarifying the underlying purpose(s) of the GATT and articulating a reason for the GATT to exist is not as simple a task as it might first appear. In what follows, we will present and critically discuss the standard approach in economics to explaining the rationale for agreements such as the GATT.

The structure of this study is as follows. Section 2.2 introduces several economic concepts that will be essential for the analysis to come. It starts by discussing the notion of an "externality." Most economists believe that trade agreements are made to address the negative international externalities that would result if governments were to set their trade policies unilaterally and without regard to their effects on actors in other countries. We then provide an introduction to the conceptually difficult idea of a "government objective function." Finally, we present the basic game-theoretic concept, that economists and others use to predict the outcomes of strategic interaction in the absence of a cooperative agreement – the "Nash equilibrium."

In Section 2.3, we introduce a stylized model of a trade agreement that is generally enough to encompass the majority of models in the literature as special cases. This Section also discusses a number of general features of trade agreements, such as their reciprocal nature, the importance of the fact that they are negotiated settlements, the need for agreements to be self-enforcing, the inevitable contractual incompleteness of trade agreements, and the fact that trade agreements are manifestly textual documents.

The generality of the model in Section 2.3 helps us to distill the commonality of a large part of the literature on trade agreements. But it has the consequence of depriving the model of more specific predictions with regard to many aspects of interest. In particular, there is very little of economic structure imposed on the model, so the model does not illuminate the exact economic reasons for the existence of trade agreements. Section 2.4 goes to the opposite extreme, and imposes several strong assumptions about market structure and government motives on the general model. This particular model, which we shall term the "national market power model," has been well developed in the economics literature, and rightfully it has been very influential in shaping the way that many economists think about trade agreements. But some observers remain dubious about the empirical plausibility of some underlying assumptions of the national market power model and so question whether it can provide a meaningful explanation for the GATT. Section 2.4 discusses their critique, and also broadly assesses the extent to which the model helps to explain core features of the GATT.

Section 2.5 lays out the so-called "commitment approach" to explaining the role of trade agreements. It sees trade agreements as means for governments to tie their own hands vis-à-vis their domestic interest groups. This commitment approach is often portrayed as the leading alternative to the international externalities approach. As we will explain, however, we believe that the two approaches are better seen as complementary.

Section 2.6 concludes.

2.2 Building Blocks for a Theory of Trade Agreements

In order to lay the groundwork for the analysis of trade agreements that follows, this Section will discuss several fundamental concepts that feature prominently in any economic analysis of trade-policy formation. In Section 2.2.1 we focus on the economic interdependence between countries in a global world economy. Most explanations for why countries enter into trade agreements cite the economic interdependence between national economies as an important motivating consideration. When national economies are mutually interdependent, governments' decisions about trade and other policies will have repercussions outside their national borders, and these repercussions may be downplayed or ignored if the governments act noncooperatively. Interdependencies exist whenever private actions and public policies in one country affect economic (and other) outcomes elsewhere. Such spillover effects are pervasive in today's world economy, and increasingly so with the globalization of so many areas of economic interaction.

Government decisions, and the scope for beneficial trade agreements, do depend not only on the way in which policy choices affect economic variables at home and abroad, but also on how the governments *evaluate* these effects.

Section 2.2.2 will discuss the treatment of government objectives and motives in models of trade agreements.

Finally, having described how decisionmakers' policy choices are mutually interrelated, and how their respective decision problems can be mathematically represented as optimizations of well-specified objective functions with certain properties, it is natural to ask what will be the outcome of these governmental interactions. This is not a trivial issue, because each decisionmaker's optimal choice of policy depends on the choices of the other decisionmakers. Section 2.2.4 introduces the concept of a Nash Equilibrium, which game theorists use to forecast the outcome of strategic interactions such as those that interdependent governments face when setting their economic policies.

2.2.1 Economic Interdependence and International Externalities

In earlier times, national economies (and even local economies) were geographically isolated. The difficulty of moving people, goods, and information meant that there was little migration from one region to another, little trade of goods, services, and capital, and little exchange of information and ideas. But with the falling costs of transportation and communication came an expanding web of economic relations. Goods farmed or manufactured in one location increasingly were shipped for consumption far from their place of production. People relocated from their nation of birth to pursue economic opportunities on distant continents. International lending provided additional sources of funding for investment beyond what could be financed with local savings. Ideas flowed from their place of creation via communication and imitation. These processes of globalization have been ongoing for centuries, and continue today. And, most recently, improved information technologies have made possible the remote delivery of services that formerly required face-to-face contact.

When residents of different countries exchange goods, services, capital, information, and ideas, the outcomes in any location are determined in part by conditions and actions elsewhere. Planting decisions in New Zealand affect the price of food in Australia. A savings glut in Japan encourages new investment in Thailand. An invention in Spain finds uses in Argentina. French films are enjoyed by moviegoers in Canada. Indian call centers respond to queries from American customers, while perhaps displacing U.S. workers from their similar jobs.

The increasing integration of national economies does not as such suffice to explain the development of multilateral trade agreements, such as the GATT and the WTO, because these agreements constrain the actions of politicians and bureaucrats, not those of actors in the private sector. Do government policies have spillover effects that might warrant some strictures in the name of international cooperation? Surely they do. Policies that restrict imports or promote exports most obviously have implications for incomes and prices abroad. Domestic policies also affect foreign citizens in a world of economic interdependence. A farm subsidy or tax on gasoline or a regional development loan will alter the allocation of resources domestically and so generate spillover effects abroad. The spillover effects of all sorts of national laws, regulations, and bureaucratic procedures provide the most plausible explanation for international agreements, including trade agreements.

At this point, we need to introduce a few fundamental economic concepts. First, economists use measures of "efficiency" in policy analysis to gauge which changes in policy are beneficial or harmful to society. There are alternative notions of economic efficiency that differ according to whether they contemplate the possibility of compensation in combination with the policy change, or whether the policy effects are considered all on their own. The Pareto criterion considers as unambiguously beneficial only those policy changes that make some individuals better off without harming any others, when the policy change is taken in isolation from any forms of compensation. Needless to say, this is a very strict criterion for efficiency gain inasmuch as most policy choices create winners and losers. A more forgiving measure of efficiency is that proposed by Kaldor and Hicks. According to the Kaldor–Hicks criterion, a policy change is considered efficiency enhancing if the winners gain more than the losers give up, in the sense that it would be possible to transfer resources ex post from the direct winners to the direct losers in such a way that no one is left worse off than before the policy change. The Kaldor–Hicks criterion is more common in policy analysis because it corresponds to the intuitive idea that policy change is (potentially) good for society if it "expands the size of the economic pie."

Second, economists use the term "externalities" to refer to the consequences of actions taken within a relationship for those on the outside. The consequences can be beneficial or harmful, giving rise to externalities that are "positive" or "negative," depending on whether they benefit the third parties or not. Externalities pose a problem for economic efficiency; whereas the parties to a relationship have means to influence actions that affect their interests (by, for example, offering or withholding payments or other counteractions), the interests of those outside a relationship can easily be overlooked in the course of decisionmaking.[3] Where government policies are concerned, the relationship at stake is between the politicians who set the policies (and the bureaucrats who implement them) on the one hand, and their domestic constituencies such as voters and interest groups on the other. Foreign citizens are external to these political relationships, so there is no direct mechanism for their interests to be taken into account. International negotiations and agreements are a means to "internalize"

---

[3] The term "efficiency" refers, roughly speaking, to the extent to which the maximum benefit is obtained from a relationship.

the externalities that flow from national politics, that is, to make decision-makers behave as if they took these beneficial or adverse external effects into account.

A distinction is sometimes drawn between "real" and "pecuniary" externalities. Real externalities flow directly from an action, such as when poisonous waste is deposited in a river, thereby affecting individuals who live or work downstream. A pecuniary externality, by contrast, is mediated by the price system; when a consumer buys an ear of corn, the consumption of the corn itself causes no harm to others, but the purchase may bid up the price of corn and so make it more expensive for others to consume. The distinction between the two types of externalities is useful in some contexts. However, the distinction carries less meaning in the context of government actions affecting world trade, since both forms of externalities can give rise to inefficiencies. Real externalities certainly are a cause for concern to the world economy, such as when greenhouse gases generated in one country cause environmental damage elsewhere. But activities by governments that cause world prices of certain goods to rise or fall can also generate inefficiencies for foreign interests, and in this sense generate (international) externalities.

There is an obvious reason why externalities can arise when governments set their trade policies: national governments often place little or no weight on the well-being of foreigners in making their policy choices. Take for example a policy that has some adverse effects on a group of consumers or firms. If the group is a domestic one, then presumably the government would weigh the harm in choosing its policy level. But if the group is foreign, there are fewer if any political mechanisms to ensure that this is so. As a result, there will be a tendency to overuse policies that generate costs abroad, and underuse those that are beneficial there. *Unilateral policy choices are therefore likely to be inefficient when evaluated from the perspective of the world as a whole.*

For example, consider some French policy that would cause the world price of wine to rise. If all wine consumers and producers resided in France, then the French government might consider the price hike to be roughly a "wash." The extra cost to French consumers would be matched by a similar rise in producer revenues and if the government weighed the two equally, it might consider this to be neither a gain nor a loss. However, we know that France, in fact, is a substantial exporter of wine, which means that its farms produce more than its households drink. It follows that French producers gain more in revenues when prices go up than French consumers pay in extra outlays. The consumer losses are, of course, shared by wine lovers abroad. Now if, as is likely to be the case, the French government puts less weight on the interests of the foreigners than on those of French citizens, it could well see the increase in wine price as bringing benefit to France. Consequently, its policies that affect wine prices would be inefficient from a global perspective. But France might be open to the idea that it changes its policies in exchange for similar concessions by foreign governments in other markets. We will see that externalities that are transmitted through world prices play a central role in the literature on trade agreements.

When governments neglect the impact of their national policies on their trading partners, they are likely to set their policies at inefficient levels even when the interventions themselves are justifiable in terms of global efficiency. Consider, for example, a situation in which the consumption of some product generates an adverse impact on the environment. In such circumstances, the government would be well justified to discourage consumption via taxation and, indeed, a consumption tax at some level would serve to improve global efficiency. However, if when choosing its tax rate, the government ignores the fact that the tax will harm producer interests in foreign, exporting countries, it is bound to choose a tax rate higher than the one associated with a globally efficient outcome. The globally optimal consumption tax balances the benefits to the local environment with the cost to producers wherever they are located, and if some produce interests are ignored, the resulting tax will be overly stringent from a global point of view.

Unilateral policy setting can also result in inefficiency in governments' discrete choices. Suppose, for example, that a national government must rule on whether a corporate merger is permissible under its national competition laws. In making this decision, the efficiency-minded government would weigh the harm to consumers resulting from any greater exploitation of market power against the benefit to the firms from any technological synergies or other productivity gains that might result from the combination. If all the parties to the proposed merger are national companies, then a consideration of national consumer and producer interests alone might be sufficient for a decision that promotes the efficient outcome. However, if some of the parties to the merger are foreign firms, and if the potential gains to these firms do not figure in the government's cost-benefit calculus, then the resulting decision on the merger might err on the side of conservatism; that is, they might disallow mergers that would, if tolerated, create (global) gains in excess of the costs to consumers. An international agreement on competition policy would be needed to ensure globally efficient decisions.[4]

---

[4] The commitment approach (to be discussed in Section 2.5) suggests that trade agreements are vehicles by which governments can commit to implement policies that might run against their short-run interests at the time when they must be carried out. But even this explanation for trade agreements requires interdependence. First, partners to an agreement would not play a role in enforcing a government's commitments if economic outcomes in their countries did not depend on the policies enacted by the government that seeks to tie its own hands. Second, a government will not be able to use a trade agreement as a vehicle for commitment unless it is concerned about the retaliatory policies that would be imposed by partners to the agreement, should it fail to honor its commitment.

In order for a unilateral policy to be internationally inefficient, it obviously must affect foreign interests. But an adverse international impact does not *necessarily* make a government's domestic policy inefficient. This can be seen in the example above in which consumption of an imported product pollutes the environment. Global efficiency can be achieved in the presence of pollution externalities by means of a consumption tax. Such a tax can further efficiency even though it may harm producers in a foreign country. It is thus not the adverse effect on foreign interests *per se* that makes a government action inefficient, but rather the failure to consider these interests in setting the level of the policy. A consumption tax will be globally inefficient in our example of a pollution externality only if the tax rate is higher than what is required to balance the effects on all interests, both local and foreign. The need to balance costs and benefits for various parties complicates the interpretation and implementation of a number of GATT features, including the provisions for National Treatment.

2.2.2 Government Objectives

Trade negotiations are conducted by officials appointed by their national governments. To predict the outcome of a negotiation, and to interpret the meaning of the language of the agreement, we need to understand the objectives of these negotiators.[5] More generally, whose preferences do negotiators represent? And how do legislators evaluate and rank alternative policies?

These are difficult questions that have perplexed economists and political scientists for decades. It is tempting to argue that negotiators in a democracy represent the aggregate preferences of society. But how do we aggregate individuals' preferences? How much weight do the views of a particular person receive? Should we weigh individuals equally in some sense? If so, how do we deal with the fact that the intensity of an individual's preferences is a personal matter and impossible to compare to that of another? Suppose citizen 1 in country A would very much like a trade agreement with some given terms, but is less enthusiastic about another agreement. Meanwhile, citizen 2 has the opposite ordering. What are the preferences of society? Even if we expect a compromise between the two, exactly which compromise would we expect the negotiator to seek? If the negotiator cannot deliver her preferred agreement because the negotiator for country B has different goals, how will the negotiators evaluate the various possible compromises between their two first choices? These questions have been at the forefront in social-choice theory, a field of economics, political science, and moral

---

[5] In our discussion below, we do not draw a distinction between the preferences of the government officials who negotiate a trade agreement and those of the government officials who select trade policies after the agreement is in place. See Section 2.5 for a discussion of this assumption.

philosophy. The theory has produced many interesting arguments but no compelling resolution to these issues.

The simplest approach – and also the most commonly used approach in
the economics literature – assumes that each government seeks to maximize the
sum of the incomes of all of its citizens. However, it is difficult to justify national
income as the appropriate government objective either descriptively or prescriptively. As a description of government objectives, simple income measures are
suspect because they neglect citizens' concerns about the prices of the goods
they buy, the insecurity they feel about potential disruptions to their income
flows, the conditions under which they work, the quality of their environment,
and so on. As a prescription, the measures suffer from these same omissions
and moreover they suggest a lack of societal concern about the distribution of
income.

An alternative approach begins with the notion of a "social welfare function." Social welfare is intended to measure overall societal well-being. A non-
paternal social-welfare function is one that reflects only the citizen's own evaluation of their happiness and well-being. A paternalistic social-welfare function
can assess an individual's plight in a given situation differently than she would
herself. In either case, the social-welfare function must impose some scheme for
aggregating individuals' well-being. Should they simply be summed and, if so,
in what units should they be measured? If summing seems inappropriate, what
weights should be applied to different individuals and what is the implicit evaluation of inequality in outcomes?

The assumption that governments maximize a measure of social welfare has
the advantage of flexibility. In principle, the social-welfare function can accommodate any considerations that the analyst deems appropriate, or descriptive
of actual government behavior. The analyst need not take a stand a priori on
what are valid concerns for members of society or how these concerns ought
to be weighed or compared. Of course, in the application of this approach, the
analyst adopts an objective function with particular arguments and so implicitly imposes restrictions on the validity and importance of alternative concerns.
Unfortunately, there is little to guide the choice of the social-welfare function;
essentially, the governments' objectives under this approach must come from
outside the analysis.

A rather different approach to specifying the governments' objective function begins with an appreciation of political interactions. In this approach,
the governments' objectives are induced by the political regime. Government
officials, like private agents, are assumed to pursue their own well-being (or
"utility") subject to constraints. Their utilities might reflect a taste for power or
a pure desire to "do good," in addition to private concerns about material goods
and perhaps the perquisites of office. After specifying the objectives of the political agents, the analyst must model the political interactions: What is the assumed

electoral system? What are the voting rules, the political institutions, the role of campaign contributions, and the behavior of voters? Given the analyst's model of the political system, and the assumed interactions between political players, the government's objectives in its trade negotiations can be derived as a political outcome. That is, the electoral system, political institutions, and rules of the political game determine, among other things, the identities of the elected leaders and the policy positions they take.

This "political-economy" approach to government objectives recognizes, for example, that elected officials might pursue more strongly the interests of some constituents than others. The favored constituencies might be residents of swing districts, voters for whom trade policy is the most salient issue, or groups with ample resources to contribute to campaign financing. In any case, it is no longer clear, or even expected, that the government will pursue the aggregate and socially-just welfare of society.

The political-economy approach also has shortcomings. First, the approach relies on the modeling of political interactions. The more explicit are the government preferences used in the analysis, the sharper are the predictions about trade negotiations, but the more dependent are they on the plausibility and reliability of the assumed political model. Second, the induced government objective function need not be stable over time. Changes in the identities of the elected leaders may change the preferences of trade negotiators; changes in political institutions in the negotiating countries almost certainly will do so. This makes it difficult to render interpretations or predictions about trade agreements without detailed information about the state of politics in all the participating countries at the time of their discussions. Third, and perhaps most troubling, the composition of governments (and thus governments' preferences) may be jointly determined with the outcome of the trade negotiations. For example, some industries that serve only local markets prior to a trade liberalization may become exporters as a result of the trade agreement. If this changes the support in these industries for political parties, the formation of the trade agreement will influence government preferences. At the same time, government preferences obviously influence the formation of the trade agreement. In such circumstances, governments' preferences must be treated as endogenous, and predictions about the results of trade negotiations must be made jointly with predictions about political outcomes.

The different approaches to describing government objectives can be useful in different ways when interpreting the WTO Agreement. For instance, as mentioned above, Art. 31.1 of the *Vienna Convention on the Law of Treaties* holds that an agreement should be interpreted "in the light of its object and purpose." Matters of interpretation may therefore require us to consider what the negotiators were trying to achieve when drafting the agreement. Their intentions surely were conditioned on their actual politically-induced preferences, and not on some ethically-defensible preferences that they might have held in some best-of-all-possible worlds. Arguably, the political-economy approach is the more useful for illuminating such aspects. But the analyst may also want to take a stand on the objectives that the WTO ought to seek to achieve. The analyst would then follow the earlier mentioned approaches, by ascribing preferences that are his or her own, or that come from outside the analysis.

We will next introduce a formal (i.e., mathematical) tool that allows us to express certain ideas concerning government preferences in a compact fashion.

2.2.3 A Formal Representation of Government Objectives[6]

A basic tenant in virtually all economic analysis is that decisionmakers, such as consumers, producers, or governments, behave purposefully to promote their own interests – this is a loosely expressed version of the economic "rationality assumption."[7] The mathematical representation of this idea rests on two key foundations.

First, it is assumed that the preferences of the decisionmaker fulfill certain properties; for example, a standard assumption is that if an option A is preferred to an option B, and B is preferred to an option C, then A is also preferred to C – this is the so-called transitivity property. It can be shown as a matter of mathematical logic, that if these basic assumptions are fulfilled, it is possible to represent the preferences of the decisionmaker by a mathematical function with certain properties – what in general terms is referred to as an "objective function" for the decisionmaker.

Second, it is commonly assumed that the decisionmaker will, when faced with a choice between several alternative policies and given the information available to him or her at the time, choose the option that best serves the objectives captured in the objective function. In what follows, the decisionmaker will typically be assumed to be a politician, and we thus assume that he or she chooses an option that maximizes the value of the objective function given informational and other constraints. This representation of the decision problem facing the decisionmaker is highly convenient from an analytical point of view, since it allows us to employ standard tools from optimization theory (the mathematical theory for how to find maxima and minima among sets of available alternatives) in order to shed light on the nature of policy choices.

In order to introduce a government welfare function to be used for trade-policy analysis, let us for simplicity (but without loss of generality) consider a world with two countries – Home and Foreign – and two goods. Each country's

---

[6] The content of this Section is slightly more technical than the rest of the study.

[7] As a side point, it can be noted that this economic approach is commonplace in legal analysis, albeit in less strict form, for instance, when evaluating motives and intent.

government will impose a tariff on its imports at some rate, denoted t for the Home government, and t^* for the Foreign government.[8] Also, let the symbol G denote the Home government's objective function. This function describes how different constellations of tariffs affect the government's perceived utility – that is, how the government evaluates the various outcomes that result. To express the dependence of the value of objective function on the tariffs that are chosen, we write this as $G(t,t^*)$, spelled out as "G is a function of the tariffs t and t^*." Note that the government's assessment of its well-being depends not only on its own tariff rate, but also on that of the other country, reflecting the interdependence between the two governments.

The function $G(t,t^*)$ is clearly a very abstract way of expressing the dependence of government well-being on the tariffs: we have not yet mentioned anything about how the tariffs affect the governments. This influence will most likely depend on a number of considerations, such as how the tariffs will affect economic variables such as trade volumes, incomes, consumption levels, employment, etc. It will also depend on how the political system rewards the government for different economic outcomes, and how the decisionmakers in the government evaluate these political rewards. All these aspects of how the tariffs affect the decisionmaker are conveniently packaged into the symbol G. In Section 2.4, we will open this black box and consider what may lie behind this general but abstract representation of the economic-*cum*-political system. However, in order to avoid losing sight of the broader picture, we will first employ the more general formulation. Accordingly, our analysis in Section 2.3 lacks institutional detail and makes only a few relatively unobjectionable assumptions about the properties of the government welfare function $G(t,t^*)$.

2.2.4 Predicting Outcomes of Strategic Interaction

In the setting we have just sketched, the Home government maximizes the value of the function $G(t,t^*)$ and the Foreign government, we assume, seeks to maximize an analogous objective function $G^*(t,t^*)$ that reflects the economics and politics abroad. What tariffs would result from these partly conflicting ambitions in the absence of any explicit trade agreement?

This is an example of a much more general question, concerning the outcome of strategic interactions in the absence of binding contracts. Mathematicians and social scientists have developed the tools of "non-cooperative game theory" to predict the outcomes of such interactions, and this body of theory is drawn upon in all fields of economic analysis to predict the outcome of strategic interaction. This theory provides the benchmark that is used in the literature on trade agreements to explain the reasons for trade negotiations and to evaluate

---

[8] We use the symbol " * " to denote a variable or a function pertaining to the Foreign country.

their success. In particular, we adopt as our benchmark the basic concept from non-cooperative game theory, the "Nash equilibrium" of a "simultaneous-move, one-shot game" – a concept that we will describe in what follows.

In this formulation, the two governments are assumed to choose from a set of feasible interventions, in this case all possible import tariff rates. Each government makes a once-and-for-all choice of policy without knowing what policy the other will choose, but recognizing the incentives that the other faces. The two policies are announced simultaneously, each selected in anticipation of the other. The Nash equilibrium is the most widely-used concept for predicting outcomes of noncooperative games; and although much has been written about its applicability in particular settings, it remains an accepted and useful starting point for the analysis of strategic interaction.

The assumption that policy choices are made simultaneously is meant to cast the players in a symmetric position with regard to timing. By this assumption, no government has the opportunity to commit to its policies before the others can act, nor can any government wait to observe its rivals' final choices before making its own decisions. This seems appropriate in our benchmark setting, because in the absence of an international agreement, governments might find it difficult to bind their policies in a way that could not subsequently be changed, and there is no natural sequence of tariff setting to be assumed.

The assumption that policies are set once and for all requires more explanation. Formally, this means that the game is solved as if the governments do not contemplate the possibility of future policy changes. Needless to say, this assumption is unrealistic and by invoking it we may be imparting undue pessimism about what the trading environment would be like without a negotiated agreement. We have several reasons for using the one-shot game as our no-agreement benchmark. First, the assumption of a single interaction delivers a simple analysis that is easy to understand, whereas dynamic games with repeated (or sequenced) interactions are much more complex. Second, if we were instead to assume that governments set policies in an indefinitely repeated sequence of periods, we would find that one possible Nash equilibrium outcome of this interaction is the indefinite repetition of the strategies invoked in the equilibrium of a one-shot game. That is, if all players realize that the game will be played repeatedly but all expect the others to act as if they are only concerned with their short-run (one-shot) interests, then no one will have any reason to behave differently from what it would do in a single play of the game. In this sense, our benchmark survives as a sensible equilibrium outcome even in a setting that allows for repeated interaction. Finally, the equilibria of the repeated game besides the one that has indefinite repetition of behavior in the one-shot game, all involve "tacit cooperation." Although the players are assumed to choose their actions independently, without consultation and without direct concern for the impact on others, they behave in these equilibria as if they were cooperating, because each believes that rivals will punish a selfish act today with retaliation tomorrow. Indeed, the structure of modern trade agreements shares many features with the tacitly-cooperative equilibria of a repeated game. As will be discussed further in Section 2.3.4.2, in both the WTO Agreement and the theoretical construct of a Nash equilibrium with tacit cooperation, there can be no legal enforcement of "good" behavior by an outside party. Both the actual agreement and the theoretical construct rely instead on internal enforcement, with bad behavior deterred by threats of retaliation and punishment. Since trade agreements mirror in many ways the game theorist's predictions about equilibria of repeated games with tacit cooperation, we choose to treat the outcome of a repeated game not as our no-agreement benchmark, but rather as informative about what might result from bargaining.[9]

Before leaving this Section, we introduce one further bit of game-theory terminology, which is that of a "best response." A player's best response to an action by his rival is a choice for his own action that best serves his interests given the action of the other player. A "best response function" identifies a player's best response to every possible action that his rival might take. A Nash equilibrium of a simultaneous-move, one-shot game can be characterized using the players' best response functions; specifically, it is the point at which the two functions intersect. In a Nash equilibrium, if player 1 takes action a and player 2 takes action b, then a must be a best response for player 1 to the action b by player 2, while b is a best response for player 2 to the action a by player 1. With mutual best responses, each player anticipates its rivals' behavior and each responds optimally in light of those expectations. Hence, in Nash equilibrium, no player is surprised by a rival's actual play and no one has any reason to alter behavior once rivals' actual actions are revealed.

2.3 A General International Externalities Model of Trade Agreements

This Section introduces a general model of how international externalities that result from unilateral policy setting may create a useful role for trade agreements. We intentionally present the model at a high level of abstraction, in order that details about government preferences, political institutions, and other aspects of the environment do not conceal the underlying nature of the strategic interactions between governments. A more detailed, but therefore also more narrow, model will be presented in Section 2.4.

In order to assess the purpose of a trade agreement, we first need to specify government objectives. We do so in Section 2.3.1, where we make a few assumptions concerning the properties of the welfare function $G(t,t^*)$ we introduced

---

[9] We will discuss the related issue concerning the similarities and differences between explicit agreements and tacit cooperation below.

in Section 2.2.3. Second, using the concept of the Nash equilibrium that we described in Section 2.2.4, Section 2.3.2 defines the benchmark policies that we would expect to see in the absence of any negotiation and cooperation. Section 2.3.3 then adopts the notion of Pareto efficiency for the two governments as a means to predict the outcome of a trade negotiation and to gauge the performance of a given agreement. That is, we assume that the outcome of the negotiation fulfills two properties: first, all parties gain from the outcome relative to how they would fare in the benchmark situation, which we take to be the (one-shot) Nash equilibrium; and second, no alternative policies can be found that would benefit one government and not harm the other. In some circumstances (that we shall describe), bargaining may be expected to yield just such an outcome. We emphasize that the predicted gains from an efficient agreement are measured relative to the objectives of the negotiators, with whatever preferences they may hold and whatever interests they may represent. An efficient agreement need not benefit all residents of a country, or even a majority of such residents.[10] In Section 2.3.4, we will point to several practical considerations that may limit the scope for achieving a fully efficient agreement, and we will point out how these practicalities might influence the design of a trade agreement.

2.3.1 Imposing Minimal Structure on Government Objectives

We now need to be a bit more specific about the governments' preferences as they enter into international negotiations. We suppose, as we mentioned before, that the Home government's preferences can be represented by a (government) welfare function $G(t, t^*)$. But now we also assume that this function has some specific properties:[11]

1. Starting from a Home tariff of zero, the Home government's welfare rises when a (small) positive Home tariff is introduced.[12]
2. As the Home tariff is increased holding the Foreign tariff rate constant, the Home government's welfare eventually reaches a peak and then declines.[13]

---

[10] Although much of the approach that we shall develop here would be applicable to any multilateral agreement, we shall limit our focus to the study of "trade agreements." Narrowly defined, such an agreement directly constrains governments' choices of policies to promote, impede, or regulate the flows of goods and services across borders. A broader definition would include constraints on policies that govern other cross-border flows, such as those of capital and technologies.

[11] Some additional, necessary assumptions are left out, being of a more technical nature.

[12] More formally, $G(t, t^*)$ is an increasing function of t when evaluated at $t = 0$ and any value of t^*.

[13] This assumption is not needed for the main points that we shall make, it ensures that the benchmark tariffs are not prohibitive, which seems realistic.

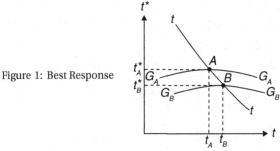

Figure 1: Best Response

3. The welfare of the Home government falls whenever the Foreign tariff is increased.[14]

The first property implies that the Home government always has a unilateral incentive to impose some positive tariff. The second ensures that the benchmark tariff is not prohibitive, which certainly seems in line with real-world observations. The final property embodies the international externality; it says that the Home government is harmed by protection abroad.

The Foreign government preferences $G^*(t, t^*)$ have the same properties, but with the roles of the tariffs being reversed. The Foreign government benefits from some positive tariffs t^*, but it suffers from any increase in the Home tariff, t.

2.3.2 The Benchmark Outcome: Unilateral Policy Decisions

In Figure 1, point A represents the Home government's best response to the foreign tariff t_A^*. That is, if the government of Foreign were to set its tariff rate at t_A^*, the Home government would maximize its own objective function by setting the Home tariff equal to t_A. The Home government might prefer this positive tariff for any one of a number of reasons – the very general formulation of the government objective function allows for a range of different interpretations, as will be seen. But in this Section, the reason why governments prefer to invoke trade barriers is not important.

Notice the curve $G_A G_A$. This curve depicts all combinations of t and t^* that generate the same level of utility for the Home government as at point A. A point directly to the right of point A (which is not on the curve) yields less utility to the Home government than does point A, because t_A is the best response to t_A^* and so any other response must be inferior to it. A point to the southeast of A could, however, yield the same level of welfare to the Home government as point A, because the loss associated with moving to the right from point A is compensated by a gain from moving t^* downward. The latter movement reflects a

---

[14] More formally, $G(t, t^*)$ is a decreasing function of t^* for any value of t.

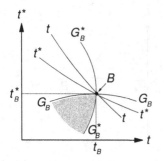

Figure 2: The Nash Equilibrium

reduction in the foreign tariff for a given home tariff and could benefit the Home government by providing improved access to the foreign market for domestic producers. Similarly, a point directly to the left of point A could not yield as great a value for $G(t,t^*)$ as point A, but a point to the southwest of A could do so by compensating the loss from a leftward move with a gain from a downward move.

The Figure also shows point B, which is the Home government's best response to a foreign tariff of t_B^*. The curve $G_B G_B$ depicts combinations of the two tariff rates that deliver the same level of utility to the Home government as it achieves at point B. We could indicate other points like A and B, and other curves of constant government utility that pass through these points. By connecting points A, B, and the others like them, we trace out the curve tt, which represents the aforementioned Home best response function; i.e., the optimal policy choices for the Home government in response to every possible value of the Foreign tariff. We have drawn the curve as downward sloping, because many economic and political-economic models suggest that the optimal home tariff shrinks as the foreign tariff grows.[15] But the slope of the curve is not important at this point.

In Figure 2, we have reproduced tt and $G_B G_B$. We have also drawn $t^* t^*$, which depicts the Foreign best response function; i.e., the optimal policy for the Foreign government in response to every tariff t that the Home government might set. This curve is derived by an analogous thought experiment to that which gave us tt. The curve $G_B^* G_B^*$ represents the combinations of t^* and t that yield the same level of political utility to the Foreign government as it would obtain with the combination of tariffs t_B^* and t_B. Its derivation mirrors that of $G_B G_B$ but uses instead the Foreign government's preferences, $G^*(t^*,t)$.

Now, at last, we are ready to identify the Nash equilibrium, which is found at point B. This pair of policies has the property that t_B is a best response by

---

[15] This could be, for example, because a higher foreign tariff shrinks the overall volume of trade and so reduces the political gains available to the Home government from providing protection.

the Home government to t_B^* while t_B^* also is a best response by the Foreign government to t_B. With these choices, neither government has any reason to alter *unilaterally* its tariff rate. If the Home government expects the Foreign government to set t_B^*, its best policy response is t_B. If the Foreign government expects t_B, its best response is t_B^*. We consider this Nash equilibrium to be the benchmark outcome that would arise in the absence of cooperation between the two governments. Although our artistic abilities (and geometry) limit us to two dimensions in the figures, the idea of a Nash equilibrium would be the same with any number of goods, any number of governments, and any number of policy instruments at their disposal.

The features of the Nash equilibrium can help us to understand some of the language that is used to describe trade negotiations. In a negotiation, governments are asked to make *concessions* to their trade partners. These are concessions, because any unilateral change in policy harms a government that has chosen a best response. For example, the Home government loses political welfare by moving horizontally from its best response curve *tt*. Governments might concede in this way only when they anticipate *reciprocity* from their partners. Whereas a movement due left from point B cannot benefit the Home government, a movement to the southwest conceivably could do so, if the political benefits from a reduced foreign tariff compensate the perceived loss from a lowering of Home barriers. The shaded area in Figure 2 illustrates such mutually beneficial, reciprocal liberalization.

2.3.3 An Efficient Trade Agreement

Starting from the benchmark situation that is depicted in Figure 2, the Home government and the Foreign government have clear reasons to negotiate. As the figure shows, the curve $G_B G_B$ has a horizontal slope at point B, whereas the curve $G_B^* G_B^*$ has a vertical slope at this point.[16] The fact that the two curves are perpendicular at B reveals an opportunity for mutual gain. Consider the policy combinations represented by points in the shaded region. These points lie *below* the curve $G_B G_B$ and so correspond to greater political welfare than at B for the Home government, and they lie *to the left of* $G_B^* G_B^*$ and so correspond to greater political welfare than at B for the Foreign government. If the governments can agree to choose policies from the shaded region, and if that agreement can be enforced, then each government stands to reap political rewards.

Why must there be scope for mutual gain? We shall address this question more fully beginning in Section 2.4, where we will describe in more detail the

---

[16] The horizontal slope of $G_B G_B$ at B is a consequence of maximization by the Home government. It anticipates the foreign policy G_B^* and chooses t to reach the highest (i.e., southernmost) welfare contour. The vertical slope of $G_B^* G_B^*$ has a similar explanation.

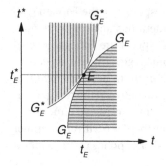

Figure 3: The Efficient Agreement

functioning of the underlying economy and government preferences, but the intuition can be explained now. When the Home government chooses its best response to t_B^* at point B, it neglects the spillover effect that its policy choice has on the welfare of the Foreign government. A small change in the Home tariff would reduce the Home government's welfare only slightly (because a near-optimal choice yields almost the same welfare as an optimal choice), but would provide clear political gains to the Foreign government.[17] Similarly, t_B^* has been chosen by the Foreign government to maximize its own objective function without regard to the adverse impact on the Home government. The Foreign government too can alter t_B^* at relatively little cost to itself and generate a non-negligible gain for its counterpart. By agreeing to reduce tariffs from t_B and t_B^* to some pair in the shaded region, the two governments can achieve mutual gains in political welfare.

Figure 3 illustrates an efficient outcome from the perspective of the Home and Foreign governments. At point E, with policies t_E and t_E^*, the curves G_E and G_E^* are tangent to one another. An improvement in the Home government's welfare relative to point E requires movement into the horizontally-shaded region, whereas an improvement in the Foreign government's welfare relative to point E requires movement into the vertically-shaded region. As is clear from the figure, there are no combinations of t and t^* that lie in both of these regions; thus, there does not exist a feasible policy change relative to point E that benefits one government without harming the other – this pair of tariffs is thus Pareto efficient.

It is important to stress the nature of the efficiency that is at issue here. The efficiency depicted in Figure 3 is defined in relation to the *governments'* objectives, as it is the government officials who conduct trade negotiations. If a negotiated trade agreement were to prescribe the policies associated with point E, neither of the negotiators could offer a proposal that its government prefers to E that would be acceptable to his counterpart. But, as we discussed in

---

[17] In many political and economic models, the Home government must gain from a reduction in the foreign tariff, as we discuss further below. However, our argument that both governments can gain from an agreement is more general than this, and applies whenever the no-agreement benchmark is the one-shot Nash equilibrium.

Section 2.2.2 the preferences of government officials are colored by the political environment in which they operate and need not coincide with measures of social welfare. So, it is impossible to say without further information about the politics in each country whether an agreement at point E best serves the citizens of the two countries, or even whether such an agreement raises aggregate welfare (somehow measured) relative to what it would be without any trade agreement.

2.3.4 The Design of Trade Agreements

In Section 2.3.3, we explained why unilateral policymaking in interdependent countries is likely to result in inefficient policies. We have shown why the governments have an incentive to cooperate, and we have identified the conditions that would need to be satisfied by a fully efficient agreement. But we have not talked about how negotiators might go about generating political welfare gains relative to the benchmark outcome, nor about whether a potential agreement would be sustainable and enforceable. Moreover, we have oversimplified the world by pretending that there are only two parties to the negotiation, that there are only two tariff rates to be discussed, that the parties' preferences are clear-cut and stable, that each side's preferences are fully known by the other, and so on. In this Section, we outline some of the issues that a theory of trade agreements must overcome in moving from an explanation of why trade agreements might exist to an explanation of what form they take and what their myriad provisions are meant to achieve.

2.3.4.1 *Trade Agreements Are Negotiated*

A salient feature of trade agreements is that they result from explicit *negotiations*. These negotiations make each party sensitive to the externalities that result from its existing policies. If the Home and Foreign governments negotiate about their respective policies measures X and Y, government B might offer to change policy Y by a certain amount in exchange for a certain change in policy X by government A. The latter can opt to continue to pursue its original level of policy X, but now it must bear a cost for doing so in terms of the foregone "concession" from its counterpart. Through the process of offers and counteroffers, negotiations can induce the parties to internalize the externalities that their unilateral choices impose.

But what policies will emerge from such a process? Here, the economic literature is less clear. Even if the parties are fully aware of the preferences of their counterparts, there are many policy combinations that are Pareto efficient. Some combinations give greater welfare to government A at the expense of government B, while others do the opposite. The economics literature on bargaining explains how the outcome will depend on a number of considerations, such as the well-being of the two parties in the status quo, who has the chance to make the first offer, the bargaining protocol that is used, and the patience of the parties to the negotiation. Although there are elegant theories to predict the outcome of a negotiation carried out with full information, these theories rely on strong assumptions about exactly how the bargaining takes place; e.g., that offers must alternate between the parties and that a fixed amount of time must pass between offers.

More worrisome, still, is the assumption of full information and common knowledge. Governments cannot easily know the political pressures that their counterparts face or exact meaning of these pressures in a foreign context. As a result, they typically enter negotiations with uncertainty about the counterparts' preferences, as well as uncertainty about how different policies will affect the economy and their own political well-being. In the face of uncertainty and imperfect information, it becomes much more difficult if not impossible to achieve an efficient outcome of the sort described above.

Imperfect information gives parties an incentive to posture and bluff in the hope of convincing negotiating partners that the cost of changing one's own policies is high or that the prospective benefit that will come from the other's concessions is small. In such an environment, it is no longer obvious that the parties will accept any offers that improve their conditions relative to the status quo. It may be optimal to decline an attractive offer in the hope of generating one later that is even better.

The history of GATT and WTO negotiations suggests that such considerations are important in the world of international trade policy. Trade negotiations are notoriously slow and seemingly are becoming more so over time. Indeed, the current negotiations in the Doha Round have been so much delayed by intransigence from many parties that it seems possible that cooperation will not be achieved.

Unfortunately, models with complete information cannot explain why negotiations take time; delays only postpone the realization of the gains from cooperation. Models of bargaining with imperfect information may explain why it takes time to conclude an agreement, or even why a negotiation ends without an agreement even if both sides know that there are potential gains from cooperation. Most theories of trade agreements nevertheless assume that the parties have full information, for two related reasons. First, models of bargaining under imperfect information are typically too complex to be useful as tools for analyzing the structure and implication of trade agreements. Second, predictions from these models are often extremely sensitive to what might seem to be somewhat arbitrary details of how the negotiations are conducted.

2.3.4.2 *Trade Agreements Must Be Self-Enforcing*

Were it not for informational problems just described, the idea of an efficient agreement might seem very compelling. Why would the parties end a negotiation and sign on to an agreement if they realized that further mutual gains were still possible? Why wouldn't some party make a further proposal if policy combinations exist that would be better for itself and also better for its counterpart? How could an outcome with ongoing inefficiency be sustained?

The literature on trade agreements offers some unsettling answers to these questions that point to the difficulty of enforcing international trade agreements. In other negotiating contexts, agreements are enforced by third parties. When private parties enter into a legal agreement, they can count on the government to enforce the terms of the contract. Then, if one side feels that the other has not fulfilled its obligations, it can sue for damages in a court of law. Once a judgment has been obtained, the aggrieved party can further rely on the police to ensure that the court's stipulated restitutions are carried out. But trade agreements are inevitably contracts between sovereign entities. There is no disinterested third party to enforce these agreements and no international police to ensure that damages are paid. Trade agreements can survive only if the parties choose to honor their terms on an ongoing, and essentially voluntary, basis.

Why should there be any need for enforcement of an agreement that all parties sign and from which all parties presumably reap benefits? Recall from Section 2.3.3 that whereas the noncooperative choices depicted in the Nash equilibrium of Figure 2 lie on the governments' respective best response functions, the efficient policy choices identified in Figure 3 do not. Indeed, by definition, the Nash equilibrium policies are the ones that leave neither party with an incentive to change behavior unilaterally. For all other policies, and especially for the efficient policies, the parties must be behaving in such a way that they do not maximize their own utility for the actions prescribed for the other. But this means, of course, that all parties to an agreement will want to "cheat," if they think they can get away with it. Starting from a point such as E in Figure 3, the Home government could benefit by raising its tariff t while the Foreign government sticks to a policy of t_E^*, and the Foreign government would benefit by increasing t^* while the Home tariff remains with t_E.

But could they get away with it? If the only policies at issue were border tariffs, then presumably they could not do so for long. The tariffs collected by a customs authority are apparent to the foreign firms that must pay them, which could almost immediately report on violations of the terms of any agreement to their national government. But governments have more ways to provide protection than only with tariffs. They often can replicate the effects of such policies, or at least nearly so, with combinations of other fiscal instruments, with quantitative restrictions, and with administrative and other impediments to trade. A violation of the terms of a trade agreement may not be as transparent and as readily observable as would be the levying of an excessive tariff charge. Some forms of cheating might go undetected for a long time and others might occur in ways that require careful and subtle investigation in order to determine whether they constitute an abrogation of the agreement or not. Considering the difficulties that are likely to arise in monitoring and detecting actions that run counter to a trade agreement, our theories of such agreements should recognize that the parties have incentives to cheat and often will have opportunities and means to do so.

The literature on trade agreements has sought to address such concerns about enforcement by looking for outcomes that satisfy a "self-enforcement" constraint. An agreement is self enforcing if the parties prefer to take the actions stipulated by the agreement to all other options open to them, considering both the likelihood that they would be "caught" behaving differently, the expected time until "detection" of such behavior, and the consequences that would ensue.

The literature on "repeated games" can guide us in understanding the implications of the self-enforcement constraint. Repeated games are strategic interactions that recur in the same form over time. In the trade-policy context, for example, we might consider the repeated game in which two governments repeatedly set tariff rates for their import goods for some period of time. At the beginning of each period, the governments would simultaneously choose the tariffs (or other similar, but less observable policies) that would apply during the period. A period in this context is the time it would take before a party would recognize a change in its rival's behavior and change its own behavior in response. The theory of repeated games has asked how much cooperation can be sustained in the Nash equilibrium of such repeated play, considering that some opportunistic actions by each party would be deterred by the threat of later retaliation by the other. The threat of retaliation means that – even in the absence of a formal agreement or contract – it may be possible to sustain more cooperative behavior than the Nash equilibrium of the one-shot game. In a repeated equilibrium with cooperation, each party refrains from pursuing its (short-run) best response to the other's action, expecting that its counterparts will do likewise. Each (implicitly) threatens to punish any opportunistic behavior by its counterparts, and each expects that any of its own opportunistic actions will invoke similar retribution by the others. Punishments must be credible in the sense that it must actually be in the interest of each party to carry out what is expected of it should some violation of the implicit agreement actually occur. By construction, the equilibrium outcomes of repeated games are self enforcing, because they require no adjudication and penalties imposed by disinterested third parties.

So, how much cooperation can be sustained by threat of punishment in repeated play? The answer depends on a number of features of the strategic environment, including the time it takes for detection of opportunistic behavior and the response to it, the size of the gains that each player can capture by cheating until detection, and how much each player would give up by forgoing some subsequent cooperation. But, however much cooperation might be possible in such a setting, the theory does not predict a unique outcome for the repeated play.[18] The theory does predict, however, that the more patient are the parties (i.e., the less they discount events in the future), the higher the maximal degree of cooperation that can be sustained. In particular, the self-enforcement constraint is likely to prevent the parties from reaching a fully efficient outcome, such as the one identified by point E in Figure 3, since it would be too tempting for any government to cheat on such an agreement. Since there are reasons to believe that governments are typically rather short-sighted, we should indeed expect the best outcome to involve much higher tariffs than what would be fully efficient.

2.3.4.3 *Trade Agreements Are Explicit and Incomplete*

The two-countries, two-product framework illustrates starkly the basic gains from an arrangement that takes the parties from an inefficient unilateral outcome, toward the efficiency frontier. But the simplicity of the analysis is deceptive, in that it appears so simple for the parties both to identify more efficient outcomes, and to maintain such outcomes through repeated interaction. In practice, the problem of designing an agreement is enormously complex: the agreement needs to cover not just two countries and two products, but many countries, and millions of goods; there are international externalities not only from trade instruments, but from a huge number of domestic policy instruments; the economic environment is highly uncertain, being bombarded by changes in the underlying conditions such as changes in technology, natural resources, tastes, weather, politics, etc. This complexity has profound implications for the design of the agreement.

A first implication is that it is necessary to come to an *explicit* agreement on the terms for the cooperation. It seems highly unlikely that the cooperation that has been implemented through the creation of the GATT/WTO could have been achieved if Members had not explicitly agreed on how to cooperate through a series of negotiation rounds, and through innumerable meetings between rounds. The reader might view this as a rather trivial observation – but it is actually an aspect of trade agreements that economics has difficulty explaining. As described above, theory shows how governments in a repeated interaction can benefit from refraining from short-run, opportunistic behavior if they believe such actions would induce other governments to retaliate in kind. But "all" this theory says is that a certain set of behaviors jointly supports a Nash equilibrium that is more efficient than the one-shot Nash equilibrium. The theory is silent on how the parties can coordinate their expectations concerning what is, and what is not, accepted as cooperative behavior. But it can be imagined

---

[18] There is a path of play sustained by players' beliefs about what is expected of them and by credible punishments for departures from expected behavior that achieves "the most cooperative equilibrium," as well as many other paths that involve lesser standards of good behavior and that achieve less (but still some) cooperation.

that a trade agreement makes explicit what would only be implicit in a tacitly-cooperative equilibrium of a repeated trade-policy game. The agreement could spell out the behavior that is expected of governments in the pursuit of cooperation and the retaliation that should ensue from opportunistic behavior. In so doing, it could coordinate expectations and help to implement one of the cooperative outcomes among those that are sustainable under repeated play. And so long as the agreement stipulates actions that would themselves be sustainable as an equilibrium outcome of a repeated game without a formal contract, it will not require any external enforcement. By taking this perspective, we again cast doubt on the feasibility of a fully efficient outcome, such as the one identified by point E in Figure 3.

Second and related, the complexity of the interaction implies that an explicit agreement between the parties would have to be an extraordinarily lengthy document, if it were to identify a fully efficient outcome. Such an agreement would have to dictate the legitimate uses of a myriad of domestic policy instruments, and it would have to be sensitive to changes in an incalculable number of economic and political conditions. The construction of such an agreement is, of course, a practical impossibility because of the time and administrative costs it would require, if at all possible. As a consequence, trade agreements are by necessity *incomplete* in various ways.[19] First, contractual bindings are less responsive to changes in the underlying economic and political environment than they should ideally be; for instance, tariff bindings are not conditioned on such changes except for through the means of escape mentioned above. Second, the agreement does not bind all policy instruments, but leaves discretion over certain policies to the parties; for instance, the GATT leaves discretion over domestic instruments to the Members, albeit with certain constraints imposed. Third, contractual provisions are expressed vaguely in order to save negotiators time.

The incompleteness of the agreement provides yet another reason why the parties cannot achieve a fully efficient outcome. It also has the important implication that the agreement would benefit from the inclusion of a *dispute-settlement mechanism*, since it will often be unclear whether undertaken measures should be seen as violating the agreement, and the parties need to agree beforehand on how to resolve such conflicts. Hence, the need for *interpretation* of the agreements largely stems from this incompleteness. The "contractual

---

[19] We here emphasize the role of contracting costs for contractual incompleteness. The economic literature points to two further reasons for incompleteness, both of which seem important for the design of the GATT: first, some aspects of the state of the world may be unverifiable by a court, and so contracts that included contingencies under such states of the world could not be enforced; and second, some aspects of the state of the world may be unforeseeable or not possible to describe, making it impossible to include these in the contract.

incompleteness" of trade agreements will be discussed in more detail in the accompanying ALI study on the treatment of domestic instruments in the GATT.

2.3.4.4 *Trade Agreements Involve Reciprocal Exchanges of Concessions*

The final property of the design of trade agreements that we will point to is that they entail *reciprocal* reductions in tariffs, and other trade barriers. In theory, it would be possible to have nonreciprocal agreements. Indeed, each pair of countries could negotiate a separate agreement for each tariff line and for each trade direction, with each such agreement specifying a tariff reduction against, say, a monetary payment. The fact that virtually all agreements we observe involve reciprocal undertakings to reduce trade barriers, strongly suggests that there are efficiency gains from reciprocal exchanges that are not captured in the model above. The economic literature offers surprisingly little by way of explanation of this feature, however. But it seems quite clear intuitively that it would be extremely costly to negotiate separate agreements for each trade barrier, since this would involve significant duplication of negotiation efforts and other resources; for instance, each of the agreements would then require a separate dispute-settlement mechanism. Furthermore, the payments require the collection of tax revenue, which is likely to distort the economy. In addition, the parties need to agree on the monetary value of each tariff concession, which might be more difficult than to agree on reciprocal tariff reductions. There are thus clear gains in terms of reduced administrative costs and negotiation costs to form a package of tariff reductions.

2.4 A Special Case: The National Market Power Model

The effects of government's economic policies cross international boundaries and impact actors residing outside their political borders. In the previous Section, we argued that the threat of such policy externalities provides a strong motivation for governments to participate in international trade agreements. To analyze the impact, we assumed that governments' decisionmaking with regard to trade policy could be represented as maximizations of the welfare functions $G(t,t^*)$ and $G^*(t,t^*)$. We made some intuitively plausible assumptions concerning the properties of these functions, illustrated in Figure 3, but we did not specify any details concerning what more specifically lay behind this function. With this very general framework, we illustrated the gains that could be had from a trade agreement. On the one hand, this shows the generality of the proposition that trade agreements solve problems arising from international externalities, since it is highly plausible that countries *will* affect each other in the assumed manner through their trade policies. On the other hand, one may wonder what underlying situations fit this description.

Most economic analysis of trade agreements are conducted in international externality frameworks with more detailed institutional structure imposed than in the general model above. Institutional details are typically added in two respects:

- a description of how tariffs affect economic outcomes, such as trade volumes, incomes, consumption levels, employment, wages, etc. These relationships are embedded in a model of the economy; and
- a description of how governments rank and choose among these different economic outcomes.

In what follows we will discuss the standard approach to model the role of trade agreements. As will be argued, this approach is broad enough to allow for many different treatments of the above two points. But the approach is defined by the assumption that governments have incentives to exploit their ability to extract surplus from trading partners by restricting imports, and that this causes an international inefficiency. Because of the close parallel with the behavior of firms with market power, we will denote this as the "national market power" approach. Section 2.4.1 will lay out the unilateral incentives for governments to employ tariffs in order to exploit national market power. The structure of the analysis will ultimately be the same as in Section 2.3.2, but we now go behind the general expressions $G(t,t^*)$ and $G^*(t,t^*)$, by making detailed assumptions concerning the structure of the economy and government behavior. The rest of the Section then discusses the theoretical generality and practical relevance of the approach.

2.4.1 When Free Trade Is Unilaterally Optimal

A theory of trade agreements requires an explanation for why countries would restrict trade if they were not bound by any treaty. A trade agreement would be unnecessary if free trade were in the unilateral interests of all countries. Trade economists have identified circumstances in which all governments would opt for free trade without needing any explicit agreement. In particular, a government will unilaterally choose free trade when:

1. all markets are perfectly competitive;
2. production occurs under constant or decreasing returns to scale;
3. there are no externalities;
4. the country as a whole does not affect the prices at which it trades internationally; and
5. the government pursues an objective of maximizing national income (or social welfare).

When these five assumptions are satisfied for both countries, the government welfare functions $G(t,t^*)$ and $G^*(t,t^*)$ have the property that $t = 0$ is a best response to any tariff t^* chosen by the foreign government and that $t^* = 0$ is a best response to any tariff t chosen by the home government. The Nash equilibrium in the absence of any trade agreement is characterized by universal free trade.

The standard approach to trade agreements may incorporate departures from several of these assumptions. Most importantly, however, all models that take this approach dispense with Assumption 4, which is known in the literature as the "small country assumption." This assumption stipulates that a country can set its national policies without any spillover effects on its trading partners. If a country were so small that its national policies had no international ramifications, then indeed there would be no need for the world trading system to restrict its actions in order to achieve global efficiency. But most countries are large enough to affect world prices in at least some markets. As we shall see, zero tariffs would not be a unilateral best response for such moderately-sized or larger countries, even if their governments took the maximization of social welfare as their objective. We will follow the literature in assuming that each country's policy choices affect at least some world prices and turn now to a closer examination of what incentives such countries have to restrict trade in such circumstances.

2.4.2 The Unilateral Incentive to Exploit National Market Power

Economists have long recognized that governments concerned with national income may have a unilateral incentive to erect barriers to trade. Robert Torrens argued for reciprocity in trade liberalization based on the potentially adverse effects of a unilateral dismantling of England's trade barriers. Endorsing Torrens's claims, John Stuart Mill demonstrated that by levying an import tariff, a country could improve its "terms-of-trade" – that is, it could increase the price of its exports relative to its price of imports – and thereby enhance its share of the gains from trade.[20,21] Charles Bickerdike (1906) formalized Mill's argument and developed a diagrammatic analysis to illustrate the determinants of the size of the welfare-maximizing trade tax.

The potential for national gains from unilateral protection are readily seen in a familiar supply-and-demand analysis of perfectly competitive markets.

---

[20] Mill recognized that the benefits from unilateral protectionism implied a need for international cooperation, writing that "it is evidently the common interest of all nations that each of them should abstain from every measure by which the aggregate wealth of the commercial world would be diminished, although of this smaller sum total it might thereby be enabled to attract itself a larger share."

[21] The terms of trade thus measures the amount of imports that can be obtained for a unit of exports. In a two-good model, where a country imports one product and exports another, the terms of trade are simply the relative price of these two products. But with more goods, it is necessary to relate an index for import prices to an index for export prices.

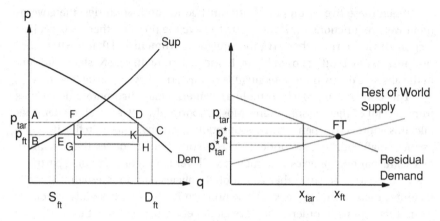

Figure 4: The Market for a Traded Product

In Figure 4, the left-hand panel depicts a country's demand for an importable good and its supply of a competing good, each drawn as a function of the domestic price. The horizontal difference between demand and supply at any price measures the demand for imports; when derived as the difference between domestic demand and supply, as is done here, it is also sometimes denoted the "residual demand." It is depicted on the right-hand panel, along with the rest of the world's residual supply of exports (i.e., the world's total supply less the sum of the internal demands). The intersection of import demand and export supply at point FT in the right-hand panel reveals the volume of trade, x_{ft}^*, and the terms of trade, p_{ft}^* when the home country practices free trade. On the left-hand panel, D_{ft} and S_{ft} represent the corresponding free-trade levels of domestic demand and supply.

Now suppose that the government of the importing country implements a small tariff at *ad valorem* rate t. This policy drives a wedge between the price received by foreign suppliers and the price paid by domestic consumers. Domestic producers are able to sell at the higher domestic price, because their output is not subject to the tax. With the tariff in place, import demand still must balance the export supply, but the quantities demanded and supplied must reflect the prices faced by the agents in each country. In the right-hand panel, we show the volume of trade that balances demand and supply when the domestic price p_{tar} exceeds the foreign price p_{tar}^* by the percentage t.

Notice that the importing country pays less to its trade partner for its imports with the tariff in place; that is, p_{tar}^* is less than p_{ft}^*. This is the terms-of-trade improvement first identified by Torrens and Mill. The tariff discourages consumption in the importing country, while the associated protection of domestic producers encourages their production. For both reasons, the demand for imports shrinks. With less demand in the world market, the world price falls.

Returning to the left-hand panel, we can gauge the implications of the tariff for aggregate welfare in the importing country. The tariff has three effects on welfare. First, consumers lose from the rise in the domestic price from p_{ft}^* to p_{tar}. The loss comprises the increased amount they pay for the goods they continue to consume at the higher price and the loss of surplus that results from their contracting consumption. Since the demand curve reveals consumers' "willingness-to-pay," the total loss to consumers is the area represented by $ABCD$ in the figure. Second, producers benefit from the protection. They gain from receiving more for the output that they originally produced and also from the expansion in production. The supply curve reveals the (marginal) cost of the resources that go into production, so $ABEF$ represents the increase in profits. Finally, the government captures revenue from the tariff. The revenue is the equal to the volume of imports, FD, times the gap between internal and foreign prices, $p_{tar} - p_{tar}^*$. In the figure, the tariff revenue is represented by $FGHD$. The government can use this revenue for instance to provide public goods valued by their constituents, to make payments to them, or to reduce their taxes. The government revenue can in turn be decomposed into two parts, reflecting the distribution of the burden of the tariff between domestic consumers and foreign producers: (i) the area $FDKJ$ represents tariff revenue that is effectively collected from domestic consumers, who are paying a higher price on the units that they continue to purchase after the tariff is imposed; and (ii) the area $JKHG$ corresponds to the reduction in foreign firms' profits stemming from the tariff-induced fall in the price these firms receive on the units they continue to sell with the tariff in place.

Neglecting the distributional implications for the time being, the net welfare effect for the importing country is the sum of the effects on consumers, producers, and the government. In the figure, this net gain is represented by the difference between the area of the rectangle $JKHG$ and the area of the two triangles, EFJ and DKC. The former is a terms-of-trade gain for the importing country – the volume of imports with the tariff in place times the amount by which the tariff causes the world price to fall. The latter is the "deadweight-loss" – the inefficiency caused by reducing consumption below the point where the willingness to pay equals the opportunity cost in terms of the payment to foreigners and by increasing production beyond the point where the marginal cost of the resources used by the domestic industry equals the opportunity cost of importing the goods from the foreign industry. The area of the triangles is small when the tariff rate is small, because a small tariff generates only a modest loss of efficiency. When the tariff rate is small, the sum of these areas cannot be as large as the area of the rectangle, so a small tariff always generates a net welfare gain for the importing country. The traditional "optimum tariff" is the tariff level that balances the marginal gain from improving the terms of trade with the marginal loss from exacerbating the deadweight loss. Or, put differently, it is the tariff level at which the marginal reduction of consumer welfare is just balanced by the marginal increase in the surplus for import-competing industry and in tariff revenue.[22]

Note that the unilateral incentive that an importing country has to impose a tariff does not hinge on the partner country pursuing any particular policy. National income-maximizing governments will perceive a benefit for restrictive policies no matter whether they expect the markets of their trade partners to be open or closed.

2.4.3 The Basic National Market Power Model

We have thus far considered the situation from the point of view of the importing country. We now ask, what is the impact of the tariff on a country's trade partner, and on global efficiency? As we just saw, for the importing country, there are two sources of deadweight loss: one stems from over production and the other from under consumption. But there is an offsetting gain, which is the portion of the tariff revenue that comes from the lowering of the international price of the imported product, or equivalently, the terms-of-trade gain on those units that continue to be traded after the imposition of the tariff. For the "Foreign" exporting country there are two types of costs. First, there is the reduction in the price of those units that continue to be traded after the imposition of the tariff. This loss is, of course, the mirror image of the importing country's gain, so in the calculus of global efficiency, the two effects cancel. The other cost borne by Foreign occurs because some units are not exported after the tariff is introduced, and the difference between the price at which they were traded under free trade and the (marginal) production costs reflects a deadweight loss imposed on the exporting country. The net effect of the tariff on global income comprises the three sources of deadweight losses. Put differently, while benefiting the importing country, the tariff necessarily is globally inefficient. Provided the exporting country could share the gains with the importing country, both governments could gain from a removal of the tariff. In the national market power approach, the basic rationale for a trade agreement is to enable such gains to be realized.

[22] The benefits that a country derives from unilaterally restricting its imports or exports are analogous to those that a firm with market power derives from restricting its supply or demand. A large firm can significantly affect the price at which it sells its output and buys its inputs. It maximizes profits by selling less than the competitive supply, or if being a larger buyer, by buying less than the competitive demand. Similarly, a large country can improve its terms of trade by selling less than the free-trade supply of its exports and buying less than the free-trade demand for imports. This could, in principle, be achieved if the many domestic buyers of the imported product were to hold back their purchases, and if the many small domestic exporters were to hold back their sales. However, they are typically not able to coordinate on such arrangements. Instead, the government effectively helps them achieve the same outcome, when it imposes a tariff.

We have so far considered the effects of the unilateral imposition of a tariff by Home, while assuming that Foreign does not pursue any interventionist trade policy of its own. But suppose that there is another sector where the roles of the two countries are reversed, so that Home exports a product to Foreign, with Foreign possibly imposing a tariff t^*. The roles of the two countries depicted in Figure 4 would then be reversed in this other market.

Due to the assumed structure of the economy and government objectives, any positive tariff would reduce global national income. Each country imposes on the other a negative externality when it unilaterally introduces a tariff, since the increase in national income for the importing country government necessarily falls short of the reduction in income for the exporting country government. This model provides an example of a setting that fulfills the assumptions made in Section 3 concerning government objective functions $G(t,t^*)$ and $G^*(t,t^*)$, as was illustrated in Figure 2. The difference between the two analyses is that the special model described here stipulates more precisely the supply and demand conditions, and government objectives, that give rise to a situation with international policy externalities.

The simple game-theoretic analysis that we developed in Section 2.3 can now be adapted to our special case. The outcome of such a policy game was first analyzed by Johnson (1953–1954). He presented a diagrammatic analysis similar to our depiction of a Nash equilibrium in Figure 2 above.[23] In the equilibrium he considered, each government imposes a tariff in order to exploit its national market power. The resulting Nash equilibrium is globally inefficient, because each government disregards the distortionary effect of its tariff. This leaves room for a trade agreement to raise aggregate welfare for both governments by increasing trade.

Although we have illustrated the argument with reference to a policy that restricts imports, a similar argument applies also to export restrictions. By taxing exports, a country reduces the supply of those goods to the world market, thereby driving up the world price and generating a terms-of-trade improvement on the export side. For a small tax, the revenue generated by the government plus the gain to local consumers from the induced fall in the domestic price must exceed the profit loss that domestic producers will suffer as a consequence. In fact, economists usually explain the terms-of-trade argument for trade policy in terms of a general equilibrium in which resources flow between and among export sectors and import-competing sectors and households allocate their budgets among exportable and import goods. In this setting, what matters for welfare is the relative price of exports in terms of imports, which is what economists

---

[23] The analysis was subsequently developed by Mayer (1981), who gave it a more rigorous game-theoretic setting.

mean by the terms of trade. Either a restriction on imports or a restriction on exports can be used to improve a country's terms of trade.

2.4.4 Discussion

Section 2.3 showed how international externalities from unilateral policy setting provide a rationale for the formation of trade agreements, relying on a few plausible general assumptions about the properties of government objective functions. But because of the lack of detail with regard to government preferences and the economy in which governments interact, the model did not shed light on the nature of these international externalities. In Sections 2.4.1 and 2.4.2, we went to the opposite extreme and presented a stylized special case of the international externalities model, which depicts national income (or social welfare) maximizing governments that interact in a two-good, perfectly competitive economy. The attraction of this model is that it illustrates, in an analytically simple way, what most economists see as the core inefficiency that trade agreements are intended to address, namely *the reduction in trade that results from unilateral tariff setting*. But the model obviously relies on some very special assumptions. In what follows, we will discuss several aspects of the model, including how it can be generalized. We will mostly focus on the assumed government behavior, but we begin with a brief discussion of the assumed structure of the economy.

2.4.4.1 *The Structure of the Economy*

With regard to the assumed structure of the economy, the simple model makes a number of strong assumptions, such as there being only two countries and two goods, all markets being perfectly competitive, etc. But the economic environment in the model can readily be generalized in various ways without changing the basic conclusion that noncooperative policy setting generates tariffs that are too high relative to what is required for global efficiency. For instance, the model can easily be expanded to include many countries and any number of goods. Also, as shown by Bagwell and Staiger (2009a,b), and as argued in the companion study *Principles of World Trade Law: Border Instruments*, similar conclusions may be drawn in settings with imperfect competition and with firm-level economies of scale. Consequently, the simplicity of the model with regard to the structure of the economy should be seen as a strength rather than a source of concern.

2.4.4.2 *Do Countries Have Sufficient Market Power?*

It is hardly controversial to claim that some large countries, like the United States or China are sufficiently important buyers of many of the products they import so that their purchase decisions affect world prices. For these countries, the assumption of national market power seems highly appropriate, although there is still a question of whether their market power is sufficiently great to explain the levels of protection that would prevail absent the GATT/WTO.[24] The more difficult issue is how to view the market power of smaller members of the WTO. Is it reasonable to assume that these countries have *some* impact on prices in world markets and that this motivates their inclusion in the trade agreement?

First note that even small countries may be important players in the markets for certain goods and may have significant market power in these markets. Transport costs may limit the geographic extent of the market for some goods, rendering the relevant market as a regional one in which relatively small countries are nonetheless big players. Many natural resources are found mainly in a small number of countries, so that the producers of these resources enjoy market power. Also, goods from different origins often are imperfect substitutes in the eyes of consumers, so that the producers of the differentiated goods can affect prices in a market niche. Moreover, most countries tend to export relatively few products compared to how many they import, and this specialization in production tends to create national (and/or firm-level) market power. For all of these reasons, even seemingly small countries may have an influence on world prices.

Be that as it may, the WTO includes as members many very small countries along with many more that are small with respect to most world markets. What incentives do such countries have to join the trade agreement, and what incentives do the large countries have to include them? One answer is that the reason for their joining and the reason for including them need be no different than for larger countries: by including a small country in the agreement, the larger trade partners can avoid a small negative spillover at a still smaller cost to themselves. By including many such countries in the agreement, the potential gains for the governments of the large countries could be substantially greater. There can thus be scope for an agreement that includes many small countries, even if the trade restrictions that these countries would apply if they were not members would be rather low.

Even if the small countries in the world trading system would not form an agreement among themselves if such an agreement did not already exist, these countries might well choose to become members of a trade agreement concluded among the larger countries in order to benefit from Most-Favored Nation treatment and to avoid facing the higher trade barriers imposed on nonmembers. Of course, an agreement designed by the larger countries need not be ideal

---

[24] We refrain from discussing a recent empirical literature that seeks to shed light on the extent to which tariffs can be explained by national market power, as exemplified by Broda, Limão, and Weinstein (2008), Bagwell and Staiger (2011), and Ossa (2011). This literature is highly relevant to the issue at stake here, but the literature is still in its infancy, and it would take our discussion into conceptually too difficult issues.

from the perspective of small-country governments, since with few valuable concessions to offer, the small countries might have little influence over the terms of a multilateral agreement.[25] The specific reductions in trade barriers agreed by the larger countries need not benefit the smaller trade countries compared to the barriers that would obtain in the absence of any multilateral agreement. But the fact that the government of a small country might prefer a world trading system without cooperation to one in which the large countries choose the terms does not imply that the small countries would prefer to stay out of any agreement that is reached; the small countries face a choice of joining or not, but do not have the means to enforce the benchmark outcome without any cooperation.

As we have seen, there are several reasons to believe that the national market power may be a driving force behind the membership of both larger and of smaller countries in trade agreements. But it does appear that many small countries erect trade barriers that are much higher than what can be explained by the potential exploitation of their world market power. This may primarily be explained by the influence of special interests in these countries, as we have noted above. But the high tariffs imposed by many small countries may be explained by several additional factors. For instance, these countries may lack capability to enact and enforce taxes on sales or income, leaving trade taxes as the administratively simplest way to government revenue. Alternatively, some countries may have a cultural reluctance to integrate into the world economy. Or, the consumer interest may be particularly weak and politically underrepresented in some small developing countries.

2.4.4.3 *Richer Descriptions of the Politics of Trade-Policy Formation*

Let us next turn to the assumptions concerning government objectives. The basic model seemingly provides an unrealistic depiction of the domestic politics of trade-policy choices. It is tempting to believe that governments rarely seek to maximize national income as their sole objective (although strictly speaking, such a claim should be verified empirically, and not simply be postulated). It therefore seems important to incorporate, into the modeling of trade agreements, a more realistic description of the political process, both as regards the incentives that governments perceive in making their policy choices absent any agreements and the incentives they have to form an agreement. Fortunately, the economics literature on trade policy has made great progress in generalizing the basic model to include richer descriptions of domestic politics.

As far back as the 1970s and even earlier, economists and political scientists have been studying how trade policies are formed via the interaction of the government, voters, and the private sector. The earlier attempts offered some

---

[25] This statement assumes that the small countries cannot band together to form a coalition. If they can do so, they can act collectively like a large country.

interesting insights and hypotheses, but they were often based on models and approaches that lacked the analytical rigor demanded in other areas of economics. But, in the last couple of decades, the research on the political economy of trade policy has made great progress, and the models of the political process that have been developed are every bit as sophisticated as those long used to model the economy. For example, Dixit and Londregan (1996) analyze policy formation in a polity in which two parties compete for votes in many electoral districts. They find that redistributive policies favor districts with relatively many "swing voters"; i.e., voters who find the ideological positions of the parties to be similarly appealing or unappealing. In the context of trade policy, their finding predicts protection for industries that are geographically concentrated in districts (or states) with many centrist voters. Grossman and Helpman (1994, 1995a, 1995b) examine trade policy formation in an environment in which politicians covet campaign contributions. When special interests offer contributions in exchange for implicit promises of policy favors, the resulting trade policy caters to the concerns of organized interests. The trade policies that emerge from the political contest are those that maximize a weighted average of aggregate welfare and the welfare of special interests in politically organized industries. Several other political-economy models of trade-policy formation have a similar feature.

Despite the wide variety of political interactions that are highlighted in these more sophisticated analyses, the models share certain features with the simple national market power model laid out in the previous Section. In particular, the models with more realistic depictions of politics still predict that unilaterally-chosen trade policies will be excessively restrictive compared to what would generate global efficiency, due to the continued presence in these models of a temptation for governments to exercise their national market power. As argued by Bagwell and Staiger (1999, 2002), the models with richer depictions of the political process offer fundamentally the same explanation for the existence of trade agreements as does the more basic model described in Section 2.4.2. Governments may set positive tariffs to cater to particular constituents, but the resulting tariffs will be even greater than what would result from constituent pressures due to the temptation they have to exploit national market power. The models with domestic politics may provide more realistic predictions about the level of protection absent an agreement, but they provide a similar explanation as models of national-income maximizing governments as concerns the incentives for international cooperation.

2.4.4.4 *The Role of Tariff Revenue*

The national market power model has been questioned by some on the grounds that it relies too heavily on the collection of tariff revenue as an incentive for governments to impose tariffs. Some observers have gone as far as to argue that tariff revenue is completely irrelevant to developed country governments when they set trade policies.[26] If one were to assume, contrary to the standard model, that the government's objective function puts no weight on tariff revenue whatsoever, then a national-income-maximizing government would have no reason to invoke positive tariffs and therefore no reason to enter into a trade agreement with other governments that behaved similarly. This can be seen from Figure 4, where the national benefit of the tariff is represented by the rectangle *JKHG*, a portion of the country's tariff revenue.

It is true that tariff revenue does not figure in the policy debates of most countries as a motive for trade restrictions, and it is rare to hear governments of developed countries refer to tariff revenue as a rationale for their tariffs. Still, we do not find the criticism to be entirely compelling.

First, as a matter of theory, while tariff revenue plays a central role in the work-horse model of trade agreements that assumes national-income-maximizing governments, it is less central in other models building on national market power. To illustrate, consider the Grossman and Helpman (1995a) model of political influence and suppose that the government puts a zero weight on social welfare and cares only about its campaign contributions. Then the tariff revenue would not directly affect the government's decisions about tariffs. Assume further that the special interests are concentrated in a very small fraction of the population, so that the members of the interests groups obtain only a negligible fraction of the redistributed tariff revenue. The special interests will then neglect tariff revenue when deciding about their campaign contributions. In this case, governments will choose their tariffs solely in view of the campaign contributions they are offered, which will in turn be based on the protection that special interests gain from tariffs and not on the revenues that are generated. Nonetheless, the tariffs that the governments will set will be inefficiently large when viewed from the perspective of the politically-influential interest groups in all countries taken together, and there will be scope for the governments to negotiate a trade agreement.

Second, governments do generally behave as if tax revenues matter to voters and constituents. Politicians need revenues to finance government spending on projects that are valuable to voters and for transfer programs that gain them political support. They are reluctant to raise income taxes and pay a political cost when they do so. On the margin, tariff revenues allow the government to spend more than it otherwise could or to maintain lower income and other tax rates than otherwise. If governments care about their finances, as surely must be the case, then they should also care about tariff revenue. It is not essential that voters and constituents recognize the link between tariffs and public spending, or between tariffs and other tax rates, for the government to behave as if the tariff

---

[26] See, for example, Ethier (2006) and Regan (2006).

revenues are valuable. Rather, it is enough that voters see benefits from public goods and that they dislike other forms of taxes. Then, a government that recognizes a (long-run) budget constraint should be expected to place a positive weight on tariff revenues as a means to provide voters and constituents with valued goods and services.

2.4.4.5 *Labeling the Government Behavior That Trade Agreements Address*

At a general level, the role of a trade agreement can be described as helping countries to prevent international externalities from unilateral tariff setting. But more descriptive labels are often used to describe the problem that trade agreements are intended to solve. The designation of a very precise role for a trade agreement is a somewhat elusive task, however.

It is common in the literature to link the role of trade agreements to the unilateral incentives facing governments. For instance, Bagwell and Staiger (1999) focus on the incentives of governments to improve the *terms of trade*: "...trade agreements are appealing to governments solely as a means to remedy the inefficient terms-of-trade-driven restrictions in trade that arise when trade policies are set unilaterally...." This notion is often criticized, however. Critics assert that the notion of terms of trade hardly ever figures in the policy debate, and that governments rarely deliberately seek to depress prices of imports, or increase the world prices of exports. Partly in response to this objection, Hillman and Moser (1996) describe the problem that trade agreements address as stemming from governments' unilateral incentives to *restrict market access* due to the perceived benefit from preserving sales in their home market for local firms. This terminology is, of course, much more in tune with what policy makers seem to care about than the notion that governments impose import restrictions in order to improve the terms of trade.

But Bagwell and Staiger (2002, p. 30) argue that there is no real distinction between the two views on the unilateral incentives for governments: because of the intrinsic interrelationship (or duality) between prices and quantities, one might equally well assume that governments worry about the terms of trade or about market access. To see how, think of the standard downward sloping schedule that relates the quantity demanded to price. We can either view the graph as illustrating the quantity that will be purchased at each price, or as illustrating the price that consumers are willing to pay for each quantity – the two formulations reveal exactly the same information. Similarly, Bagwell and Staiger would argue, it is immaterial whether we assume that governments are concerned with the price of their imports for any imported quantity – the terms of trade – or about the quantities being traded at a given price – the market access. The alternative terms just reflect two sides of the same coin: an improvement in the terms of trade goes hand in hand with an improvement in market access; when governments request better access for their firms to foreign markets, they are also requesting higher export prices for the initial volume of exports, or equivalently, better terms of trade. Negotiations about market access can thus be regarded as negotiations about the terms of trade, even if the governments are unaware of this equivalence.[27]

Regardless of how we view government motives, it is not the change in terms of trade as such that is the problem with unilateral tariff setting: when both countries impose tariffs, the effects on the terms of trade will tend to counteract one another. It is even possible that the two, offsetting tariffs will leave the terms of trade approximately where they would have been under free trade. But the tariff-ridden equilibrium will still yield less welfare for the parties compared to what could be achieved with free trade, or with an efficient trade agreement, because the lesser volume of trade means fewer gains from trade. The more fundamental problem caused by unilateral tariff setting is that governments reduce trade volumes in order to achieve their objectives, whatever they may be. Consequently, it seems appropriate to identify the fundamental rationale for trade agreements as to *induce governments to internalize the externalities that result from their unilateral reductions of import demand and export supply.*

2.4.5 Are Predictions from the National Market Power Model Compatible with the Design of the GATT?

A minimal requirement for our theory of trade agreements is that it should identify a plausible rationale for the existence of the GATT (or WTO). But it is also highly desirable that the theory should be compatible with the salient features of the GATT, and in particular that the theory should explain how some of these features contribute to solving the problem that the theory identifies as the rationale for the agreement. This is desirable for at least two related reasons. First, the extent to which the model seems to explain core features serves as a "reality check," in the sense that if most core features of the GATT seemed incompatible with model's predictions, it would be difficult to argue that it captures the essential rationale for the existence of the GATT. Second, the purpose of this project is not to explain the existence of the GATT – although this would be a worthy task on its own – but to contribute to improving the interpretation of the text. We would be much abetted in this task if theory could help us to explain the broad purposes of the provisions to be analyzed.

[27] This argument might not adequately reflect protectionist motives for being concerned about market access. For instance, Regan (2006) argues that for a protectionist government, the increase in domestic production is the desirable consequence of the imposition of a tariff. But for a government that seeks to improve the terms of trade, the reduction of the imported volume is undesirable as such, but is the means through which the improvement in terms of trade is achieved. Accordingly, the two views do not seem to simply reflect two sides of the same coin.

In this Section, we will point to a number of features of the GATT that are notable when the agreement is viewed from an economic perspective and we will very briefly discuss the extent to which a national market power approach can shed light on these features. By necessity, the analysis will have to be superficial; however, most of the features mentioned here are discussed more fully in the accompanying study *Legal and Economic Principles of World Trade Law: Border Instruments*. Whether a feature is deemed "notable" is of course highly subjective, and other observers might point to different features than those mentioned here. Moreover, the national market power approach encompasses a large number of different contributions, and it is not possible to evaluate the contributions of each separate model. Instead, we will discuss in broader terms whether national market power seems to be an important part of the rationale for a variety of observed features. Our general conclusion is that the national market power model does provide plausible explanations for a number of core features of the GATT, or is at least broadly compatible with these features. But we will also point to some aspects of the GATT that are harder to fit into the model.

2.4.5.1 *Border Instruments Are Regulated, But Alternative Policies Are Treated Differently*

The basic restrictions imposed by the GATT are ceilings on permissible levels of border instruments. Such ceilings make eminent sense from the perspective of the national market power model, since a basic proposition from the model is that governments will impose trade measures that are too restrictive if they are chosen unilaterally. But not all border measures are treated similarly by the GATT/WTO. Quantitative trade restrictions are illegal by virtue of GATT Article XI on both the import and the export side, while fiscal measures are treated much less categorically. Meanwhile, export subsidies were treated rather permissively in the early GATT years (under GATT Articles XVI and VI), but are now illegal by virtue of the WTO *Agreement on Subsidies and Countervailing Measures* (SCM). In contrast, export taxes are treated symmetrically with import tariffs under GATT Articles II and XXVIII *bis*, and therefore are legal. In principle, export taxes could be bound just like tariffs (although Art. II GATT refers only to importation), but in practice they are not; we return to export taxes and subsidies below. Somewhere in between these extremes are tariffs, which are legal, but the maximum height of the taxes are bound through negotiation.

The GATT's hostile attitude toward quantitative trade restrictions is superficially compatible with the general theoretical proposition that quantitative trade restrictions are more distortionary than fiscal measures when employed to achieve the same objective.[28] But in order to explain why the GATT prohibits

---

[28] Although an import quota and an import tariff can be made equivalent in all respects under very special circumstances – essentially those that are assumed in the basic national market

such measures, we need to explain why they are used at all, since if they are not used, there is little reason to prohibit them. We also need to explain why the externalities from quantitative import restrictions are likely to be worse than those from tariffs – if they are not, we have no explanation for why the parties would steer permissible protection over to tariffs. It is far from obvious how to explain either of these features, however. The extra distortionary costs from quantitative measures that theory identifies are typically borne by the country imposing them. This suggests that countries should prefer to employ tariffs rather than quotas. It also suggests that countries might impose less protection in case they have to rely on quotas, these being more costly to the importing country than tariffs. If so, it would seem appropriate that the agreement bans *tariffs* rather than quotas, in order to reduce international externalities.[29] We are led to conclude that the national market power approach does not provide a simple explanation for one of the more fundamental aspects of the GATT, namely its preference for fiscal measures over direct regulation of trade volumes.

2.4.5.2 *The Emphasis on Reciprocity*

Reciprocity arises in two forms in the GATT/WTO, referring as it does to a balance of concessions between parties. First, it appears in the rules concerning renegotiations of tariff bindings: Art. XXVIII.2 GATT stipulates that such renegotiation must maintain the reciprocal balance of concessions that had been agreed previously. Second, reciprocity is frequently mentioned in more general statements concerning tariff negotiations. For instance, after listing a number of objectives that the GATT is to achieve, the Preamble of the GATT states the following:

> Being desirous of contributing to these objectives by entering into reciprocal and mutually advantageous arrangements directed to the substantial reduction of tariffs and other barriers to trade and to the elimination of discriminatory treatment in international commerce. ...

Here, reciprocity has been interpreted more as a norm than as a legal requirement. The more precise meaning of this norm has not been well developed in the GATT/WTO, however.

---

power model, but with only one country being policy active – in many situations it will be less costly in terms of distortions to employ tariffs rather than import quotas to achieve a given level of imports.

[29] An additional layer of complexity appears when we take into consideration the self-enforcement constraints. As discussed above, the degree of liberalization that can be achieved through a self-enforcing agreement depends on the extent to which the parties have incentives to punish deviations from the agreement, and the effectiveness of these punishments. It seems to be an open question whether quantitative restrictions perform better in this regard.

Reciprocity in the second sense could be given a rather strict interpretation. Such a stance is illustrated by the following passage from the final report by the USTR on the Kennedy Round of GATT negotiations, which explains the various criteria used by the USTR in measuring reciprocity:

> In order to simplify the presentation, the results of U.S. participation in the Kennedy Round tariff negotiations are presented in this report solely in terms of the value of trade covered by the concessions and the depth of the tariff reductions. However, in the course of the negotiations, numerous other factors were considered in evaluating the balance of concessions – the height of duties, the characteristics of individual products, demand and supply elasticities, and the size and nature of markets, including the reduction in the disadvantage to U.S. exports achieved through reductions in the tariffs applied to the exports of the United States and other non-member countries by the European Economic Community (EEC), the European Free-trade Area (EFTA) and those countries in the British Commonwealth preferential system. (U.S. Office of Special Representative for Trade Negotiations, Report on United States Negotiations, 1967, Vol. I, p. iii.)

Alternatively, "reciprocity" could be seen more as a bargaining norm, and this is the path that the bureaucrats have followed in later work. For instance, a GATT Working Party responded to a proposal by Brazil to adopt a definition of reciprocity as follows:

> ...the Working Party noted that there was nothing in the Agreement, or in the rules for tariff negotiations which has been used in the past, to prevent governments from adopting any formula they might choose, and therefore considered that there was no need for the CONTRACTING PARTIES to make any recommendation in this matter. (GATT, BISD, Third Supplement, p. 22)[30]

Evidently, the emphasis on reciprocity extends as a negotiating norm to general GATT/WTO tariff negotiations, and seems to reflect the balance between the trade effects of concessions offered and received.

Both notions of reciprocity can be explained within a national market power model.[31] It is an intrinsic nature of any negotiated settlement in a situation where parties expose each other to externalities, that the parties exchange concessions. It may appear as a rather self-evident feature to demand of any model of the formation of trade agreements that it should feature this form of reciprocity.

---

[30] This and the previous quote are from Hoda (2001).

[31] For instance, Bagwell and Staiger (1999) argue that reciprocal tariff reductions in the GATT context can be understood as reductions that maintain the terms of trade. This interpretation sheds light on both Art. XXVIII GATT renegotiations, and general tariff negotiations.

But, as discussed in Section 2.5, not all models purporting to explain the existence of trade agreements share this feature.

2.4.5.3 *Border Instruments Are Regulated, But Domestic Instruments Are Not*

Section 2.3.4.3 points to a fundamental difference in how GATT treats internal domestic policies and border instruments. The use of policies that apply to goods as they cross international borders typically is regulated by the trade agreement. But the GATT leaves governments with broad discretion to set their own internal policies, only imposing general constraints on how this discretion can be exercised. It is clearly desirable that a theory to be used to interpret the GATT contributes to explaining this characteristic of the agreement.

There is a fairly large body of literature that studies various aspects of the incompleteness of trade agreements. This literature assumes almost exclusively that the basic role of trade agreements is to prevent governments from seeking to exploit national market power, and it focuses on the extent to which the agreements prevent governments from using domestic instruments for such purposes. National market power does not as such explain the incompleteness of trade agreements – most of the literature studies the impact of exogenously imposed restrictions on what governments can regulate in an agreement, although there are recent attempts to explain the structure of trade agreements from a contract-theoretic perspective.[32] But the models that explore the implications of contractual completeness do make use of the national market power approach as their explanation for the existence of a trade agreement in the first place.

2.4.5.4 *The Most-Favored Nation Principle*

While the GATT/WTO prohibits the use of certain border measures, it leaves significant room for the member governments to either negotiate bindings on other policies – as in the case of tariffs – or to set the levels of policies unilaterally. The parties are not completely unconstrained in this regard, however. Two nondiscrimination clauses constitute basic restrictions on permissible policies. These are the *Most-Favored Nation* (MFN) clause in Art. I GATT and the *National Treatment* (NT) clause in Art. III. The MFN clause applies to any type of border measure, and (by virtue of the reference to Art. III GATT, which we discuss below) also to any type of domestic measure. It stipulates that an imported product originating from one member country must be treated no less favorably than a like imported product from any other country with regard to virtually any government policy. The provision is widely viewed as one of the cornerstones of the GATT/WTO.

---

[32] Early papers in this literature include Copeland (1990) and Hungerford (1991), which highlight consequences of exogenously imposed contractual incompleteness. Horn, Maggi, and Staiger (2010) show how contracting costs may explain why border instruments are bound but not domestic instruments.

There is a fairly large literature on MFN. Most studies build on the national market power model, and analyze its consequences for trade, and for tariff liberalization. Some contributions to this literature also suggest reasons for the inclusion of this provision in trade agreements. From the point of view of the national market power approach, this is of course reassuring. But interesting insights into the rationale of MFN are also provided by studies using alternative approaches.[33]

2.4.5.5 *The National Treatment Principle*

Although the NT clause shares certain general features with MFN, its ambit is different. Whereas the MFN clause applies to all policies, whether pursued at the border or domestically, NT applies only to domestic policies. Moreover, whereas the MFN clause applies to a comparison of similar products from different sources of imports, NT restricts the relative policy treatment of imported versus domestically-produced products.

There is a small economics literature on NT. As in the case of MFN, most of this literature is compatible with, and builds on, the national market power approach.[34] This literature is described in more detail in the accompanying study *Legal and Economic Principles of World Trade Law: National Treatment*.

2.4.5.6 *Rules Concerning Preferential Trading Agreements*

While the MFN provision is seen as a cornerstone of the GATT/WTO, it is singled out almost as often for its exceptions as its rule. The main exception can be found in Art. XXIV GATT, which allows for the formation of preferential trading arrangements (PTAs). These arrangements are by their very nature discriminatory, as is acknowledged through the term "preferential." They allow subsets of GATT/WTO member countries to eliminate tariffs on one another's trade while maintaining positive (but common) tariffs against other GATT/WTO member countries who are not part of the arrangement. The apparent contradiction between the MFN principle and Art. XXIV GATT raises fundamental questions about the purposes of the various provisions, and also about the precise way in which the rules governing the formation of PTAs have been formulated.

A large economic literature – too vast to cite here – studies various aspects of PTA formation, in a large variety of different economic settings. This literature often employs models with similar mechanisms as in the national market power model. It thus seems fair to say that the mechanisms that are captured in the national market power model help to explain the incentives that countries have to form PTAs, and to some extent also the GATT rules that regulate their terms (such as the requirement that tariffs against non-PTA countries must not

[33] For a discussion of the literature, and for references, see Horn and Mavroidis (2001), and Schwartz and Sykes (2002).

[34] Horn (2006), and Saggi and Sara (2008), analyze implications of exogenously imposed NT-like provisions. Horn, Maggi, and Staiger (2010) show how contracting costs might explain the existence of such a provision.

increase as a result of the formation of the PTA). But we are not aware of any analyses of the rationale for Art. XXIV that point to national market power as the underlying force.

2.4.5.7 *Possibilities to Escape Bindings*

From the inception of the GATT it was anticipated that governments might need to escape from negotiated tariff commitments. Flexibility is provided by Art. XIX GATT for temporary escape and in Art. XXVIII GATT for permanent escape. The WTO Agreement contains additional understandings and agreements related to each Article. Of particular significance is the accompanying *Agreement on Safeguards*, which represents an attempt to clarify and strengthen the mechanism for members to unilaterally withdraw concessions with regard to tariffs for a limited period of time.

The economic literature contains some analysis of safeguards and renegotiations in trade agreements. To the best of our knowledge, most of the literature develops frameworks that are based on the national market power model. In these models, governments have incentives to impose tariffs in order to exploit national market power, thus exposing trade partners to negative externalities, and the basic purpose of the agreement is to induce governments to internalize these effects. But the design of the optimal agreement is more complicated than usual, because it is assumed that random exogenous events can affect the efficient degree of trade liberalization. The literature considers various aspects of this contracting problem, such as for example the balance between the need to check members' unilateral incentives to pretend injury in order to exploit national market power and the desire to allow them to escape bindings in situations where this is efficient.[35]

The national market power model does not by itself explain the inclusion in the agreement of possibilities for temporary escape and for permanent renegotiations in the GATT. But the focus in this approach on international efficiency makes it a natural starting point to study such mechanisms.

2.4.5.8 *Gradual Trade Liberalization*

A direct application of any of the international externalities models discussed above would suggest that the founders of the GATT should have negotiated efficient tariffs once and for all. Instead, one of the distinguishing features of the GATT/WTO has been its very gradual process of tariff liberalization, agreed

---

[35] For a recent extensive analysis and for references, see Bagwell and Staiger (2005), and Herzing (2005). A number of reports in the case-law part of this project discuss the role of safeguards in the WTO, See, e.g., Bagwell and Sykes (2004), Grossman and Mavroidis (2004a), Grossman and Sykes (2006), and Horn and Mavroidis (2004a). See also Regan (2006) for a critical discussion of the ability of the national market power model to capture salient features of WTO safeguards.

upon through a series of tariff negotiations since its inception. This gradualism does not apply only to the rate at which tariffs on individual goods have been lowered; it applies as well to a number of other dimensions of the GATT/WTO, including the gradual expansion of GATT/WTO coverage to additional product categories and issue areas and the gradual expansion of GATT/WTO membership. Clearly, the gradual nature of trade liberalization in the GATT/WTO represents an important feature of the multilateral agreement.

A fairly sizeable literature seeks to explain gradualism in trade negotiations. The gradualism might stem from various causes, but a common assumption is that certain factors of production, such as human capital, move sluggishly from one sector to another in response to changes in prices. As a result, it may be desirable to lower trade barriers slowly, to allow time for the factors to adjust. Several of these models assume that the purpose of a trade agreement is to internalize externalities from exploitation of national market power, although the gradualism in the model does not stem from this particular objective for an agreement.[36]

2.4.5.9 Export Taxes Are Legal

The national market power model is compatible with, or can even be used to plausibly explain, most of the core features of the GATT that we have pointed to above. We now come to a pair of characteristic features of the GATT/WTO that are much more difficult to reconcile with this approach. These problems go to the heart of the national market power model, since they directly concern government incentives and possibility to change the terms of trade in their favor.

Before pointing to the problem, let us briefly explain a feature of trade policies that is known as "Lerner symmetry."[37] It appears in general equilibrium analysis and takes its sharpest form in a standard two-good, two-country framework. The Lerner symmetry theorem states that, in such a setting, an export tax at some ad valorem rate has exactly the same effects on resource allocation and welfare as an import tariff at the same rate. To gain some intuition for this somewhat surprising symmetry property, note that the direct effect of an import tariff is to increase the domestic prices in the import-competing sector. This will have the general equilibrium ramification of attracting productive resources in the export sector to shift into the import-competing sector, while discouraging consumption of this good. The direct effect of an export tax rather is to reduce domestic prices in the export sector, which stimulates resources to move out of the export industry and encourages consumption of the export good. In short, the alternative measures have the same influence on the *relative* price, they encourage resources to move in the same direction, and they induce similar

---

[36] See, e.g., Bagwell (2009), Chisik (2003), and Maggi and Rodríguez-Clare (2007), for analyses and further references to the literature.

[37] See Lerner (1936).

incentives for consumers to substitute in their purchases. The complete symmetry between an import tariff and an export tax breaks when there are more than two goods.[38] But it will still be possible to use export taxes to stimulate production in import-competing industries.

With this background, let us now turn to the role of export taxes in the GATT. As noted above, governments' use of export taxes is hardly restricted by the GATT. It would be possible to negotiate bindings, just like those for tariffs, but this has not occurred to any significant degree. As noted by Ethier (2004, 2006), this feature of the GATT does not seem to fit very well with the national market power model. The model proposes that tariffs are bound in order to prevent governments from restricting imports that can be used to exploit national market power. But Members have the economic and legal possibility to use export taxes for a similar purpose. It might seem implausible in the light of the GATT's failure to regulate export taxes that the purpose of the agreement could be to prevent the exploitation of national market power.

In our view, the GATT's failure to regulate export taxes is not fully consistent with the national market power model. But there are several reasons why the critique is not as severe as is sometimes argued, and why the incentives to use export taxes may not be as strong as the argument above suggests.

First, the fact that GATT Members largely abstain from using export taxes even absent any legal restrictions can be explained within a national market power model, such as the one of Grossman and Helpman (1995a), if it is assumed that the weight on domestic interests relative to aggregate welfare in governments' objective functions is sufficiently high. The governments would then refrain from imposing export taxes, even if they were perceived as beneficial from an aggregate welfare point of view, due to the harm they do to special interests in export industries.

Second, export taxes might have politically unattractive features: the direct effect is to push resources in the export sectors into unemployment, and depress the rents to the specific factors in these sectors. Then as the rewards to these factors fall, they will gradually move to other sectors. This process is likely to take considerable time, and will be a hard sell from a political point of view for any government with a short time horizon. The process would be further delayed to the extent that there are nominal rigidities, in the form of inflexible prices and wages. It is thus doubtful whether there would be political gains to be had from taxing or other restrictions on exports. Indeed, as argued by Ethier (2004), the political process seems to disproportionately reward the direct effects of policy measures, and the direct effects of export taxes are likely to have adverse implications for the popularity of incumbent governments.

---

[38] According to a weaker Lerner Symmetry theorem, applying to the case of more than two goods, a uniform import tariff at the same rate on all import goods is equivalent to a uniform export tax at that rate on all export goods.

Third, it would require a very good understanding of the workings of the general equilibrium system in order to replace a system of tariffs by a corresponding system of export taxes, if the two systems are to have the same economic effects. Tariffs are bound in the WTO mostly at the six-digit Harmonized System level, with many countries binding thousands of tariff levels. It is simply not a practical possibility to compute a system of export taxes that would come anywhere near having the same effects. Of course, this argument presupposes that imposing import barriers is simpler. But intuitively, this seems to be the case, and in any event, this is the historical record with which countries become members of the GATT/WTO.

Fourth, even if governments rarely use export taxes, there are still instances when they do – the recent *China–Raw Materials* dispute is an example of this. But governments also sometimes use other forms of export restraints that generate terms-of-trade gains, just like export taxes would. For instance, some countries have more permissive approaches toward cartels in export industries than in other sectors. An export cartel can achieve similar allocational effects as would an export tax, the main difference being that the surplus of the measure shows up as increased profits for cartelized firms, rather than as tax revenue for the government. The *US–Export Restraints* dispute concerned yet another form of export restraint.[39]

Finally, the fact that there are hardly any bindings of export taxes in the GATT does not by itself imply that governments are free to use export taxes freely. If countries started using export taxes, they would likely be bound through negotiations just like tariffs. Hence, while the lack of export tax bindings may say something about the desire of governments to impose such taxes, it does not say much about what would be the eventual treatment of such instruments if they were to be used more extensively.

2.4.5.10 *Subsidies Are Restricted*

The MFN and NT provisions place broad limitations on discrimination by WTO Members in their choices of both border and internal measures. But the existing trade agreements also place specific limits on the use of domestic and export subsidies. We have already mentioned the prohibition on the use of export subsidies in the GATT/WTO, observing that this treatment evolved from one of relative permissiveness in the early GATT years to outright prohibition under the WTO *SCM Agreement*. The *SCM Agreement* prohibits also a second type of subsidy, one that is conditioned on the use of a domestically produced import. The *SCM Agreement* does not make domestic (production or factor-use) subsidies illegal per se, but it does designate some such subsidies as "actionable" based on the external harm they induce. This harm can arise both when an importing

---

[39] Janow and Staiger (2003a) provide an economic analysis of issues raised in this dispute.

country displaces imports by subsidizing a domestic industry producing a like product, and when the subsidy adversely affects an exporter of a like product in a third market. Again the treatment of these domestic subsidies has evolved over the years: in the GATT years, the domestic subsidies of a member government could be challenged, but only if they upset the legitimate expectations of market access negotiated with another member government.

A fundamental aspect of export subsidies is that they *worsen* the terms of trade of the subsidizing country. As pointed out by, e.g., Ethier (2011), this does not square well with the notion that the purpose of the GATT is to steer countries away from seeking unilaterally to improve their terms of trade. But the prohibition of export subsidies can still be understood within an international externalities framework, such as the Grossman and Helpman (1995a) model: Suppose that each politically motivated government has strong preferences for its import competing interests, but also subsidizes exports, due to a strong weight on profits of export interests. These subsidies will then generate negative externalities, being set without consideration of the harm they do to foreign import competing interests, and there will consequently be scope for an agreement between the governments to internalize these externalities.

A prohibition of export subsidies can also partly be understood even for governments that maximize social welfare or national income, especially in markets that are imperfectly competitive. In such a setting, each government may face a unilateral incentive to subsidize exports in order to shift profits to its domestic producers. But the subsidies by each exporting government will worsen the terms of trade for other countries that export similar goods. It may be that all exporting countries lose as a result of their collective subsidies even though each alone has an incentive to do so. If so, the export subsidizing governments might prefer to prohibit subsidies. However, note that such a prohibition would adversely affect the interests of import-competing countries, and so a prohibition on subsidies might not be reached if all governments (and not just those of exporting countries) are parties to the international negotiation.

2.4.5.11 *Anti-dumping*

The most difficult feature of the GATT for the national market power model to explain are the agreement's rules concerning anti-dumping duties as embodied in Art. VI GATT and in the *Agreement on the Implementation of Article VI of the General Agreement on Tariffs and Trade 1994*. These complex rules can loosely be described as permitting importing countries to impose duties when foreign firms price discriminate by charging lower prices in their export markets than at home, or when these firms set export prices that are below some constructed measure of production costs. The problem that the national market power approach has in explaining these provisions is, of course, that importing countries should welcome low import prices. There would not be any deeper inconsistency between the treatment of dumping in the GATT/WTO and the national market power approach if the exporting firms did not change their pricing behavior in response to the threat of anti-dumping duties; with export prices constant, anti-dumping duties would serve to transfer revenues from the exporting firms to the importing government, which would represent an improvement in the terms of trade. However, anti-dumping duties are intended not to raise revenue, but to induce the foreign firms to *increase* their export prices, since these can avoid paying the duty by doing so. As formulated, the anti-dumping regime thereby generates a deterioration of the importing country's terms of trade. Accordingly, these provisions stand in sharp conflict with the logic of the national market power model.

2.5 Trade Agreements as Government Commitment Devices Vis-à-Vis Constituent Interests

In the discussion thus far, the overriding purpose of trade agreements has been to mediate the strategic interaction between governments. A smaller economic literature highlights what sometimes is presented as an alternative view of trade agreements, according to which the purpose of these agreements is to provide a mechanism for governments to commit to liberal trade policies, and thereby resist the pressures from their own domestic interests. This literature is often referred to as the "commitment approach" to explaining the role of trade agreements. The possibility for governments to gain from committing to certain policies is well-known from a number of strands in the economic literature, as well as from actual policymaking. For instance, this notion is an important reason why many governments have left the control over monetary policy to independent central banks.

We will briefly present two illustrations of how a commitment mechanism may help a government in the context of its trade-policy setting. We will then explain why we believe the commitment approach should be seen as complementing the national market power approach, rather than as being an alternative explanation for the existence of trade agreements.

Example 1: Suppose that wages in an industry are influenced by the actions of a labor union. The union can push up wages in order to increase incomes for employed members, but doing so will also tend to create unemployment. The unemployment would be mitigated, however, if the government subsequently imposes a tariff. The union finds most desirable an outcome that combines high wages tariff protection. But it prefers lower wages to high wages in the absence of import protection in recognition of the unemployment that high wages would then cause. The government in turn prefers low wages and free trade. But it will protect the industry with a tariff when wages are high, to avoid unemployment. In such a setting, and absent any commitment to trade policy, the labor union will push up wages, to exploit the government's aversion against unemployment, and the government will respond by protecting the domestic industry.

Now suppose that the government can commit to free trade by entering into a trade agreement. If the union sees the agreement as credible and binding, it will know that the government has no discretion to respond to the threat of high unemployment with protection. Realizing that high wages will cause unemployment, the union will now opt for lower wages. The outcome with the agreement will thus be more favorable to the government, since it can avoid unemployment without having to bear the associated costs of the protection.

The example is special, but illustrates two more general points. First, the government benefits from the *commitment* that the agreement provides: the fact that the government can no longer control the tariff policy changes the incentives facing the union, causing it to take actions that are beneficial to the government's interests. Second, this benefit from the agreement does *not* hinge on any exploitation of national market power. Indeed, we could assume that the country in the example is "small" in the sense discussed above, thus completely removing any national market power motivation for imposing a tariff. The agreement would still be beneficial to the government, by affecting the behavior of the union.

Example 2: Suppose that a government derives welfare both from domestic social welfare, as well as from the campaign contributions. The campaign contributions are offered by the import-competing sector in return for promises of protection. The industry benefits more from protection the more capital is invested there, and therefore the contributions vary with the size of the industry capital stock. If the government makes no commitments about its trade policy, the opportunity that the industry has to lobby for protection will lure capital to the import-competing industry, which in turn will induce the government to grant a high level of protection. If the government instead enters a trade agreement that compels free trade, the investment in the import-competing sector will be smaller and the industry's motive for campaign contributions will vanish. From the government's perspective, the loss of contributions is a negative consequence of the commitment, but the deterrence to overinvestment in the industry is a potential benefit. Depending on the weights in the government's objective function, it may prefer an outcome with zero contributions but a smaller resource misallocation to one with positive contributions but a gross misallocation of capital.[40]

---

[40] This is an extremely simplified account of the Maggi and Rodríguez-Clare (1998) model.

These two examples thus show how a *restriction* on a government's ability to freely choose its future policy actually benefits the government by changing the behavior of private interest groups with which it interacts. The trade policy literature contains other examples of situations in which governments may benefit from a similar type of commitments.[41] The unifying theme is that the commitments solve a "time consistency" problem for the government: the government prefers ex ante the outcome that results from a "tough" stance ex post, but a mere threat to act tough is not effective, because the interest group knows that the government would not actually wish to carry out the threat. By signing a trade agreement that locks in its future level of protection, the government buys credibility for its threat to act tough, and so can induce better behavior from the special interests.

The commitment approach is often seen as representing a conceptually distinct explanation for why countries form trade agreements, since it does not rely on international externalities. But this does not seem to us to be correct. The basic idea of the commitment approach is that governments will be punished by trade partners, should they increase tariffs beyond bound levels. But how can such punishment be administered if countries lack market power? If the deviating importing country is small, trade partners would not be affected by the deviation, and would for this reason have little incentive to impose retaliatory tariffs that would be costly to itself. And if the trade partner is small, the imposition of retaliatory tariffs would be ineffective, since it would not hurt the deviating import country. It thus appears that in order for the commitment to be effective, both the country making the commitment, and the trade partners that are to enforce it, must have some national market power.

It should also be noted that several core features of the GATT/WTO seem difficult to understand were commitment the only reason for a trade agreement:

1. If there is one single feature that more than anything else characterizes multilateral trade liberalization, it is the difficulty to find mutually acceptable *concessions* in terms of tariff cuts and adoption of regulations. Countries seem genuinely unwilling to liberalize unilaterally, and they seem to desire other countries to liberalize.
2. As argued by Ethier (2001), many of the rules concerning dispute settlement in the GATT/WTO *restrict* the possibilities for members to take countermeasures. For instance, countermeasures cannot be taken by other members than those affected by an illegality; countermeasures typically come with a significant delay because of the need to go through the formal process of adjudication, and a recalcitrant responding country can, through legal measures, delay countermeasures by several years; and when countermeasures

---

[41] See, for instance, Maggi and Rodríguez-Clare (2007) and references cited there.

are finally imposed, they have to be commensurate with the ongoing deviation.

3. The GATT/WTO incorporates several forms of safeguards that allow members to escape their commitments. While it would be possible to construct a rationale for safeguards in a commitment contract, it does appear as if the scope to use them would be more limited than if the purpose of the agreement were to internalize externalities.

4. If the purpose of the GATT/WTO were to serve as a commitment device, the legal text would presumably insist on the *obligations* of the parties toward the other parties. There are indeed frequent references to obligations, but these obligations create rights for other parties, not restrictions on what they can do. Indeed, Art. XXIII GATT, which specifies the circumstances under which a member can successfully pursue a complaint against another member, reads:

> "If any contracting party should consider that any benefit accruing to it directly or indirectly under this Agreement is being nullified or impaired...."

This core provision gives a right to a member to take action if the member believes that *its* rights have been denied. It does not *request* the member to do so, should other parties fail to live up to their obligations. Of course, it could be argued that if trade partners always protected their interests, the two things would amount to the same thing in practice. But it would still seem odd that an agreement purportedly serving the role of a commitment device, should instead emphasize the rights of trade partners.

5. Related to the previous point, Art. XXIII GATT only allows a member to take countermeasures when benefits accruing to this member have been nullified or impaired, that is, when it has been adversely *affected* by another member. But, as was argued above, if countries are small, how could a deviation by a single member affect trade partners? This fundamental provision indeed seems squarely designed to address situations where there *are* externalities of some form, but the commitment approach alone does not explain what these are.

To conclude, the commitment approach captures interesting aspects of the interaction between governments and their constituent interests. But it does not provide an independent explanation for the existence of trade agreements; it should thus better be seen as complementing some form of national market power approach. While there may well be countries that have acceded to the WTO in order to achieve commitment, this cannot be true for all of the countries in the multilateral system, or even for the largest and most important members of the WTO.

2.6 Concluding Remarks

The purpose of this study has been to introduce the reader to an approach used by most economists to study trade agreements – what we denoted as the international externalities approach. The analytical core of this approach is the notion that governments expose one another to externalities when they set their trade policies unilaterally, and that trade agreements provide a way to help governments coordinate on more efficient outcomes. Section 2.3 illustrated this idea in a very general form, making only a few assumptions about the functioning of the economy and political systems of the trade partners under study. The Section also discussed several intrinsic features of trade agreements, such as the fact that they are negotiated, reciprocal, self-enforcing, explicit, and incomplete.

The depiction of trade agreements in Section 2.3 illustrated the basic externality problem that trade agreements address, but it was too general to yield any more specific predictions concerning the properties of equilibrium agreements or outcomes. Section 2.4 described how the international externalities approach is typically operationalized within a particular model of the economy and polity. The Section first laid out the simplest model of trade-agreement formation, which assumes national income maximizing governments and perfectly competitive markets. In this setting, governments impose negative externalities in their attempts to exert their national market power. We argued that the simple baseline model can be modified to capture more realistic economic structures and government objectives, and that the model is compatible with many core features of the GATT. But we also discussed some of the criticism that has been directed toward the model, and noted that certain features of the GATT are hard to reconcile with the model. Finally, Section 2.5 briefly discussed the commitment approach, which often is seen as the main alternative explanation to the role of trade agreements. But as argued, this approach should rather be seen as a complement to the national market power approach.

So where does this leave us? In our view, the fundamental rationale for the GATT is to help governments avoid externalities from unilateral determination of policies. These externalities arise when governments reduce import demand in order to achieve their domestic policy objectives. When import demand is reduced, exporters face lower prices for any volume they sell, and they sell smaller volumes for any price they charge, and as a consequence export less. A reduced import demand is not necessarily negative, as a matter of theory – a reduction may be desirable for instance if the consumption of imports causes environmental harm. However, since the full costs of tariffs are not factored into governments' unilateral decisions, tariffs will typically be set too high from a global point of view. In such circumstances, reciprocal reductions of tariffs can be found that benefit all governments. The central role of the GATT is to help governments achieve this. This vision of the role of GATT can be harbored reasonably well within the national market power approach.

REFERENCES

Bagwell, Kyle. 2009. Self-Enforcing Trade Agreements and Private Information, NBER Working Paper 14812, National Bureau of Economic Research, Inc.

Bagwell, Kyle, and Robert W. Staiger. 1999. An Economic Theory of the GATT. American Economic Review 89(1), pp. 215–248.

Bagwell, Kyle, and Robert W. Staiger. 2002. The Economics of the World Trading System, MIT Press : Cambridge, Mass.

Bagwell, Kyle, and Robert W. Staiger. 2005. Enforcement, Private Political Pressure and the GATT/WTO Escape Clause, The Journal of Legal Studies 34(2).

Bagwell, Kyle, and Robert W. Staiger. 2006. Will International Rules on Subsidies Disrupt the World Trading System?, American Economic Review, 96(3), June 2006, pp. 877–895(19).

Bagwell, Kyle, and R. W. Staiger. 2009a. Profit Shifting and Trade Agreements in Imperfectly Competitive Markets, NBER Working Paper 14803.

Bagwell, Kyle, and R. W. Staiger. 2009b, Delocation and Trade Agreements in Imperfectly Competitive Markets, unpublished manuscript, Stanford University.

Bagwell, Kyle, and Robert W. Staiger. 2011. What Do Trade Negotiators Negotiate About? Empirical Evidence from the World Trade Organization. American Economic Review 101(4), pp. 1238–1273.

Bagwell, Kyle, and Alan O. Sykes. 2004. Chile – Price Band System and Safeguard Measures Relating to Certain Agricultural Products, in Henrik Horn and Petros C. Mavroidis (eds.), The WTO Case Law of 2002: The American Law Institute Reporters' Studies, Cambridge: Cambridge University Press.

Bickerdike, Charles 1906. The Theory of Incipient Taxes, Economic Journal XVI (December), pp. 529–535.

Broda, Christian, Nuno Limão, and David E. Weinstein, 2008. Optimal Tariffs and Market Power: The Evidence. American Economic Review 98(5), pp. 2032–2065.

Chisik, Richard. 2003. Gradualism in Free Trade Agreements: A Theoretical Justification, Journal of International Economics 59(2), pp. 367–397.

Copeland, Brian R., 1990. Strategic enhancement and destruction of fisheries and the environment in the presence of international externalities, Journal of Environmental Economics and Management 19(3), pp. 213–226.

Crowley, Meredith A., and David Palmeter. 2009. Japan – Countervailing Duties on Dynamic Random Access Memories from Korea (DS 336 and Corr.1, adopted 17 December 2007), World Trade Review 8(1), pp. 259–272.

Dixit, Avinash K., and John Londregan. 1996. The Determinants of Success of Special Interests in Redistributive Politics, Journal of Politics 58, pp. 1132–1155.

Ethier, Wilfred J. 2001. Theoretical problems in negotiating trade liberalization, European Journal of Political Economy 17(2), pp. 209–232.

Ethier, Wilfred J. 2004. Political Externalities, Nondiscrimination, and a Multilateral World, Review of International Economics 12(3), pp. 303–320.

Ethier, Wilfred J. 2006. The Theory of Trade Policy and Trade Agreements: A Critique, Penn Institute for Economic Research Working Paper 06-013.

Ethier, Wilfred J. 2011. The Political Economy of Protection, in Bernhofen, Daniel, Rod Falvey, David Greenaway, and Udo Kreickemeier (eds.), Palgrave Handbook of International Trade.

Grossman, Gene M., and Elhanan Helpman. 1994. Protection for Sale, American Economic Review 84(4), pp. 833–850.

Grossman, Gene M., and Elhanan Helpman. 1995a. Trade Wars and Trade Talks, Journal of Political Economy 103(4), pp. 675–708.

Grossman, Gene M., and Elhanan Helpman. 1995b. The Politics of Free-Trade Agreements, American Economic Review 85(4), pp. 667–690.

Grossman, Gene M., and Petros C. Mavroidis. 2003. United States – Imposition of Countervailing Duties on Certain Hot-Rolled Lead and Bismuth Carbon Steel Products Originating in the United Kingdom: Here Today, Gone Tomorrow? Privatization and the Injury Caused by Non-Recurring Subsidies, The WTO Case Law of 2001: The American Law Institute Reporters' Studies, Cambridge: Cambridge University Press, pp. 170–200.

Grossman, Gene M., and Petros C. Mavroidis. 2004a. United States – Definitive Safeguard Measures on Imports of Circular Welded Carbon Quality Line Pipe from Korea, in Henrik Horn and Petros C. Mavroidis (eds.), The WTO Case Law of 2002: The American Law Institute Reporters' Studies, Cambridge: Cambridge University Press.

Grossman, Gene M., and Petros C. Mavroidis. 2004b. United States – Countervailing Measures Concerning Certain Products from the European Communities: Recurring Misunderstanding of Non-Recurring Subsidies, in Henrik Horn and Petros C. Mavroidis (eds.), The WTO Case Law of 2002: The American Law Institute Reporters' Studies, Cambridge: Cambridge University Press.

Grossman, Gene M., and Alan O. Sykes. 2006. United States – Definitive Safeguard Measures on Imports of Certain Steel Products, in Henrik Horn and Petros C. Mavroidis (eds.), The WTO Case Law of 2003: The American Law Institute Reporters' Studies, Cambridge: Cambridge University Press.

Grossman, Gene M., and Alan O. Sykes. 2011. 'Optimal' Retaliation in the WTO – a commentary on the Upland Cotton Arbitration, World Trade Review 10, pp. 133–164.

Herzing, Mathias. 2005. Essays on Uncertainty and Escape in Trade Agreements, Monograph No. 50, Institute for International Economic Studies, Stockholm University.

Hillman, Arye L., and Peter Moser. 1996. Trade Liberalization as Politically Optimal Exchange of Market Access, in Canzoneri, Mathew, Wilfed J. Ethier, and Vittorio Grilli (eds.), The New Transatlantic Economy, Cambridge: Cambridge University Press, pp. 295–312.

Hoda, Anwarul. 2001. Tariff Negotiations and Renegotiations under the GATT and the WTO: Procedures and Practices, Cambridge: Cambridge University Press.

Hoekman, Bernard, and Robert L. Howse. 2008. EC – Sugar, World Trade Review, Cambridge University Press, vol. 7(01), pages 149–178.

Hoekman, Bernard M., and Michel M. Kostecki. 2009. The Political Economy of the World Trading System: The WTO and Beyond, Oxford University Press.

Horn, Henrik. 2006. National Treatment in Trade Agreements, American Economic Review 96(1), pp. 394–404.

Horn, Henrik, and Petros C. Mavroidis. 2001. Legal and Economic Aspects of MFN, European Journal of Political Economy 17, pp. 233–279.

Horn, Henrik, and Petros C. Mavroidis. 2004a. US Safeguard Measures on Imports of Fresh, Chilled or Frozen Lamb Meat from New Zealand and Australia: what should be required of a safeguard investigation?, World Trade Review 2(3), pp. 395–430.

Horn, Henrik, and Petros C. Mavroidis. 2004b. United States – Preliminary Determination with Respect to Certain Softwood Lumber from Canada: What is a Subsidy?, in Henrik Horn and Petros C. Mavroidis (eds.), The WTO Case Law of 2002: The American Law Institute Reporters' Studies, Cambridge: Cambridge University Press.

Horn, Henrik, and Petros C. Mavroidis. 2006. United States – Final Determination with Respect to Certain Softwood Lumber from Canada. In Henrik Horn and Petros C. Mavroidis (eds.), The WTO Case Law of 2002: The American Law Institute Reporters' Studies, Cambridge: Cambridge University Press.

Horn, Henrik, Giovanni Maggi, and Robert W. Staiger. 2010. The GATT as an Endogenously Incomplete Contract, American Economic Review 100(1), pp. 394–419.

Hungerford, Thomas L. 1991. GATT: A cooperative equilibrium in a noncooperative trading regime?, Journal of International Economics 31(3–4), pp. 357–369.

Janow, Merit E., and Robert W. Staiger. 2003a. United States – Measures Treating Export Restraints as Subsidies, in Henrik Horn and Petros C. Mavroidis (eds.), The WTO Case Law of 2001: The American Law Institute Reporters' Studies, Cambridge: Cambridge University Press, pp. 201–235.

Janow, Merit E., and Robert W. Staiger. 2003b. Canada – Measures Affecting the Importation of Dairy Products and the Exportation of Milk, in Henrik Horn and Petros C. Mavroidis (eds.), The WTO Case Law of 2001: The American Law Institute Reporters' Studies, Cambridge: Cambridge University Press, pp. 236–280.

Johnson, Harry G. 1953–1954. Optimum Tariffs and Retaliation, Review of Economic Studies 21, pp. 142–153.

Lerner, Abba P. 1936. The Symmetry Between Import and Export Taxes, Economica 3(11), pp. 306–313.

Mayer, Wolfgang. 1981. Theoretical Considerations of Negotiated Tariff Adjustments, Oxford Economic Papers 33, pp. 135–153.

Magee, Stephen P. 1994. Endogenous Protection: A Survey, in: Mueller, D. C. (ed.), Handbook of Public Choice, Cambridge, MA: Basil Blackwell.

Maggi, Giovanni, and Andrés Rodriguez-Clare. 1998. The Value of Trade Agreements in the Presence of Political Pressures, Journal of Political Economy 106(3), pp. 574–601.

Maggi, Giovanni, and Andrés Rodríguez-Clare. 2007. A Political-Economy Theory of Trade Agreements, American Economic Review 97(4), pp. 1374–1406.

Nelson, David. 1988. Endogenous Tariff Theory: A Critical Survey, American Journal of Political Science 32, pp. 796–837.

Ossa, Ralph. 2011. Trade Wars and Trade Talks with Data. NBER Working Paper Series No. 17347, Boston, Mass.

Regan, Donald H. 2006. What Are Trade Agreements For? – Two Conflicting Stories Told by Economists, With a Lesson for Lawyers, Journal of International Economic Law 9(4), pp. 951–988.

Rodrik, Dani. 1995. Political Economy of Trade Policy, in Grossman, G., and K. Rogoff (eds.), Handbook of International Economics III, Amsterdam: North-Holland, pp. 1457–1495.

Saggi, Kamal, and Nese Sara. 2008. National Treatment at the WTO: The Roles of Product and Country Heterogeneity, International Economic Review 49(4), pp. 1365–1394.

Sapir, Andre, and Joel P. Trachtman. 2008. Subsidization, price suppression, and expertise: causation and precision in Upland Cotton, World Trade Review 7(1), pp. 183–209.

Schropp, Simon. 2009. Trade Policy Flexibility and Enforcement in the WTO: A Law & Economics Analysis, Cambridge University Press.

Schwartz, Warren F., and Alan O. Sykes. 2002. The Economics Structure of Renegotiation and Dispute Resolution in the WTO/GATT System, Journal of Legal Studies 31(1), pp. 179–204.

Staiger, Robert W. 1995. International Rules and Institutions for Trade Policy, in Grossman, Gene M., and Kenneth Rogoff (eds.), Handbook of International Economics III, Amsterdam: North-Holland, pp. 1495–1551.

Sykes, Alan O. 2005. The Economics of WTO Rules on Subsidies and Countervailing Measures, in A. Appleton, P. Macrory & M. Plummer eds., The World Trade Organization: Legal, Economic and Political Analysis, Vol. II, New York: Springer Verlag.

WTO. 2008. World Trade Report 2008: Trade in a Globalizing World, World Trade Organization, Geneva.

KYLE BAGWELL, ROBERT W. STAIGER, AND ALAN O. SYKES

3 Border Instruments

3.1 Introduction

The objective of this study is to analyze the treatment of border instruments in the WTO/GATT system from both a legal and economic perspective. Our goals are both positive and normative. From a positive perspective, we will draw on the economic theory of international trade and relevant aspects of economic history to explain the legal treatment of border instruments in the WTO/GATT system as it has evolved over time. From a normative perspective, we will build on an economic understanding of the function of the various legal disciplines to critique elements of the treaty text and the case law.

We limit our focus to the disciplines on traditional instruments of import protection and export promotion that are applicable to all WTO Members. Because such border instruments are mainly relevant to trade in goods, we focus here on the GATT – GATS and TRIPs are outside the scope of the current study. We consider the core tariff bindings of GATT (Articles II and XXVIII pertaining to renegotiation), restrictions on quantitative restrictions and "other measures" (Article XI), and the nondiscrimination or "most-favored-nation" (MFN) obligations that apply to these measures (Article I) as well as brief attention to the exceptions created for preferential trading arrangements (Article XXIV) and special or differential treatment for developing countries. We also consider the disciplines applicable to export subsidies in both the original GATT (as amended) and the Agreement on Subsidies and Countervailing Measures (SCMs Agreement).

The study is organized as follows. In the remainder of this Section, we present the key treaty text. Section 3.2 concerns the rationale for negotiated constraints on the traditional instruments of protection, while Section 3.3 follows with an analysis and critique of the pertinent case law in these areas. Section 3.4 concerns the rationale for the MFN requirement and its exceptions, while Section 3.5 addresses the case law on these subjects. Sections 3.6 and 3.7 provide a parallel discussion of the rationale for disciplines on export subsidies and the relevant case law.

3.1.1 The Treaty Text

3.1.1.1 *Tariff Commitments*

The basic tariff commitments of GATT are contained in Article II, and in the associated tariff-commitment schedules of all WTO Members to which Article II makes reference. In addition, GATT contains provisions for renegotiation of tariff commitments in Article XXVIII.

Article II of GATT provides:

Schedules of Concessions

1. (a) Each contracting party shall accord to the commerce of the other contracting parties treatment no less favourable than that provided for in the appropriate Part of the appropriate Schedule annexed to this Agreement.

   (b) The products described in Part I of the Schedule relating to any contracting party, which are the products of territories of other contracting parties, shall, on their importation into the territory to which the Schedule relates, and subject to the terms, conditions or qualifications set forth in that Schedule, be exempt from ordinary customs duties in excess of those set forth and provided therein. Such products shall also be exempt from all other duties or charges of any kind imposed on or in connection with the importation in excess of those imposed on the date of this Agreement or those directly and mandatorily required to be imposed thereafter by legislation in force in the importing territory on that date.

   (c) The products described in Part II of the Schedule relating to any contracting party which are the products of territories entitled under Article I to receive preferential treatment upon importation into the territory to which the Schedule relates shall, on their importation into such territory, and subject to the terms, conditions or qualifications set forth in that Schedule, be exempt from ordinary customs duties in excess of those set forth and provided for in Part II of that Schedule. Such products shall also be exempt from all other duties or charges of any kind imposed on or in connection with importation in excess of those imposed on the date of this Agreement or those directly or mandatorily required to be imposed thereafter by legislation in force in the importing territory on that date. Nothing in this Article shall prevent any contracting party from maintaining its requirements existing on the date of this Agreement as to the eligibility of goods for entry at preferential rates of duty.

2. Nothing in this Article shall prevent any contracting party from imposing at any time on the importation of any product:

   (a) a charge equivalent to an internal tax imposed consistently with the provisions of paragraph 2 of Article III* in respect of the like domestic product or in respect of an article from which the imported product has been manufactured or produced in whole or in part;

(b) any anti-dumping or countervailing duty applied consistently with the provisions of Article VI;*

(c) fees or other charges commensurate with the cost of services rendered.

3. No contracting party shall alter its method of determining dutiable value or of converting currencies so as to impair the value of any of the concessions provided for in the appropriate Schedule annexed to this Agreement.

4. If any contracting party establishes, maintains or authorizes, formally or in effect, a monopoly of the importation of any product described in the appropriate Schedule annexed to this Agreement, such monopoly shall not, except as provided for in that Schedule or as otherwise agreed between the parties which initially negotiated the concession, operate so as to afford protection on the average in excess of the amount of protection provided for in that Schedule. The provisions of this paragraph shall not limit the use by contracting parties of any form of assistance to domestic producers permitted by other provisions of this Agreement.*

5. If any contracting party considers that a product is not receiving from another contracting party the treatment which the first contracting party believes to have been contemplated by a concession provided for in the appropriate Schedule annexed to this Agreement, it shall bring the matter directly to the attention of the other contracting party. If the latter agrees that the treatment contemplated was that claimed by the first contracting party, but declares that such treatment cannot be accorded because a court or other proper authority has ruled to the effect that the product involved cannot be classified under the tariff laws of such contracting party so as to permit the treatment contemplated in this Agreement, the two contracting parties, together with any other contracting parties substantially interested, shall enter promptly into further negotiations with a view to a compensatory adjustment of the matter.

6. (a) The specific duties and charges included in the Schedules relating to contracting parties members of the International Monetary Fund, and margins of preference in specific duties and charges maintained by such contracting parties, are expressed in the appropriate currency at the par value accepted or provisionally recognized by the Fund at the date of this Agreement. Accordingly, in case this par value is reduced consistently with the Articles of Agreement of the International Monetary Fund by more than twenty per centum, such specific duties and charges and margins of preference may be adjusted to take account of such reduction; provided that the CONTRACTING PARTIES (i.e., the contracting parties acting jointly as provided for in Article XXV) concur that such adjustments will not impair the value of the concessions provided for in the appropriate Schedule or

elsewhere in this Agreement, due account being taken of all factors which may influence the need for, or urgency of, such adjustments.

(b) Similar provisions shall apply to any contracting party not a member of the Fund, as from the date on which such contracting party becomes a member of the Fund or enters into a special exchange agreement in pursuance of Article XV.

7. The Schedules annexed to this Agreement are hereby made an integral part of Part I of this Agreement.

Article II also has a few "footnotes" (denoted in the text by an asterisk) contained in Ad Article II, which reads:

Paragraph 2 (a)
The cross-reference, in paragraph 2 (a) of Article II, to paragraph 2 of Article III shall only apply after Article III has been modified by the entry into force of the amendment provided for in the Protocol Modifying Part II and Article XXVI of the General Agreement on Tariffs and Trade, dated September 14, 1948.

Paragraph 2 (b)
See the note relating to paragraph 1 of Article I.

Paragraph 4
Except where otherwise specifically agreed between the contracting parties which initially negotiated the concession, the provisions of this paragraph will be applied in the light of the provisions of Article 31 of the Havana Charter.

Each WTO member has its own schedule of tariff commitments in accordance with Article II:1(a), embodying, *inter alia*, the obligations undertaken in the course of its tariff negotiations with other members. In addition, the obligation in paragraph 1(b) of Article II respecting "other duties or charges of any kind" has been elaborated by a WTO Understanding on the Interpretation of Article II:1(b), which we omit in the interest of brevity.

Because tariffs are most often expressed as "ad valorem" charges (a percentage of the value of the imported good), the method by which customs authorities compute the value of imported merchandise becomes quite important. Indeed, it is not difficult to find examples of importing nations that have apparently inflated the value of imported goods to impose higher tariffs. Likewise, importers have an incentive to under-report the true value of goods to reduce tariff liability. This problem can become particularly acute if the importer is affiliated with the exporter. GATT addresses these issues in Article VII, which we again omit in the interest of brevity.

GATT also contains a number of provisions permitting the modification of tariff commitments. Temporary withdrawal of commitments in the face of an import surge causing "serious injury" to an import-competing industry – so-called safeguard measures – are the province of Article XIX and the WTO Agreement on Safeguards. We do not consider these measures. Provisions for the permanent withdrawal or modification of tariff commitments are contained in Article XXVIII, which provides:

Modification of Schedules*

1. On the first day of each three-year period, the first period beginning on 1 January 1958 (or on the first day of any other period* that may be specified by the CONTRACTING PARTIES by two-thirds of the votes cast) a contracting party (hereafter in this Article referred to as the "applicant contracting party") may, by negotiation and agreement with any contracting party with which such concession was initially negotiated and with any other contracting party determined by the CONTRACTING PARTIES to have a principal supplying interest* (which two preceding categories of contracting parties, together with the applicant contracting party, are in this Article hereinafter referred to as the "contracting parties primarily concerned"), and subject to consultation with any other contracting party determined by the CONTRACTING PARTIES to have a substantial interest* in such concession, modify or withdraw a concession* included in the appropriate schedule annexed to this Agreement.

2. In such negotiations and agreement, which may include provision for compensatory adjustment with respect to other products, the contracting parties concerned shall endeavour to maintain a general level of reciprocal and mutually advantageous concessions not less favourable to trade than that provided for in this Agreement prior to such negotiations.

3. (a) If agreement between the contracting parties primarily concerned cannot be reached before 1 January 1958 or before the expiration of a period envisaged in paragraph 1 of this Article, the contracting party which proposes to modify or withdraw the concession shall, nevertheless, be free to do so and if such action is taken any contracting party with which such concession was initially negotiated, any contracting party determined under paragraph 1 to have a principal supplying interest and any contracting party determined under paragraph 1 to have a substantial interest shall then be free not later than six months after such action is taken, to withdraw, upon the expiration of thirty days from the day on which written notice of such withdrawal is received by the CONTRACTING PARTIES, substantially equivalent concessions initially negotiated with the applicant contracting party.

   (b) If agreement between the contracting parties primarily concerned is reached but any other contracting party determined under paragraph 1 of this Article to have a substantial interest is not satisfied, such other contracting party shall be free, not later than six months after action under such agreement is taken, to withdraw, upon the expiration of thirty days from the day on which written notice of such withdrawal is received by the CONTRACTING PARTIES, substantially equivalent concessions initially negotiated with the applicant contracting party.

4. The CONTRACTING PARTIES may, at any time, in special circumstances, authorize* a contracting party to enter into negotiations for modification or withdrawal of a concession included in the appropriate Schedule annexed to this Agreement subject to the following procedures and conditions:

(a) Such negotiations* and any related consultations shall be conducted in accordance with the provisions of paragraph 1 and 2 of this Article.

(b) If agreement between the contracting parties primarily concerned is reached in the negotiations, the provisions of paragraph 3 (b) of this Article shall apply.

(c) If agreement between the contracting parties primarily concerned is not reached within a period of sixty days* after negotiations have been authorized, or within such longer period as the CONTRACTING PARTIES may have prescribed, the applicant contracting party may refer the matter to the CONTRACTING PARTIES.

(d) Upon such reference, the CONTRACTING PARTIES shall promptly examine the matter and submit their views to the contracting parties primarily concerned with the aim of achieving a settlement. If a settlement is reached, the provisions of paragraph 3 (b) shall apply as if agreement between the contracting parties primarily concerned had been reached. If no settlement is reached between the contracting parties primarily concerned, the applicant contracting party shall be free to modify or withdraw the concession, unless the CONTRACTING PARTIES determine that the applicant contracting party has unreasonably failed to offer adequate compensation.* If such action is taken, any contracting party with which the concession was initially negotiated, any contracting party determined under paragraph 4 (a) to have a principal supplying interest and any contracting party determined under paragraph 4 (a) to have a substantial interest, shall be free, not later than six months after such action is taken, to modify or withdraw, upon the expiration of thirty days from the day on which written notice of such withdrawal is received by the CONTRACTING PARTIES, substantially equivalent concessions initially negotiated with applicant contracting party.

5. Before 1 January 1958 and before the end of any period envisaged in paragraph 1 a contracting party may elect by notifying the CONTRACTING PARTIES to reserve the right, for the duration of the next period, to modify the appropriate Schedule in accordance with the procedures of

paragraph 1 to 3. If a contracting party so elects, other contracting parties shall have the right, during the same period, to modify or withdraw, in accordance with the same procedures, concessions initially negotiated with that contracting party.

The lengthy footnotes in Ad Article XXVIII provide:

The CONTRACTING PARTIES and each contracting party concerned should arrange to conduct the negotiations and consultations with the greatest possible secrecy in order to avoid premature disclosure of details of prospective tariff changes. The CONTRACTING PARTIES shall be informed immediately of all changes in national tariffs resulting from recourse to this Article.

Paragraph 1

1. If the CONTRACTING PARTIES specify a period other than a three-year period, a contracting party may act pursuant to paragraph 1 or paragraph 3 of Article XXVIII on the first day following the expiration of such other period and, unless the CONTRACTING PARTIES have again specified another period, subsequent periods will be three-year periods following the expiration of such specified period.
2. The provision that on 1 January 1958, and on other days determined pursuant to paragraph 1, a contracting party "may...modify or withdraw a concession" means that on such day, and on the first day after the end of each period, the legal obligation of such contracting party under Article II is altered; it does not mean that the changes in its customs tariff should necessarily be made effective on that day. If a tariff change resulting from negotiations undertaken pursuant to this Article is delayed, the entry into force of any compensatory concessions may be similarly delayed.
3. Not earlier than six months, nor later than three months, prior to 1 January 1958, or to the termination date of any subsequent period, a contracting party wishing to modify or withdraw any concession embodied in the appropriate Schedule, should notify the CONTRACTING PARTIES to this effect. The CONTRACTING PARTIES shall then determine the contracting party or contracting parties with which the negotiations or consultations referred to in paragraph 1 shall take place. Any contracting party so determined shall participate in such negotiations or consultations with the applicant contracting party with the aim of reaching agreement before the end of the period. Any extension of the assured life of the Schedules shall relate to the Schedules as modified after such negotiations, in accordance with paragraphs 1, 2, and 3 of Article XXVIII. If the CONTRACTING PARTIES are arranging for multilateral tariff negotiations to take place within the period of six months before 1 January 1958, or before any other day determined pursuant to paragraph 1, they

shall include in the arrangements for such negotiations suitable procedures for carrying out the negotiations referred to in this paragraph.

4. The object of providing for the participation in the negotiation of any
   contracting party with a principal supplying interest, in addition to any
   contracting party with which the concession was originally negotiated, is
   to ensure that a contracting party with a larger share in the trade affected
   by the concession than a contracting party with which the concession
   was originally negotiated shall have an effective opportunity to protect
   the contractual right which it enjoys under this Agreement. On the other
   hand, it is not intended that the scope of the negotiations should be
   such as to make negotiations and agreement under Article XXVIII unduly
   difficult nor to create complications in the application of this Article
   in the future to concessions which result from negotiations thereunder.
   Accordingly, the CONTRACTING PARTIES should only determine that
   a contracting party has a principal supplying interest if that contracting party has had, over a reasonable period of time prior to the nego- ·
   tiations, a larger share in the market of the applicant contracting party
   than a contracting party with which the concession was initially negotiated or would, in the judgement of the CONTRACTING PARTIES, have
   had such a share in the absence of discriminatory quantitative restrictions maintained by the applicant contracting party. It would therefore
   not be appropriate for the CONTRACTING PARTIES to determine that
   more than one contracting party, or in those exceptional cases where
   there is near equality more than two contracting parties, had a principal
   supplying interest.

5. Notwithstanding the definition of a principal supplying interest in note
   4 to paragraph 1, the CONTRACTING PARTIES may exceptionally determine that a contracting party has a principal supplying interest if the
   concession in question affects trade which constitutes a major part of
   the total exports of such contracting party.

6. It is not intended that provision for participation in the negotiations of
   any contracting party with a principal supplying interest, and for consultation with any contracting party having a substantial interest in the
   concession which the applicant contracting party is seeking to modify or
   withdraw, should have the effect that it should have to pay compensation
   or suffer retaliation greater than the withdrawal or modification sought,
   judged in the light of the conditions of trade at the time of the proposed
   withdrawal or modification, making allowance for any discriminatory
   quantitative restrictions maintained by the applicant contracting party.

7. The expression "substantial interest" is not capable of a precise definition and accordingly may present difficulties for the CONTRACTING
   PARTIES. It is, however, intended to be construed to cover only those
   contracting parties which have, or in the absence of discriminatory

quantitative restrictions affecting their exports could reasonably be expected to have, a significant share in the market of the contracting party seeking to modify or withdraw the concession.

Paragraph 4

1. Any request for authorization to enter into negotiations shall be accompanied by all relevant statistical and other data. A decision on such request shall be made within thirty days of its submission.
2. It is recognized that to permit certain contracting parties, depending in large measure on a relatively small number of primary commodities and relying on the tariff as an important aid for furthering diversification of their economies or as an important source of revenue, normally to negotiate for the modification or withdrawal of concessions only under paragraph 1 of Article XXVIII, might cause them at such time to make modifications or withdrawals which in the long run would prove unnecessary. To avoid such a situation the CONTRACTING PARTIES shall authorize any such contracting party, under paragraph 4, to enter into negotiations unless they consider this would result in, or contribute substantially towards, such an increase in tariff levels as to threaten the stability of the Schedules to this Agreement or lead to undue disturbance of international trade.
3. It is expected that negotiations authorized under paragraph 4 for modification or withdrawal of a single item, or a very small group of items, could normally be brought to a conclusion in sixty days. It is recognized, however, that such a period will be inadequate for cases involving negotiations for the modification or withdrawal of a larger number of items and in such cases, therefore, it would be appropriate for the CONTRACTING PARTIES to prescribe a longer period.
4. The determination referred to in paragraph 4 (d) shall be made by the CONTRACTING PARTIES within thirty days of the submission of the matter to them unless the applicant contracting party agrees to a longer period.
5. In determining under paragraph 4 (d) whether an applicant contracting party has unreasonably failed to offer adequate compensation, it is understood that the CONTRACTING PARTIES will take due account of the special position of a contracting party which has bound a high proportion of its tariffs at very low rates of duty and to this extent has less scope than other contracting parties to make compensatory adjustment.

The obligations of Article XXVIII are further elaborated in an Understanding on the Interpretation of Article XXVIII, again omitted in the interest of brevity.

Finally, the GATT anticipated the prospect of regular multilateral negotiations toward further tariff liberalization. The authority for these negotiations is contained in Article XXVIIIbis, which we omit.

3.1.1.2 *Quantitative Restrictions and "Other Measures"*

We will focus in this study on the disciplines of general applicability to quantitative restrictions and similar measures. We will not, however, linger on all of the exceptions to these disciplines. Accordingly, we are not concerned here with the exceptions allowing quantitative restrictions for balance of payments and related development purposes (GATT Articles XII, XIV, and XVIII) or the general exceptions to GATT (Article XX). Likewise, we will not linger on any special rules in the Agreement on Agriculture.

The core limitations on quantitative restrictions and similar measures is found in GATT Article XI:

General Elimination of Quantitative Restrictions

1. No prohibitions or restrictions other than duties, taxes or other charges, whether made effective through quotas, import or export licences or other measures, shall be instituted or maintained by any contracting party on the importation of any product of the territory of any other contracting party or on the exportation or sale for export of any product destined for the territory of any other contracting party.
2. The provisions of paragraph 1 of this Article shall not extend to the following:
    (a) Export prohibitions or restrictions temporarily applied to prevent or relieve critical shortages of foodstuffs or other products essential to the exporting contracting party;
    (b) Import and export prohibitions or restrictions necessary to the application of standards or regulations for the classification, grading or marketing of commodities in international trade;
    (c) Import restrictions on any agricultural or fisheries product, imported in any form,* necessary to the enforcement of governmental measures which operate:
         (i) to restrict the quantities of the like domestic product permitted to be marketed or produced, or, if there is no substantial domestic production of the like product, of a domestic product for which the imported product can be directly substituted; or
         (ii) to remove a temporary surplus of the like domestic product, or, if there is no substantial domestic production of the like product, of a domestic product for which the imported product can be directly substituted, by making the surplus available to certain groups of domestic consumers free of charge or at prices below the current market level; or
         (iii) to restrict the quantities permitted to be produced of any animal product the production of which is directly dependent, wholly or mainly, on the imported commodity, if the domestic production of that commodity is relatively negligible.

Any contracting party applying restrictions on the importation of any product pursuant to subparagraph (c) of this paragraph shall give public notice of the total quantity or value of the product permitted to be imported during a specified future period and of any change in such quantity or value. Moreover, any restrictions applied under (i) above shall not be such as will reduce the total of imports relative to the total of domestic production, as compared with the proportion which might reasonably be expected to rule between the two in the absence of restrictions. In determining this proportion, the contracting party shall pay due regard to the proportion prevailing during a previous representative period and to any special factors* which may have affected or may be affecting the trade in the product concerned.

The footnotes in Ad Article XI are:

Paragraph 2 (c)
The term "in any form" in this paragraph covers the same products when in an early stage of processing and still perishable, which compete directly with the fresh product and if freely imported would tend to make the restriction on the fresh product ineffective.

Paragraph 2, last subparagraph
The term "special factors" includes changes in relative productive efficiency as between domestic and foreign producers, or as between different foreign producers, but not changes artificially brought about by means not permitted under the Agreement.

As the "general elimination" of quantitative restrictions and similar measures in Article XI is qualified by a number of exceptions, rules aimed at promoting the nondiscriminatory application of measures covered by such exceptions are found in Article XIII, the "quota-MFN" article. We will not have much to say about Article XIII and omit it in the interest of brevity.

3.1.1.3 *MFN and Exceptions*

The MFN obligation in GATT is found in Article I, which provides:

General Most-Favoured-Nation Treatment

1. With respect to customs duties and charges of any kind imposed on or in connection with importation or exportation or imposed on the international transfer of payments for imports or exports, and with respect to the method of levying such duties and charges, and with respect to all rules and formalities in connection with importation and exportation, and with respect to all matters referred to in paragraphs 2 and 4 of Article III, any advantage, favour, privilege or immunity granted by any contracting party to any product originating in or destined for any other

country shall be accorded immediately and unconditionally to the like product originating in or destined for the territories of all other contracting parties.

2. The provisions of paragraph 1 of this Article shall not require the elimination of any preferences in respect of import duties or charges which do not exceed the levels provided for in paragraph 4 of this Article and which fall within the following descriptions:

   (a) Preferences in force exclusively between two or more of the territories listed in Annex A, subject to the conditions set forth therein;

   (b) Preferences in force exclusively between two or more territories which on July 1, 1939, were connected by common sovereignty or relations of protection or suzerainty and which are listed in Annexes B, C and D, subject to the conditions set forth therein;

   (c) Preferences in force exclusively between the United States of America and the Republic of Cuba;

   (d) Preferences in force exclusively between neighbouring countries listed in Annexes E and F.

3. The provisions of paragraph 1 shall not apply to preferences between the countries formerly a part of the Ottoman Empire and detached from it on July 24, 1923, provided such preferences are approved under paragraph 5, of Article XXV which shall be applied in this respect in the light of paragraph 1 of Article XXIX.

4. The margin of preference on any product in respect of which a preference is permitted under paragraph 2 of this Article but is not specifically set forth as a maximum margin of preference in the appropriate Schedule annexed to this Agreement shall not exceed:

   (a) in respect of duties or charges on any product described in such Schedule, the difference between the most-favoured-nation and preferential rates provided for therein; if no preferential rate is provided for, the preferential rate shall for the purposes of this paragraph be taken to be that in force on April 10, 1947, and, if no most-favoured-nation rate is provided for, the margin shall not exceed the difference between the most-favoured-nation and preferential rates existing on April 10, 1947;

   (b) in respect of duties or charges on any product not described in the appropriate Schedule, the difference between the most-favoured-nation and preferential rates existing on April 10, 1947.

   In the case of the contracting parties named in Annex G, the date of April 10, 1947, referred to in subparagraph (a) and (b) of this paragraph shall be replaced by the respective dates set forth in that Annex.

At the founding of GATT, the most important exceptions to the MFN obligation were contained in Article I(2) and Article II(1)(c), set forth above, which allowed for the retention of many colonial preferences. In more modern times, the exceptions for preferential trading arrangements – customs unions and free trade areas – have become much more important. The authority for such arrangements is contained in GATT Article XXIV, which provides:

> Territorial Application – Frontier Traffic – Customs Unions and Free-trade Areas
>
> 1. The provisions of this Agreement shall apply to the metropolitan customs territories of the contracting parties and to any other customs territories in respect of which this Agreement has been accepted under Article XXVI or is being applied under Article XXXIII or pursuant to the Protocol of Provisional Application. Each such customs territory shall, exclusively for the purposes of the territorial application of this Agreement, be treated as though it were a contracting party; provided that the provisions of this paragraph shall not be construed to create any rights or obligations as between two or more customs territories in respect of which this Agreement has been accepted under Article XXVI or is being applied under Article XXXIII or pursuant to the Protocol of Provisional Application by a single contracting party.
> 2. For the purposes of this Agreement a customs territory shall be understood to mean any territory with respect to which separate tariffs or other regulations of commerce are maintained for a substantial part of the trade of such territory with other territories.
> 3. The provisions of this Agreement shall not be construed to prevent:
>   (a) Advantages accorded by any contracting party to adjacent countries in order to facilitate frontier traffic;
>   (b) Advantages accorded to the trade with the Free Territory of Trieste by countries contiguous to that territory, provided that such advantages are not in conflict with the Treaties of Peace arising out of the Second World War.
> 4. The contracting parties recognize the desirability of increasing freedom of trade by the development, through voluntary agreements, of closer integration between the economies of the countries parties to such agreements. They also recognize that the purpose of a customs union or of a free-trade area should be to facilitate trade between the constituent territories and not to raise barriers to the trade of other contracting parties with such territories.
> 5. Accordingly, the provisions of this Agreement shall not prevent, as between the territories of contracting parties, the formation of a customs union or of a free-trade area or the adoption of an interim agreement necessary for the formation of a customs union or of a free-trade area; Provided that:
>   (a) with respect to a customs union, or an interim agreement leading to a formation of a customs union, the duties and other regulations of

commerce imposed at the institution of any such union or interim agreement in respect of trade with contracting parties not parties to such union or agreement shall not on the whole be higher or more restrictive than the general incidence of the duties and regulations of commerce applicable in the constituent territories prior to the formation of such union or the adoption of such interim agreement, as the case may be;

(b) with respect to a free-trade area, or an interim agreement leading to the formation of a free-trade area, the duties and other regulations of commerce maintained in each of the constituent territories and applicable at the formation of such free trade area or the adoption of such interim agreement to the trade of contracting parties not included in such area or not parties to such agreement shall not be higher or more restrictive than the corresponding duties and other regulations of commerce existing in the same constituent territories prior to the formation of the free-trade area, or interim agreement as the case may be; and

(c) any interim agreement referred to in subparagraphs (a) and (b) shall include a plan and schedule for the formation of such a customs union or of such a free-trade area within a reasonable length of time.

6. If, in fulfilling the requirements of subparagraph 5 (a), a contracting party proposes to increase any rate of duty inconsistently with the provisions of Article II, the procedure set forth in Article XXVIII shall apply. In providing for compensatory adjustment, due account shall be taken of the compensation already afforded by the reduction brought about in the corresponding duty of the other constituents of the union.

7. (a) Any contracting party deciding to enter into a customs union or free-trade area, or an interim agreement leading to the formation of such a union or area, shall promptly notify the CONTRACTING PARTIES and shall make available to them such information regarding the proposed union or area as will enable them to make such reports and recommendations to contracting parties as they may deem appropriate.

(b) If, after having studied the plan and schedule included in an interim agreement referred to in paragraph 5 in consultation with the parties to that agreement and taking due account of the information made available in accordance with the provisions of subparagraph (a), the CONTRACTING PARTIES find that such agreement is not likely to result in the formation of a customs union or of a free-trade area within the period contemplated by the parties to the agreement or that such period is not a reasonable one, the CONTRACTING PARTIES shall make recommendations to the parties to the agreement. The parties shall not maintain or put into force, as the case may be, such agreement if they are not prepared to modify it in accordance with these recommendations.

(c) Any substantial change in the plan or schedule referred to in paragraph 5 (c) shall be communicated to the CONTRACTING PARTIES, which may request the contracting parties concerned to consult with them if the change seems likely to jeopardize or delay unduly the formation of the customs union or of the free-trade area.

8. For the purposes of this Agreement:

(a) A customs union shall be understood to mean the substitution of a single customs territory for two or more customs territories, so that

   (i) duties and other restrictive regulations of commerce (except, where necessary, those permitted under Articles XI, XII, XIII, XIV, XV, and XX) are eliminated with respect to substantially all the trade between the constituent territories of the union or at least with respect to substantially all the trade in products originating in such territories, and,

   (ii) subject to the provisions of paragraph 9, substantially the same duties and other regulations of commerce are applied by each of the members of the union to the trade of territories not included in the union;

(b) A free-trade area shall be understood to mean a group of two or more customs territories in which the duties and other restrictive regulations of commerce (except, where necessary, those permitted under Articles XI, XII, XIII, XIV, XV, and XX) are eliminated on substantially all the trade between the constituent territories in products originating in such territories.

9. The preferences referred to in paragraph 2 of Article I shall not be affected by the formation of a customs union or of a free-trade area but may be eliminated or adjusted by means of negotiations with contracting parties affected.* This procedure of negotiations with affected contracting parties shall, in particular, apply to the elimination of preferences required to conform with the provisions of paragraph 8 (a)(i) and paragraph 8 (b).

10. The CONTRACTING PARTIES may by a two-thirds majority approve proposals which do not fully comply with the requirements of paragraphs 5 to 9 inclusive, provided that such proposals lead to the formation of a customs union or a free-trade area in the sense of this Article.

11. Taking into account the exceptional circumstances arising out of the establishment of India and Pakistan as independent States and recognizing the fact that they have long constituted an economic unit, the contracting parties agree that the provisions of this Agreement shall not prevent the two countries from entering into special arrangements with respect to the trade between them, pending the establishment of their mutual trade relations on a definitive basis.*

12. Each contracting party shall take such reasonable measures as may be available to it to ensure observance of the provisions of this Agreement by the regional and local governments and authorities within its territories.

The brief footnotes to Article XXIV state:

Paragraph 9
It is understood that the provisions of Article I would require that, when a product which has been imported into the territory of a member of a customs union or free-trade area at a preferential rate of duty is re-exported to the territory of another member of such union or area, the latter member should collect a duty equal to the difference between the duty already paid and any higher duty that would be payable if the product were being imported directly into its territory.

Paragraph 11
Measures adopted by India and Pakistan in order to carry out definitive trade arrangements between them, once they have been agreed upon, might depart from particular provisions of this Agreement, but these measures would in general be consistent with the objectives of the Agreement.

Finally, GATT contains various provisions relating to special and differential treatment for developing countries. We will devote only brief attention to them and omit them here in the interest of brevity.

3.1.1.4 *Export Subsidies*
GATT disciplines on export subsidies have tightened over time. Originally, the only disciplines were a loose reporting requirement in the first paragraph of Article XVI, coupled with authority for the use of countervailing duties in Article VI. Additional provisions on export subsidies were added to Article XVI in the 1954–1955 review session. Further rules were negotiated in the Tokyo Round as part of the first Subsidies Code, and these rules were extended and tightened in the WTO Agreement on Subsidies and Countervailing Measures (SCMs).

GATT Article XVI, as amended, provides:

Subsidies
Section A – Subsidies in General

1. If any contracting party grants or maintains any subsidy, including any form of income or price support, which operates directly or indirectly to increase exports of any product from, or to reduce imports of any product into, its territory, it shall notify the CONTRACTING PARTIES in writing of the extent and nature of the subsidization, of the estimated effect of the subsidization on the quantity of the affected product or products

imported into or exported from its territory and of the circumstances making the subsidization necessary. In any case in which it is determined that serious prejudice to the interests of any other contracting party is caused or threatened by any such subsidization, the contracting party granting the subsidy shall, upon request, discuss with the other contracting party or parties concerned, or with the CONTRACTING PARTIES, the possibility of limiting the subsidization.

Section B – Additional Provisions on Export Subsidies*

2. The contracting parties recognize that the granting by a contracting party of a subsidy on the export of any product may have harmful effects for other contracting parties, both importing and exporting, may cause undue disturbance to their normal commercial interests, and may hinder the achievement of the objectives of this Agreement.
3. Accordingly, contracting parties should seek to avoid the use of subsidies on the export of primary products. If, however, a contracting party grants directly or indirectly any form of subsidy which operates to increase the export of any primary product from its territory, such subsidy shall not be applied in a manner which results in that contracting party having more than an equitable share of world export trade in that product, account being taken of the shares of the contracting parties in such trade in the product during a previous representative period, and any special factors which may have affected or may be affecting such trade in the product.*
4. Further, as from 1 January 1958 or the earliest practicable date thereafter, contracting parties shall cease to grant either directly or indirectly any form of subsidy on the export of any product other than a primary product which subsidy results in the sale of such product for export at a price lower than the comparable price charged for the like product to buyers in the domestic market. Until 31 December 1957 no contracting party shall extend the scope of any such subsidization beyond that existing on 1 January 1955 by the introduction of new, or the extension of existing, subsidies.*
5. The CONTRACTING PARTIES shall review the operation of the provisions of this Article from time to time with a view to examining its effectiveness, in the light of actual experience, in promoting the objectives of this Agreement and avoiding subsidization seriously prejudicial to the trade or interests of contracting parties.

The footnotes of AD Article XVI state:

The exemption of an exported product from duties or taxes borne by the like product when destined for domestic consumption, or the remission of such duties or taxes in amounts not in excess of those which have accrued, shall not be deemed to be a subsidy.

Section B

1. Nothing in Section B shall preclude the use by a contracting party of multiple rates of exchange in accordance with the Articles of Agreement of the International Monetary Fund.
2. For the purposes of Section B, a "primary product" is understood to be any product of farm, forest or fishery, or any mineral, in its natural form or which has undergone such processing as is customarily required to prepare it for marketing in substantial volume in international trade.

Paragraph 3

1. The fact that a contracting party has not exported the product in question during the previous representative period would not in itself preclude that contracting party from establishing its right to obtain a share of the trade in the product concerned.
2. A system for the stabilization of the domestic price or of the return to domestic producers of a primary product independently of the movements of export prices, which results at times in the sale of the product for export at a price lower than the comparable price charged for the like product to buyers in the domestic market, shall be considered not to involve a subsidy on exports within the meaning of paragraph 3 if the CONTRACTING PARTIES determine that:
   (a) the system has also resulted, or is so designed as to result, in the sale of the product for export at a price higher than the comparable price charged for the like product to buyers in the domestic market; and
   (b) the system is so operated, or is designed so to operate, either because of the effective regulation of production or otherwise, as not to stimulate exports unduly or otherwise seriously to prejudice the interests of other contracting parties.

   Notwithstanding such determination by the CONTRACTING PARTIES, operations under such a system shall be subject to the provisions of paragraph 3 where they are wholly or partly financed out of government funds in addition to the funds collected from producers in respect of the product concerned.

Paragraph 4

The intention of paragraph 4 is that the contracting parties should seek before the end of 1957 to reach agreement to abolish all remaining subsidies as from 1 January 1958; or, failing this, to reach agreement to extend the application of the standstill until the earliest date thereafter by which they can expect to reach such agreement.

The SCMs Agreement provides, in pertinent part:

Article 1
Definition of a Subsidy

1.1 For the purpose of this Agreement, a subsidy shall be deemed to exist if:

(a)(1) there is a financial contribution by a government or any public body within the territory of a Member (referred to in this Agreement as "government"), i.e. where:

> (i) a government practice involves a direct transfer of funds (e.g. grants, loans, and equity infusion), potential direct transfers of funds or liabilities (e.g. loan guarantees);

> (ii) government revenue that is otherwise due is foregone or not collected (e.g. fiscal incentives such as tax credits)[1];

> (iii) a government provides goods or services other than general infrastructure, or purchases goods;

> (iv) a government makes payments to a funding mechanism, or entrusts or directs a private body to carry out one or more of the type of functions illustrated in (i) to (iii) above which would normally be vested in the government and the practice, in no real sense, differs from practices normally followed by governments;

or

(a)(2) there is any form of income or price support in the sense of Article XVI of GATT 1994;

and

(b) a benefit is thereby conferred.

1.2 A subsidy as defined in paragraph 1 shall be subject to the provisions of Part II or shall be subject to the provisions of Part III or V only if such a subsidy is specific in accordance with the provisions of Article 2.

---

[1] (original note 1) In accordance with the provisions of Article XVI of GATT 1994 (Note to Article XVI) and the provisions of Annexes I through III of this Agreement, the exemption of an exported product from duties or taxes borne by the like product when destined for domestic consumption, or the remission of such duties or taxes in amounts not in excess of those which have accrued, shall not be deemed to be a subsidy.

Article 2
Specificity

...

2.3 Any subsidy falling under the provisions of Article 3 shall be deemed to be specific...

Article 3
Prohibition

3.1 Except as provided in the Agreement on Agriculture, the following subsidies, within the meaning of Article 1, shall be prohibited:

(a) subsidies contingent, in law or in fact,[2] whether solely or as one of several other conditions, upon export performance, including those illustrated in Annex I[3] ...

3.2 A Member shall neither grant nor maintain subsidies referred to in paragraph 1.

Article 4
Remedies

4.1 Whenever a Member has reason to believe that a prohibited subsidy is being granted or maintained by another Member, such Member may request consultations with such other Member.

4.2 A request for consultations under paragraph 1 shall include a statement of available evidence with regard to the existence and nature of the subsidy in question.

4.3 Upon request for consultations under paragraph 1, the Member believed to be granting or maintaining the subsidy in question shall enter into such consultations as quickly as possible. The purpose of the consultations shall be to clarify the facts of the situation and to arrive at a mutually agreed solution.

4.4 If no mutually agreed solution has been reached within 30 days[4] of the request for consultations, any Member party to such consultations may

---

[2] (original note 4) This standard is met when the facts demonstrate that the granting of a subsidy, without having been made legally contingent upon export performance, is in fact tied to actual or anticipated exportation or export earnings. The mere fact that a subsidy is granted to enterprises which export shall not for that reason alone be considered to be an export subsidy within the meaning of this provision.

[3] (original note 5) Measures referred to in Annex I as not constituting export subsidies shall not be prohibited under this or any other provision of this Agreement.

[4] (original note 6) Any time periods mentioned in this Article may be extended by mutual agreement.

refer the matter to the Dispute Settlement Body ("DSB") for the immediate establishment of a panel, unless the DSB decides by consensus not to
establish a panel.

4.5 Upon its establishment, the panel may request the assistance of the Permanent Group of Experts[5] (referred to in this Agreement as the "PGE") with
regard to whether the measure in question is a prohibited subsidy. If so
requested, the PGE shall immediately review the evidence with regard to the
existence and nature of the measure in question and shall provide an opportunity for the Member applying or maintaining the measure to demonstrate
that the measure in question is not a prohibited subsidy. The PGE shall
report its conclusions to the panel within a time limit determined by the
panel. The PGE's conclusions on the issue of whether or not the measure
in question is a prohibited subsidy shall be accepted by the panel without
modification.

4.6 The panel shall submit its final report to the parties to the dispute. The
report shall be circulated to all Members within 90 days of the date of the
composition and the establishment of the panel's terms of reference.

4.7 If the measure in question is found to be a prohibited subsidy, the panel
shall recommend that the subsidizing Member withdraw the subsidy without delay. In this regard, the panel shall specify in its recommendation the
time period within which the measure must be withdrawn.

4.8 Within 30 days of the issuance of the panel's report to all Members, the
report shall be adopted by the DSB unless one of the parties to the dispute
formally notifies the DSB of its decision to appeal or the DSB decides by
consensus not to adopt the report.

4.9 Where a panel report is appealed, the Appellate Body shall issue its decision within 30 days from the date when the party to the dispute formally
notifies its intention to appeal. When the Appellate Body considers that it
cannot provide its report within 30 days, it shall inform the DSB in writing of the reasons for the delay together with an estimate of the period
within which it will submit its report. In no case shall the proceedings exceed
60 days. The appellate report shall be adopted by the DSB and unconditionally accepted by the parties to the dispute unless the DSB decides by consensus not to adopt the appellate report within 20 days following its issuance to
the Members.[6]

---

[5] (original note 7) As established in Article 24.
[6] (original note 8) If a meeting of the DSB is not scheduled during this period, such a meeting
shall be held for this purpose.

4.10 In the event the recommendation of the DSB is not followed within the time period specified by the panel, which shall commence from the date of adoption of the panel's report or the Appellate Body's report, the DSB shall grant authorization to the complaining Member to take appropriate[7] countermeasures, unless the DSB decides by consensus to reject the request.

4.11 In the event a party to the dispute requests arbitration under paragraph 6 of Article 22 of the Dispute Settlement Understanding ("DSU"), the arbitrator shall determine whether the countermeasures are appropriate.[8]

4.12 For purposes of disputes conducted pursuant to this Article, except for time periods specifically prescribed in this Article, time periods applicable under the DSU for the conduct of such disputes shall be half the time prescribed therein...

ANNEX I

ILLUSTRATIVE LIST OF EXPORT SUBSIDIES

(a) The provision by governments of direct subsidies to a firm or an industry contingent upon export performance.
(b) Currency retention schemes or any similar practices which involve a bonus on exports.
(c) Internal transport and freight charges on export shipments, provided or mandated by governments, on terms more favourable than for domestic shipments.
(d) The provision by governments or their agencies either directly or indirectly through government mandated schemes, of imported or domestic products or services for use in the production of exported goods, on terms or conditions more favourable than for provision of like or directly competitive products or services for use in the production of goods for domestic consumption, if (in the case of products) such terms or conditions are more favourable than those commercially available[9] on world markets to their exporters.

---

[7] (original note 9) This expression is not meant to allow countermeasures that are disproportionate in light of the fact that the subsidies dealt with under these provisions are prohibited.
[8] (original note 10) This expression is not meant to allow countermeasures that are disproportionate in light of the fact that the subsidies dealt with under these provisions are prohibited.
[9] (original note 57) The term "commercially available" means that the choice between domestic and imported products is unrestricted and depends only on commercial considerations.

(e) The full or partial exemption remission, or deferral specifically related to exports, of direct taxes[10] or social welfare charges paid or payable by industrial or commercial enterprises.[11]

(f) The allowance of special deductions directly related to exports or export performance, over and above those granted in respect to production for domestic consumption, in the calculation of the base on which direct taxes are charged.

(g) The exemption or remission, in respect of the production and distribution of exported products, of indirect taxes in excess of those levied in respect of the production and distribution of like products when sold for domestic consumption.

(h) The exemption, remission or deferral of prior stage cumulative indirect taxes on goods or services used in the production of exported products in excess of the exemption, remission or deferral of like prior stage cumulative indirect taxes on goods or services used in the production of like products when sold for domestic consumption; provided, however, that prior stage cumulative indirect taxes may be exempted,

---

[10] (original note 58) For the purpose of this Agreement:

The term "direct taxes" shall mean taxes on wages, profits, interests, rents, royalties, and all other forms of income, and taxes on the ownership of real property;

The term "import charges" shall mean tariffs, duties, and other fiscal charges not elsewhere enumerated in this note that are levied on imports;

The term "indirect taxes" shall mean sales, excise, turnover, value added, franchise, stamp, transfer, inventory and equipment taxes, border taxes and all taxes other than direct taxes and import charges;

"Prior stage" indirect taxes are those levied on goods or services used directly or indirectly in making the product;

"Cumulative" indirect taxes are multi staged taxes levied where there is no mechanism for subsequent crediting of the tax if the goods or services subject to tax at one stage of production are used in a succeeding stage of production;

"Remission" of taxes includes the refund or rebate of taxes;

"Remission or drawback" includes the full or partial exemption or deferral of import charges.

[11] (original note 59) The Members recognize that deferral need not amount to an export subsidy where, for example, appropriate interest charges are collected. The Members reaffirm the principle that prices for goods in transactions between exporting enterprises and foreign buyers under their or under the same control should for tax purposes be the prices which would be charged between independent enterprises acting at arm's length. Any Member may draw the attention of another Member to administrative or other practices which may contravene this principle and which result in a significant saving of direct taxes in export transactions. In such circumstances the Members shall normally attempt to resolve their differences using the facilities of existing bilateral tax treaties or other specific international mechanisms, without prejudice to the rights and obligations of Members under GATT 1994, including the right of consultation created in the preceding sentence.

Paragraph (e) is not intended to limit a Member from taking measures to avoid the double taxation of foreign source income earned by its enterprises or the enterprises of another Member.

remitted or deferred on exported products even when not exempted, remitted or deferred on like products when sold for domestic consumption, if the prior stage cumulative indirect taxes are levied on inputs that are consumed in the production of the exported product (making normal allowance for waste).[12] This item shall be interpreted in accordance with the guidelines on consumption of inputs in the production process contained in Annex II.

(i) The remission or drawback of import charges in excess of those levied on imported inputs that are consumed in the production of the exported product (making normal allowance for waste); provided, however, that in particular cases a firm may use a quantity of home market inputs equal to, and having the same quality and characteristics as, the imported inputs as a substitute for them in order to benefit from this provision if the import and the corresponding export operations both occur within a reasonable time period, not to exceed two years. This item shall be interpreted in accordance with the guidelines on consumption of inputs in the production process contained in Annex II and the guidelines in the determination of substitution drawback systems as export subsidies contained in Annex III.

(j) The provision by governments (or special institutions controlled by governments) of export credit guarantee or insurance programmes, of insurance or guarantee programmes against increases in the cost of exported products or of exchange risk programmes, at premium rates which are inadequate to cover the long term operating costs and losses of the programmes.

(k) The grant by governments (or special institutions controlled by and/or acting under the authority of governments) of export credits at rates below those which they actually have to pay for the funds so employed (or would have to pay if they borrowed on international capital markets in order to obtain funds of the same maturity and other credit terms and denominated in the same currency as the export credit), or the payment by them of all or part of the costs incurred by exporters or financial institutions in obtaining credits, in so far as they are used to secure a material advantage in the field of export credit terms.

Provided, however, that if a Member is a party to an international undertaking on official export credits to which at least twelve original Members to this Agreement are parties as of 1 January 1979 (or a successor undertaking which has been adopted by those original Members), or if in practice a Member applies the interest rates provisions of the

---

[12] (original note 60) Paragraph (h) does not apply to value-added tax systems and border-tax adjustment in lieu thereof; the problem of the excessive remission of value-added taxes is exclusively covered by paragraph (g).

relevant undertaking, an export credit practice which is in conformity with those provisions shall not be considered an export subsidy prohibited by this Agreement.

(l) Any other charge on the public account constituting an export subsidy in the sense of Article XVI of GATT 1994.

In addition to the remedy provided by WTO action in accordance with Article 4 of the SCMs Agreement, export subsidies are subject to the imposition of "countervailing duties" by an importing nation in an amount calculated to offset the value of the subsidy. These duties are authorized by GATT Article VI, which provides, among other things, that duties may be imposed only if "the effect of the . . . subsidization . . . is to cause or threaten material injury to an established domestic industry, or is such as to retard materially the establishment of a domestic industry." The SCMs Agreement contains extensive rules and procedures governing the imposition and administration of countervailing duties, which we omit here as we will not be focused on them. We also omit general obligations under the SCMs Agreement concerning the notification of subsidies to the WTO and WTO surveillance of subsidies matters.

3.1.2 Note on GATT 1994

The text reproduced above is from the GATT 1947, that is, the original GATT. GATT 1994 is not the same agreement, and was substantially modified through negotiations during the Uruguay Round. GATT 1994 comprises the following elements:

(a) the provisions in the General Agreement on Tariffs and Trade, dated 30 October 1947, annexed to the Final Act Adopted at the Conclusion of the Second Session of the Preparatory Committee of the United Nations Conference on Trade and Employment (excluding the Protocol of Provisional Application), as rectified, amended or modified by the terms of legal instruments which have entered into force before the date of entry into force of the WTO Agreement;

(b) the provisions of the legal instruments set forth below that have entered into force under the GATT 1947 before the date of entry into force of the WTO Agreement:

   (i) protocols and certifications relating to tariff concessions;

   (ii) protocols of accession (excluding the provisions (a) concerning provisional application and withdrawal of provisional application and (b) providing that Part II of GATT 1947 shall be applied provisionally to the fullest extent not inconsistent with legislation existing on the date of the Protocol);

    (iii) decisions on waivers granted under Article XXV of GATT 1947 and still in force on the date of entry into force of the WTO Agreement;

    (iv) other decisions of the CONTRACTING PARTIES to GATT 1947;

(c) the Understandings set forth below:

    (i) Understanding on the Interpretation of Article II:1(b) of the General Agreement on Tariffs and Trade 1994;

    (ii) Understanding on the Interpretation of Article XVII of the General Agreement on Tariffs and Trade 1994;

    (iii) Understanding on Balance-of-Payments Provisions of the General Agreement on Tariffs and Trade 1994;

    (iv) Understanding on the Interpretation of Article XXIV of the General Agreement on Tariffs and Trade 1994;

    (v) Understanding in Respect of Waivers of Obligations under the General Agreement on Tariffs and Trade 1994;

    (vi) Understanding on the Interpretation of Article XXVIII of the General Agreement on Tariffs and Trade 1994; and

(d) the Marrakesh Protocol to GATT 1994.

With reference to the term "other decisions of the CONTRACTING PARTIES to GATT 1947" in item (b)(iv) above, there is some ambiguity. It is clear, however, that GATT dispute-settlement reports do not come under its purview.

3.2 The Rationale for Negotiated Constraints on Traditional Instruments of Protection (Tariffs and QRs)

The preamble (chapeau) of the GATT sets out the major purposes of the agreement, at least in the eyes of the founders:

> Recognizing that their relations in the field of trade and economic endeavour should be conducted with a view to raising standards of living, ensuring full employment and a large and steadily growing volume of real income and effective demand, developing the full use of the resources of the world and expanding the production and exchange of goods,
> Being desirous of contributing to these objectives by entering into reciprocal and mutually advantageous arrangements directed to the substantial reduction of tariffs and other barriers to trade and to the elimination of discriminatory treatment in international commerce, ...

We take these statements at face value, but in this Section seek to go beyond them. We begin with a survey of the negotiating history, and then turn to modern economic theory.

3.2.1 The Negotiating History[13]

To understand the origins of the GATT, one must appreciate the traumatic events of the 1920s and 1930s. The period between World War I and World War II was a political and economic disaster, scarred by the Great Depression and the rise of fascism. Although monetary and financial factors were primarily responsible for allowing the recession of 1929 to turn into the Great Depression of the early 1930s,[14] the spread of trade restrictions aggravated the problem. The commercial policies of the 1930s became characterized as "beggar-thy-neighbor" policies because many countries sought to insulate their own economy from the economic downturn by raising trade barriers. Blocking imports proved to be a futile method of increasing domestic employment because one country's imports were another country's exports. The combined effect of this inward turn of policy was a collapse of international trade and a deepening of the slump in the world economy.

The United States bore considerable responsibility for this turn of events. What started out in 1929 as a legislative attempt to protect farmers from falling agricultural prices led to the enactment of higher import duties across the board in 1930. The Hawley–Smoot tariff of that year pushed already high protective tariffs even higher and triggered a similar response by other countries. Many countries also turned to discriminatory trade arrangements in the early 1930s, both for economic and political reasons. At a conference in Ottawa in 1932, the United Kingdom and its dominions (principally Australia, Canada, New Zealand, and South Africa) agreed to give preferential tariff treatment for one another's goods. This scheme of imperial preferences involved both higher duties on non-British Empire goods and lower duties on Dominion goods and drew the ire of excluded countries for discriminating against their trade. Meanwhile, under the guidance of Reichsbank President Hjalmar Schacht, Nazi Germany concluded a series of bilateral clearing arrangements with central European countries that effectively created a new trade bloc, orienting the trade of these countries toward Germany at the expense of others. In Asia, Japan created the Greater East Asia Co-Prosperity sphere to extend its political and economic influence throughout the region and siphon off trade for its own benefit.

Having initiated the move toward greater protectionism in the 1930s, the United States also became one of the first countries to try to reverse these developments. Recognizing that it could not undertake a unilateral reduction in American tariffs in the midst of the depression, the Roosevelt administration sought to negotiate bilateral trade agreements to reduce tariffs in concert with others. In 1934, the Congress enacted the Reciprocal Trade Agreement Act (RTAA),

---

[13] The material in this subsection draws heavily on Irwin, Mavroidis and Sykes (2008) (hereafter Genesis).
[14] See Genesis for a more detailed history of this period.

which allowed the president to reduce American tariffs by up to 50% in the context of bilateral trade agreements that employed the unconditional most-favored-nation (MFN) clause. With this authority, originally granted for three years and subsequently renewed, the Roosevelt administration concluded more than 20 trade agreements during the 1930s.

During the 1940s, the United States sought to establish a new multilateral institutional architecture, a component of which would be devoted to the reconstruction of world trade. The United States took concrete steps to bring this about: in February 1946, the U.S. delegate to the United Nations proposed that a resolution be adopted in order to convene a United Nations Conference on Trade and Employment, the purpose of which would be to draft the Charter for an International Trade Organization (ITO), also referred to as the Havana Charter. The General Agreement on Tariffs and Trade (GATT) would be an off-shoot of the broader and more ambitious ITO project. The ITO project foundered, of course, leaving GATT to govern multilateral commercial policy for nearly a half century.

3.2.1.1 *The Negotiation Process*

The GATT was first negotiated at the London Conference in 1946. However, the London Conference did not disentangle the GATT from the wider ITO negotiation. Indeed, the negotiation of the GATT, as we know it, was the work of Committee II, a committee established during the conference to deal with commercial policy. Other committees were established to deal with issues that were supposed to come under the ITO, such as employment, restrictive business practices, international commodity agreements, and organizational issues. The actual ambit of the GATT was not definitively agreed at the London Conference. Quoting from the relevant documents, Jackson (1969, 43) suggests that it was agreed that the GATT would include "such other provisions as may be appropriate." Other refers, of course, to provisions other than those dealing directly with tariff concessions. The London negotiations were inconclusive as to the scope of GATT, however, and the issue carried over to the New York Conference in Lake Success, New York (which served as the temporary headquarters of the United Nations from 1946 to 1951).

The working assumption during negotiations was that the GATT was not to be an institution; rather, it was simply a trade agreement that was to eventually come under the aegis of the ITO, once that institution was established and its Charter entered into force. Consequently, the GATT did not contain provisions creating any sort of bureaucracy or secretariat. The Drafting Committee also decided to exclude detailed provisions dealing with pure domestic-policy issues.

The London Conference ended with a decision to appoint a Drafting Committee that was entrusted with formalizing the text of the agreement reached in

London. The Drafting Committee, originally convened in New York, in Lake Success in January – February 1947, and then completed its work in Geneva later in the same year. It comprised 53 national delegates, as well as eight observers (one from Mexico, one from Colombia, one from the ILO, one from the WB, one from the IMF, and three from the FAO). The size of the Drafting Committee was kept intentionally limited in order to speed up the process. In New York, the first textual separation of the GATT from the ITO was made.

At the end of the New York Conference, it was clear that negotiators would reconvene in Geneva to finalize their agreement on the GATT text, as well as hold the first round of multilateral trade negotiations.

The plan for the negotiations on tariff concessions had already been agreed to during the London Conference. In brief:

(a) negotiations should be based on reciprocity, which meant that countries should not be expected to grant concessions unilaterally;
(b) prior international commitments, with respect to tariff treatment, should not stand in the way of the negotiations;
(c) stand-still provisions should be agreed regarding residual preferences (they could not be increased after that date), new tariffs, and other restrictive measures;
(d) negotiations should take place between a small subset of the members of the Preparatory Committee (two to four), the concessions agreed, nevertheless, should be extended to all members;
(e) negotiations should take place in accordance with the principal supplier rule: countries should be expected to grant concessions on products of which the other members of the Preparatory Committee were likely to be the principal supplier;
(f) additionally, concessions should also be granted on products for which no single principal supplier existed among the members of the Preparatory Committee, but a principal part of which was supplied by various members of the Preparatory Committee;
(g) negotiations would roll over four stages, which largely reflect a (bilateral) request and offer, and a multilateral review of concessions made;
(h) 16 schedules would be completed that would incorporate the MFN and the preferential rates of duty.

As described in detail in Gardner (1956), Jackson (1969), and Irwin, Mavroidis and Sykes (2008), the original GATT negotiations focused intently on two related issues – tariff reductions and tariff discrimination – both of which had come to be perceived as severe problems during the interwar years. The result of the negotiations on these issues was Part One of the GATT, containing Article I (the MFN obligation) and Article II (the basic tariff commitments). The basic tariff commitments took the form of legal ceilings ("bindings") on applied tariffs, and the negotiations on this issue were considered broadly successful. The push for nondiscrimination was only partly successful, however, as many of the colonial preferences that had emerged prior to World War II were preserved in Article I despite the general MFN obligation.[15]

The drafters were also keenly aware that other policy instruments could readily substitute for tariffs as a source of trade protectionism. Accordingly, and perhaps because the future of the ITO was already in some doubt by 1947, the GATT contained numerous provisions designed to prevent the substitution of alternative forms of protection for tariffs. Most notable among these provisions were Article XI, concerning quantitative restrictions and similar measures, and Article III, concerning discriminatory domestic taxation and regulation.

The GATT negotiations were successfully concluded on October 30, 1947, and the GATT entered into force on January 1, 1948. Its original 23 members were: Australia, Belgium, Brazil, Burma, Canada, Ceylon, Chile, Republic of China, Cuba, Czechoslovak Republic, France, India, Lebanon, Luxembourg, Netherlands, New Zealand, Norway, Pakistan, Southern Rhodesia, Syria, South Africa, the United Kingdom, and the United States.

According to GATT (1949, p. 11), in the first Geneva negotiation the 23 participating countries made no fewer than 123 bilateral agreements covering 45,000 tariff items related to about one half of the value of world trade. However, in terms of its effect on tariff levels, the outcome of the Geneva negotiations has been difficult to assess. The best information concerns the United States. The U.S. Tariff Commission (1948, p. 18) calculated that had the tariff cuts from the first GATT round in Geneva (finalized in October 1947, implemented in January 1948) been applied to actual imports in 1947, the average tariff would have declined 21.1%, from 19.4% to 15.3%. Thus, the United States reduced its tariff by about 20% in the Geneva conference. The actual U.S. tariff fell by a somewhat greater margin because of the impact of import price inflation in reducing the ad valorem equivalent of specific duties.

Shortly after GATT entered into force, political support for the ITO waned. Among other things, the U.S. Congress became more protectionist, and the effort to establish the ITO was eventually abandoned.

As a consequence, GATT gradually evolved into an institution "by default." It developed a support-staff bureaucracy, established a Secretariat, and was headed by a Director-General. And with the passage of time, opportunities for additional multilateral trade negotiations presented themselves. Additional tariff reductions were negotiated over the course of seven more GATT negotiating "rounds," concluding with the Uruguay Round from 1986 to 1994. The Uruguay Round, of course, replaced the GATT with the WTO, greatly elaborated GATT

---

[15] GATT also contained an authorization for customs unions and free-trade areas, Article XXIV, which over time has proven a far greater source of discrimination.

obligations through a number of additional agreements (some built on pluri-lateral agreements from the GATT years), and added services and intellectual property obligations to the set of commitments undertaken by WTO Members. At this writing, further negotiations are ongoing under the rubric of the WTO "Doha Round," with the outcome quite uncertain.

3.2.1.2 *Negotiations on Quantitative Restrictions (QRs)*

From the outset, GATT negotiators recognized that there are many ways to impose trade protection, and that tariff negotiations alone would not ensure lib-eralization. QRs were a particular focus of concern.[16]

At the London Conference, a main goal of the developing countries – partic-ularly Australia, along with India, China, Brazil, and Chile – was to shift attention toward employment and economic development and to ensure that rules did not prevent them from using quantitative import quotas to promote those goals. As a result, new chapters of the draft ITO charter were included on both issues. Aus-tralia also joined with India in demanding a "developing country exception" that would permit the use of QRs to foster industrialization. To accommodate this, the U.S. delegation drafted a new chapter on economic development that permitted the ITO to allow the limited use of import quotas by developing countries.

At the same time, the United States sought to impose greater disciplines on the use of QRs than in some of the proposals. Indeed, the U.S. negotiator Clair Wilcox argued that:

> The major objective of the United States was the adoption of a rule that would outlaw the use of import quotas and other quantitative restrictions as a matter of principle, permitting them only with international approval in exceptional cases and requiring that they be administered, in such cases, without discrimination. In the absence of such a rule, it is virtually certain that all other nations will impose quotas on imports and that many nations will so administer these quotas as to discriminate against American goods.

The United States sought to end the transition period that allowed QRs for balance-of-payments purposes in December 1949, after which QRs would be permitted only in cases of severe balance-of-payments difficulties and only in conformity with the principle of nondiscrimination. Furthermore, after 1949, a country seeking to impose QRs for balance-of-payments reasons would be obliged to consult with the ITO. If the ITO members requested the removal of the QRs and the country did not comply, the members could retaliate. Britain resisted this provision and held out for more discretionary use of QRs for balance-of-payments purposes. Although they were concerned that widespread

---

[16] For additional detail on these issues and complete documentation, see Genesis, Chapter 2.

use of QRs would have an adverse effect on their exports, British officials wanted a longer transition period and no ITO consultation.

At the Geneva Conference, the main area of dispute continued to be quantitative restrictions on imports, and Wilcox noted the "continuous assaults that are being made from all sides upon the controls developed at the London meeting dealing with the use and imposition of quantitative restrictions." In London, the United States reluctantly agreed to broaden the permission given to countries to introduce quantitative restrictions in the event of balance-of-payments difficulties. In Geneva, there was further pressure to widen the scope for using quantitative measures including general permission for developing countries to use them for the purpose of economic development. There was also pressure to eliminate the requirement that countries seeking to impose QRs had to justify their action and receive permission from the ITO before doing so. While the United States did not want to see a weakening in the discipline of QRs, countries such as New Zealand, Cuba, China, Chile, India, and Czechoslovakia wanted them for reasons dealing with state trading, economic development, and balance of payments. The United States found that it had little choice but to accede to these demands.

The result was Article XI, creating a "general elimination" of QRs, married with exceptions for various purposes, most notably balance-of-payments issues (Article XXIV) and economic development (Article XVIII). Because of the various exceptions, the prospect of discrimination in the use of QRs remained, which would be disciplined by Article XIII.

3.2.1.3 Foreign-Policy Considerations in the Negotiations

Later subsections will consider the rationale for trade agreements from the economic perspective, but here we note the existence of considerable evidence indicating that tariff liberalization was viewed as important to avoid the economic conditions that led to armed conflict in Europe.[17] The liberal argument that trade promotes peace goes back at least to the 18th century and is associated with Baron de Montesquieu and Immanuel Kant. The idea was later expounded by 19th-century liberal thinkers, such as Richard Cobden and John Stuart Mill.

During the inter-war years before GATT, U.S. Secretary of State Cordell Hull enthusiastically embraced this view. As Hull wrote in 1934: "The truth is universally recognized that trade between nations is the greatest peace-maker and civilizer within human experience." The Roosevelt administration's program

> to secure trade agreements with the principal nations is the first step in a
> broad movement to increase international trade. Upon this program, rests
> largely my hope of insured peace and the fullest measure of prosperity.

---

[17] For detailed citations and further discussion, see Genesis, Chapter 3.

Indeed, Schatz (1970) points out that Hull envisioned the reciprocal-trade-agreements program in the 1930s as the first step in a worldwide campaign to restore political stability.

Was Hull correct in his view that international trade promotes peace and cooperation among nations? At the time, Hull was certainly perceived as being correct in the eyes of many. In 1945, he was awarded the Nobel Peace Prize for his efforts to promote international political and economic cooperation. In the opening public statements at the Geneva conference, there is much support for the view that economic cooperation would promote political cooperation. In particular, countries that had been directly involved in World War II, and that had suffered great material damage and casualties, saw the GATT as a part of a new era of international cooperation that would reduce the risks of war in the future. In the view of Baron van der Straten-Waillet (Belgium), the economic union between his country, the Netherlands, and Luxembourg offered an appropriate example of how economic nationalism can be defeated; it should be extrapolated to the world sphere. While acknowledging the leading role that the U.S. government was playing, he argued in favor of emulating at the world level his own country's experience. Wilgress (Canada) offered a similar view to that of the Benelux countries: he preached in favor of relaxing (to the extent necessary) one's national sovereignty in order to promote the common good. Philip (France) stressed the positive role that bilateral trade agreements could play, and argued in favor of ensuring that they coexist with ITO, since they share the same objective: to open up markets. Huysmans (Netherlands) urged the ITO to open up to enemies as well, since, in his view, the contribution to world peace would be increased as more and more joined the ranks of the ITO.

Sir Stafford Cripps (UK) started by stressing that "we all failed to appreciate sufficiently the direct relation between international economic policies and the danger of war." In his view, the GATT and ITO project demonstrated the will for international cooperation and the abandonment of dangerous unilateral policies. Finally, Wilcox (United States) emphasized the links between the GATT/ITO with the other Bretton Woods institutions, and the wider peace process. Echoing the spirit of Hull, he explained his government's view that the establishment of the world trading system was a major contribution to the new world order that nations would be jointly building in order to break with the past.

Finally, a month before the start of the Geneva conference, President Truman threw his support behind the meeting in a major speech at Baylor University in Waco, Texas. In a strong statement, Truman argued:

> If the nations can agree to observe a code of good conduct in international
> trade, they will cooperate more readily in other international affairs. Such
> agreement will prevent the bitterness that is engendered by an economic

war. It will provide an atmosphere congenial to the preservation of peace. As a part of this program we have asked the other nations of the world to join with us in reducing barriers to trade. We have not asked them to remove all barriers. Nor have we ourselves offered to do so. But we have proposed negotiations directed toward the reduction of tariffs, here and abroad, toward the elimination of other restrictive measures and the abandonment of discrimination. These negotiations are to be undertaken at the meeting which opens in Geneva next month. The success of this program is essential to the establishment of the International Trade Organization [and] to the strength of the whole United Nations structure of cooperation in economic and political affairs.... The negotiations at Geneva must not fail.[18]

The empirical relationship between trade and peace may never be determined precisely, and we note that it is controversial in the modern international-relations literature.[19] But Hull and many of his generation strongly believed that cooperation to establish more liberal trade policies would not only bring economic benefits, but lay the groundwork for political cooperation in other areas and hence reduce the chances of military conflict. Indeed, if there was one overarching rationale for the GATT, as envisioned by its founders, it was simply one component of a broad effort to avoid the problems of the 1930s and establish conditions that might increase the chances for world peace after World War II.

We also observe that, even though the economic rationale for trade agreements that we review below does not emphasize the implications of trade agreements for world peace, this rationale is certainly consistent with a "peace dividend" associated with trade agreements. This follows from a basic tenet of the economic rationale: trade agreements exist to eliminate inefficiencies associated with unilateral policy choices as those inefficiencies are perceived by governments. Therefore, according to the economic rationale, international trade agreements create value for member governments. And this value would presumably be lost in times of war, thereby raising the cost of war to governments who are members of a successful international trade agreement.

3.2.2 The Rationale According to Case Law

Statements in the case law about the general "rationale" for tariff bindings are limited. Perhaps the clearest statement is to be found in some of the cases relating to "nonviolation" claims under GATT Art. XXIII(1)(b). The GATT

---

[18] (State Department Bulletin, March 16, 1947, 483).

[19] For discussion of the modern international relations literature on the subject, see Id.

Panel in *EEC–Oilseeds*,[20] quoted approvingly by the WTO Panel in *Japan–Film*,[21] remarked as follows:

> The idea underlying [nonviolation claims] is that the improved competitive opportunities that can legitimately be expected from a tariff concession can be frustrated not only by measures proscribed by the General Agreement but also by measures consistent with that Agreement... The Panel considered that the main value of a tariff concession is that it provides an assurance of better market access through improved price competition. Contracting parties negotiate tariff concessions primarily to obtain that advantage. They must therefore be assumed to base their tariff negotiations on the expectation that the price effect of the tariff concessions will not be systematically offset. If no right of redress were given to them in such a case they would be reluctant to make tariff concessions and the general Agreement would no longer be useful as a legal framework for incorporating the results of trade negotiations.

A bit more has been said about the rationale for the "general elimination" of QRs. Perhaps the clearest statement in that regard is to be found in the Panel Report on *Turkey–Textiles*, in connection with a finding not reviewed by the Appellate Body:

> The prohibition on the use of quantitative restrictions forms one of the cornerstones of the GATT system. A basic principle of the GATT system is that tariffs are the preferred and acceptable form of protection. Tariffs, to be reduced through reciprocal concessions, ought to be applied in a non-discriminatory manner independent of the origin of the goods (the 'most-favoured-nation' (MFN) clause). Article I, which requires MFN treatment, and Article II, which specifies that tariffs must not exceed bound rates, constitute Part I of GATT. Part II contains other related obligations, inter alia to ensure that Members do not evade the obligations of Part I. Two fundamental obligations contained in Part II are the national treatment clause and the prohibition against quantitative restrictions. The prohibition against quantitative restrictions is a reflection that tariffs are GATT's border protection 'of choice'. Quantitative restrictions impose absolute limits on imports, while tariffs do not. In contrast to MFN tariffs which permit the most efficient competitor to supply imports, quantitative restrictions usually have a trade distorting effect, their allocation can be problematic and their administration may not be transparent.[22]

---

[20] *EEC–Oilseeds*, adopted January 25, 1990, BISD 37S/86, paras. 144 and 148.

[21] *Japan – Measures Affecting Consumer Photographic Film and Paper*, WT/DS44/R, adopted April 22, 1998, para. 10.35.

[22] Panel Report, *Turkey – Restrictions on Imports of Textile and Clothing Products*, WT/DS34/R, adopted November 19, 1999, para. 9.63.

The cases also speak briefly about the underlying logic of GATT Article XXVIII renegotiations. In *EC–Poultry*, Brazil claimed that the MFN principle in Articles I and XIII did not apply to tariff-rate quotas resulting from compensation negotiations under Article XXVIII. The Panel rejected this argument and in the process suggested that the goal of Article XXVIII is to preserve the balance of negotiated concessions:

> [I]f a preferential treatment of a particular trading partner not elsewhere justified is permitted under the pretext of 'compensatory adjustment' under Article XXVIII:2, it would create a serious loophole in the multilateral trading system. Such a result would fundamentally alter the overall balance of concessions Article XXVIII is designed to achieve.[23]

The Appellate Body upheld the finding at issue in this passage.

3.2.3 The Rationale According to Economic Theory

We now provide an overview of the economics of international trade agreements and the reasons suggested by economic theory as to why governments might wish to cooperate to constrain traditional instruments of protection.[24] We begin with the general rationale for trade liberalization agreements, followed by a more detailed analysis of their structure.

To organize our discussion, we proceed in two steps. First, we consider the basic rationale for a trade agreement. In particular, we organize our discussion around the following fundamental question: What can governments achieve with a trade agreement that they are unable to achieve when they set their trade policies in a unilateral fashion? To explore this question in the simplest possible context, we frame our discussion in terms of a simple economic environment in which two countries trade two goods. In most of our discussion, we assume as well that the trade policy for each government consists of a tariff that is applied to imports. In response to the question raised above, we observe that trade agreements can help to remove inefficiencies that arise under unilateral policies as a consequence of international externalities and that trade agreements can also better enable governments to make policy commitments to their private sectors. Our review of the economics literature, however, suggests that the primary purpose of a trade agreement is to eliminate the inefficiencies that arise under unilateral policies as a consequence of a particular international externality, which is commonly referred to as the "terms-of-trade" externality.

---

[23] Panel Report, *European Communities – Measures Affecting the Importation of Certain Poultry Products*, WT/DS69/R, adopted July 23, 1998, para. 215.

[24] Portions of our discussion of the economics of international trade agreements parallel that in Bagwell (2008) and in Bagwell and Staiger (2010a).

We then proceed to our second step and consider the implications of the terms-of-trade theory of trade agreements for the broad design of a trade agreement and its legal rules. Building on the legal and historical discussion found in previous subsections, we recall that the design of the WTO/GATT agreement emphasizes reciprocal tariff adjustments, tariff bindings, renegotiation and negotiation rounds (gradualism), and we argue that these features can be readily interpreted from the perspective of the terms-of-trade theory of trade agreements. Finally, an important feature of the WTO/GATT system is that protection is largely concentrated in the form of tariffs rather than quotas and other quantitative measures. We thus also discuss the advantages that tariffs offer over quotas in facilitating mutually beneficial and reciprocal trade agreements between governments.

In later Sections we will return to the theory and use it to interpret further aspects of the legal rules. For example, after describing their legal implementation we will revisit some of the details of WTO/GATT tariff bindings and offer interpretations from the perspective of the terms-of-trade theory. In addition, after extending the economic framework to allow for more than two countries, we use this theory to interpret and evaluate the principle of nondiscrimination. We also later consider export-policy instruments in greater detail. The SCM agreement in the WTO imposes strong restrictions on the use of export subsidies. We argue that, from the perspective of the terms-of-trade theory, the treatment of export subsidies in the WTO is somewhat puzzling. We also discuss other potential interpretations of the treatment of export subsidies in the WTO. As well, we describe recent work that emphasizes the "firm-delocation" effects of export subsidies and that generates predictions that are somewhat more in line with the treatment of export subsidies in the WTO. Our discussion there also considers the effects of export tariffs and explores the possible reason that such tariffs are not often used.

The Purpose of Trade Agreements   A trade agreement is an agreement among governments. Consequently, if governments form a trade agreement, then we may presume that governments anticipate enjoying higher "welfare" with a trade agreement than they would enjoy without a trade agreement. (As we discuss further below, the government preferences that we have in mind may reflect a variety of political/distributional concerns beyond standard economic welfare as conventionally defined.) A trade agreement can be mutually beneficial for governments, however, only if an inefficiency arises when trade policies are set unilaterally.[25] In seeking to understand the purpose of a trade agreement, we are

---

[25] When we say that unilateral trade policies are "inefficient" from the perspective of governments, we follow the economics literature and utilize the conventional Pareto criterion. Thus, unilateral trade policies are inefficient relative to the preferences of governments when alternative trade policies exist under which both governments would achieve higher welfare.

thus naturally led to consider the reason that unilateral trade policies would be inefficient relative to the preferences of governments.

Economic Model and Government Preferences To make progress on this issue, we require two ingredients. First, we must put forth an economic model. The model describes the manner of trade between countries and the way in which import tariffs may affect prices and trade volumes. Second, we must also describe the preferences of governments. Governments may have a range of economic, distributional, and political concerns, and it is thus important that our specification of government preferences be general.

We begin with the economic model. Taking the simplest possible economic setting, let us suppose that the world is comprised of two countries that trade two goods. Both goods are consumed and produced in both countries, and the home country imports one good from the foreign country while the foreign country imports the other good from the home country. We assume as well that the goods are supplied in each country by perfectly competitive markets. Thus, in each country, every firm takes the prevailing local prices as given when deciding on a level of output to produce, and every consumer likewise takes local prices as given when making consumption choices. We assume further that the government of each country has available an ad valorem import tariff instrument. We assume for now that other trade-policy instruments, such as import quotas and export tariffs, are unavailable to governments. Given the import tariffs that governments select, prices are set to equate supply and demand, so that for each good the export supply from one country equals the import demand from the other country.

In this simple economic setting, we may now consider the tradeoffs that a government confronts when determining its optimal unilateral tariff. A higher import tariff naturally raises the relative local price of the import good in the domestic economy. This local-price effect creates winners and losers at home: import-competing firms win, whereas consumers of the import good may lose. Additionally, a higher import tariff results in a change in the level of tariff revenue. If the initial import tariff is below the level that maximizes tariff revenue, then a (slightly) higher import tariff generates greater tariff revenue, and this additional revenue can be distributed to individuals in the economy. When contemplating a higher unilateral tariff, then, a government balances the benefit to import-competing firms and the possible gain in tariff revenue against the cost to consumers of the import good.

The exact manner in which the government aggregates these various effects depends on the specific nature of the government's preferences. We can imagine many potential specifications for government preferences. A government may maximize national welfare, for example, but it is also plausible that a government's preferences over local prices derive in part from distributional and/or political concerns. Such concerns might lead a government to weigh more

heavily the profit in the import-competing industry than the welfare of consumers, for instance. As we seek here to develop a general rationale for a trade
agreement among governments, we do not restrict our attention to any particular specification for government preferences.

International Externalities To this point, we have considered the domestic
benefits and costs that a government entertains when determining its optimal
unilateral tariff. The existence of domestic costs and benefits on their own do not
constitute a reason for a trade agreement with the governments of other countries. To provide a rationale for a trade agreement, we must identify the reason
that a trade agreement would enable governments to achieve higher welfare than
they could achieve without a trade agreement. As we now explain, such a reason
is present if the trade policy of each government imposes an international externality on the welfare of the other government.

To identify the international externality, let us return to the domestic government's calculations when determining its optimal unilateral tariff. These calculations are domestic in nature and do not entertain any effect of the domestic import tariff on foreign exporters. What form might such an effect take? As
we discuss in further detail below, when a government selects a higher import
tariff, the world price (i.e., the offshore price) of the import good is expected to
fall.[26] Foreign exporters thus receive diminished profits on their exported units
following an increase in the domestic import tariff. Since the foreign government
naturally suffers to some degree when its export sector is harmed, we may thus
anticipate that an increase in the domestic import tariff leads to a decline in the
welfare of the foreign government.[27] In this way, when a government imposes
a higher import tariff, a negative international externality is imposed upon its
trading partner's government welfare. Governments fail to internalize this externality when they set their policies in a unilateral fashion; thus, in the absence
of a trade agreement, import tariffs are higher and trade volumes are lower than
would be efficient, where efficiency is measured relative to the preferences of
governments.

We have now determined a problem that a trade agreement might solve.
In particular, when governments set their trade policies unilaterally, they end
up setting import tariffs too high. The source of this inefficiency is that a negative international externality flows from each government's import tariff policy
through the world price to the other government's welfare function. This externality is not internalized when trade policies are set in a noncooperative fashion.

---

[26] The world price is the price that prevails prior to the imposition of the import tariff. It is
thus the price at which foreign exporters sell their product.

[27] An increase in the domestic import tariff is sure to lead to a drop in the welfare of the foreign
government, if the foreign government has selected its import tariff so as to maximize its
own welfare. For a formal demonstration, see Bagwell and Staiger (2002, p. 192).

From this vantage point, the purpose of a trade agreement is to facilitate a reciprocal reduction in import tariffs and thereby an expansion in trade volume, so
that the participating governments can achieve a more efficient (i.e., mutually
beneficial) outcome.

The Terms-of-Trade Rationale for Trade Agreements   The role for a trade
agreement that we describe above is sometimes referred to as the terms-of-trade
rationale for trade agreements. A country's terms of trade is the relative price on
the world market of its export good to its import good. Intuitively, when a country engages in international trade, it offers units of its export good in exchange
for units of its trading partner's export good. When a country's terms of trade
improve, a unit of its export good can be exchanged for a greater number of units
of the import good; thus, a country naturally benefits when its terms of trade
improve. Of course, in a two-country setting, a terms-of-trade gain for one country corresponds exactly to a terms-of-trade loss for the other country. Viewed in
this context, our discussion above indicates that a country can engineer a terms-
of-trade gain for itself by raising its import tariff, since a higher import tariff
induces a reduction in the relative price of its import good on the world market. Given that the government does not internalize the cost of the corresponding terms-of-trade loss for its trading partner, the government sets its tariff at a
higher level than would be efficient.[28] In this general manner, we may interpret
the international externality described above as a terms-of-trade externality.

   The terms-of-trade rationale for trade agreements has a long history in economics. Mill (1844) and Torrens (1844) offer early arguments that a higher import
tariff can improve a country's terms of trade, and Johnson (1953–1954) provides
the first formal analysis of the terms-of-trade rationale for trade agreements.
Johnson develops his arguments in a model in which governments maximize
national welfare. Bagwell and Staiger (1999, 2002) develop the rationale further,
by allowing for a wide range of government preferences. In particular, Bagwell
and Staiger allow that a government's preferences may be a general function of
the local prices that prevail in its country and its country's terms of trade. Their
general specification allows that a government maximizes national welfare, but
it includes as well the government preferences that arise in the leading political–
economy models of trade policy.

---

[28] Put differently, if the government of a country did internalize the terms-of-trade loss for its
   trading partner, then the government would not be motivated by the terms-of-trade implications of its trade policies, since a terms-of-trade gain for its country would be offset in its
   welfare by the terms-of-trade loss of its trading partner. When a government does not internalize the terms-of-trade loss for its trading partner, however, the terms-of-trade gain for its
   country is not offset, and so its unilateral tariff selection is in part motivated by terms-of-
   trade considerations.

At a more formal level, we can follow Bagwell and Staiger and summarize the arguments presented above in terms of three findings. First, when governments select their import tariff in a unilateral fashion, the resulting unilateral tariffs are inefficient relative to the preferences of governments. Second, a trade agreement that is mutually beneficial to governments (i.e., that is efficient relative to the unilateral tariffs) must involve tariff reductions by both governments. This second finding confirms that unilateral tariffs are higher than is efficient. Third, the "politically optimal" tariffs that governments would choose if, hypothetically, they were not motivated by the terms-of-trade effects of their trade policies are efficient. This last finding confirms a sense in which the international externality associated with the terms of trade represents the fundamental rationale for a trade agreement.

The Practical Relevance of the Terms-of-Trade Rationale   Having described the theoretical foundations of the terms-of-trade rationale for trade agreements, we now consider the practical relevance of this rationale. To this end, we first identify the key assumptions that underlie the theory. We then consider the intuitive and empirical foundations for these assumptions.

The terms-of-trade rationale for trade agreements rests on only two key assumptions. The first assumption is that, all else equal, a government's welfare falls when its terms of trade deteriorate. This assumption seems relatively uncontroversial. It holds when a government maximizes national welfare, and it also holds in the leading political–economy models of trade policy. Importantly, we impose no assumption about the preferences that a government holds as to the local price in its country. The second assumption is that each government can achieve an improvement in its country's terms of trade by raising its import tariff. This assumption holds if each country is "large" and merits further discussion.

When a government raises its import tariff, the local price of the imported good in the domestic market rises. As a consequence, for any given world price, the higher import tariff leads to a diminished demand in the domestic market for the import good. If the importing country is large, then the diminished import demand makes the good more abundant on the world market, with the result that the world price of this good must then drop to restore a balance between import demand and export supply. In this way, the government of a large country can improve its terms of trade, and thus reduce the terms of trade of its trading partner, by raising its import tariff. In effect, the government of a large country is like a monopsonist, in that it can exercise its market power by reducing volume so as to generate a more favorable purchase (i.e., world) price.

For the purpose of comparison, let us now suppose instead that the importing country is small. Once again, a higher import tariff results in diminished import demand; however, in the case of a small country, the reduced import demand does not have an appreciable effect in making the import good more abundant on the world market. Consequently, the world price of the import good is not affected when the government of a small country raises its import tariff. For a small country, then, the entire tariff increase is passed through as an increase in the local price. This means that no international externality flows from the import tariff of a small country through the terms of trade to the welfare of the government of the exporting country. Thus, the second assumption mentioned above is indeed critical for the terms-of-trade theory of trade agreements.

The distinction between large and small countries serves well at a pedagogical level, but the distinction is most likely one of degree. By this we mean that most countries are large, to some degree, with respect to at least some of the goods that they import. As noted, a country is literally small with regard to some good that it imports, if a hike in its ad valorem import tariff of, say, 5% is fully passed through to its consumers and thus results in a local price increase of 5%. The same country, however, may be large with regard to some other product that it imports. Such a product, for example, may be supplied by a neighboring country, perhaps because the product entails high transportation costs or is perishable in nature. An increase in the ad valorem tariff of 5% for a product of this kind may be incompletely passed through to consumers and may thus lead to a local price increase of only, say, 3%. In that case, the price received by foreign exporters (that is, the world price for this product) falls by 2%, and the importing country has achieved a terms-of-trade gain through an import tariff increase.

The hypothesis that governments are able to alter the terms of trade with their tariff selections also finds support in a growing body of empirical research. As Bagwell and Staiger (2010a) report in their survey, a number of empirical studies offer compelling evidence that unilateral tariff changes can significantly alter a country's terms of trade, even for countries like Mexico that might be thought to be small. Further, a large body of research as surveyed by Goldberg and Knetter (1997) reports that exchange-rate shocks are not fully passed through to consumers. If the cost increase experienced by foreign exporters as a consequence of an exchange-rate shock is analogous to the cost increase that is experienced when a higher import tariff is confronted, then this body of work supports the view that the terms-of-trade effects of import tariffs are likely to be quantitatively significant and widespread across countries.

A related but different empirical question is whether governments respond to their terms-of-trade motivations in the way that the theory predicts, when governments set their policies in a unilateral fashion. An important recent paper by Broda, Limao and Weinstein (2008) argues that the answer to this question is yes. Broda, et al. consider 15 countries that were never GATT members and which thus adopted optimal unilateral trade policies prior to joining the WTO.

Broda, et al. first estimate the market power possessed by these countries (specifically, they estimate the foreign export supply elasticities faced by these countries). Their estimates here confirm the findings of early studies: most countries, and even seemingly small countries, have the ability to use their import tariffs so as to achieve significant changes in the world prices for many of their imported goods. Broda, et al. then go further and compare their estimates of market power with the actual unilateral import tariffs selected by governments. Their finding is striking: prior to joining the WTO, these countries on average had tariffs that were 9% higher on imported goods for which they had significant market power in comparison to the tariffs set on goods for which market power was limited. The apparent implication of this study is that governments respond to terms-of-trade motivations in a way that is broadly consistent with the theory, when they set their policies in a unilateral fashion.

A further empirical question concerns whether the pattern of tariff cuts negotiated in WTO/GATT align well with the pattern of tariff cuts that would be predicted by the terms-of-trade theory of trade agreements. In effect, the central issue here is whether negotiated tariffs can be understood as reflecting the removal of the portion of a government's optimal unilateral tariff that embodies the terms-of-trade motive. This issue can be addressed in a couple of ways. A first approach is to focus on WTO/GATT Members and posit that their unbound tariffs are set in a unilateral fashion while the tariffs that they bound in WTO/GATT negotiations are set at efficient levels. If estimates of market power are useful in predicting the levels of unbound tariffs but are not useful in predicting the levels of bound tariffs, then we would have empirical support for the hypothesis that tariffs bound in WTO/GATT negotiations are determined in the manner predicted by the terms-of-trade theory. Broda, et al. (2008) focus on the United States and offer support of exactly this nature. A second approach is to consider countries that joined the WTO subsequent to its creation in 1995 and compare the tariffs selected by the governments of these countries prior to joining the WTO with those selected after joining the WTO. Under the assumption that the former tariffs are set at optimal unilateral levels while the latter tariffs are set at efficient, politically optimal levels, Bagwell and Staiger (2011) show that the terms-of-trade theory can be used to predict negotiated tariff levels based on pre-negotiation tariff levels, import volumes and prices, and measures of market power. For example, when demand and supply functions are linear, the theory predicts that the magnitude of the negotiated tariff cut should be larger when the ratio of pre-negotiation import volume to world price is larger. They report robust support for this relationship and thereby provide empirical support for the central predictions of the terms-of-trade theory of trade agreements.[29]

---

[29] Further results consistent with these findings are reported by Eicher and Henn (2011), who find that the trade effects associated with WTO membership are largest for countries that

Stepping away from the formal empirical studies, one might still ask whether it is plausible that governments set their unilateral trade policies in a way that reflects the terms-of-trade benefits that are associated with higher tariffs. After all, as Regan (2006) emphasizes, government trade-policy officials rarely mention the terms of trade. To this concern, we offer two responses. First, at its core, the terms-of-trade theory of trade agreements builds from the idea that foreign exporters bear some of the incidence of an import tax. The empirical studies cited above suggest that the tax incidence borne by foreign exporters is often significantly different from zero. In this light, if a government seeks to implement a higher local price on an import good, whether for economic, distributional, or political reasons, then it would seem quite plausible that the government would be tempted to shift some of the costs of achieving a higher local price onto foreign exporters. Unlike domestic groups, foreign exporters do not have a "voice" in the determination of domestic unilateral tariff policies, and consequently they represent a particularly tempting group on which to shift the tax burden. Second, while real-world trade-policy officials rarely mention the "terms of trade," they do frequently mention "market access." But the terms-of-trade theory of trade agreements can be recast entirely in the language of market access. When a government raises its import tariff, it shifts in the import demand curve. The associated "price effect" under which the domestic country enjoys a terms-of-trade gain is accompanied by a "volume effect" whereby the foreign government experiences reduced access to the domestic market. Once this link between price and volume effects is forged, we can reinterpret the terms-of-trade theory entirely in the language of market access that is employed by trade-policy negotiators.[30]

Imperfect Competition and Other International Externalities Our discussion to this point has employed an economic model in which markets are perfectly competitive. This model provides a valuable benchmark for understanding the purpose of trade agreements. In many markets, however, firms possess market power and markets are thus imperfectly competitive. Correspondingly, a large literature in economics characterizes optimal unilateral trade policies for governments when markets are imperfectly competitive. This literature emphasizes novel "profit-shifting" and "firm-delocation" effects of trade policy. The existence of such effects suggests that other international externalities in addition to the terms-of-trade externality may arise in imperfectly competitive markets. We may thus ask: How, if at all, would the rationale for a trade agreement change if instead markets were imperfectly competitive?

were large in world markets at the time of their accession to the WTO/GATT (and hence would be expected to have a significant terms-of-trade component in their unilateral tariffs and therefore to negotiate large tariff reductions in the WTO/GATT according to the terms-of-trade theory).

[30] For further discussion of this point, see Bagwell and Staiger (2002).

This question is addressed in several recent papers. Ossa (2011) relaxes the assumption of perfectly competitive markets and assumes instead that the economic setting is described by monopolistic competition and two-way trade in similar products. In this economic setting, the number of firms located in each country is determined endogenously, firms sell differentiated products, and firms compete for sales in both the home market and the foreign market. For exported units, a firm incurs trade costs comprised of a transport (shipping) cost and any trade taxes. In earlier work, Venables (1987) considers optimal unilateral trade policy in this setting and shows that a novel firm-delocation motive for trade policy is present. Intuitively, if the government of the home country imposes an import tariff or an export subsidy, then more firms enter the home market while fewer firms establish their locations in the foreign market. In this sense, an import tariff or export subsidy can "delocate" firms to the domestic market. For a domestic government that maximizes national welfare, the benefit of such delocation is that domestic consumers then save on trade costs and enjoy a lower overall price index. The downside of delocation to the home market is experienced by foreign consumers, who then experience a higher price index. Ossa's interesting contribution is to show that the associated negative international externality does not travel through the terms of trade.

The international externality identified by Ossa is instead a local-price externality. Intuitively, in this economic setting, a government that maximizes national welfare is directly concerned with the local price in its own country, the world prices, *and* the local price in the other country.[31] In turn, the equilibrium pattern of firm location across countries is endogenously determined in the model and depends on local prices in both countries. Since each government would prefer to have more of the world's firms located locally in order to save on transport costs, each government thus has a direct interest in the local prices at home and abroad.

Recent work has also demonstrated that a local-price externality arises in other imperfectly competitive markets as well. Building on work by Venables (1985), Bagwell and Staiger (2009a) also identify a firm-delocation effect and associated local-price externality in a model with endogenous entry, segmented markets, and two-way trade in a homogeneous product.[32] In other work, Bagwell and Staiger (2009b) consider imperfectly competitive markets with an exogenous number of firms, in which the presence of a monopoly or oligopoly is associated with positive profits. Earlier work by Brander and Spencer (1981, 1984a,b, 1985) considers the determination of unilateral trade policies in this economic setting and identifies a novel profit-shifting motive for trade-policy intervention.

---

[31] For further development of this formalization of preferences in Ossa's model, see Bagwell and Staiger (2009a).

[32] We discuss this model in greater detail in Section 3.4, when we address the treatment of export policies in the WTO.

In this setting as well, each government is directly interested in the local price in its own country, world prices, *and* the local price in the other country. A local-price externality arises in this model, since the profit enjoyed on exports by the home monopoly or oligopoly is determined in part by the volume of export sales, which is in turn determined by the local price in the foreign market.

In short, when markets are imperfectly competitive, the international policy environment is more complex. International externalities flow through world prices as before, but they also now travel through local prices. Accordingly, the possibility arises that the rationale for a trade agreement may be more complex in imperfectly competitive markets.

To assess this possibility, we consider whether the three findings reported above for perfectly competitive markets continue to hold when the economic setting is characterized by imperfect competition. Not surprisingly, the first finding – when governments select their trade policies in a unilateral fashion, the resulting unilateral policies are inefficient – continues to hold. The inefficiency of unilateral policies is expected, since the economic setting with imperfect competition includes the terms-of-trade (world-price) externality that delivers the inefficiency of unilateral policies in the model with perfect competition as well as a new local-price externality. A version of the second finding holds as well. In particular, a trade agreement that is mutually beneficial to governments must involve a reduction in the net trade impediment (i.e., the import tariff less any export subsidy) along any trade channel. Thus, a mutually beneficial agreement must again expand trade volumes. Finally, and perhaps more surprisingly, the third finding continues to hold as well: the politically optimal tariffs are efficient, and so the fundamental rationale for a trade agreement is again the terms-of-trade externality.[33]

Given that international externalities flow through world and local prices when markets are imperfectly competitive, the third finding requires further discussion. Recall that the political optimum corresponds to the unilateral trade policies that governments would choose if they did not value gains or losses attributable to movements in their terms of trade. Thus, at a political optimum, along any trade channel, each government sets its corresponding trade policy so as to deliver its preferred mix of home and foreign local prices. Starting at the political optimum, therefore, if the foreign government were to slightly change its trade policy, then the resulting change in local prices would not generate a first-order change in the welfare of the home government. In effect, then, at the political optimum, each government sets its trade policies so that local-price externalities are "shut down." Of course, a slight change in the trade policy of the foreign government would alter the terms of trade, but this alteration cannot

---

[33] These findings are shown for firm-delocation models in Bagwell and Staiger (2009a) and for profit-shifting models in Bagwell and Staiger (2009b).

be the source of mutual gain since the governments have opposite preferences as to the preferred direction for the terms of trade to move. Arguing in this way, we may conclude again that the politically optimal tariffs are efficient. Hence, if governments could be induced not to value the terms-of-trade implications of their trade policies, then they would again achieve an efficient outcome.

It is important to emphasize, though, that the preceding argument relies on the assumption that, for every trade channel, each government has a trade policy. Thus, for a good that is exported from the home country to the foreign country, our assumption is that the government of the home country has an export subsidy and the foreign country has an import tariff. If instead we were to eliminate the use of export subsidies in the imperfect-competition models, then the government of the exporting country for a particular good would be unable to set its export policy so as to achieve its preferred mix of home and foreign local prices. Accordingly, at a political optimum, the local-price externality that flows from the foreign import tariff to the home-government welfare function would not be shut down, and as a consequence the political optimum in an imperfect-competition setting in which export instruments are prohibited may be inefficient. We can thus conclude that local-price externalities represent an additional rationale for a trade agreement when markets are imperfectly competitive, if we assume that export policies are unavailable. We note, though, that this local-price rationale for a trade agreement is incomplete, since it appeals to the existence of an agreement that prohibits export subsidies in order to provide an alternative rationale for a trade agreement (and what is then lacking is an explanation for why a prohibition on export subsidies would arise in the first place).

Finally, in the perfect- and imperfect-competition economic settings considered above, prices are determined by market-clearing conditions. In some markets, though, prices may be determined by bilateral bargaining between a foreign exporter and a domestic purchaser. Antras and Staiger (2008) consider a model of this kind and find that a novel "political externality" may arise that represents an independent problem for a trade agreement to solve.[34] The full implication of this analysis for the theory of trade agreements is not yet fully developed and warrants further investigation.

Returning now to the question raised at the beginning of our discussion of imperfectly competitive markets, we may conclude that, for economic settings with imperfectly competitive markets and in which prices are set by a standard market-clearing mechanism, international externalities flow through local prices as well as through the terms of trade; however, if governments have export and import trade policies at their disposal, then the terms-of-trade externality continues to provide the fundamental rationale for a trade agreement. If instead

---

[34] See also Ethier (2004) for an early discussion of political externalities.

prices are set by a bilateral bargaining process, then unilateral trade policies may be inefficient even if governments do not value terms-of-trade movements, and so an additional non-terms-of-trade rationale for a trade agreement may be available.

The Commitment Theory of Trade Agreements In our discussion above, we examine models in which the rationale for a trade agreement stems from an international externality. We now briefly turn to an alternative and possibly complementary approach, under which the rationale for a trade agreement is as an external commitment device that better enables a government to make commitments to economic actors within its own country.

To develop this perspective, let us consider the government of a small country. We can imagine a variety of commitment problems that might confront this government. For example, the government might wish to commit to a low import tariff in order to induce capital to move from an import-competing sector into an export sector. Relatedly, it might wish to commit to a low import tariff in order to induce firms in an import-competing industry to adopt more efficient technologies. The problem confronting the government is one of credibility: if capital fails to move from the import-competing sector, or if the desired technologies are not adopted, the government may be unable to resist setting a high import tariff. The lack of commitment in turn may mean that private actors are not motivated to take the desired actions, leaving the government with lower welfare than it would enjoy were it able to make credible policy commitments.

A government might address its commitment problem through a trade agreement. In particular, if a government makes a commitment in a trade agreement to maintain a low tariff, then the government may be able to maintain the low tariff, even if the private sector does not take the desired action. Foreseeing this possibility, the private sector may take the desired action. As a result, the government may enjoy higher welfare with a trade agreement than without a trade agreement.

It is important to ask exactly how a trade agreement enables a government to keep its commitments. The most natural interpretation is that the government achieves commitment through a trade agreement, since the rules of the agreement provide that other governments will raise the tariffs that they apply to exports from the government's country in the event that the government raises its tariff. We might then ask why the government would find the possibility of retaliatory tariffs sufficient to enable it to resist the temptation to protect. For the threat of retaliatory tariffs to be meaningful to the government, the most likely scenario is that the retaliatory tariffs would lower the profits of exporters and thereby diminish the welfare of the government. In a standard economic setting with perfectly competitive markets, retaliatory tariffs lower exporters' profits by inducing a fall in the (world) price at which exporters sell. The commitment theory in this instance thus relies on the presence of a terms-of-trade externality.[35]

More generally, while the commitment role of trade agreements has been identified in the economics literature, research featuring the commitment role has for the most part not pushed forward to interpret and evaluate the design of WTO/GATT.[36] In Section 3.2.4, we thus put the commitment theory of trade agreements to the side and focus on the terms-of-trade rationale for trade agreements.

3.2.4 From Economic Theory to Interpretation of Legal Rules

Having presented the terms-of-trade theory of trade agreements, we now proceed to our second step and consider the implications of this theory for the design of a trade agreement. We consider some of the key design features of the WTO/GATT system and argue that these features can be readily interpreted from the perspective of the terms-of-trade theory. In particular, we confront the theory with the fact that WTO/GATT negotiations entail reciprocal tariff reductions achieved through negotiations over tariff bindings while allowing for renegotiation. We also note that liberalization in the WTO/GATT system occurs over time through rounds of negotiation, and we discuss possible interpretations of "gradualism" in trade negotiations. And we offer an economic interpretation for the fact that protection in the WTO/GATT system is largely concentrated in the form of tariffs rather than quotas and other quantitative measures. Finally, a key feature of the WTO/GATT is the principle of nondiscrimination and, as already mentioned, we will in later Sections extend the economic framework to allow for more than two countries, and we interpret and evaluate the principle of nondiscrimination in the extended model.

Reciprocal Tariff Liberalization Through WTO/GATT negotiation rounds, governments achieve agreements to reduce tariffs. In practice, these agreements often reflect a norm of reciprocity and entail a "balance of concessions," whereby one government makes the concession of lowering its import tariff in exchange for receiving the benefit of a similar concession from a trading partner.[37] This

---

[35] Even in the presence of a terms-of-trade externality, there remains the further question of whether a trade agreement such as the WTO/GATT can effectively "tie the hands" of its member governments and so provide them with the desired commitment, especially in light of the ample opportunities for "escape" and renegotiation that we have described in earlier Sections.

[36] Maggi and Rodriguez-Clare (2007) is an important exception.

[37] Recent work by Karacaovali and Limao (2008), Limao (2006, 2007), and Shirono (2004) offers evidence in support of the hypothesis that tariff-bargaining outcomes in WTO/GATT satisfy a reciprocity norm.

practice is difficult to reconcile with arguments that unilateral liberalization is always in a country's best interest. As we now argue, reciprocal tariff liberalization is readily interpreted using the terms-of-trade theory of trade agreements. To develop this point, we use the simple economic model developed above, in which two countries trade two goods and markets are perfectly competitive.

At a broad level, our presentation of the terms-of-trade theory above already offers an interpretation of the emphasis that negotiating governments place on reciprocal tariff liberalization. As we explain above, in the absence of a trade agreement, governments set tariffs that are inefficiently high, due to the terms-of-trade externality. Governments can then mutually gain from forming a trade agreement if the agreement facilitates a reciprocal reduction in import tariffs. The theory also provides an interpretation for the language that associates a tariff cut with a concession. Starting from its optimal unilateral tariff, a government of course cannot gain from a unilateral reduction in its tariff. More generally, when a government cuts its tariff in a unilateral fashion, its country suffers a terms-of-trade loss, and this loss must be balanced against any potential benefit that a lower local price might offer.

We can also interpret the value of reciprocal tariff liberalization at a more specific level. To this end, let us say that a negotiated reduction in tariffs between two governments satisfies the principle of reciprocity if each country's increase in the volume of imports is equal in value to its increase in the volume of exports, where all trade volumes are valued using the world prices that prevail under the initial tariffs. As Bagwell and Staiger (1999, 2002) establish, when trade is balanced, the principle of reciprocity is satisfied if and only if the negotiated tariff reduction leaves the terms of trade unaltered. Intuitively, the reduction in the import tariff of the home country serves to raise the price of the home import good on the world market, while the reduction in the import tariff of the foreign country serves to raise the price of the home export good on the world market. When the negotiated tariff reductions satisfy the principle of reciprocity, the world price of the home export good relative to that of the home import good is unchanged.

Now suppose that governments initially set their optimal unilateral tariffs and then consider forming a trade agreement in which they lower their tariffs in a manner that satisfies the principle of reciprocity. At the original tariffs, each government has set its tariff at a level so that the costs and benefits of a slight unilateral tariff cut would be exactly offsetting. The cost of a unilateral tariff cut is that the country's terms-of-trade would deteriorate. Since this cost must be offset by a benefit, we know that at this particular configuration of tariffs the government would gain from the reduced local price for the import good that a unilateral tariff cut would imply. The key point is that the government resists a unilateral tariff cut, despite the advantageous reduction in the local price, since a unilateral tariff cut would imply a terms-of-trade loss. On the other hand, if governments form a trade agreement and lower their tariffs in a manner that conforms to the principle of reciprocity, then each government enjoys the benefit of a reduced local price on its import good without suffering a terms-of-trade loss.[38] Starting from their optimal unilateral tariffs, therefore, governments are sure to enjoy mutual gains from a trade agreement in which they lower their tariffs a small degree in a fashion that satisfies the principle of reciprocity.[39]

Tariff bindings WTO/GATT tariff negotiations concern bound rates rather than exact rates for applied tariffs. Why would governments find it advantageous to negotiate over tariff ceilings rather than tariff floors or exact tariff levels?

Our discussion above indicates that mutual gains for governments are possible only if a trade agreement ensures a reciprocal reduction in tariffs. In fact, we may understand a trade agreement as a solution to a Prisoners' Dilemma problem. Governments jointly gain if they both agree to lower their tariffs below the unilateral tariff levels that would be selected in the absence of an agreement. When tariffs are set at efficient levels, however, each government has an incentive to "cheat" and raise its tariff to the unilaterally optimal level. From this perspective, it is immediately plausible that governments would regard ceilings on tariffs as more valuable than floors on tariffs. Nevertheless, we may still ask why governments do not simply negotiate exact tariff levels rather than ceilings.

Relatively little research in economics has formally analyzed the benefits that are associated with a trade agreement that utilizes tariff ceilings ("weak bindings"). Some recent research, however, suggests that tariff ceilings may be an attractive design feature of a trade agreement when governments are subject to preference shocks.[40] For example, at the time of negotiation, a government may be unsure about the importance it will place on profits in an import-competing

---

[38] Of course, governments impose import protection precisely to raise local prices of the import good, so it might seem unlikely that a government could ever view a reduced local price for the import good as a good thing. But if a government were told that the costs of its protection were higher than it had initially believed was the case, then it is natural to expect that the government would wish to revise downward its chosen tariff level and thereby reduce its local price of the import good. In effect, reciprocity is simply a means by which governments are faced with the full costs of their tariff choices.

[39] See Bagwell and Staiger (1999, 2002) for a formal demonstration of this point. We note also that the theory does *not* indicate that any degree of reciprocal tariff liberalization is mutually beneficial to governments. For any government, once tariffs are reciprocally liberalized to a sufficient degree, the government no longer benefits from a reduction in the local price of its import good. When tariffs are reciprocally liberalized beyond this point, the government actually loses from a further reduction in its local price and thus loses overall from further reciprocal liberalization.

[40] See, for example, Amador and Bagwell (2011), Bagwell and Staiger (2005a), and Horn, et al. (2010).

industry relative to consumer welfare. The government's optimal unilateral tariff and also the efficient tariff are higher when the weight that the government attaches to profits in the import-competing industry is larger. If government preference shocks were publicly observable, then governments might attempt to develop a state-contingent agreement, under which a government is allowed to apply the higher efficient tariff in the event that the well-being of import-competing firms is of particular importance to the government. A government is likely, however, to have some private information about its actual preferences; furthermore, even if preference shocks are publicly observable, it may be costly to write a detailed state-contingent "contract."

Given the difficulty of designing a contract that is fully state-contingent, governments might consider other means of disciplining tariffs. At one extreme, governments might simply agree to apply the tariff that is efficient on average. The problem with agreeing to a rule that specifies an exact tariff, however, is that it would be efficient for a government to select a higher tariff for some preference shocks. This flexibility is lost when agreements are made to specific tariff levels. At the other extreme, another possibility would be for governments to attempt to implement efficient tariffs by granting one another complete discretion to adjust tariffs after preference shocks are experienced. This approach is also problematic. A government would be tempted to claim that the well-being of import-competing firms is of paramount importance, even if this were not the case, since it could thereby effectively cheat and set its tariff at a high level that is closer to its optimal unilateral tariff. In light of these difficulties, an agreement to impose a tariff ceiling offers important advantages. The ceiling can limit the ability of governments to cheat upward in the direction of their optimal unilateral tariffs. It thereby serves to limit the extent to which a government can adopt a high tariff and impose a terms-of-trade externality on the other country. At the same time, a ceiling gives a government downward discretion. If the government receives a preference shock that makes lower tariffs more attractive, the government is free to adopt the lower tariff.[41]

Renegotiation   The principle of reciprocity also appears in WTO/GATT rules that pertain to instances where one government takes an action which nullifies

---

[41] A government may preserve some degree of upward flexibility for the tariff that it applies on a given import good, if its current applied rate lies below its bound rate. Interestingly, some countries joined the WTO with negotiated tariff bindings that exceeded applied rates. An alternative approach for a new member would be to join the WTO with a bound rate which equals the applied rate, and then to use WTO/GATT renegotiation or escape-clause provisions in the event that upward flexibility is desired. We may speculate that even a new member may value a gap between bound and applied rates, if the use of such provisions at a later date could entail transactions costs.

or impairs the benefits expected under the agreement by another country. In particular, under GATT Article XXVIII, a government may propose to modify or withdraw a concession that its country agreed to in a previous round of negotiation. The government may then offer compensation to its trading partner. Compensation, for example, might take the form of a reduction in the tariff of some other import good. If an acceptable level of compensation is not agreed upon, then the country is permitted to undertake the proposed change anyhow, with the understanding that its trading partner is then entitled to reciprocate by withdrawing a "substantially equivalent" concession of its own. In this application, the principle of reciprocity is used to moderate the response of the trading partner.

In the context of our economic model, when a government initiates a renegotiation under Article XXVIII, the reciprocal withdrawal of concessions serves to preserve the terms of trade. While neither country experiences a change in its terms of trade, the local prices in each country are altered following the tariff hikes. In particular, in each country, the relative price of the import good is higher after tariffs are renegotiated to higher levels. An interesting question is whether an efficient pair of tariffs exists that is robust against the potential for renegotiation.

In fact, there exists exactly one pair of efficient tariffs that are such that neither government would choose to initiate a renegotiation under GATT Article XXVIII. This tariff pair is the politically optimal tariff pair. Intuitively, at the political optimum, each government has selected its tariff so as to achieve its preferred local price. If a government were to raise its tariff and initiate thereby a renegotiation to a higher tariff pair, then the reciprocal withdrawal of a tariff concession by the other government would ensure that the renegotiation process fails to alter the terms of trade. Renegotiation would lead to a rise in the relative local price of the import good, however. At the political optimum, though, each government already has its preferred local price; thus, starting at the politically optimal tariff pair, neither government can gain by initiating a renegotiation to a higher tariff pair. The political optimum is in this sense robust even when renegotiation is possible. By contrast, at any other efficient tariff pair, holding fixed the associated terms of trade, one government would prefer to have a higher relative local price for its import good. This government would thus initiate the renegotiation process, and as a consequence efficient tariff pairs other than the politically optimal tariff pair would be renegotiated to higher (and inefficient) tariffs.[42]

This discussion suggests that renegotiation provisions may play a role in limiting power asymmetries across countries. Imagine that one country is more powerful and attempts to force an agreement to an efficient tariff pair that is favorable to this country. In comparison to the politically optimal tariff pair, the resulting tariff pair involves a higher tariff for the more powerful country and a

---

[42] For a formal demonstration of these points, see Bagwell and Staiger (1999, 2002).

lower tariff for the less powerful country. At the associated terms of trade, the weaker country then has a greater volume of imports than it would prefer. Under GATT Article XXVIII, the government of the weaker country could initiate a renegotiation leading to a reciprocal increase in tariffs by both governments. The government of the weaker country would thereby enjoy an unaltered terms of trade but obtain a more favorable local price that results in the desired reduction in the volume of trade. In this way, an efficient outcome that favors one country leads to renegotiation to higher tariffs that are inefficient. As a result, some of the benefit to the government of the powerful country of pushing the negotiation outcome away from the political optimum and to an efficient outcome that it favors would be given up in the subsequent renegotiation. When renegotiation of this kind is possible, the government of a powerful country may thus be less tempted to push negotiations away from the political optimum in the first place.

Negotiation Rounds: Gradualism We argue above that governments can achieve an efficient outcome only if they reduce their tariffs from the unilateral levels that they would choose in the absence of an agreement. This argument might suggest that a trade agreement should involve one negotiating round. Yet, in fact, trade policies have been liberalized gradually over time in several rounds of negotiation. What accounts for the gradual nature of trade-policy liberalization?

Research in economics suggests that gradualism is expected when an initial tariff round of tariff liberalization results over time in changes in the economic environment, where these changes in turn alter governments' preferences and thereby lead to future liberalization efforts.[43] For example, in the years that follow an initial round of tariff liberalization, workers may gradually relocate from the import-competing industry to the export industry. After this relocation occurs, the government may find that it now prefers a lower local price for the import good relative to the local price for its export good. Thus, after a period of time, the government may be willing to return to the bargaining table and offer to lower its import tariff further in exchange for a further reduction in the foreign country's import tariff. A reciprocal exchange of this kind maintains the terms of trade and lowers the local price of the import good relative to the export good in each country.

A related theory of gradualism highlights the role of learning by doing in the production process. After an initial round of tariff liberalization, exporting firms in each country produce a greater volume of output. Over time, they thus "learn by doing" and thereby enjoy lower costs of production. In turn, the reduced costs

---

[43] For further discussion of economic research on gradualism in trade agreements, see Bagwell and Staiger (2002).

of production may raise the benefits to each country of obtaining a further reduction in the import tariff applied by the other country. Eventually, production costs have fallen to a sufficient extent that each government finds it worthwhile to participate in a new round of tariff negotiations.

The common feature in these models is that government preferences change over time, once an initial round of tariff liberalization is achieved. The initial round of liberalization triggers changes in the underlying economic environment, with the result that government preferences as regards local prices evolve as well. Eventually, the initial round of liberalization induces a "virtuous cycle," whereby governments' preferences change in a way that leads to a preference for further liberalization. The liberalization process is thus necessarily gradual, since the underlying changes in the economic environment occur slowly over time.

Tariffs vs. Quotas   With certain exceptions, members of WTO/GATT agree to concentrate protective measures into tariffs. We consider here the advantages of a trade agreement in which quantitative measures such as quotas must undergo a process of "tariffication," whereby they are converted into tariff equivalents. Economic theory indicates that, in some situations, import tariffs and quotas have similar economic effects. We argue, though, that tariffication can facilitate mutually beneficial and reciprocal trade liberalization between governments. Our discussion thus provides support for the tariffication of quantitative restrictions.

To begin, we describe a famous "tariff-quota equivalence" result: in perfectly competitive markets, the price and quantity effects of tariffs and quotas are equivalent. To see this point, let us suppose that the home country imports a given good from the foreign country and imposes an import tariff. The tariff on this good drives a wedge between the local price in the home country paid by domestic consumers and the price received on the world market by foreign exporters. Due to the resulting increase in the domestic price, the volume of imports is less when the tariff is in place than would be the case were the home government to adopt a policy of free trade. Imagine now that the government of the home country removes the import tariff and replaces it with an import quota, where the quota is set equal to the import volume under the original tariff. At the world price, domestic import demand exceeds foreign export supply. The domestic price is thus bid up until the market clears; hence, the local price paid by domestic consumers ends up being the same under the quota as it was under the tariff.

The tariff-quota equivalence result seems to suggest that tariffs and quotas are interchangeable. In fact, however, this conclusion does not follow. First, while in perfectly competitive markets tariffs and quotas can generate equivalent prices and outputs, the allocation of rents may differ significantly depending upon whether a tariff or quota is used. When a specific tariff is imposed, the volume of imports times the price wedge equals the amount of tariff revenue that the government of the importing country collects. By contrast, when an import quota is imposed, the rents that would have been received as government revenue under a tariff are now collected by the individuals who hold the import quota licenses. These individuals can buy imports at the world price and resell them locally at the domestic price. If these licenses are distributed to individuals in the home country, then quota rents are like tariff revenue in that the rents stay at home. But if the quota licenses are assigned to the government of the exporting country, then the quota rents are transferred to the foreign country. From the point of view of the home country, an import tariff is then preferred to an import quota when the quota licenses are assigned to the foreign government.

Second, while the price and quantity effects of tariff and quotas are equivalent in perfectly competitive markets, the tariff-quota equivalence may fail under other market structures. Suppose, for example, that the home country has a domestic monopoly that competes for domestic sales against a competitive foreign export supply. In the presence of a modest import tariff, the existence of foreign export supply (or perhaps even the threat of foreign export supply) limits the monopolist's ability to exercise market power and raise its price. By contrast, if the home government replaces an import tariff with an import quota that delivers the same level of imports, then the monopolist has the option of raising prices further and monopolizing the residual demand (i.e., the demand that remains after foreign exporters reach their quota). An equivalent quota thus creates more domestic monopoly power and may thus lead to a higher domestic price and lower domestic output. Accordingly, tariff-quota equivalence fails to hold in the presence of a domestic monopoly.[44]

Third, and more importantly for our present purposes, the process of "tariffying" quantitative measures like quotas acts to facilitate mutually beneficial and reciprocal trade liberalization between governments. Following Bagwell and Sykes (2004), we support this claim by highlighting here three benefits of the tariffication process for facilitating trade liberalization. First, when governments have a range of nontariff trade-policy instruments that affect trade in a given product, it becomes more difficult for a government to estimate the actual market-access gains that might be achieved through the modification or removal of any one foreign instrument. When governments face higher transactions costs in evaluating the offers of other countries, it is likely that fewer deals will get finalized in a given negotiation window. Second, some trade-policy instruments have less predictable effects on trade volumes than do others. With an import tariff, foreign exporters know exactly the tax that they must pay to sell in a given market. While they may face uncertainty about various factors that

---

[44] For further discussion, see Bhagwati (1965).

affect domestic demand and supply, the magnitude to the tariff that they face is known. With an import quota, on the other hand, foreign exporters may face additional uncertainty, since the quota may be filled by other exporters or the importing country may allocate the quota in a way that is disadvantageous to an exporter. If governments are risk averse with regard to the export volumes of firms, then they will offer a smaller concession to secure a given expected volume of trade when the uncertainties associated with this volume are greater. Third, our discussion above indicates that trade-policy interactions between governments take the form of a Prisoners' Dilemma game. At an efficient trade agreement, each government thus has a temptation to "cheat" on the agreement and limit the volume of imports to some degree. If governments' trade policies were nontransparent and thus difficult to monitor, then the temptation for a government to (secretly) cheat would be increased. Tariffication thus facilitates trade liberalization, since tariffs are transparent and cheating thus becomes a less tempting option.

And finally, as was pointed out in Section 3.2.2 above, a key rationale in the WTO/GATT for the general elimination of quantitative restrictions is their almost-inherent inconsistency with the principle of nondiscrimination as embodied in MFN. As we later describe in Section 3.4, there is a strong economic rationale for MFN in the WTO/GATT, and hence by implication this rationale for the WTO/GATT preference of tariffs over quotas as the protective measure of choice is also strong.

3.3 Implementation in WTO Law: Tariffs and QRs

Having considered at length the rationale for constraints on traditional instruments of protection, we now turn to the legal implementation of those constraints in the case law and in subsequent practice and understanding. Tariff Commitments are considered first, followed by a discussion of QRs.

3.3.1 Key Features of the Law on Tariff Commitments

As we have previously noted and will detail further below, a WTO/GATT tariff binding specifies a legal ceiling for the applied tariffs which it covers. Why would governments find it advantageous to negotiate over tariff ceilings rather than tariff floors or exact tariff levels? We have argued in Section 3.2 that the terms-of-trade theory of trade agreements provides a rationale for this approach: a ceiling is preferred to a floor, since governments have an incentive to cheat on the agreement and shift costs onto their trading partners by *raising* tariffs; furthermore, a ceiling is preferred to a rigid tariff, because a ceiling provides downward flexibility in response to preference shocks and thereby permits efficiency-enhancing reductions in tariffs.

Given this broad rationale for tariff bindings, we begin our consideration of implementation in WTO law with a more detailed discussion of tariff bindings and how they are negotiated. We then discuss the interpretation of tariff commitments, before turning to a review of the legal requirements regarding changes in tariff commitments. Finally, we will explain what fees and formalities (besides tariffs) a customs authority can legitimately impose on imports, and conclude with a discussion of customs valuation.

The Mechanics of Tariff Bindings

The Harmonized System (HS)   To facilitate the negotiation of tariff commitments, it is extremely useful to have a common system for the classification of goods. Efforts to develop a harmonized nomenclature began early in the history of GATT (although the negotiations were conducted under the auspices of a separate entity, the Customs Cooperation Council), and culminated with the Harmonized Commodity Description and Coding System (the Harmonized System).

The Harmonized System (HS) comprises about 5000 commodity groups, each identified by a six-digit code. The description of goods can also be expressed in two and four digits: the lower the number of digits, the more generic the product category (for example, at the two-digit-level one might find the term 'motor vehicles'); the higher the number of digits, the more specific the product category (for example, at the six-digit-level, one might find the term 'passenger cars of less than 2 tons'). The HS thus provides the standardized component in national schedules of tariff concessions; the variable component will be the tariff treatment. The system is used by more than 190 countries as the basis for their customs tariffs.

The language used in the HS is often quite generic, and disputes may arise as to the appropriate classification of a particular good. Disputes will be submitted to the HS Committee which will consider the dispute and make recommendations to the parties. The HS Committee will base its decision not only on the text of the HS Convention, but also on various General Interpretative Rules (GIR) that it has adopted over the years, as well as their Explanatory Notes. GIR 3(a), for example, stipulates that the heading which provides the most specific description shall be preferred to headings providing a more general description. There are also specific GIRs for composite goods [GIR 3(b)].

Ordinary Customs Duties (OCD) and Other Duties and Charges (ODC)   Based on the HS classification, WTO Members negotiate their tariff concessions on various goods. As noted, the resulting commitments are termed "bindings." A binding is a *ceiling* on the permissible tariff rate – WTO Members are free to charge a lower tariff. GATT Art. II thus provides that goods will not be burdened with an ordinary customs duty (OCD) in an amount higher than that reflected in a

member's schedule of concessions. Art. II:1(b) further provides that "such products" shall be exempt from "other duties or charges of any kind" (ODCs) higher
than those applicable when the GATT entered into force or otherwise required
by mandatory legislation in place at that time.

GATT Art. II:7 states that the national tariff schedules negotiated by GATT
members are an "integral part of this Agreement." The practical importance of
this principle is to make the schedules part of the treaty text, subject to the same
rules and principles of interpretation (such as those of the Vienna Convention
on the Law of Treaties).

The terms OCD and ODC are not defined in the treaty text, but have been
addressed in the case law. In *Chile–Price Band* (§§ 264ff.), the Appellate Body
suggested that for a charge to constitute an OCD, it must simply be expressed in
a particular form. In practice, OCDs may be expressed as:

(1) ad valorem duties;
(2) specific duties;
(3) compound duties;
(4) alternative duties (or mixed duties); and
(5) technical duties.

A duty is ad valorem when it is a percentage of the value of the imported
product (e.g., 15% of the import price). A duty is specific when it is related to the
weight, volume, surface, etc. of the good at hand (e.g., $20 per ton of imported
wheat). A duty is compound when it comprises an ad valorem duty to which the
customs authority adds, or from which it subtracts a specific duty (e.g., 10% on
the import price of wheat plus $2 per imported kg of wheat). A duty is alterna-
tive or mixed when it ensures a minimum or maximum tariff protection through
the choice between, in most cases, an ad valorem and a specific duty (e.g., 10%
on the import price of or $2 per imported kg of wheat whichever is the maxi-
mum). Finally, and particularly relevant to agricultural products, a technical duty
is determined by factors, such as alcohol or sugar content or other variables.

With respect to the meaning of the term ODCs, the GATT Secretariat offered
some clarification in a document prepared during the negotiation of the Understanding on the Interpretation of GATT Art II.1(b). Among other things, the Secretariat concluded that ODCs are charges applicable only to imports – they do not
include charges applied to imports and domestic goods alike. In addition, there
is no agreed or exhaustive definition of ODCs and, indeed, it is always possible
for governments to invent new charges.

The subsequently negotiated Understanding concerning Art. II:(1)(b) establishes a few additional principles: First, to improve transparency, members were
required to record ODCs applicable to goods with bound tariffs in their schedules
of concessions (there is no obligation to record ODCs on goods with unbound
tariffs). Second, the obligation of GATT Art. II:1(b) was clarified to provide that

ODCs could not be imposed in an amount higher than those imposed on the date that the first tariff binding on the good in question entered into force – if the first binding was negotiated during the Tokyo Round, for example, the entry into force of the Tokyo Round concession would establish the date on which the ceiling on any applicable ODCs became applicable. Third, the Understanding afforded members a period of three years to challenge ODCs as excessive in relation to the ODCs in place at the time of an earlier (pre-Uruguay Round) concession on the item in question. Fourth, members could at any time challenge an ODC as inconsistent with some other provision of GATT. Challenges can be brought in accordance with these rules despite the fact that schedules are normally "certified" by the WTO Membership at the end of a negotiating round – in other words, certification does not cleanse a recorded ODC of any potential violations.

An illustration of this system is provided in the Panel Report on *Dominican Republic–Import and Sale of Cigarettes*[45]: Honduras challenged the legality of an ODC over three years after the Dominican Republic's schedule had entered into force. The Dominican Republic argued that no challenge could be mounted after the three-year period. The Panel rejected this argument, holding that the three-year period covered only challenges to an ODC based on the proposition that the amount recorded in the schedule exceeded the amount applicable at the time of a pre-Uruguay Round tariff concession on the item in question, or to a challenge based on the proposition that no ODC existed at that point in time. By contrast, Honduras challenged the ODC on the grounds that no such ODC was applied at the time of the Uruguay Round, and hence that it violated a distinct obligation to record ODCs at the level actually applied at the conclusion of the Round. The Panel thus proceeded to examine the claim by Honduras that the relevant ODC did not exist at the conclusion of the Uruguay Round (§§ 7.54–7.79).

Multilateral Negotiating Rounds   Tariff concessions are usually exchanged in the context of multilateral trade negotiations, the so-called trade rounds. GATT Art. XXVIII bis makes clear that the WTO Membership decides when to initiate these multilateral talks. At this writing, we are in the midst of the ninth negotiating round since the inception of the GATT, the Doha Round.

Originally, tariff round negotiations proceeded in a "request-offer" fashion with bilateral discussions followed by offers and counter-offers item by item. As GATT grew in size, however, the challenges of negotiating in this fashion became more acute, and some later rounds relied on more formulaic, "across-the-board" techniques (particularly the Kennedy and Tokyo Rounds). For example, each nation might begin from the premise that all tariffs will be reduced by an agreed

---

[45] *Dominican Republic – Measures Affecting the Importation and Internal Sale of Cigarettes,* WT/DS302/R, Panel Report adopted May 19, 2005.

percentage, and then negotiate backward from that point to restore higher tariffs on more politically sensitive items.

At the end of a round, all national schedules of concessions will be deposited for review by all parties, and thereafter "certified" (validated) through a multilateral process. Usually, schedules will be annexed to a protocol which will be open for signature to all WTO Members. Clarifications may be sought and, eventually, the Protocol will be registered in accordance with the provisions of Art. 102 of the UN Charter. This process can raise some interesting legal questions. For example, the question arises whether WTO Members, by accepting the protocol have impliedly also accepted that all schedules annexed are GATT-consistent. The case law as we will see has answered this question in the negative.

The number of tariff lines bound is not identical across WTO Members. It is commonly the case that larger, wealthier markets such as the European Community and the United States have made the largest number of tariff commitments. Developing countries have on average made fewer commitments. It is also important to note that some WTO Members have a significant gap between some of their bound tariff rates and their applied tariff rates (i.e., the applied rates are lower), a situation known as "water in the bindings."

The history of the WTO/GATT system reflects steady and often dramatic liberalization of tariffs over the course of these negotiating rounds. To take the example of the United States, the average tariff rate on dutiable imports was 53.2% after the Hawley-Smoot Tariff Act of 1930. This average fell to 12.1% by 1951, 4.9% after the Tokyo Round of GATT negotiations, and 4.5% after the Uruguay Round.[46]

As we note in Section 3.2, the terms-of-trade theory of trade agreements provides a natural interpretation of reciprocal trade liberalization negotiated gradually over a series of rounds. According to this theory, governments can achieve mutual gains from a trade agreement if they *lower* their import tariffs below the levels that they would select in the absence of a trade agreement. Consequently, a trade agreement should systematically facilitate reciprocal trade liberalization and should not encourage greater restrictions in trade.[47] And an initial round of trade liberalization induces subsequent changes in the economic environment and thus government preferences. Over time, these changes may lead to a preference for further liberalization and result in another round of trade-liberalization negotiations.

---

[46] See Jackson, Davey and Sykes (2008), Chapter 1.

[47] This prediction might seem to be an obvious and inevitable feature of any theory of trade agreements, but it is not necessarily implied by the main alternative to the terms-of-trade theory, the commitment theory of trade agreements. According to the commitment theory, whether a government would want to use a trade agreement to help it commit to a lower tariff or rather to a higher tariff would depend on the circumstances.

Concessions outside Multilateral Rounds   Concessions have, on occasion, been exchanged in mini-rounds when only a sub-set of the WTO Membership participated. For instance, the Information Technology Agreement (ITA) was concluded at the Singapore Ministerial Conference in December 1996. At that time, 29 (including the then 15 member states of the European Union[48]) countries or separate customs territories signed the declaration. The Declaration stipulated that participants representing approximately 90% of world trade would have to notify their acceptance of the ITA by 1 April 1997. The original 29 signatories did not reach this 90% trade-coverage criterion, but a number of other countries expressed an interest in becoming participants in the ITA and notified their acceptance. The 90% criterion was met and the ITA entered into force with the first staged reduction in tariffs occurring on July 1, 1997. The ITA has now 69 members (counting the European Community as 25), out of which 35 are developing countries. Together, the 69 members of the ITA represent approximately 97% of world trade in IT products.

Export Tariffs (Taxes)   The discussion so far has focused on the treatment of import tariffs under GATT. Export tariffs do exist, however, albeit not with the same frequency as import tariffs. GATT Art. XXVIII bis makes it clear that not only import tariffs, but export tariffs as well, can be negotiated: "negotiations on a reciprocal and mutually advantageous basis, directed to the substantial reduction of the general level of tariffs and other charges on imports and exports … are of great importance to the expansion of international trade."

The process for consolidating export concessions is not spelled out in the GATT – there is no Art. II-equivalent for export tariffs. This does not mean, however, that export concessions cannot be negotiated on an ad hoc basis. An appropriate illustration is offered in the Report of the Working Party on the Accession of Ukraine to the WTO, which states in § 240:

> The representative of Ukraine confirmed that … Ukraine would reduce export duties in accordance with the binding schedule contained in Table 20(b). He also confirmed that as regards these products, Ukraine would not increase export duties, nor apply other measures having an equivalent effect, unless justified under the exceptions of GATT 1994.

Export taxes are relatively rare and those that do exist are usually aimed at hindering exports of commodities. The 1943 interim report of the (U.S.) Special Committee on Relaxation of Trade Barriers remarked:[49]

---

[48] We use the term EU to refer to Europe today following the adoption of the Lisbon Treaty on December 1, 2009. References to Europe in WTO documents prior to that date (and thus in cases that we cite) are to the EC.

[49] Report of 8 December 1943, International Trade Files, Lot File 57D-284, p. 34.

Except during wartime, governmentally-imposed export duties, and prohibitions and quantitative restrictions on exports have had relatively little
influence in limiting the over-all movement of commodities in world trade,
although they have seriously affected the movement of specific products.
Export taxes and quantitative restrictions on exports have been instituted
for a variety of reasons. Some, such as export taxes on coffee in certain
Latin American countries, have been imposed for revenue purposes. Some
have been imposed for indirect protective reasons: for example, the United
States prohibition on commercial exports of tobacco seed for the purpose
of preventing the cultivation abroad of American types of tobacco. In a different category are the Mexican export taxes, which are used for revenue
purposes and, in combination with an export tax-rebate system to enforce
Membership in export cooperatives. Some, such as the United States control
of helium exports, have been imposed for security reasons. Some have been
imposed pursuant to international agreements; for example, the undertaking by Cuba, in connection with the trade agreement with the United States,
to prohibit the exportation of avocados to the United States except during
the months of July through September...

In the same report, the Committee suggested that it would be useful to regulate or abolish certain objectionable export taxes. In its view, however, export
taxes for revenue purposes, taxes enforced pursuant to international agreements, taxes imposed under the conditions of famine or severe domestic short-
age in the exporting country, or taxes designed to regulate the trade in military
supplies under specified conditions, should not be regarded as objectionable.
The eventual GATT compromise, as shall be seen, disallowed export quantitative restrictions but not export taxes. Consequently, WTO Members are, absent a
commitment otherwise, free to impose export taxes to their liking. Export taxes
are thus treated symmetrically with import tariffs – they are not prohibited, but
may be bound. In practice, however, export tax bindings are rare.

A notable exception is to be found in the Chinese Protocol of Accession to
the WTO. China undertook to eliminate export duties except on certain products
listed in Annex 6 to the Protocol. In *China–Raw Materials*, the United States, Mexico, and the European Communities challenged various restrictions imposed by
China on a range of raw mineral exports, including export duties. The Panel and
the Appellate Body ruled in favor of the complainants on this issue.[50]

Interpreting Tariff Commitments   Tariff commitments often embody ambiguities. Moreover, a certified national schedule of concessions is not necessarily

---

[50] *China – Measures Related to the Exportation of Various Raw Materials* (WT/DS394, 395,
and 398/AB/R, adopted February 22, 2012; WT/DS394, 395, and 398/R and Corr. 1, adopted
February 22, 2012).

GATT-consistent. In what follows, we will briefly examine the most important cases regarding the interpretation of tariff commitments.

The Legal Relevance of the HS   The Panel Report on *EC–Chicken Cuts*[51] held that the HS provides the context, in the sense of the term as used in the Vienna Convention on the Law of Treaties Art. 31.2, for the schedules of concessions submitted by WTO Members. As such, Panels must always take it into account when the issue of interpretation of a particular concession arises. The Appellate Body confirmed this finding (§ 199). The relevant facts are described in §§ 7.2 and 7.3 of the Panel Report:

> The EC Schedule provides for a tariff of 102.4€/100kg/net for products covered by subheading 0207.14.10 and allows the European Communities to use special safeguard measures under Article 5 of the Agreement on Agriculture in respect of such products. The EC Schedule provides for a tariff of 15.4% ad valorem for products covered by subheading 0210.90.20 and there is no reservation for the use of special safeguard measures under Article 5 of the Agreement on Agriculture in respect of such products.
>
> Brazil and Thailand (the complainants) submit that less favourable treatment has been accorded to frozen boneless salted chicken cuts in violation of Article II:1(a) and Article II:1(b) of the GATT 1994 because, through the relevant EC measures, the European Communities changed its customs classification so that those products, which had previously been classified under subheading 0210.90.20 and were subject to an ad valorem tariff of 15.4%, are now classified under subheading 0207.14.10 and are subject to a tariff of 102.4€/100kg/net as well as being potentially subject to special safeguard measures pursuant to Article 5 of the Agreement on Agriculture.

Salted meat exported from Brazil suffered from the change in classification. The European Community defended the change in classification with the argument that salted meat, if not salted for preservation purposes (which did not apply to the Brazilian exports), could not be classified under em 0210.90.20 since this tariff line was intended to cover meat salted for preservation purposes only. The Panel rejected the arguments advanced by the European Community, noting that nothing in the HS description of this item conditioned the classification on the purpose of salting (that is, preservation). In reaching that conclusion, it went through all the interpretative elements of the Vienna Convention, paying particular attention to the HS system as context for the tariff negotiations and

---

[51] WT/DS269/R, Panel Report adopted September 27, 2005.

the resulting schedules (§§ 7.104ff). The AB upheld the Panel's findings in this respect (§§ 199ff).

Scheduling of Concessions Must Be WTO-Consistent GATT Art. II.1(b) states that goods are imported "subject to the terms, conditions or qualifications set forth in [a member's] Schedule." At first glance, this language would seem to imply that concessions are conditional on whatever the negotiators might agree. The extent of the contractual autonomy in this respect was discussed in Panel Reports both in the GATT and in the WTO era. During the *EC–Bananas III* dispute between the European Community and various banana-exporting countries, the question arose as to whether a WTO member can specify conditions of importation in its schedule of concessions in a discriminatory fashion that would otherwise violate the MFN obligation. The European Community had included in its schedule of concessions a condition specifying that certain WTO Members would receive a preferential rate on bananas. A series of banana-exporting WTO Members complained, and the European Community argued in response that its regime was permissible under Art. II.1(b) because it had been notified to the WTO Membership and had gone through the certification process without any WTO Member raising an issue as to its legality. The Appellate Body rejected the argument, holding that a WTO Member can, through conditions attached to its schedule, grant other WTO Members rights but cannot diminish its obligations (§§ 154–158), notwithstanding the fact that nothing in the pertinent language of Article II (or in the Agreement on Agriculture, which was also at issue) specifically prohibits "conditions" that clash with other provisions of GATT.[52]

The outcome is not unreasonable. Were one to introduce a comprehensive legal review of all schedules at the end of a negotiation, the process would perhaps be excessively burdened as it would become necessary for WTO Members to check each other's schedules from a GATT consistency perspective before certification. It perhaps makes more sense from a policy standpoint to conclude that the multilateral review occurring with the exchange of schedules is limited to verification of the accuracy of commitments and not to an assessment of their overall GATT consistency.

The Relevance of a Member's Expectations The LAN dispute (*EC–Computer Equipment*) between the United States and the European Community involved a disagreement between the two parties as to the proper classification of certain computer equipment. The particular commodity (LAN equipment) could, conceivably, come under two different HS classifications, and the United States

---

[52] *European Communities – Regime for the Importation, Sale and Distribution of Bananas*, WT/DS27/AB/R, adopted September 25, 1997.

(exporters) of course preferred that it be classified under the heading with the lower import duty. There had been divergent practice with respect to the classification of LAN equipment among individual European Community member states. The United States argued that the practice of some states in affording LAN equipment the more favorable tariff treatment created a legitimate expectation that they would continue to do so, and further argued that this expectation should be relevant to the interpretation of ambiguous tariff headings. The Panel agreed with the United States, but was reversed by the Appellate Body, which held that the expectations of a single member could not be the basis for interpretation, only the expectations of the WTO Membership as a whole[53] (§§ 80–96).

GATT Art. II:5 further provides that if a member believes that another member is not affording the tariff treatment "contemplated by a concession," and if the other member concurs but is unable to afford the contemplated treatment "because a court or other proper authority has ruled to the effect that the product involved cannot be classified under the tariff laws … so as to permit the treatment contemplated," then the other member must "promptly" enter into negotiations for the purpose of making a compensatory adjustment. Such compensation could involve some tariff reduction on another product, or a reduction on the tariff rate on the product whose classification has been altered by the "court or other proper authority."

Changes in Tariff Protection post-Certification   WTO Members cannot introduce unilateral modifications to their schedule of concessions unless they respect the 1980 Decision on Procedures for Modification and Rectification of Schedules of Tariff Concessions. WTO Members can withdraw concessions negotiated with WTO Members that have withdrawn from the institution under GATT Art. XXVII. More importantly, WTO Members can renegotiate their tariff protection with WTO Members provided that the requirements of Art. XXVIII GATT are respected.

Rectifications and Modifications of Schedules   The 1980 Decision distinguishes modifications, which imply substantive change of a concession (§ 1 of the 1980 Decision), from rectifications, which should imply no such change (§ 2 of the 1980 Decision). Both modifications and rectifications are certified and communicated to the Director-General of the WTO (the former within three months, the latter within six months). The new (modified or rectified) schedules will be definitive if no objection has been raised by a WTO member within three months (§ 3 of the 1980 Decision).

---

[53] *European Communities – Customs Classification of Certain Computer Equipment*, WT/DS62/AB/R, adopted June 22, 1998.

It is unclear whether WTO Members will lose their legal right to challenge the consistency of the notified rectification (or modification) with the multilateral rules at the end of the three- or six-month period. Recall that, in *EC–Bananas III*, the Appellate Body held that WTO Members, when certifying national schedules, do not necessarily waive objections to their consistency with other GATT provisions. If a similar rule were to apply here, then WTO Members would not, by virtue of the 1980 Decision, give up their right to challenge the consistency of modified (or rectified) schedules with the multilateral rules.

There is no litigation thus far under the 1980 Decision, but one older case under GATT did involve a challenge to a tariff modification. Spain introduced a modification into its schedules that distinguished various types of unroasted, nondecaffeinated coffees and charged different tariff rates on them (the tariffs were unbound). Brazil complained because its coffee exports to the Spanish market were being negatively affected, and the Panel ruled for Brazil, finding that the various coffees were all "like products" and that discrimination among them thus violated the MFN obligation of GATT Art. I.[54] We will have more to say about the like-product issue below.

Renegotiating Tariff Protection   A WTO member can increase its bound protection on a given item, but in doing so it shall, according to GATT Art. XXVIII, "endeavour to maintain a general level of reciprocal and mutually advantageous concessions not less favourable to trade than that provided for in this Agreement prior to such negotiations." Thus, in the typical case, the member wishing to raise its duties on a bound item will attempt to negotiate compensation (that is, a lowering of tariffs on other items) with a sub-set of the WTO Membership that will be most severely affected by the tariff change. The agreed compensation will be applied on an MFN basis.

Regarding the timing of negotiations, there are three possibilities. An "open season" negotiating window occurs every three years beginning on January 1, 1958 (thus again on January 1, 1961, etc.). Alternatively, a member can reserve the right to renegotiate at other times as part of its tariff concession. Finally, a member can ask the WTO Membership as a whole for permission to engage in "out of season" renegotiations.

All renegotiations will occur between the party proposing to raise a bound tariff on the one hand, and other WTO Members with whom the tariff concession at issue was "initially negotiated," as well as any other member deemed to have a "principal supplying interest." The identification of these parties is often a difficult task and involves some rules and principles that would take us beyond what is necessary here.[55] Roughly speaking, however, the objective is to include

---

[54] 28th Supp. BISD 102 (1982) (Panel Report adopted June 11, 1981).

[55] For much more detail on these and other issues under Article XXVIII, see Mavroidis (2005).

in the negotiations the parties who were directly involved in negotiating the concession that is to be withdrawn, along with perhaps one or two other parties that
have become major suppliers to the importing nation in question even if they
were not involved in negotiating the initial concession. But a balance must be
struck between including the parties seriously affected by the withdrawal of a
concession on the one hand, and introducing an excessive number of parties
into the negotiation on the other so as to complicate the likelihood of a successful outcome. Accordingly, members that merely have a "substantial interest" in
the concession (short of a principal supplying interest) are simply to be "con-
sulted" during the negotiation process but need not formally sign off before a
deal can be reached.

In the event that no agreement is reached on compensation, the requesting WTO Member will still be free to increase its tariff protection.[56] At that point,
however, members with whom a concession was initially negotiated, as well as
all members with a principal supplying interest or substantial interest, have the
right (within a specified time) to withdraw "substantially equivalent concessions
initially negotiated with" the member raising the bound tariff. Likewise, even if
the negotiations on compensation do reach a successful conclusion, those members with a substantial interest (and thus barred from the negotiating table) may
make such a withdrawal if they are not "satisfied" with the negotiation outcome.

The text of the agreement leaves unanswered the question whether any
withdrawal of concessions will be on a bilateral or MFN basis. Logically, it seems
that retaliation should be bilateral, lest it also potentially triggers an obligation
by the retaliating nation to compensate "innocent bystanders" who have been
harmed by increases in the retaliator's own bound tariffs. This issue remains
unsettled, however, and at times in the history of the system nations have at least
contemplated retaliation that would be implemented on an MFN basis.

Another difficulty raised by the treaty text is the suggestion that retaliation
take the form of concessions "initially negotiated" with the party that raises a
bound tariff. With 153 members now in the WTO, and concessions that date
back decades to a time when many nations were not members (or did not even
exist), cases can arise in which a member with the right to retaliate does not
have any concessions of any importance that were "initially negotiated" with the
member that raises its bound tariff. Historical practice suggests that this limitation on retaliation is not observed assiduously, however, and members threaten-
ing retaliation under Article XXVIII have identified goods that did not meet this
test.

---

[56] In the case of an "out of season" negotiation authorized by the WTO membership under
Article XXVIII(4), the right to proceed with the withdrawal of the tariff concession is lost if
the membership determines that the party in question failed to make an offer of adequate
compensation.

More broadly, on economic grounds we may ask two related questions. First, why does GATT permit renegotiation of tariff commitments at all? Here we simply observe that an agreement must allow for renegotiation if it is to continue delivering efficient outcomes following changes in the environment that alter the locus of efficient tariffs.[57] A second and related question is, What is the logic of permitting the withdrawal of "substantially equivalent" concessions if renegotiations over the withdrawal of a tariff commitment break down? In answer to this second question, we note that some rules concerning renegotiation may be desirable, in order to limit the scope for opportunistic renegotiations. In this regard, an attractive feature of GATT Article XXVIII is that a trading partner may withdraw a "substantially equivalent" concession and thereby, as we indicate in Section 3.2, ensure that its terms of trade are preserved.[58] Equivalently, GATT Article XXVIII deters terms-of-trade opportunism: a country cannot achieve a terms-of-trade gain through a renegotiation, if its trading partner withdraws a substantially equivalent concession. As we explain in Section 3.2, this feature of GATT Article XXVIII makes the politically optimal tariff pair more focal and may also limit the extent to which negotiations reflect power asymmetries across countries.

Switching Between Different Types of Duties   The question of whether WTO Members can switch from one particular type of import tariffs (say ad valorem) to another (say specific duties), following certification of tariff schedules was a central issue in *Argentina–Footwear, Textiles and Apparel*.[59] Argentina was imposing

---

[57] We note that, if it were assumed that governments maximize real national income with their tariff choices, then free trade policies would be efficient regardless of changes in the underlying environment, and there would in that case be no need for the capacity of governments to renegotiate tariff commitments in order to maintain efficient levels of protection. But when governments are assumed to employ tariffs for achieving goals beyond real national income maximization, as allowed by the terms-of-trade theory and as we have assumed throughout our discussion here, the locus of efficient tariffs shifts with changes in the underlying environment, and as we have indicated this then provides a reason for GATT to permit renegotiation of tariff commitments. It should also be pointed out that opportunities to renegotiate tariff commitments could be potentially devastating to a trade agreement according to the commitment theory that we have reviewed above, because such opportunities would tend to undermine the ability of the trade agreement to credibly "tie the hands" of its member governments.

[58] This is not to say, however, that a trading partner is made "whole" when it withdraws a substantially equivalent concession. The trading partner's terms of trade are unaltered; however, the trading partner raises its own tariff, which leads to a higher local price for the import good and thus a lower trade volume. The associated "local-price" effect could diminish the trading partner's welfare, if the partner prefers greater trade volume at the initial tariffs, given the terms of trade.

[59] *Argentina – Measures Affecting Imports of Footwear, Textiles, Apparel and Other Items*, WT/DS56/AB/R, adopted April 22, 1998.

on imports of various products either an ad valorem duty (35% or less), or a specific duty which was calculated to equal 35% of a "representative international price" for each category of product, whichever was higher. It had bound its duties on the relevant products during the Uruguay Round at an ad valorem rate of 35%. The Appellate Body ultimately held that switching from one form of protection to another is acceptable as long as the overall 35% binding was not violated (§§ 44–55). Argentina had, however, violated Article II because the alternative specific duty equal to 35% times the representative international price could exceed 35% of the actual value of certain imports.

The "Carve Out" of GATT Art. II.2 GATT Art. II.2 reads:

Nothing in this Article shall prevent any contracting party from imposing at any time on the importation of any product:

(a) a charge equivalent to an internal tax imposed consistently with the provisions of paragraph 2 of Article III in respect of the like domestic product or in respect of an article from which the imported product has been manufactured or produced in whole or in part;
(b) any anti-dumping or countervailing duty applied consistently with the provisions of Article VI;
(c) fees or other charges commensurate with the cost of services rendered.

Charges Equivalent to Internal Taxes The Panel on *India–Additional Import Duties*[60] dealt with the interpretation of this provision. The facts of the case, as well the U.S. challenge against them, are described in §§ 7.3–7.5 of the Panel Report:

India's Central Government imposes several types of border charges ("duties"), including: the basic customs duty (hereinafter the "BCD"); the additional duty (hereinafter the "AD"), which its statutory basis states is related to the excise duty for the time being leviable on like domestic products in India; as well as "such additional duties as would counter-balance the sales tax, value added tax, local tax or any other charges" (hereinafter the "SUAD") for the time being leviable on a like domestic product in India.

India has indicated that there are no recorded "other duties or charges," within the meaning of Article II:1(b) of the GATT 1994 in India's Schedule of Concessions, which are applicable to any of the products subject to the measures at issue in these proceedings.

---

[60] *India – Additional and Extra-Additional Duties on Imports from the United States*, WT/DS360/R, adopted November 17, 2008.

The measures being challenged in this case are the AD and the SUAD, respectively. The United States alleges that the AD, when imposed in conjunction with the BCD, results in a breach of India's obligations under Article II:1(a) and (b) of the GATT 1994 because it results in ordinary customs duties or other duties or charges imposed on or in connection with importation that exceed those set out in India's Schedule of Concessions. The United States similarly alleges that the SUAD, when imposed in conjunction with the BCD, results in a breach of India's obligations under Article II:1(a) and (b) of the GATT 1994 because it results in ordinary customs duties or other duties or charges imposed on or in connection with importation that exceed those set out in India's Schedule of Concessions. Accordingly, there follows a brief description of the BCD, the AD and the SUAD as well as the provisions of Indian law identified by the United States as those through which India levies these duties.

The Panel rejected the U.S. claim on the grounds that both measures were protected by Article II:2(a). In so doing, it effectively held that charges imposed on imports that are related to internal taxes imposed on like domestic products are not ODC covered by the obligation in Article II:1(b).

The Appellate Body reversed the Panel, framing the issue in the following terms (§ 155):

> We note, at the outset, that the Panel's interpretative analysis was guided by what it characterized as the "issue presented in this case:" that is, whether the residual category of ODCs reflected in the second sentence of Article II:1(b) includes, as argued by the United States, "any and all charges imposed on the importation of a product" other than OCDs, or whether it was, as India argued, limited to "a subset of all such duties and charges."

The Appellate Body then found that ODC includes *any* charges imposed on imports that do not comply with Art. II(2). It was thus insufficient to conclude "qualitatively" that the import charges were "related" to internal taxes on domestic products, but it was further necessary to compare the amount of the duties and domestic taxes quantitatively. Accordingly, to the extent that the charges applied by the Indian government exceed the corresponding taxes applied to like domestic products, India violated its obligations under Art. II.

Fees and Charges for Services Rendered　In addition to permitted OCDs and ODCs, WTO Members may impose additional fees that comply with Art. II:2(c) and with GATT Art. VIII (Fees and Formalities connected with Importation and Exportation). Fees that comply with Art. VIII will not be regarded as ODCs subject, for example, to the requirement that they be recorded and bound at the level applied at the time of a tariff concession.

The most important piece of litigation in this area was a pre-WTO case, *US–Customs User Fee*.[61] The United States imposed in 1986 a 0.22% ad valorem charge on all imports to finance the operations of the U.S. Customs Service. It defended the fee with reference to Arts. II and VIII.

One issue in the case was whether "services rendered" had to be requested by or of value to importers. The Panel held not (§ 77):

> In referring to these customs-related government activities as 'services rendered,' the drafters of Articles II and VIII were clearly not employing the term 'services' in the economic sense. Granted that some government regulatory activities can be considered as 'services' in an economic sense when they endow goods with safety or quality characteristics deemed necessary for commerce, most of the activities that governments perform in connection with the importation process do not meet that definition. They are not desired by the importers who are subject to them. Nor do they add value to the goods in any commercial sense. Whatever governments may choose to call them, fees for such government regulatory activities are, in the Panel's view, simply taxes on imports. It must be presumed, therefore, that the drafters meant the term 'services' to be used in a more artful political sense, i.e., government activities closely enough connected to the processes of customs entry that they might, with no more than the customary artistic licence accorded to taxing authorities, be called a 'service' to the importer in question. No other interpretation can make Articles II:2(c) and VIII:1(a) conform to their generally accepted meaning.

On the other hand, the Panel also concluded that the fee charged for services rendered must be linked to the cost of processing the particular import transaction in question (§ 81):

> Granted that the terms 'commensurate with' and 'approximate' were intended to confer a certain degree of flexibility in the requirement that fees not exceed costs, the range of fees permitted under the US merchandise processing fee could by no stretch of language be considered a matter of mere flexibility. Moreover, the United States contention that 'cost of services rendered' referred only to the total cost of the relevant government activities would leave Articles II:2(c) and VIII:1(a) without any express standard for apportioning such fees among individual importers, thereby committing the issue of apportionment, at best, to an implied requirement of equitable (or non-protective) apportionment that would be neither predictable nor capable of objective application. Finally, if 'cost of services rendered' meant the total cost of customs operations, the 'fiscal purposes' criterion of Article VIII:1(a) would be rendered largely redundant.

---

[61] 35th Supp. BISD 245 (Panel Report adopted February 2, 1988).

Based on this analysis, the Panel went on to find that the U.S. system was GATT inconsistent because the ad valorem fee structure bore no apparent relation to the cost of processing each transaction (low-value imports would be taxed far less than high-valued imports for potentially the same service) (§§ 84–86). Subsequent WTO Panels have borrowed heavily from this analysis and cited it favorably. The Panel Report in *Argentina–Measures Affecting Imports of Footwear*[62] in particular confronted a very similar ad valorem charge and, applying the same logic as in *US–Customs User Fee*, found the Argentine measure to be GATT-inconsistent.

On economic grounds, one may ask why other charges such as taxes equivalent to internal taxes on domestic products and fees for customs processing are exempt from the GATT disciplines over tariff bindings. While we are not aware of much specific work by economists that addresses this question, we can speculate that a sensible answer might proceed along the following lines.

First, we emphasize that GATT tariff disciplines *do* extend to the related category of charges that are applicable only to imports (ODCs), albeit in a somewhat different form: the discipline on ODCs is activated once a tariff is bound, at which point such charges cannot be raised beyond their existing levels. As ODCs represent a catch-all for the infinite variety of creative charges that governments could invent and apply at the border, it seems sensible that the disciplines applied to these charges take a form that is somewhat different from those that apply to a bound tariff.

Second, while the discipline of tariff bindings does not extend to other charges such as taxes equivalent to internal taxes on domestic products and fees for customs processing, we note that it is not that such charges and fees are entirely without discipline under WTO/GATT rules, only that the disciplines take a form that is quite distinct (and significantly weaker) than the disciplines that apply to a bound tariff. The WTO/GATT discipline on fees for customs processing derives from the fact that such fees must reflect actual costs of customs processing; and the discipline on charges such as taxes equivalent to internal taxes on domestic products is the same discipline that is placed on internal taxes (as contained in the national-treatment provision of GATT Art. III:2). With regard to this last category of charges in particular, there is a question as to why more stringent disciplines are not imposed under the WTO/GATT (and of course the same question arises with regard to the WTO/GATT treatment of internal taxes). There is recent research in economics that suggests that a rationale for such treatment can be offered under certain conditions on the basis of costly contracting, but whether those conditions are consistent with the WTO/GATT contracting

---

[62] WT/DS56/R, adopted April 22, 1998.

environment is an open question.[63] In any event, with these observations, we may speculate that the different disciplines across tariffs, OCDs, charges such as taxes equivalent to internal taxes on domestic products, and fees for customs processing may reflect a practical method for securing meaningful commitments over the protective effect of border instruments while limiting the scope of negotiations over border instruments to tariffs alone.

Plugging Other Loopholes   The remaining three paragraphs of Article II not yet mentioned address some additional "loopholes" in tariff commitments. Paragraph 3 concerns the "method of determining dutiable value or of converting currencies," and indicates that such methods should not be altered in a fashion that impairs the value of negotiated concessions. Thus, for example, if a nation changed the method of converting prices in foreign currency into its domestic currency for purposes of calculating an ad valorem duty in a way that systematically increased the amount of duty payable, it could run afoul of paragraph 3. The obligation in that paragraph is broader, however, and extends to all aspects of the way that dutiable value is determined – we note some further issues relating to customs valuation below.

Paragraph 6 was drafted at a time of fixed exchange rates, and concerns the allowable adjustments to specific duties and charges when the par value of currency changes under the system administered by the International Monetary Fund. It has little practical importance today.

Paragraph 4, in contrast, retains considerable importance, and concerns the behavior of government import monopolies. These entities are fairly common in a number of sectors, and have been particularly at issue with the importation of alcoholic beverages. The basic obligation in paragraph 4 is that the import monopoly should not "operate so as to afford protection on the average in excess of the amount of protection provided for in [its national Schedule]." During GATT, Panels twice examined the pricing policies of Canadian liquor import monopolies, which had allegedly followed a policy of imposing higher markups on imported spirits than on domestic spirits. These additional markups apparently could not be justified in relation to scheduled tariff commitments, leading Canada to argue instead that the import monopoly was maximizing revenue by taking advantage of lower demand elasticities for imported products. This argument was rejected by the Panel, which held that Canada could only justify additional markups on the imported goods if it could show that they reflected

---

[63] On a costly-contracting rationale for national-treatment-like disciplines on internal taxes, see Horn, Maggi and Staiger (2010).

"additional costs necessarily associated with the marketing of the imported products."[64]

Customs Valuation Customs valuation procedures are necessary when imported items face ad valorem duties. GATT Art. VII, now elaborated by an Agreement on Implementation that is contained in an Appendix to this study, requires that the value for customs purposes of imported merchandise be based on the actual value of the imported merchandise and not on the value of similar merchandise of domestic origin or on arbitrary or fictitious values.

The value of goods will ordinarily be determined by the "transaction value," which is simply the price paid by the importer, perhaps adjusted for certain items such as the cost of containers or selling commissions not already included in transaction value. In some instances, however, the transaction value is potentially distorted. Most importantly, if the import and exporter are related companies, they may have a powerful incentive to understate the transaction price – doing so could reduce the duty while shifting accounting profits from one related entity to the other. Transaction value might also be distorted by certain contractual situations (such as a prohibition on resale). Where the transaction price is unreliable, the Agreement provides for five alternative methods to be applied (in the prescribed hierarchical order): the transaction value of identical goods; the transaction value of similar goods; a deductive method (that looks for a downstream arm's-length sale and backs out various costs); and a computed method (estimating cost of production). The hierarchy of methods is based essentially on considerations relating to their accuracy and costs of administration.

The Nonviolation Doctrine GATT Article XXIII, governing the "nullification and impairment" of benefits under GATT, makes clear that benefits can be nullified or impaired by measures that do not violate GATT [see Art. XXIII:1(b)]. This provision has given rise to a small line of cases holding that tariff concessions can be impaired by certain practices that do not violate the letter of GATT, but that nevertheless upset reasonable expectations associated with the negotiations over concessions. In such instances, aggrieved GATT members are entitled to receive trade compensation or to "retaliate," much as they could in response to a GATT violation (although they are not entitled to a ruling that the policy in question should be discontinued).

To date, nonviolation claims have been successful with respect to two types of phenomena: changes in subsidy policies, and changes in tariff classifications. Thus, for example, if a nation negotiates a tariff concession on a good, and subsequently introduces a new subsidy program for domestic producers of that good,

---

[64] Canada – Import, Distribution and Sale of Alcoholic Drinks by Canadian Provincial Marketing Agencies, 35th Supp. BISD 37, 88 (Panel Report adopted March 22, 1988).

a valid nonviolation claim can be made. Likewise, if changes in tariff classifications are made that upset reasonable expectations that competing goods will be treated comparably, a nonviolation claim is possible. For example, in *Treatment by Germany of Imports of Sardines*,[65] Germany changed its tariff schedules so that higher tariffs were imposed on imports of sardines and herring than on sprats. Norway complained about the less favorable treatment of sardines. The Panel held that the negotiating history on the various products established a reasonable expectation on Norway's part that the three products would be treated similarly.

3.3.2 The Case Law on QRs

Economic theory indicates that, in some situations, import tariffs and quotas have similar economic effects. We argue in Section 3.2, though, that tariffication can facilitate mutually beneficial and reciprocal trade liberalization between governments. Our discussion thus provides support for the tariffication of quantitative restrictions. In the WTO/GATT the relevant legal rules are contained in GATT Article XI.

The general prohibition of Article XI covers a broad range of practices – "no prohibitions or restrictions other than duties, taxes or other charges, whether made effective through quotas, import or export licenses or other measures, shall be instituted or maintained on...importation...or...exportation." Its scope plainly extends to familiar quotas and import licensing schemes, but also to any "other measures" distinct from "duties, taxes or other charges." As a shorthand, we refer to the measures covered by Article XI as QRs.

Covered Measures Perhaps the most contentious issue under Article XI relates to the scope of the measures that it covers. In this regard, several distinctions are of note.

Duties and Taxes Why omit "duties, taxes and other charges" from the ambit of Article XI? The obvious answer is that GATT seeks to channel import protection (as well as export restraint) into the tariff mechanism. Subject to some exceptions that permit QRs under specified circumstances, GATT members remain free to protect their import-competing industries with tariffs, subject to product specific tariff bindings that they may choose to negotiate as described above under Article II. In this sense, GATT may be said to encourage a process of "tariffication," the benefits of which we discuss in Section 3.2. Likewise, to the degree that domestic taxation may be a burden on international commerce,

---

[65] 1st Supp. BISD 53 (1953), Report adopted October 31, 1952.

it is disciplined by the nondiscrimination obligations of Article III on national treatment.

International Trade Restrictions versus Domestic Restrictions   To fall under Article XI, a measure must be maintained "on importation or exportation." It is not enough that a measure merely has some effect on imports or exports. Thus, purely domestic restrictions are not covered. For example, as part of an agricultural price-support plan, a government might set an aggregate production quota for some crop and allocate it among domestic farmers. Such a measure could well have an impact on, for example, export prices and quantities, but would not fall within the Article XI prohibition.

A more subtle and unsettled distinction exists between domestic regulatory measures and measures that regulate imports. A footnote to GATT Article III provides:

> Any...law, regulation or requirement...which applies to an imported product and to the like domestic product and is...enforced in the case of the imported product at the time or point of importation, is nevertheless to be regarded as an internal...law, regulation or requirement...and is accordingly subject to the provisions of Article III.

In other words, when regulatory requirements that affect and may well restrict imports are enforced at the border, but are nevertheless parallel to regulations that apply as well to domestically produced products, they are subject to the nondiscrimination rules of GATT Article III rather than to the "general prohibition" of Article XI. This principle has obvious rationale in the fact that Article XI is aimed at dismantling protective border measures, not at undermining the capacity of nations engaged in international trade to engage in evenhanded regulation for other purposes.

The question whether a measure falls under Article XI or Article III is not always obvious and, indeed, the possibility arises that both Articles may at times be applicable. The GATT Panel in its Report on *Canada–Provincial Liquor Boards*,[66] suggested that in some circumstances, such as state trading entities whose behavior can be interpreted as a regulation of imports or a regulation of the domestic market, a dividing line cannot readily be drawn between measures covered by Art. III by Art. XI. See also the GATT Panel Report in *Canada–Foreign Investment Review Act.* (FIRA) A later WTO Panel in its Report on *India–Autos* also suggested that concurrent application of both Art. III and Art. XI might be appropriate if different facets of the same measure could be regarded as border measures and as internal measures.

---

[66] 35th Supp. BISD 37, Panel Report adopted March 22, 1988.

In most cases, however, measures will be classified as one or the other. In *France–Asbestos*,[67] for example, the question arose whether a French prohibition on the importation or sale of asbestos products was an import QR or a domestic regulation subject to Article III. Canada argued that the import ban was formally a border measure covered by Article XI, and further that since no asbestos mining existed in France, the ban on sale of asbestos-containing products was the equivalent of a ban on imports of asbestos. The Panel determined that Article III was applicable, however, essentially relying on the fact that France also prohibited any domestic production or sale of asbestos-containing products.

The GATT Panel in *Canada–FIRA*[68] relied on a somewhat fuzzy line between measures that affect "importation" and measures that affect "imported products." For example, a law stating that a company can only import goods in an amount bearing some proportion to the value of its exports comes under Article XI. A law requiring that a company purchase some proportion of its input supply from local sources, by contrast, merely "affects imports" and falls under Article III. These distinctions were effectively codified in the illustrative list to the WTO Agreement on Trade Related Investment Measures (TRIMs). See also the WTO Panel Report on *India–Autos* (concerning the "trade balancing condition" relating permissible import volumes to exports).[69]

Export Restrictions   It is worth underscoring that Article XI applies to export QRs as well (but not to export taxes). A common practice that would fall under Article XI, for example, would be a prohibition on the exportation of an unprocessed product, perhaps enacted for the purpose of lowering the price of the unprocessed product to the local processing industry.

Governmental Measures Only   Like the rest of GATT, Article XI applies only to measures maintained by WTO Members – i.e., member governments. Purely private conduct is not covered. Thus, for example, to take a stylized fact from the *Japan–Film*[70] dispute (popularly known as the *Kodak–Fuji* case), it does not violate Article XI for Fuji, a private company, to enter into exclusive dealing arrangements with Japanese film retailers under which the retailers promise to sell only Fuji film, thereby foreclosing imports of Kodak products.

---

[67] *European Communities – Measures Affecting Asbestos and Asbestos-Containing Products*, WT/DS135/R, adopted April 5, 2001.
[68] 30th Supp. BISD 140, Panel Report adopted February 7, 1984.
[69] *India – Measures Affecting the Automotive Sector*, WT/DS146/R, Panel Report adopted April 5, 2002.
[70] WT/DS44/R, adopted April 22, 1998.

In some cases, however, private conduct may be influenced by government policy in such a way as to bring it within the ambit of "other measures." The leading case remains that GATT dispute involving the U.S.–Japan semiconductor agreement. The Panel in *Japan–Semi-conductors*[71] was called upon to address a situation in which the government of Japan, as a result of an agreement it had reached to settle antidumping proceedings, adopted a series of measures which allegedly induced Japanese companies producing semi-conductors to raise their prices when exporting to the European market. There were no European producers of the same product during that period in the mid- to late 1980s, and consumers of semi-conductors were required to pay higher prices. Europe argued that Article XI had been violated, but Japan responded that its actions did not amount to covered measures because they placed no quantitative restriction on exports and required no increase in their prices. Rather, Japan simply required semi-conductor producers to report their prices to the government, and "encouraged" them to price their products in a manner that would avoid dumping. The Ministry of International Trade and Industry also monitored the market, but did not dictate export prices or quantities. The Panel nevertheless found sufficient government involvement to find that "measures" were in place for purposes of Article XI:

> In order to determine this, the Panel considered that it needed to be satisfied on two essential criteria. First, there were reasonable grounds to believe that sufficient incentives or disincentives existed for non-mandatory measures to take effect. Second, the operation of the measures to restrict export of semi-conductors at prices below company-specific costs was essentially dependent on Government action or intervention. The Panel considered each of these two criteria in turn. The Panel considered that if these two criteria were met, the measures would be operating in a manner equivalent to mandatory requirements such that the difference between the measures and mandatory requirements was only one of form and not of substance, and that there could be therefore no doubt that they fell within the range of measures covered by Article XI.1 ...
>
> [T]he Panel [concluded] that an administrative structure had been created by the Government of Japan which operated to exert maximum possible pressure on the private sector to cease exporting at prices below company-specific costs. This was exercised through such measures as repeated direct requests by MITI, combined with the statutory requirement for exporters to submit information on export prices, the systematic monitoring of company and product-specific costs and export prices and the institution of the supply and demand forecasts mechanism and its

---

[71] 35th Supp. BISD 116, Panel Report adopted May 4, 1988.

utilization in a manner to directly influence the behaviour of private companies. These measures operated furthermore to facilitate strong peer pressure to comply with requests by MITI and at the same time to foster a climate of uncertainty as to the circumstances under which their exports could take place. The Panel considered that the complex of measures exhibited the rationale as well as the essential elements of a formal system of export control. The only distinction in this case was the absence of formal legally binding obligations in respect of exportation or sale for export of semi-conductors. However, the Panel concluded that this amounted to a difference in form rather than substance because the measures were operated in a manner equivalent to mandatory requirements. The Panel concluded that the complex of measures constituted a coherent system restricting the sale for export of monitored semi-conductors at prices below company-specific costs to markets other than the United States, inconsistent with Article XI:1.

Subsequent GATT and WTO cases have consistently referred favorably to this ruling.

Must a Complainant Show Trade Effects? The long-standing general view under GATT is that a complainant need not demonstrate adverse trade effects in order to establish a violation. This view applies, in particular, to Article XI.

For example, the GATT Panel in *US–Superfund*[72] examined the imposition of a discriminatory tax on imported petroleum (an Article III issue rather than an Article XI issue to be sure). The United States argued that the tax differential was effectively *de minimis* and did not affect imports, and that no violation of GATT existed without an adverse trade impact. The Panel disagreed, reciting what was by then familiar rubric that the purpose of GATT was not to "protect expectations on export volumes" (§ 5.1.9). Rather, "[t]he general prohibition of quantitative restrictions under Article XI, which the Panel on Japanese Measures on Imports of Leather examined, and the national-treatment obligation of Article III, which Canada and the EEC invoked in the present case, have essentially the same rationale, namely to protect expectations of the contracting parties as to the competitive relationship between their products and those of the other contracting parties (§ 5.2.2).

The Superfund Panel also embraced a familiar distinction in the GATT case law between "mandatory" and "discretionary" legislation.[73] Because the tax differential was mandatory (administrators had no discretion to avoid

---

[72] 34th Supp. BISD 136 (1988), Panel Report adopted June 17, 1987.

[73] This distinction has less vitality in WTO law today. See, e.g., *United States – Sections 301–310 of the Trade Act of 1974*, WT/DS152/R, Panel Report adopted January 27, 2000.

imposing it), it could be challenged in advance of its taking effect under U.S. law:

> [GATT Articles XI and III] are not only to protect current trade but also to create the predictability needed to plan future trade. That objective could not be attained if contracting parties could not challenge existing legislation mandating actions at variance with the General Agreement until the administrative acts implementing it had actually been applied to their trade. Just as the very existence of a regulation providing for a quota, without it restricting particular imports, has been recognized to constitute a violation of Article XI:1, the very existence of mandatory legislation providing for an internal tax, without it being applied to a particular imported product, should be regarded as falling within the scope of Article III:2, first sentence. (Id.)

A slightly different view was taken by the WTO Panel in *Argentina–Hides and Leather*.[74] Argentina allowed representatives of the leather-processing industry to be present during the processing by its customs officials of leather for exportation. The European Community argued that the result was to create a de facto QR on exportation, because the industry representatives could see who was exporting unprocessed leather and penalize them in some fashion. Under these circumstances, the Panel held that the complainant was required to demonstrate that the measure in question (permitting the presence of representatives from the processing industry) actually had an impact on exports:

> Article XI:1, like Articles I, II and III of the GATT 1994, protects competitive opportunities of imported products, not trade flows ... the European Communities need not prove actual trade effects. However, it must be borne in mind that Resolution 2235 is alleged by the European Communities to make effective a de facto rather than a de jure restriction. In such circumstances, it is inevitable, as an evidentiary matter, that greater weight attaches to the actual trade impact of a measure.
>
> Even if it emerges from trade statistics that the level of exports is unusually low, this does not prove, in and of itself, that that level is attributable, in whole or in part, to the measure alleged to constitute an export restriction. Particularly in the context of an alleged de facto restriction and where, as here, there are possibly multiple restrictions, it is necessary for a complaining party to establish a causal link between the contested measure and the low level of exports. In our view, whatever else it may involve, a demonstration of causation must consist of a persuasive explanation of precisely

---

[74] *Argentina – Measures Affecting the Export of Bovine Hides and Import of Finished Leather*, WT/DS155/R, adopted February 16, 2001.

how the measure at issue causes or contributes to the low level of exports. §§ 11.21 and 11.22

The Panel then rejected the EC claim, since the only evidence before the Panel merely demonstrated the presence of downstream industry representatives during customs clearance. The Panel allowed that such presence might have a QR-effect, but refused to find a violation based solely on that evidence. The Panel Report was not appealed.

Argentina–Hides and Leather might be taken to suggest that a showing of trade effects is necessary in general. That interpretation is open to question, however, since the argument of the EC was that the Argentine practice amounted to the "equivalent" of an export QR. Plainly, nothing in WTO law prohibits the presence of processing industry representatives, and if a complainant wishes to establish that a nonprohibited practice has effects equivalent to a prohibited practice, some requirement to show trade effects indeed seems sensible.

As for the broader question whether trade effects should in general be shown to prove a violation, WTO law distinguishes between "violations" and the concept of "nullification or impairment" of benefits. A right to redress arises in the WTO whenever benefits are nullified or impaired; a violation creates a prima facie presumption of nullification or impairment that can in principle be rebutted by the respondent member that has committed a violation. (See Article 3(8) of the WTO Dispute Settlement Understanding). Logically, if such a rebuttal is possible, a member that has violated the letter of the law has done no harm, and the violation is likely to be a Pareto improvement since the member in question presumably benefits from the violation. Accordingly, the opportunity to rebut the existence of any harm seems a sensible option in the system, although as yet no member has been able to make a successful rebuttal.

Exceptions to the "General Prohibition" Although we will not explore them in any detail in this study, a number of exceptions to the prohibition on QRs exist in GATT. Some are contained in Article XI itself. These include "export prohibitions or restrictions temporarily applied to prevent or relieve critical shortages of foodstuffs or other products essential to the exporting contracting party" (XI:2(a)), a provision that has never been litigated but that has potentially broad applicability. Article XI:2(b) allows import and export restrictions necessary to the "classification, grading or marketing of commodities" in international trade. Article XI:2(c) permits import restrictions on agriculture and fisheries products "imported in any form" that are "necessary" to the enforcement of, for example, domestic price-support schemes. As an illustration, a nation that was undertaking to support the price of wheat by restricting domestic production of wheat could also restrict imports to prevent an import surge from undercutting the target price.

Other applicable exceptions include those for balance-of-payments issues (GATT Arts. XII and XVIII Part B), infant-industry protection in developing countries (Art. XVIII Part C), national security (Art. XXI), and of course the general exceptions to GATT contained in Art. XX.

Nondiscriminatory Administration of QRs   When a QR is justified by some exception to the prohibition in Article XI, it must nevertheless obey certain nondiscrimination principles. These are contained in GATT Article XIII, colloquially known as the "quota-MFN" provision, and in the WTO Import Licensing Agreement. We briefly sketch the requirements of Article XIII here; the Import Licensing Agreement involves a level of detail that would take us unnecessarily afield.

Although Article XIII is entitled "non-discriminatory administration of QRs," it is not really an obligation not to discriminate. It is instead, in the first instance, an obligation to administer quotas transparently and, where quotas are to be allocated among supplier countries (rather than administered on a first-come, first-served basis), an obligation to seek negotiated agreement on respective country shares. In the event that no agreement can be reached between the importing state and the WTO Members having a substantial interest in exporting the restricted good, the importing state must allocate quotas based on historical market shares during a "representative period." [Art. XIII.2(d)].

In *EC–Bananas III*, a dispute between the European Community and a group of banana exporters, the issue arose as to whether Art. XIII applies to all imports of a particular product or just to the imports coming in under a particular "quota regime." The European Community had in place two quota regimes for imports of bananas, one for the ACP (African, Caribbean, Pacific) countries and another for the rest of the world. The Panel and the Appellate Body both upheld the claim advanced by the complainants that the obligations of Article XIII applied to imports of bananas in the aggregate, and hence that it could condemn discrimination across "regimes" as well as within them.

3.4 The Rationale for MFN and Its Exceptions

This Section focuses on the rationale for the most-favored-nation (MFN) obligation contained in Article I of GATT, as well as the reasons why GATT included a number of exceptions to it. As noted earlier, the political impetus for GATT arose in significant part because of the network of discriminatory trade preferences that emerged prior to World War II, often connected with colonial empires. Accordingly, the MFN obligation of GATT was considered the "cornerstone" obligation [Jackson (1969)], and was enshrined in Article I of the agreement. From its inception, however, the MFN obligation was qualified by important exceptions. Most importantly at the outset, major colonial powers (especially Britain) prevailed on the negotiators to preserve many of their preferential tariffs. The significance of these exceptions, however, is now dwarfed by the modern proliferation of preferential trade agreements (customs unions and free-trade areas) such as the EU, NAFTA, and MERCOSUR. These arrangements are made possible by GATT Article XXIV. In addition, the concept of special and differential treatment for developing countries became an increasing part of GATT over time, including the authority for the modern Generalized System of Preferences.

3.4.1 The Negotiating History[75]

We discussed earlier how the extensive protectionist measures of the 1930s were perceived to have contributed to the Great Depression and in turn to the outbreak of World War II. But the level of trade protection was not the only concern. The United States, in particular, sought to reduce the tariff discrimination and other trade preferences that had proliferated. The preferences within the British Commonwealth were a particular irritant. U.S. Secretary of State Cordell Hull, for example, was a sharp critic of these "imperial preferences" because of their adverse effect on U.S. exports, particularly to the United Kingdom and Canada, two of America's most important markets. Testifying before Congress in 1940, Hull called imperial preferences "the greatest injury, in a commercial way, that has been inflicted on this country since I have been in public life."

Given its concerns about trade discrimination, the United States had made it a priority to seek MFN commitments in its bilateral trade agreements under the Reciprocal Trade Agreements program that began in the 1930s. The United States also included an unconditional MFN clause in its "trade template" proposal, which was an initial cut at the text for a broader post-war agreement. The term "like product" or "like article" could be found in earlier bilateral treaties. The London negotiations leading up to GATT included a reference to like products, but the negotiators consciously chose not to define the term, leaving the matter for further negotiations relating to the ITO.

The attitude toward trade discrimination of Britain – the other primary player in the original GATT negotiations – was quite different. Conservatives in Britain believed strongly in retaining the preferences and a means of maintaining strong ties within the British Empire, and the support of conservatives appeared essential to the success of any major trade agreement. Throughout the negotiations leading up to GATT, therefore, U.S. and British negotiators wrangled over the preservation of imperial preferences, and disagreement over this issue at

---

[75] For further discussion and detailed citations, see Genesis, Chapters 1 and 2.

times threatened to scuttle the entire process. Ultimately, however, the United States capitulated on the matter during the course of the Geneva negotiations and allowed the preferences to remain intact via GATT Articles I(2) and II(1)(c).

Customs unions and free-trade areas were a less contentious issue, perhaps because they were of relatively minor importance at the time. A Benelux union was in place, and a Syro-Lebanon union as well, but the beginning of European integration was a few years off (which would initially be limited to coal and steel in any event). Some recent research suggests that the United States was secretly negotiating a free-trade agreement with Canada around the time of the GATT negotiations as well, although those negotiations did not bear fruit. It also appears that France and Italy were considering the possibility of a customs union as early as the Havana conference that occurred shortly after GATT took effect.[76]

In any event, the draft text in the London conference included an exception for customs unions and arrangements leading to a customs union, which was incorporated into the original GATT without much controversy. The principal legal requirements were that there be substantial trade liberalization within the customs union, and that the general level of duties applied to trade with non-members should not increase. Shortly after GATT took effect, at the Havana conference, Article XXIV was amended to allow for free-trade areas as well (perhaps because of the U.S. negotiations).

The negotiating history thus suggests that Article XXIV was designed to accommodate existing and potential future preferential arrangements, and that the negotiators at the time did not regard this deviation from the MFN principle as seriously problematic. This posture is somewhat puzzling given the hostility of some members toward colonial preferences and their vestiges, but is perhaps best understood in light of the fact that customs unions and free-trade areas were of minor importance at the time. We also note that the seminal economic work on the matter by economists such as Jacob Viner, which highlighted the problem of "trade diversion," had not yet been done.

Finally, with regard to special and differential treatment of developing countries, the main issue in the original GATT negotiations concerned the use of QRs for balance-of-payments purposes, and for purposes of promoting the development of infant industries. These issues were central for many of the developing-country participants, who allied with a few of the developed-country delegations (such as Australia). The remaining developed nations eventually acceded to some of these proposals, but the developing countries were by no means satisfied. Further amendments were negotiated concerning both balance-of-payments measures and development assistance during the review session of the mid-1950s, producing the current versions of Articles XII and XVIII. Development was also on the agenda during the Kennedy Round of the 1960s, which

---

[76] See GATT, Analytical Index, Vol. I, p. 847.

produced part IV of the GATT, a largely hortatory set of provisions urging developed nations to afford special treatment. Clear authority for tariff preferences in favor of developing nations – the Generalized System of Preferences – came through a temporary GATT waiver in 1971, which became permanent through the "Enabling Clause" in 1979.

Thus, from the beginnings of GATT, the idea that special and differential treatment is justified to promote development in lower-income countries, or to assist developing countries in times of balance-of-payments crises, has been generally (if at times grudgingly) accepted. Preferences, in particular, were viewed as a mechanism to allow developing countries to generate export earnings that might then be used to finance important development initiatives. We consider the soundness of this view in due course.

3.4.2 The Rationale According to Case Law

As we saw with tariff bindings, the case law provides relatively little discussion of the general rationale for MFN or its exceptions. Perhaps the broadest statement is to be found in *Canada–Autos* where, in support of its interpretation of Article I:1 as covering de facto discrimination, the Appellate Body stated:

> Th[e] object and purpose [of Article I] is to prohibit discrimination among like products originating in or destined for different countries. The prohibition of discrimination in Article I:1 also serves as an incentive for concessions, negotiated reciprocally, to be extended to all other Members on an MFN basis.[77]

This passage does not contribute much to our understanding of the rationale, as the first sentence simply states the obvious, and the second is rather murky. In particular, the use of the term "incentive" hints that the MFN obligation induces concessions to be negotiated, a proposition that is not entirely obvious and to which we return later in this Section (a possible counter argument is that the MFN obligation creates free riders and may discourage concessions). Alternatively, if the Appellate Body simply means that given the existence of a concession, the MFN obligation provides an "incentive" to extend it to other members, it is understating the point – there is not merely an incentive but a binding legal obligation.

Statements in the case law about the general rationale for Article XXIV and for special and differential treatment are also limited. Perhaps the clearest recent statement regarding Article XXIV is contained instead in the 1994 Understanding on its interpretation. Its preamble recites, inter alia:

---

[77] *Canada – Certain Measures Affecting the Automotive Industry*, WT/DS139 and 142AB/R, adopted June 19, 2000, para. 84.

Recognizing that customs unions and free trade areas have greatly increased in number and importance since the establishment of GATT 1947 and today cover a significant proportion of world trade;

Recognizing the contribution to the expansion of world trade that may be made by closer integration between the economies of the parties to such agreements;

Recognizing also that such contribution is increased if the elimination between the constituent territories of duties and other restrictive regulations of commerce extends to all trade, and diminished if any major sector of trade is excluded;

Reaffirming that the purpose of such agreements should be to facilitate trade between the constituent territories and not to raise barriers to the trade of other Members with such territories; and that in their formation or enlargement the parties to them should to the greatest possible extent avoid creating adverse effects on the trade of other Members...

The premise seems to be that preferential arrangements create a desirable "expansion" of world trade, which is all the greater when the preferential liberalization is more comprehensive, as long as they do not raise barriers to trade with outsiders.

This view is echoed by the Appellate Body in *Turkey–Textiles*, which we discuss at some length in Section 3.5. In the course of its opinion in the case, the Appellate Body stated:

[T]he purpose of a customs union is 'to facilitate trade' between the constituent members and 'not to raise barriers to the trade' with third countries. This objective demands that a balance be struck by the constituent members of a customs union. A customs union should facilitate trade within the customs union, but it should not do so in a way that raises barriers to trade with third countries. We note that [the preamble of] the Understanding on Article XXIV explicitly reaffirms this purpose of a customs union, and states that in the formation or enlargement of a customs union, the constituent members should 'to the greatest possible extent avoid creating adverse effects on the trade of other Members'.[78]

3.4.3 The Rationale According to Economic Theory

As we have indicated above, a fundamental feature of the WTO/GATT system is the principle of nondiscrimination. According to this principle, when a country imports a given product, it must apply the same tariff rate regardless of the country from which the product is imported. Since no exporting country is

---

[78] *Turkey – Restrictions on Imports of Textile and Clothing Products*, WT/DS34/AB/R, adopted November 19, 1999, para. 57.

treated worse than any other, this principle is sometimes referred to as the most-favored nation (MFN) principle.

To interpret and evaluate the principle of nondiscrimination, we must extend our economic model of Section 3.2 to include a third country. Let us suppose therefore that our two-good model now entails three countries: the home country, foreign country 1, and foreign country 2. We imagine that the home country imports a given good from each of the two foreign countries, while each of the two foreign countries imports the other good from the home country. For simplicity, we assume that the two foreign countries do not trade with one another. The home country is then the only country with the potential to apply discriminatory tariffs across different exporters. If the home country's tariff policy satisfies the principle of nondiscrimination, then the same tariff is applied to the home country's import good regardless of whether the particular unit of the good is exported from foreign country 1 or foreign country 2.

At a basic level, we can already anticipate that the principle of nondiscrimination offers important advantages. When the home country adopts MFN tariffs, the world price of the home country's import good is the same whether the good originates in foreign country 1 or foreign country 2. As the home country alone exports its export good, the home-country export good has a single world price. It follows that the home country has the same terms of trade with foreign country 1 as with foreign country 2, when the home country's tariff policy satisfies the principle of nondiscrimination. The principle of nondiscrimination thus ensures that the three-country model continues to exhibit the same structure as the two-country model. Accordingly, when the home-country tariffs satisfy the principle of nondiscrimination, it can be shown that, starting at their optimal unilateral tariffs, all governments gain from a reduction in tariffs that satisfies the principle of reciprocity. In addition, the MFN politically optimal tariffs are efficient and robust against the possibility of renegotiation.[79]

At the same time, new issues arise in the three-country model. These issues relate to strategic concerns that may affect efficiency and that arise when a government negotiates over time with different partners. One issue is that a government may worry that the value of a concession received in an initial negotiation may be later eroded if the negotiation partner subsequently negotiates with another country. The associated fear of "concession erosion" potentially could undermine a government's willingness to offer significant concessions of its own in the initial negotiation. In this context, a key question is whether the principle of nondiscrimination can facilitate efficiency by mitigating the fear of concession erosion. A related but distinct issue is that, when a government must use nondiscriminatory tariffs and negotiates with different partners over time, the government may fear that the subsequent partner may free ride on the tariff

---

[79] For formal demonstrations of these points, see Bagwell and Staiger (1999, 2002).

concession that the government offers in the initial negotiation. The subsequent partner may then offer little or no tariff concession of its own. When free riding of this kind is a concern, the government may respond with a strategy whereby it offers "bargaining tariffs" in the initial negotiation. Under this strategy, the government offers a modest tariff cut to its first partner, in order to preserve "bargaining chips" for its subsequent partner.[80]

Interestingly, the strategic concerns highlighted here both relate to the third-party effects of a bilateral negotiation. Whether the issue is concession erosion or free riding, we can expect that the efficiency implications of the associated strategic behavior would be small if third-party effects were also small. We thus now focus on the nature of the third-party effects of bilateral negotiations.

To this end, let us suppose that the governments of the home country and foreign country 1 negotiate an initial trade agreement. Just as we explain above for the two-country model, the governments of the home country and foreign country 1 can achieve mutual gains in welfare by exchanging reciprocal tariff reductions that preserve the terms of trade between them. Adding a new element to our discussion, let us suppose further that the government of the home country has a subsequent opportunity to negotiate reciprocal tariff cuts with the government of foreign country 2. Now, if the government of the home country were free to use discriminatory tariffs, then it might offer a lower tariff to exporters from foreign country 2 than it had previously offered to exporters from foreign country 1. This would have the effect of reducing the demand in the home country for exports from foreign country 1, leading to a terms-of-trade loss for foreign country 1. Put differently, the subsequent negotiation would erode the market access that foreign country 1 obtained in the initial negotiation. If the government of foreign country 1 were to anticipate this possibility of concession erosion, then it might hesitate to offer access to its own market in the initial negotiation. As Schwartz and Sykes (1997) argue, a nondiscrimination rule may thus be efficiency enhancing, by protecting the interests of early negotiating partners and thus facilitating trade liberalization across partners over time.

As Bagwell and Staiger (2005b) demonstrate, however, the nondiscrimination rule on its own is not sufficient to completely protect the interests of the early negotiation partner. To see why, suppose that the subsequent negotiation fails to satisfy the principle of reciprocity in that the government of foreign country 2 offers a concession of greater magnitude than does the government of the home country. The nondiscrimination rule would ensure that exporters from foreign country 1 receive the home country's concession just as do exporters from foreign country 2. In this respect, the exporters from foreign country 1 would enjoy a modest gain. But consider now the effects of the large concession offered

---

[80] For a discussion of concession-erosion and bargaining-tariff concerns as they arose in bilateral trade negotiations from the pre-GATT era, see Bagwell and Staiger (2010a).

by the government of foreign country 2. This concession would generate a large increase in the price of the home country's export good on the world market. The subsequent negotiation thus implies a large loss for consumers in foreign country 1 of the home export good. In this case, the net effect of the subsequent negotiation is that foreign country 1 suffers a terms-of-trade loss: the world price of foreign country 1's export good rises by a modest amount while the world price of foreign country 1's import good rises by a large amount. Thus, even though the subsequent negotiation satisfies the principle of nondiscrimination and brings forth a further reduction in the home country's (MFN) tariff, the subsequent negotiation results in a terms-of-trade loss for foreign country 1. The welfare of the government of foreign country 1 may thus fall as a consequence of the subsequent negotiation.

Finally, suppose that the subsequent negotiation satisfies the principles of nondiscrimination *and* reciprocity. As discussed previously, the principle of reciprocity ensures that the subsequent negotiation preserves the terms of trade between the home country and foreign country 2. Under the principle of nondiscrimination, the world price of the home country's import good is the same for units exported from foreign country 1 as for units exported from foreign country 2. Thus, the home country has the same terms of trade with foreign country 1 as with foreign country 2, when the home-country tariff policy satisfies the principle of nondiscrimination. We may thus conclude that the subsequent negotiation does not alter the terms of trade between the home country and foreign country 1. As a consequence, the welfare of the government of foreign country 1 is completely protected when the subsequent negotiation satisfies the principles of nondiscrimination and reciprocity.[81]

It may seem surprising that the subsequent negotiation generates a reduced (MFN) tariff for exporters from foreign country 1 and yet the government of foreign country 1 experiences no change in welfare. To understand why, recall that the subsequent negotiation also entails a tariff cut by the government of foreign country 2. This tariff cut induces resources to move in foreign country 2 from the import-competing sector into the export sector. If the exchange of tariff cuts in the subsequent negotiation satisfies the principle of reciprocity, then the growth in import demand within the home country is completely met by the expanded export supply in foreign country 2. Thus, even though foreign country 1 faces a reduced (MFN) tariff from the home country, exports from foreign country 1 do not increase.

Our analysis to this point has focused on the possibility of concession erosion. The analysis, however, may also be used to consider the possibility of free riding and the associated potential for the strategic use of bargaining tariffs. In particular, if in the initial negotiation the governments of the home country and

---

[81] For a formal demonstration of this point, see Bagwell and Staiger (2005b).

foreign country 1 exchange tariff cuts that satisfy the principles of nondiscrimination and reciprocity, then the initial negotiation has no effect on the terms of trade of foreign country 2. Consequently, the initial negotiation then has no impact on the welfare of the government of foreign country 2. Thus, we may conclude that the potential for free riding is eliminated when bilateral negotiations satisfy the principles of nondiscrimination and reciprocity.

In total, our discussion here suggests that the principle of nondiscrimination can facilitate tariff liberalization that occurs across partners and over time, by mitigating the fear of concession erosion. The principle of nondiscrimination, however, can also introduce free-riding incentives and thereby encourage the strategic use of bargaining tariffs. If bilateral negotiations satisfy the principles of nondiscrimination and reciprocity, then third-party welfare is completely insulated. Thus, the principle of nondiscrimination eliminates concession erosion fears without creating free-riding incentives and thus encouraging the strategic use of bargaining tariffs when bilateral negotiations also satisfy the principle of reciprocity.

In practice, while the principle of reciprocity is a norm of negotiation, WTO/GATT rules do not require that negotiations satisfy the reciprocity principle. To the extent that bilateral negotiations do not strictly satisfy the reciprocity principle, some degree of free riding may in fact emerge. Governments may thus strategically adopt various bargaining tactics to preserve their bargaining chips and thereby limit free riding. For example, a government may order its negotiations in accordance with the principal-supplier rule, so that any tariff concession is offered first to the government which most values the concession. The potential for strategic behavior is also limited when agreements in initial negotiations may be modified or renegotiated at later dates.[82]

We next transition from our theoretical treatment of the nondiscrimination principle to a discussion of related empirical evidence. First, Subramanian and Wei (2007) find that WTO/GATT Membership is associated with a large and significant increase in trade volumes for developed countries; however, membership in WTO/GATT is associated with little or no increase in trade volumes for most developing countries. Given that trade liberalization through WTO/GATT negotiations has been largely sponsored by developed countries, one possible interpretation of their finding in light of the theory just presented is that WTO/GATT rules indeed limit third-party effects.[83] A second form of empirical evidence looks to see whether bilateral tariff concessions are more likely in settings where MFN free-riding incentives are expected to be less severe.

---

[82] For further analysis of this possibility, see Bagwell and Staiger (2010b).

[83] An alternative interpretation is that developed countries use trade policies that discriminate against developing countries. In the specific context of WTO/GATT bilateral dispute settlement negotiations, however, Bown (2004) offers evidence that countries do abide by the MFN rule.

Ludema and Mayda (2007, 2009) consider measures of the concentration of foreign exporters into a given country's market and present evidence of a potentially significant MFN free-rider effect. Bagwell and Staiger (2011) conduct a related investigation in the context of accession negotiations in the WTO and report little evidence of free-riding behavior in this context. Finally, the theory presented above suggests that evidence of concession-erosion concerns may be expected in settings where discriminatory tariffs are allowed under WTO rules. Limao (2006, 2007) and Karacaovali and Limao (2008) report evidence of this kind. They find evidence that the preference-erosion fears of U.S. and EU partners in preferential trade agreements may retard the MFN tariff cuts that the U.S. and EU might otherwise offer to other countries.

3.4.3.1 Customs Unions, Free-Trade Agreements, and the Generalized System of Preferences

As we have described in the previous Section, the economic rationale for MFN in the WTO/GATT is quite strong. What, then, are we to make of the major exceptions to MFN that permit the formation of customs unions and free-trade agreements and the granting of preferences under the Generalized System of Preferences?

The literature in economics on preferential trade agreements (i.e., customs unions and free-trade agreements) is usefully divided into two categories. The first category considers the effects on global economic welfare of preferential trade agreements, while the second category addresses the potential implications of preferential trade agreements for multilateral tariff cooperation.[84] We consider these two categories of economic research in turn.

As is well known, under conditions of perfect competition, global economic welfare is maximized when all countries adopt free-trade policies. Beginning in a situation in which countries adopt positive import tariffs, it therefore might be expected that a partial movement to free trade in the form of a preferential trade agreement would raise global economic welfare. In fact, however, when a subset of countries form a preferential trade agreement in which they impose no tariff on exports from member countries and leave in place positive tariffs on exports from nonmember countries, global economic welfare may fall. The key insight is due to Viner (1950), who notes that a preferential trade agreement may induce both trade-creation and trade-diversion effects. The trade-creation effect is associated with the possibility that efficient firms from member countries may increase their exports once the preferential trading agreement is in place and barriers to trade among member countries are thereby removed. The

---

[84] Following Bhagwati (1991), the second category of research is sometimes organized around the question of whether preferential trade agreements are "stumbling blocks" or "building blocks" for multilateral tariff cooperation.

trade-diversion effect, on the other hand, refers to the possibility that efficient firms in nonmember countries may reduce their exports after the agreement, since their exports are then treated less favorably than are exports from member countries. Whether a preferential trade agreement raises or lowers overall world welfare thus depends on the relative magnitudes of the trade-creation and trade-diversion effects. If the trade-diversion effect is significant, then it is possible that world welfare is lower following a partial movement to free trade in the form of a preferential trade agreement.[85]

Turning to the second category of research, our discussion above suggests the possibility that preferential trade agreements may frustrate the ability of governments to achieve multilateral liberalization through WTO/GATT negotiations. This suggestion follows since preferential trade agreements represent an important exception to the MFN rule and since, as we explain above, the economic rationale for MFN is quite strong. Consider, for example, the issue of concession erosion. We argue above that the principle of nondiscrimination can facilitate efficiency by mitigating the fear of concession erosion. If, however, a government were to worry that its current negotiating partner might later enter into a preferential trade agreement with another country, then the fear of concession erosion might be substantial. In our three-country model, for instance, we may imagine a current negotiation between the governments of the home country and foreign country 1 that might be followed by a preferential trade agreement between the home country and foreign country 2. If the later agreement were to occur, then the implication at that point for foreign country 1 would be a terms-of-trade loss, as the world price of its export good would fall and the world price of its import good would rise. Anticipating that the value of a current negotiation might be eroded as a consequence of a later preferential trade agreement to which it is not party, the government of foreign country 1 might well approach the current negotiation in a cautious and restrained manner.

A further dimension of the second category of research is associated with the idea that the WTO/GATT is a self-enforcing agreement. In other words, since the WTO/GATT has no police force of its own, a government may be presumed to honor its WTO/GATT commitments because it gains from doing so. Consequently, a multilateral trade agreement is self-enforcing if and only if for each government the short-term benefit of cheating is less than the long-term cost of a resulting deterioration in cooperation. This "self-enforcement constraint" may limit the extent to which governments can negotiate and enforce more efficient tariffs: if tariffs get too low, then a less patient government may find that

---

[85] See Freund and Ornelas (2010) for a recent survey of theoretical and empirical research on the economics of preferential trade agreements. Freund and Ornelas (2010, p. 140) conclude that the "broad picture that emerges is one of trade creation, with diversion limited to relatively few specific sectors and agreements." They thus express "guarded optimism" about preferential trade agreements.

the temptation to cheat is overwhelming. In this context, a preferential trade agreement may also affect multilateral tariff cooperation by making the self-enforcement constraint easier or harder to satisfy. For example, it may be more difficult for two governments to cooperate, if they each anticipate that their countries will soon enter into preferential trade agreements with other countries and thus trade less with one another. In this case, the prospect of future preferential trade agreements makes the self-enforcement constraint harder to satisfy for the two governments, since the long-term cost of a diminishment in cooperation between the two countries is less concerning when the two countries expect in any case to trade less with one another in the future. On the other hand, the governments may find that they face less incentive to cheat once they have entered into their respective preferential trade agreements, since their countries then trade less with one another and so a government's short-term benefit from a tariff hike is correspondingly reduced as well. In light of these and other considerations, the literature that considers the effect of preferential trade agreements on the enforcement of multilateral tariff cooperation suggests that the direction of the effect varies across circumstances and is in general ambiguous.[86]

Since the economic rationale for MFN is quite strong, we may expect that other GATT/WTO exceptions to MFN also have the potential to frustrate the ability of governments to achieve multilateral liberalization through WTO/GATT negotiations. Consider, for example, the exception to MFN that is allowed under the Generalized System of Preferences (GSP). Following up on our discussion of concession erosion just above, let us suppose that foreign countries 1 and 2 are two large developing countries, and that the government of the home country may select discriminatory tariffs as part of its GSP scheme. As suggested by our discussion above, foreign country 1 suffers a terms-of-trade loss when the governments of the home country and foreign country 2 enter into an agreement in which the home country offers a discriminatory tariff cut to exports from foreign country 2. Such an agreement may lower overall efficiency by generating benefits for the negotiating governments that come at the expense of a welfare loss for the government of foreign country 1. Furthermore, and as above, if the government of foreign country 1 foresees the possibility of such a future negotiation, then it may be hesitant to offer concessions in an earlier negotiation. Thus, discrimination in GSP schemes may also frustrate multilateral tariff liberalization. At the same time, heavy restrictions on GSP schemes might have a chilling effect on the extent to which developed countries are willing to offer GSP benefits in the form of unilateral concessions to developing countries. Thus, as Grossman and Sykes (2005) emphasize, an assessment as to the optimal degree and form of discrimination to allow must balance the costs of negative third-party externalities against the potential benefits of a larger number of "donated" GSP schemes.

---

[86] For further discussion of this literature, see Bagwell and Staiger (2002, Chapter 7).

3.5 Implementation in WTO Law: MFN and Exceptions

Our economic discussion in Section 3.4 has provided a basis for answering two key questions regarding the logic of the nondiscrimination principle. First, why would the drafters of GATT require that tariff concessions and other "advantages" be extended unconditionally to all members? Our discussion above employs the terms-of-trade theory of trade agreements and establishes that the principle of nondiscrimination alone can be beneficial as a means of limiting concession-erosion fears. We argue, however, that concession-erosion fears are completely eliminated only when the principle of nondiscrimination is joined with the principle of reciprocity. Accordingly, the theory that we employ offers an interpretation for the prominent role played in the WTO/GATT by the principle of nondiscrimination, but it also suggests that this principle might be more effective when joined with a reciprocity requirement. We reach a related answer with regard to a second question: Does the requirement that tariff concessions be extended unconditionally create a serious free-rider problem during the course of negotiating rounds? We have argued that the principle of nondiscrimination can give rise to a free-rider problem, but this problem would be removed if the principle were joined with a reciprocity requirement. As we explain, in the absence of such a requirement, the principal-supplier rule and other bargaining tactics are also expected to limit the scope for free riding.

Having established an economic basis for understanding the logic of the nondiscrimination principle, we now consider the most important issues that have arisen in WTO disputes relating to the MFN obligation and its exceptions. As shall be seen, the case law is somewhat sparse, but several important and thorny issues have surfaced.

3.5.1 MFN and Article I

Article I carries a broad sweep. It applies to (a) "customs duties and charges of any kind imposed on or in connection with importation or exportation," (b) "the method of levying such duties and charges," (c) "all rules and formalities in connection with importation or exportation," and (d) the matters covered by the national-treatment obligation of Article III:2 and 4, namely internal domestic taxation and "laws, regulations and requirements" affecting the sale of imported products. With respect to all such measures, any "advantage, favour, privilege or immunity" afforded to a product originating in or destined to "any other country" must also be afforded "immediately and unconditionally" to the "like products" originating in or destined to any WTO member.

Covered Measures   In light of items (a) – (d) above, virtually any governmental measure that affects the competitive position of imported or exported goods falls within the MFN obligation. Measures that were held during the GATT years to produce disadvantages in violation of the MFN obligation include consular taxes applied to imported goods, customs user fees, the methods of computing antidumping and countervailing duties, and the requirement of an injury test in countervailing-duty cases. In WTO litigation, the Panel found in *EC–Bananas III*,[87] *inter alia*, that the use of a less complicated licensing procedure for imports from some sources (§§ 7.188ff.), and the granting of licenses only to operators representing producers from certain countries (§§ 7.251ff.) were all matters covered by Article I. The Appellate Body held in *EC–Poultry* (§§ 96ff.) that Art. I covers tariff-rate quotas as well.[88]

We also note that Article I applies irrespective of whether a tariff concession exists on the good in question. See the GATT Panel on *Spain–Unroasted Coffee*, discussed further below in relation to "like products." Similarly, when a binding does exist and a nation nevertheless applies a lower tariff rate to imports from some source, it must apply that same rate to imports from all WTO Members (absent an applicable exception). Finally, it matters not whether the "advantage" in question is extended to a WTO member or to a nonmember – an advantage given to goods originating in or destined to "any other country" must be extended to all WTO Members.

"Immediately and Unconditionally" WTO Members must extend any advantage (as understood above) immediately and unconditionally to all WTO Members. The term "immediately" raises no serious interpretive issues, but the term "unconditionally" has given rise to conflicting interpretations.

The GATT Panel on *Belgium–Family Allowances*[89] was the first GATT case to deal with the substantive interpretation of the term "unconditionally." Belgium had enacted a policy of levying certain charges on goods purchased by public authorities if they originated in a country that did not have a system of family allowances (welfare payments) that was deemed satisfactory by the Belgian government. The Panel was of the view that this system was inconsistent with Art. I.1:

> According to the provisions of paragraph 1 of Article I of the General Agreement, any advantage, favour, privilege or immunity granted by Belgium to any product originating in the territory of any country with respect to all matters referred to in paragraph 2 of Article III shall be granted immediately and unconditionally to the like product originating in the territories of all contracting parties. Belgium has granted exemption from the levy under consideration to products purchased by public bodies when they

---

[87] WT/DS27/AB/R, adopted September 25, 1997.
[88] WT/DS69/AB/R, adopted July 23, 1998.
[89] 1st Supp. BISD 59 (1953), Panel Report adopted November 7, 1952.

originate in Luxemburg and the Netherlands, as well as in France, Italy, Sweden and the United Kingdom. If the General Agreement were definitively in force in accordance with Article XXVI, it is clear that that exemption would have to be granted unconditionally to all other contracting parties (including Denmark and Norway). The consistency or otherwise of the system of family allowances in force in the territory of a given contracting party with the requirements of the Belgian law would be irrelevant in this respect, and the Belgian legislation would have to be amended insofar as it introduced a discrimination between countries having a given system of family allowances and those which had a different system or no system at all, and made the granting of the exemption dependent on certain conditions. (§ 3)

This seemingly straightforward analysis in fact hides a rather subtle issue. Does the requirement to provide an advantage "unconditionally" mean that it is impossible to offer an "advantage" that is in any way made conditional on the actions of the recipient? Take the facts of the *Family Allowances* case as an illustration. Belgium could argue that its policy is nondiscriminatory on its face – any country with an acceptable system of family allowances is entitled to a waiver of the levies on goods procured by public agencies. Likewise, any country with an adequate system of allowances will "immediately and unconditionally" benefit from the waiver of levies. Thus, the argument might run, there is no "discrimination" at all by Belgium and thus no violation of Article I.

Putting it slightly differently, the interpretation of the term "unconditionally" has implications for the extent to which Article I condemns measures that might be characterized as *de facto* (as opposed to *de jure*) discrimination. Numerous WTO/GATT Panels (and working parties) have suggested that any sort of conditionality attaching to an "advantage" creates impermissible *de facto* discrimination. The GATT Panel Report on *EEC–Imports of Beef*,[90] for example, held that conditioning a duty waiver upon a certain type of certification by a particular government violated Article I. The Working Party Report on *Accession of Hungary*[91] found that to condition tariff treatment upon the prior acceptance of a cooperation agreement was a violation. The WTO Panel Report on *Indonesia–Autos*[92] (§§ 14.143ff.) found that Indonesian practices granting tax advantages to Korean companies which had entered into certain arrangements with Indonesian companies were inconsistent with Art. I.

The view implicit in these decisions is not the only possible interpretation of "unconditionally." In a case involving a dispute with India over its Generalized System of Preferences (GSP) program, the European Community argued that

---

[90] 28th Supp. BISD 92, adopted March 10, 1981.
[91] BISD 20S/34, adopted July 30, 1973.
[92] *Indonesia – Certain Measures Affecting the Automobile Industry*, WT/DS64/R, adopted July 23, 1998.

"unconditionally" was simply intended to prohibit reciprocity requirements – advantages that would be extended only if the recipient provided some benefit in return. The Panel Report on *EC–Tariff Preferences*[93] rejected this argument:

> In the Panel's view, moreover, the term 'unconditionally' in Article I:1 has a broader meaning than simply that of not requiring compensation. While the Panel acknowledges the European Communities' argument that conditionality in the context of traditional MFN clauses in bilateral treaties may relate to conditions of trade compensation for receiving MFN treatment, the Panel does not consider this to be the full meaning of 'unconditionally' under Article I:1. Rather, the Panel sees no reason not to give that term its ordinary meaning under Article I:1, that is, 'not limited by or subject to any conditions.'
>
> Because the tariff preferences under the Drug Arrangements are accorded only on the condition that the receiving countries are experiencing a certain gravity of drug problems, these tariff preferences are not accorded 'unconditionally' to the like products originating in all other WTO Members, as required by Article I:1. The Panel therefore finds that the tariff advantages under the Drug Arrangements are not consistent with Article I:1 of GATT 1994. (§§ 7.59–7.60)

Other cases, however, offer some support for the EC's position. The GATT Panel Report on *EEC–Minimum Import Prices*[94] dealt with the following issue: the EC authorities required the payment of a duty deposit from all countries that could not guarantee a specified minimum import price. Because the deposit was requested by all exporting countries falling into this category, the EC scheme was not considered to be a violation of Art. I.1 GATT. Likewise, the WTO Panel Report in *Canada–Autos* explicitly adopted the view that the term "unconditionally" simply means that MFN treatment shall not be conditioned on reciprocal conduct:

> In our view, whether an advantage within the meaning of Article I:1 is accorded 'unconditionally' cannot be determined independently of an examination of whether it involves discrimination between like products of different countries...
>
> In this respect, it appears to us that there is an important distinction to be made between, on the one hand, the issue of whether an advantage within the meaning of Article I:1 is subject to conditions, and, on the other, whether an advantage, once it has been granted to the product of any country, is accorded 'unconditionally' to the like product of all other Members. An advantage can be granted subject to conditions without necessarily

---

[93] *European Communities – Conditions for the Granting of Tariff Preferences to Developing Countries*, WT/DS246/R, adopted April 20, 2004.
[94] 25th Supp. BISD 68, adopted October 18, 1978.

implying that it is not accorded 'unconditionally' to the like product of other Members. More specifically, the fact that conditions attached to such an advantage are not related to the imported product itself does not necessarily imply that such conditions are discriminatory with respect to the origin of imported products. We therefore do not believe that, as argued by Japan, the word 'unconditionally' in Article I:1 must be interpreted to mean that making an advantage conditional on criteria not related to the imported product itself is per se inconsistent with Article I:1, irrespective of whether and how such criteria relate to the origin of the imported products. (§§ 10.22 and 10.24)

These two different approaches to interpreting "unconditionally" have not been resolved definitively by the Appellate Body – its Reports in *Canada–Autos* and in *EC–Tariff Preferences* do not specifically address the issue.[95] What is clear from the discussion above, however, is that a measure need not discriminate on its face to run afoul of Article I. As the Appellate Body stated in its Report *Canada–Autos*:

> In approaching this question, we observe first that the words of Article I:1 do not restrict its scope only to cases in which the failure to accord an 'advantage' to like products of all other Members appears on the face of the measure, or can be demonstrated on the basis of the words of the measure. Neither the words 'de jure' nor 'de facto' appear in Article I:1. Nevertheless, we observe that Article I:1 does not cover only 'in law', or de jure, discrimination. As several GATT panel reports confirmed, Article I:1 covers also 'in fact', or de facto, discrimination. Like the Panel, we cannot accept Canada's argument that Article I:1 does not apply to measures which, on their face, are 'origin-neutral.' (§ 78)

The unsettled question is whether any type of "condition" amounts to *de facto* discrimination. In the abstract, one can perhaps imagine "conditions" that are not objectionable as a policy matter. Suppose, for example, that two trading nations are signatories to an endangered species treaty covering, among other things, endangered turtles. Nation A imports turtle soup from nation B, and provides under its national laws that a tariff below the bound rate shall apply to imports from all nations that can certify that its turtle soup exports were produced in a manner that did not threaten endangered turtles. Nation B cannot offer such certification, and so is charged a higher tariff rate (but still within any applicable binding). Should nation B have a valid claim for a violation of Article I under these circumstances? A plausible argument can be made that such a "condition" for the more favorable rate, especially in light of the two nations'

---

[95] The Panel's interpretation of "unconditionally" in *Canada–Autos* was not appealed, while the issues in *EC–Tariff Preferences* were resolved under the Enabling Clause.

mutual assent to an endangered species agreement, ought be permissible under Article I. A counterargument, perhaps, is that such matters should be adjudicated under Article XX with respect to the exceptions for the protection of animal health or for conservation of scarce resources. The question whether GATT should take the policy rationale for a discriminatory measure into account in deciding whether de facto "discrimination" exists, or instead only under the Article XX exceptions, is an intriguing and challenging one. A possible advantage of adjudication under Article XX is that it provides a list of acceptable bases for deviation from GATT commitments, along with further guidance in the form of the chapeau and requirements like "necessity." Article I, by contrast, offers no basis for deciding what types of "conditionality" might be acceptable on policy grounds. The portion of this study that deals with the national-treatment obligation will address this set of questions in much greater detail.

Like Products   Covered advantages must be extended to the "like products" originating in or destined to WTO Members. The term "like product" appears in many places in WTO treaty text, and the question arises whether decisions concerning the concept in one context have applicability to another. The Appellate Body has indicated that "like product" does not have the same meaning in each instance, however, and so one must be cautious in drawing inferences about its meaning in GATT Article I based on decisions pertaining to its meaning elsewhere.

GATT does in various places draw a distinction between "like products" and "directly competitive or substitutable" products [see, for example, Articles III and XIX]. The GATT Panel Report in *EEC–Animal Feed Proteins* noted the fact that Art. I applies only to "like products," and inferred from this observation that the drafters must have intended a narrower scope for the obligation in Art. I than, say, the obligation in Article III:2 (see § 4.20). The Appellate Body has not spoken to this issue, however, although it seems certain that the set of "like products" in any given context is at least no broader than the set of "directly competitive or substitutable" products.

The only other relevant jurisprudence that addresses "like products" with particular reference to Article I also comes from the days of GATT. In *Treatment by Germany of Imports of Sardines*, a dispute arose when Germany reclassified certain species of fish (sprats, herring, and sardines) under different headings subject to different tariffs. Norway complained because the species it exported were disadvantaged. The Panel was unable to conclude that the products were "like," however, noting that the history of the negotiations did not indicate that the parties considered the products to be like.[96] Thus, this Panel seemed to focus

---

[96] 1st Supp. BISD 53, Panel Report adopted October 31, 1952. The Panel did decide the case for Norway, however, holding that the negotiations had created a reasonable expectation

on the understanding of trade negotiators as the key to understanding what is "like."

The GATT Panel on *Spain–Tariff Treatment of Unroasted Coffee*[97] confronted a claim that Spain's reclassification of unroasted, nondecaffeinated coffees into different tariff headings with different tariffs resulted in tariff discrimination among "like products." The Panel found against Spain, relying on two observations:

> The Panel furthermore found relevant to its examination of the matter that unroasted coffee was mainly, if not exclusively, sold in the form of blends, combining various types of coffee, and that coffee in its end-use, was universally regarded as a well-defined and single product intended for drinking.
>
> The Panel noted that no other contracting party applied its tariff régime in respect of unroasted, non-decaffeinated coffee in such a way that different types of coffee were subject to different tariff rates. (§§ 4.7–4.8)

Thus, the Coffee Panel introduced considerations relating to consumer substitutability as a possible dimension of "likeness," as well as a focus on common practice as to tariff classification.

The GATT Panel Report on *Japan-Spruce-Pine-Fir Dimension Lumber*[98] also emphasizes the relevance of tariff classification to establish likeness. In rejecting a claim by Canada that Japan's classification of dimension lumber by species (e.g., spruce, pine, or fir) resulted in tariff discrimination among like products, the Panel remarked:

> The Panel noted in this respect that 'dimension lumber' as defined by Canada was a concept extraneous to the Japanese Tariff . . . nor did it belong to any internationally accepted customs classification. The Panel concluded therefore that reliance by Canada on the concept of dimension lumber was not an appropriate basis for establishing 'likeness' of products under Article I:1 of the General Agreement. (§ 5.12)

In decisions relating to other provisions of GATT, WTO/GATT jurisprudence on "likeness" often looks to a set of factors developed by a GATT working party on Border Tax Adjustments in 1970. In addition to tariff classification, the so-called "border tax factors" include "the product's end uses in a given market; consumers' tastes and habits, which change from country to country; [and] the product's properties, nature and quality."[99]

on Norway's part that the tariff treatment of the three products would remain comparable (a nonviolation ruling).

[97] 28th Supp. BISD 102, Panel Report adopted June 11, 1981.

[98] 36th Supp. BISD 167 (1990), adopted July 19, 1989.

[99] See, e.g., *Japan – Taxes on Alcoholic Beverages*, WT/DS 8, 10, and 11/AB/R, Appellate Body Report adopted November 1, 1996.

The concept of "like products" is fundamental to the implementation of the nondiscrimination principle, yet as our discussion here has indicated the WTO/GATT leaves open a number of important questions, among them: Is the WTO system best served by a broader or narrower interpretation of the "like product" concept?; and of the guidelines developed by GATT Panels to assess "likeness," which make the most sense? While we are not aware of specific work by economists who address these questions, we can use the economic discussion from Section 3.4 to speculate about the main forces that might shape the answers. On the one hand, the broader the interpretation of the like-product concept, the more effective will be the MFN restriction in preventing the possibility of concession erosion and its associated distortions. This suggests that a broad interpretation of "likeness" is desirable. On the other hand, under a broad interpretation of the like-product concept the prospect of free riding in the presence of MFN becomes more likely, suggesting that a narrow interpretation of likeness is desirable. Finally, an overly-broad interpretation of likeness could also interfere with a government's ability to use its tariff policy to pursue legitimate product- or sector-specific national objectives. This too suggests that a more narrow interpretation of likeness is desirable. Taken together, we may speculate that these forces combine to create subtle trade-offs in the determination of the appropriate breadth and definition of the "like product" concept, and that this concept could reasonably depend on a variety of factors such as those that have been considered by GATT Panels, including the understanding of negotiators, tariff-classification practices, and indicia of consumer substitutability.

In short, the current jurisprudence under Article I affords a somewhat imprecise test for the concept of "likeness," and the extent to which it may be supplemented by jurisprudence regarding the meaning of likeness elsewhere in GATT is unclear. The uncertainty is not surprising given the decision of the GATT negotiators to leave the term undefined. As we discussed above, economic analysis does not point clearly to a more precise definition. A narrower scope for the term reduces free riding in negotiations and makes the outcome of negotiation more predictable, whereas a broader definition may serve to rein in differentiations that generate concession erosion. The balance of these competing considerations is hardly obvious and may well vary from case to case, although we do believe that the factors emphasized by the GATT cases – particularly tariff classification and consumer substitutability – are relevant.

Originating in a WTO Member WTO Members must extend any advantage granted to a product originating in one country, to all like goods originating in all WTO Members (absent an applicable exception). The difficulty arises when a good has been processed in, or has components from, multiple countries. The WTO Agreement on Rules of Origin does not pin down the rules to be applied in such cases, but generally requires nondiscrimination and transparency in the application of rules of origin, and establishes a work program (still ongoing) toward elaborating additional rules.

The WTO Agreement on Rules of Origin contemplates that the emphasis in origin determinations will be the locus of the last "substantial transformation" of the good in question. Factors that are commonly relevant to this issue under existing national customs laws include, among other things, whether the good has undergone a change in tariff classification, whether it has been altered from a producer good to consumer good, and the amount of value added to the good in the last processing stage.

Because fewer and fewer countries of any significance in the trading system are outside the WTO, the importance of decisions holding that a good comes from a nonmember state is minimal. The more important matter concerns determinations that a good originates in a country entitled to some trade preference. That issue is difficult for the WTO to police, in part because various preferential trade agreements have developed their own rules of origin. The ongoing work program does not attempt to address the rules of origin in preferential arrangements. Likewise, we are not aware of any economic analysis that bears squarely on the issue of "optimal" rules of origin.

3.5.2 Article XXIV

Despite their substantial and growing importance, preferential trading arrangements (PTAs) have received relatively little attention in the dispute system over the history of the WTO/GATT system. Whenever a new arrangement is formed and notified to the membership, the standard procedure has been to form a working party to examine its consistency with GATT. The resulting working party reports typically declined to draw firm conclusions, and most PTAs were not formally approved by the membership (including, most notably, the EU).

Part of the problem lies in the fact that Article XXIV authorizes not only PTAs but also interim agreements leading to a PTA, and it had been unclear how long the parties to such an agreement would be allowed to bring their arrangement into full compliance. The WTO Understanding on Article XXIV, noted in Section 3.4, provides that the transition period should not exceed 10 years except in "exceptional cases."

In more recent years, the review process shifted from working parties to the Committee on Regional Trade Agreements (CRTA). In principle, CRTA could declare that a new PTA was GATT-inconsistent, but it has not done so, and it now does little more than provide a forum for WTO members to discuss issues raised by PTAs in a more transparent way.[100]

---

[100] See Mavroidis (2011).

Thus, the prospects for extensive central supervision over the process of PTA formation remain poor, and perhaps unsurprisingly. The standards under Article XXIV are exceedingly vague in important respects (such as the "substantially all" requirement of Article XXIV(5)). Moreover, hundreds of PTAs already exist. Whatever level of supervision the GATT drafters may have contemplated, the horse has already left the barn. Mavroidis (2011) defends the regime nonetheless on the grounds that the overall decline in MFN tariff rates has reduced the potential for trade diversion, the consequences of vigorous enforcement of Article XXIV might actually cause greater trade diversion, and the available empirical evidence indicates that many PTAs are welfare enhancing.

It nevertheless remains possible to raise the GATT-consistency of a PTA in the course of WTO dispute resolution. Paragraph 12 of the Understanding makes clear that the consistency of a PTA with GATT is fair game:

> The provisions of Articles XXII and XXIII of GATT 1994 * * * may be invoked with respect to any matters arising from the application of those provisions of Article XXIV relating to customs unions, free-trade areas or interim agreements leading to the formation of a customs union or free-trade area.

The most important case to date in this regard is *Turkey–Textiles*.[101] In connection with its accession to the European Community, Turkey imposed QRs on a number of textile products from India. Of course, such measures violate the prohibition on QRs in GATT Article XI, but Turkey could not appeal to any of the exceptions in Article XI itself, to balance of payments concerns, or to any of the general exceptions in Article XX to justify its QRs. Rather, it argued that the QRs were necessary to secure duty-free treatment on its textile exports to the rest of the EC. Absent the QRs, Turkey claimed, the other members of the EC would have been so concerned about trans-shipment of products from India through Turkey (with ostensible Turkish origin) that they would have been unwilling to grant Turkey duty-free treatment on its own exports. Such a scenario, Turkey argued further, would put the members of the EC in violation of Article XXIV(8)(a)(1), which states that a customs union must eliminate "substantially all" barriers to trade among its constituent members (subject to some exceptions). In Turkey's view, this requirement could not be met without duty-free treatment on its textile exports as they comprised 40% of its exports to the EC. Thus, carrying the argument further, Turkey claimed that the QRs were necessary to the formation of the customs union, and, therefore, authorized by Article XXIV(5), which states that "the provisions of this Agreement shall not prevent, as between the territories of contracting parties, the formation of a customs union...."

---

[101] *Turkey – Restrictions on Imports of Textile and Clothing Products*, WT/DS34/AB/R, adopted November 19, 1999.

The Appellate Body agreed that, in principle, this provision creates an exception to GATT obligations for measures that would "prevent" the formation of a customs union. This exception is in the nature of an affirmative defense on which the party claiming the exception has the burden of proof. The Appellate Body also pointed to the language in XXIV(5) immediately following that quoted above, and to the words "Provided that." This language indicates that the subsequent requirements in XXIV(5) must be met for the exception to apply. The key requirement is that the barriers to trade with nonmembers not "on the whole" be higher than before. The Appellate Body also held that the customs union must satisfy the definition of a customs union in Article XXIV(8), and eliminate barriers to trade on "substantially all" trade among the constituent territories. Finally, the Appellate Body pointed to the word "formation" as the basis for a principle that the exception can only be invoked for measures taken at the time of the formation of the customs union, and not to later measures.

The Appellate Body then affirmed the Panel ruling in favor of India on the grounds that if Turkey had not imposed QRs against Indian textile exports, the customs union could still have been formed and thus the absence of the QRs would not have "prevented" it. It reasoned that Turkey could have employed less intrusive measures, such as rules and certificates of origin to prevent any transshipment of Indian products through Turkey claiming Turkish origin.

The ruling seems broadly consistent with the rationale for Article XXIV as articulated in the WTO Understanding and by the Appellate Body – to expand internal trade without raising barriers to outside trade. Nevertheless, it is subject to some criticisms. For example, the principle that any exception applies only to measures at the time of the "formation" of a customs union seems to rule out the following type of development: Suppose that a customs union is formed eliminating barriers to trade on 95% of the intra-union trade, and assume that this meets the "substantially all" test. A few years later, the parties propose to eliminate all remaining barriers to trade. Do nonmembers at that point have a valid claim of an MFN violation, in that the elimination of the remaining barriers discriminates against non-members and is not introduced on "formation" of the customs union? Such a principle seems quite peculiar, and potentially at odds with the notion that the purpose of Article XXIV is to expand intra-union trade.

Aside from this peculiarity, the deeper issue raised by the decision concerns the competence of the dispute-settlement process to evaluate PTAs under the standards of Article XXIV. The "substantially all" standard remains vague and undefined, as does the no more restrictive "on the whole" standard for the trade barriers against outsiders. How can Panels reasonably apply such principles? And is it in the interest of the system for dispute Panels and the Appellate Body to pass judgment on the legality of PTAs, when the membership as a whole has seemed incapable of doing so since the formation of GATT? The political fallout and disruption from a decision declaring some PTA to be illegal seems enormous and potentially destabilizing. One suspects that Panels and the Appellate Body will look for other ways to decide any cases that come before them, much as in *Turkey–Textiles* itself.

3.5.3 Special and Differential Treatment

The WTO/GATT system has seen only modest litigation over issues relating to special and differential treatment. Several reasons account for the dearth of cases. First, with respect to the obligations in Part IV of GATT, their language is hortatory and not really subject to effective enforcement. Second, with respect to measures taken for purposes of developing a "particular industry" under Article XVIII (infant industry measures), most such measures are taken by relatively "small" countries and have minimal impact on trading partners. Third, developing countries have historically made relatively modest tariff commitments, and thus to a great extent retained the flexibility to protect sensitive industries without need for a GATT exception.

Most of the conflict through the years has instead related to measures taken for balance-of-payments reasons, including the one important case under Article XVIII in the WTO: *India–Quantitative Restrictions*.[102] Both the Panel and the Appellate Body found that India's QRs could not be justified for balance-of-payments reasons in that proceeding. We will not discuss the case in detail, however, because the conceptual issues relate to international monetary affairs and go to matters beyond the scope of this study.

The other important case in the WTO pertaining to special and differential treatment involved a challenge by India to the EC's Generalized System of Preferences (GSP).[103] The GSP scheme of the EC was complex, but the provisions at issue in the dispute involved certain additional preferences given to countries that were combatting drug trafficking, including 11 South or Central American countries, plus Pakistan. They received additional margins of tariff preference on a range of products.[104]

The text at issue in the dispute was the "Enabling Clause," an Understanding adopted during the Tokyo Round and incorporated into GATT 1994, which provides an exception to GATT Article I for GSP schemes. It reads in pertinent part:

1. Notwithstanding the provisions of Article I of the General Agreement, contracting parties may accord differential and more favourable

---

[102] *India – Quantitative Restrictions on Imports of Agricultural, Textile and Industrial Products,* WT/DS90, adopted September 22, 1999.

[103] *European Communities – Conditions for the Granting of Tariff Preferences to Developing Countries,* WT/DS246, adopted April 20, 2004.

[104] Our discussion here draws heavily on Grossman and Sykes (2005).

treatment to developing countries, without according such treatment to other contracting parties.

2. The provisions of paragraph 1 apply to the following:

    (a) Preferential tariff treatment accorded by developed contracting parties to products originating in developing countries in accordance with the Generalized System of Preferences...3 (original footnote)...

3. Any differential and more favourable treatment provided under this clause...

    (c) shall in the case of such treatment accorded by developed contracting parties to developing countries be designed and, if necessary, modified, to respond positively to the development, financial and trade needs of developing countries.

    3 (original footnote) As described in the Decision of the CONTRACTING PARTIES of 25 June 1971, relating to the establishment of "generalized, non-reciprocal and non discriminatory preferences beneficial to the developing countries."

A key issue concerned the importance of footnote 3, which referred back to the "generalized, non-reciprocal and non discriminatory" system of preferences first discussed under the auspices of UNCTAD and then established by a GATT waiver in 1971. The UNCTAD discussion, which began in the 1960s, arose in part because developing countries confronted a patchwork of preferential policies at the time that included much discrimination.

In the litigation, India focused on the requirement of nondiscriminatory preferences. According to India, when a nation granted a preference on a particular product, it must extend that preference to all developing countries (subject only to a proviso that least-developed nations can receive greater preferences). The drug-related preferences did not meet this test.

The EC put forth several arguments, and we will focus on two. First, it argued that India misinterpreted the requirement in footnote 3 that preferences be "non discriminatory." For Europe, "discrimination" involved arbitrary differences in the treatment of similarly situated entities – as long as differences in treatment could be justified by a legitimate objective, and the differences were reasonable in pursuit of that objective, no "discrimination" should be found.

In addition, the EC argued that paragraph 2(a) of the Enabling Clause, which authorizes "preferential tariff treatment accorded by developed contracting parties to products originating in developing countries," does not require preference-granting nations to afford preferences to all developing countries. Had the drafters meant to require that preferences be extended to all, Europe suggested, they could have inserted the word "all" into the text.

The Panel rejected the EC's arguments, essentially holding that the nondiscrimination requirement prohibited GSP schemes from discriminating among developing countries. It relied heavily on the context of the 1971 waiver and the preceding negotiations in UNCTAD, which were clearly aimed at reducing the discrimination that had arisen previously.

On appeal, the Appellate Body found that the ordinary meaning of the term "non discriminatory" did not permit it to choose between the competing views of discrimination put forth by India and the European Communities. Both parties agreed that "discrimination" entails disparate treatment of those "similarly situated," but disagreed on what it means to be "similarly situated" – an appeal to the ordinary meaning of the term "discrimination" does not resolve such a disagreement.

The Appellate Body then turned to paragraph 3(c) of the Enabling Clause to provide further context for the interpretation of the nondiscrimination obligation, and accepted the European argument that the absence of the word "all" before "developing countries" implies that the text imposes no obligation to treat all developing countries alike. Further, both parties apparently conceded that the development needs of various countries may differ. Accordingly, the Appellate Body was "of the view that, by requiring developed countries to 'respond positively' to the 'needs of developing countries', which are varied and not homogeneous, paragraph 3(c) indicates that a GSP scheme may be 'non discriminatory' even if 'identical' tariff treatment is not accorded to 'all' GSP beneficiaries." It thus reversed the Panel's finding to the contrary. Likewise, the Appellate Body reversed the Panel's finding that the reference to "developing countries" in paragraph 2(a) was to all developing countries. It held that preference-granting countries are permitted to treat beneficiaries differently when such differences "respond positively" to varying "development, financial and trade needs."

The nondiscrimination requirement was not without bite in the view of the Appellate Body, however, because it does require "that identical tariff treatment must be available to all GSP beneficiaries with the 'development, financial [or] trade need' to which the differential treatment is intended to respond." The Appellate Body then held that the European Communities failed to carry the burden of proof on this issue. It emphasized that the drug-related preferences were available only to a "closed list" of 12 countries. The regulation creating the preferences did not set out any criteria for the selection of the countries, and it did not provide any mechanism for adding or deleting countries as their circumstances changed. Under these conditions, Europe failed to demonstrate that its preferences were nondiscriminatory.

The case is hard as a legal matter because, as both the Panel and the Appellate Body acknowledged, the text of the Enabling Clause is ambiguous. Even assuming that footnote 3 was intended to create a binding nondiscrimination obligation, as did the parties to the case, the absence of any definition for the concept opens the door to a wide range of interpretations. In the face of such ambiguity, the Panel relied primarily on historical context and the UNCTAD negotiations to give footnote 3 some definitive content, and inferred that any discrimination in GSP schemes had to be limited to what was expressly contemplated in UNCTAD.

The Panel's approach resonates somewhat with our economic perspective on the MFN obligation.[105] As noted, the MFN obligation helps to avert certain negative externalities that would otherwise arise relating to bilateral opportunism and to erosion of the value of trade concessions. The situation prior to the UNCTAD negotiations was one in which the problems addressed by the MFN obligation had resurfaced because of a patchwork of discriminatory preferences in the trade policies of developed nations, often dating from the colonial era. If developed nations are allowed to engage in whatever degree of discrimination they wish without legal constraint, an essential purpose of the UNCTAD negotiations is clearly jeopardized. And even if nations are only allowed to afford differential treatment according to their assessment of the individual "development, financial and trade needs" of beneficiary countries, the danger still arises that they will use such authority to justify discriminatory policies that benefit countries they favor rather than for any legitimate purpose.

But an important counterargument must be acknowledged. The parties to the UNCTAD negotiations were aware of the potential political impediments to the implementation of GSP, and might well have thought that compromise on various margins, in ways not fully anticipated during the negotiations, would be mutually preferable to political impasse and the status quo ante. GSP benefits are in the nature of a "gift" by developed countries, and if extensive conditions are placed on such gifts, they may not be made at all. It is also noteworthy that major GSP schemes put in place after UNCTAD from the outset contained exemptions and restrictions that were not contemplated at the time of the UNCTAD discussions. Had it been the intention of the Tokyo Round negotiators to outlaw the sort of discrimination and conditionality that had emerged following the 1971 waiver, they might well have done so more forcefully than by a somewhat oblique reference in footnote 3. In short, even if discrimination was at odds with what the developing nations had hoped to achieve through the UNCTAD process, it may have been a necessary political price to pay for any preferences at all.

The aftermath of the dispute is instructive. The EC complied with the ruling by eliminating the drug-related preferences, and instead affording special preferences to countries that had signed a certain set of treaties relating to various environmental and human-rights issues. The resulting list of beneficiaries was almost identical to the group that received the drug-related preferences, except that Pakistan was now excluded. India was pacified, the dispute came to

---

[105] Another important issue, of course, is whether tariff preferences actually promote economic development. For further discussion, including reasons to be skeptical in this regard, see Grossman and Sykes (2005).

an end, and no further challenges to GSP schemes have been brought despite the "discrimination" that remains in many of them.

3.6 The Rationale for Disciplines on Export Subsidies and Export Tariffs

The GATT system from the outset has distinguished between export subsidies – which are in some manner conditional on the exportation of goods by the recipient of the subsidy – and domestic subsidies, which are not conditional on exportation. Because our focus is on border instruments, here we consider only the disciplines applicable to export subsidies. We also briefly consider the limited disciplines on export tariffs.

3.6.1 The Negotiating History

WTO/GATT discipline of export subsidies has evolved greatly over the history of the system. During the negotiations leading up to GATT, the United States wished to preserve flexibility to use export subsidies, especially in agriculture. Britain, by contrast, wished to eliminate export subsidies but preserve the right to use domestic agricultural subsidies. The London draft of what would become GATT included an export-subsidies prohibition, but when the GATT was divorced from the prospective ITO charter in the New York conference, the prohibition on export subsidies was dropped from GATT. In all likelihood, the negotiators believed that the nonviolation complaint mechanism would be enough to protect the initial GATT tariff concessions from being undermined by new subsidies, and the issue of export subsidies was left to be resolved in the ITO.[106]

GATT Article XVI contains the limited original obligations on subsidies. It consisted originally of one paragraph (XVI:1), with a loose obligation to report all subsidies which operate to increase exports or decrease imports. The article was amended extensively during the GATT 1954–1955 review session. Four paragraphs were added to Article XVI, containing two key obligations: one obligation (paragraph 3) prohibits using an export subsidy on primary products which results in obtaining more than "an equitable share of world export trade in that product"; a second obligation (paragraph 4) prohibits a subsidy on the export of nonprimary products which results in an export price lower than the comparable price for like goods which are not exported (the so-called "bi-level pricing" condition). These Article XVI amendments, however, were accepted only by certain industrialized nations of GATT. These conditions are now obsolete in light of the new WTO agreements relating to subsidies.

In 1960, the GATT Contracting Parties adopted a Report of a working party which included an "illustrative list" of practices that would be considered as

---

[106] See Genesis, Chapters 1–2.

"export subsidies" for purposes of GATT Article XVI, paragraph 4.[107] This list has been very important for the interpretation of GATT subsidy obligations and has carried forward into WTO treaty text.

The disciplines on export subsidies were further tightened in the Tokyo Round Subsidies Code, which again was accepted by only a subset of GATT members. That Code has now given way to the WTO Agreement on Subsidies and Countervailing Measures (SCMs), which is binding on all WTO Members.

The SCMs initially exempted agricultural subsidies, leaving them to the Agreement on Agriculture. In that Agreement, both export subsidies and domestic subsidies to agriculture are subject to a complex set of commitments for their reduction over a period of years. It treats agricultural subsidies much like bound tariffs, with country-by-country schedules indicating what is permissible, coupled with formulas for the phase down of permissible subsidies. The provision of the Agreement on Agriculture exempting agricultural subsidies from many of the disciplines of the SCMs Agreement – the so-called peace clause in Article 13 – has now expired. The future treatment of agricultural subsidies remains a central issue in the ongoing Doha Round. In what follows, we focus on the generally applicable disciplines on export subsidies and for the most part ignore the special provisions relating to agriculture.

Regarding export taxes, the history of the WTO/GATT system shows rather little attention to them. During negotiations between the United States and Britain over loans to Britain after the expiration of the Lend-Lease program – negotiations that were a precursor to GATT negotiations – the United States urged Britain to agree to abolish all export taxes. The British resisted, arguing that instead they should be the subject of case-by-case negotiations much like import tariffs. Later, in the London conference, the United States again put forward a proposal that would eliminate export taxes, but it was ultimately left out of the ensuing drafts of GATT.[108]

Members of GATT have always been free, however, to negotiate limits on export taxes just as they negotiate tariff bindings. Historically, however, such limits have proved to be of little importance. The major exception relates to the negotiations between WTO members and China regarding China's accession. China agreed not to use export taxes on most goods, and preserved its rights to use them subject to a ceiling on a list of other goods contained in Annex 6 to the Protocol.

3.6.2 The Rationale (or Lack Thereof) in Modern Economic Theory

The SCM Agreement in the WTO represents a considerable strengthening of the disciplines on subsidies in comparison to those that were present in GATT.

---

[107] GATT, 9th Supp. BISD 185 (1961).
[108] Genesis, pp. 69–70, 136.

Indeed, except as otherwise provided in the Agreement on Agriculture, export subsidies are completely prohibited in the SCM Agreement. By contrast, and as we discuss in detail above, import tariffs are legal under WTO rules, and governments undertake voluntary negotiations to lower the tariff bindings that they apply to one another. The differing treatments of import tariffs and export subsidies in the WTO would seem to suggest that the economic case for disciplines on export subsidies must be stronger than that for import tariffs. We argue below, however, that this conclusion does not follow from the terms-of-trade theory of trade agreements; in fact, if anything, the terms-of-trade theory suggests that export subsidies should be treated with *greater* leniency than import tariffs. From the perspective of this theory, we may thus regard the treatment of export subsidies in the WTO as somewhat puzzling.[109]

After developing this conclusion, we discuss alternative perspectives concerning the appropriate treatment of export subsidies. As we explain, many of these perspectives come into play when the assumptions of our model are relaxed. We also discuss a model with two-way trade of a homogeneous good in which trade policies generate firm-delocation effects. An important feature of this model is that it generates predictions that offer a partial interpretation of the treatment of export subsidies in the WTO. The model, however, has some special features and does not apply to all markets. We conclude the Section by discussing the economic effects of export tariffs. While export tariffs can be attractive unilateral instruments for governments that maximize national welfare, the use of export tariffs is relatively rare. We discuss possible reasons that export tariffs are not more often used and consider as well potential implications of export tariffs for the terms-of-trade theory of trade agreements.

3.6.2.1 *Export subsidies*

We begin by considering export subsidies, first in the standard economic two-country model that we have explored above, and then in a sequence of alternative models that permit further exploration of some relevant considerations.

Export Subsidies in a Two-Country Model   Let us again consider the economic model described in Section 3.2 with two (large) countries and two goods and perfectly competitive markets, except that we now suppose that governments select export policies rather than import policies. In particular, we imagine that the government of the home country selects an export subsidy for the export good of the home country while the government of the foreign country likewise selects an export subsidy for the export good of the foreign country. In the event that a government selects a negative export subsidy, we may understand that the government in fact has selected an export tariff.

---

[109] Our discussion here is related to and extends Bagwell (2008).

We now come to a key observation: an increase in a country's export subsidy has the same effect on local and world prices as does a decrease in a country's import tariff.[110] To see why, recall that a decrease in a country's import tariff induces a terms-of-trade loss for the country (and thus a terms-of-trade gain for its trading partner) and also implies a fall in the local price of the import good relative to the local price of the export good. Now consider the effects on local and world prices of an increase in a country's export subsidy. The country's export good then becomes more abundant on the world market, and so the world price of the export good falls. An increase in a country's export subsidy thus induces a deterioration in the terms of trade for the subsidizing country, and hence generates a terms-of-trade gain for its trading partner. In addition, a higher export subsidy makes the export good more scarce in the domestic market; consequently, an increase in a country's export subsidy causes the local price of a country's import good to fall relative to the local price of its export good. We conclude that an export-subsidy increase has the same effect on relative local and world prices – and thus on domestic and foreign government welfare – as does an import tariff decrease.

Given this equivalence, we may easily restate our earlier conclusions about the rationale for and design of a trade agreement for the setting in which governments select export policies as opposed to import policies. In particular, when governments choose export policies, the terms-of-trade theory of trade agreements indicates that governments would mutually benefit from a trade agreement that facilitates a reciprocal *increase* in export subsidies. Intuitively, when a government selects its optimal unilateral trade policy, it does not internalize the terms-of-trade externality that its policy imposes on the government of the other country. In the absence of a trade agreement, governments thus "over-supply" policies that induce a terms-of-trade loss for the trading partner and "under-supply" policies that generate for the trading partner a terms-of-trade gain. Hence, unilateral import tariffs are too high when governments select import policies, and unilateral export subsidies are too low when governments select export policies.

As regards export policy, the general point here is that, in the absence of a trade agreement, governments do not promote exports to the extent that would be efficient, where again efficiency is measured relative to the preferences of governments. For this point, whether governments select export tariffs or export subsidies is not fundamental. If they select export subsidies when policies are set unilaterally, then they could achieve mutual gains if higher export subsidies were agreed upon. Alternatively, if their unilateral export policies are export

---

[110] This is an instance of the Lerner symmetry theorem. We discuss this theorem in further detail below.

tariffs, then they could achieve mutual gains by adopting lower export tariffs or perhaps even export subsidies.

A couple of examples may be helpful. Suppose first that a government maximizes the national welfare of its country. The optimal unilateral export policy is then an export tariff. Intuitively, national welfare is maximized if the export industry produces the same export output as would a monopolist, as then the export industry effectively monopolizes foreign consumers. Since the export industry is in fact perfectly competitive, the export volume provided by this industry under free trade exceeds the monopoly output. With an appropriately selected export tariff, however, a government can induce its export sector to produce a lower export volume and thereby guide the export volume down to the monopoly level. The monopoly profits in this case are retained in the form of tariff revenue. Notice that the export tariff raises the price of the export good on the world market and thereby effects a terms-of-trade improvement for the exporting country. If the other government also maximizes national welfare, then in the absence of a trade agreement it would also select an export tariff. The governments' unilateral export policies then support monopoly trade volumes for each good. It is thus not surprising that both governments would benefit if they were to form a trade agreement and expand trade volume by reducing export tariffs. Indeed, given that both governments maximize national welfare, an efficient trade agreement would set export policies at free trade.

Our second example is similar, except that we now suppose that each government values the profit of firms in the export sector more heavily than it values government revenue and consumer welfare. We can imagine that a government with political–economic motivations might have such preferences. If a government with these preferences offers an export subsidy, then the local price of the export good rises. On domestically traded units, this price increase amounts to a transfer from domestic consumers to producers of the export good. Similarly, on internationally traded units, the export subsidy results in a transfer from the treasury to the export industry. For a politically motivated government, the transfers associated with a higher local price for the export good generate a net welfare gain that must be balanced against the loss in government welfare that is attributable to the fall in national welfare that accompanies the ensuing deterioration in the country's terms of trade. If the government's political motivations are sufficiently strong, then the government's unilaterally optimal export policy would be an export subsidy. In this case, a trade agreement would call for an even larger export subsidy, in recognition of the benefit that a lower world price would bring to foreign consumers of the domestic export good.

In light of our discussion to this point, trade-agreement rules that serve to *limit* trade volumes are perplexing. Under the terms-of-trade theory of trade agreements, whether the governments of large countries select import or export policies, they use their policies in part to exercise market power, and as a consequence unilateral trade policies result in trade volumes that are lower than would be efficient for governments. Accordingly, governments can enjoy mutual gains if they form a trade agreement that encourages greater rather than less trade volume. Viewed in this light, the WTO prohibition of export subsidies is puzzling.

Export Subsidies in a Competing-Exporters Model with Perfect Competition Our discussion above emphasizes that an export subsidy offered by one country generates a lower world price for consumers in the other country. An export subsidy then generates a positive terms-of-trade externality for the other country. In this setting, it is perhaps not surprising that governments acting independently "under-supply" export subsidies relative to the level that would maximize their joint welfare. A limitation of the two-country model, though, is that it does not include the negative international externality that an export subsidy offered in one country implies for another country with competing exporters. We thus now extend our modeling framework to allow for three countries, so that we may consider competing exporters from different countries.

To convey the main ideas, we utilize a simple three-country model with competing exporters. In particular, let us suppose that countries A and B both have perfectly competitive export sectors that supply a given product to country C. Let us suppose further that all consumers are located in country C. This model is sometimes called a "third-country model," and it is useful as a simple setting within which to consider the role of strategic export policies when international competition occurs between exporters from different countries. In line with our discussion above, we suppose that the governments of countries A and B have political–economic preferences, in that each government places greater weight in its welfare function on the profit of its export industry than on its subsidy expenses. As before, if this weight is sufficiently large, then the optimal unilateral policy for each government is an export subsidy. For simplicity, we assume that the government of country C refrains from using an import tariff and simply follows a policy of free trade.

In this model, when a country uses an export subsidy, the sign of the terms-of-trade externality varies depending on which of the other two countries that one considers. Suppose that the government of country A or B offers an export subsidy. This depresses the price of the export good on the world market. Then, as in the two-country model discussed above, the importing country (i.e., country C) enjoys a terms-of-trade gain. At the same time, the other exporting country suffers a terms-of-trade loss.

Having discussed unilateral export policies, let us now consider the possibility of a trade agreement. A first possibility is that the governments of countries A and B form a trade agreement that reflects their joint interests. The governments can achieve mutual gains from a trade agreement in which they limit their use of export subsidies. With such an agreement, they internalize the negative terms-of-trade externality that they impose on one another with their export subsidies. The exact level at which the trade agreement caps export subsidies depends on the specific weights that the governments of countries A and B place upon export interests in their welfare functions. We can be sure, though, that the agreement results in a reciprocal reduction in export subsidies as compared to the export subsidies that these governments would select in the absence of a trade agreement. Importantly, while the governments of countries A and B gain from their trade agreement, the government of country C loses.[111] Consumers in country C pay a higher price for the good once the trade agreement is in place.

A second possibility is that the governments of all three countries form a trade agreement so as to maximize their combined welfare. A trade agreement would then also internalize the positive terms-of-trade externality that export subsidies induce for country C. Bagwell and Staiger (2001) examine a model of this kind with linear demands and supplies. In a trade agreement that maximizes the combined welfare of all three governments, they find that the agreed-upon export policies lead to greater trade volume than occurs when governments set their policies unilaterally. Thus, and in line with our finding for the two-country model, a trade agreement that is mutually beneficial to all governments calls for greater trade volume rather than less. Consequently, if governments use export subsidies when policies are set unilaterally, an efficient trade agreement for all governments would encourage even greater export subsidies.

Of the two possible trade agreements, the one that caps export subsidies and thus resembles the SCM Agreement is the first trade agreement. This is the agreement that reflects the interests of the governments of the exporting countries but not the interests of government of the importing country, and this agreement caps export subsidies at a level that is lower than would be efficient were consumer interests considered. The competing-exporters model thus suggests that an agreement to restrict export subsidies represents a victory for governments of exporting countries that comes at the expense of importing-country – and global – government welfare. An efficient agreement that also reflects the interests of consumers would call for more expansionary export policies than governments of exporting countries would otherwise provide.

Given these findings, if a rationale for a trade agreement that calls for less expansionary export policies is to be found, then the model must depart in some significant way from the competing-exporters model with perfectly competitive export industries. We consider next whether similar conclusions arise when exporting firms possess market power.

---

[111] For this simple model, we can imagine that the welfare function of the government of country C is described entirely by the welfare of consumers in country C.

Export Subsidies in a Competing-Exporters Model with Imperfect Competition We now follow Brander and Spencer (1985) and introduce market power into the competing-exporters model. In the simplest version of the Brander–Spencer model of strategic trade policies, country A has one exporting firm and country B likewise has one exporting firm. We can refer to these firms as firm A and firm B, respectively. After observing export policies in countries A and B, firms A and B select their respective output levels for export. For simplicity, we again assume that country C follows a policy of free trade when setting its import policy. Consumers in country C thus purchase the export good at the world price, which is set so that the demand in country C equals the overall supply of the export good from firms A and B.[112]

In this oligopoly model, a standard market-power distortion is present. In particular, the market-clearing price exceeds the marginal cost of production, where we may assume for simplicity that firms A and B face the same marginal production cost (in the absence of any subsidy). From a world welfare point of view, then, the presence of oligopolist market power ensures that the market provides too little output. This market distortion arises under free trade, and we thus refer to it as a "pre-existing" market distortion.

Suppose now that the governments of countries A and B, which we now refer to as governments A and B, respectively, maximize national welfare. If government B adopts an export policy of free trade, what is the optimal unilateral export policy for government A? The introduction of an export subsidy has three effects. First, the subsidy is a transfer from country A's treasury to firm A. Holding fixed the output levels of firms A and B, this transfer itself has no effect on government A's welfare, given our assumption that government A maximizes national welfare.[113] The second effect is that firm A produces a greater output when its effective marginal cost is lowered due to the export subsidy. Holding fixed the output level of firm B, this own-output effect actually lowers slightly government A's welfare. The reason is that a policy of free trade induces firm A to produce the output level that maximizes unsubsidized profit on exports and that thus maximizes the national welfare of country A. A slight export subsidy causes firm A to produce a slightly larger output and thereby introduces a "second-order" loss to government A's welfare. If there were no rival firm in country B, so that firm A is a monopoly exporter, then we would stop here and conclude that free trade

---

[112] In other words, firms A and B are Cournot competitors for sales to consumers in country C.

[113] It should also be noted that our implicit assumption here is that governments have available a lump-sum tax instrument with which to raise revenue in order to fund any export subsidy. This is of course a strong assumption, but we proceed for now under this assumption since our purpose is to focus on the effects of an export subsidy on international oligopolistic competition. We return to this assumption below, when we acknowledge and discuss omitted considerations.

is the optimal export policy for government A. But the presence of firm B introduces a novel third effect, which is strategic in nature. Specifically, when firm A receives an export subsidy, it becomes more aggressive in the sense that it is more inclined to produce a greater output. Consequently, for any output that firm B might contemplate, firm B now anticipates a lower world price for its sales. For a large set of demand functions, this implies in turn that firm B's best response is to reduce its output somewhat. This is an advantageous reaction from firm A's and similarly government A's point of view that has the effect of "shifting profit" from country B to country A. This strategic benefit represents a "first-order" gain to government A from a small export subsidy and ensures that government A's optimal unilateral export subsidy is positive, when it expects that government B will adopt an export policy of free trade.

Of course, government B can also play this game. When governments A and B simultaneously select their export subsidy levels, the resulting "Nash" equilibrium in export policies involves both governments behaving strategically and subsidizing exports. From the point of view of the exporting countries, the end result is not appealing: export subsidies from governments A and B lead to greater export volumes from firms A and B, depress the world price, and thus decrease true (unsubsidized) profit for countries A and B. In short, and as in the third-country model with competitive exporters above, exporting countries suffer a terms-of-trade loss and reduced national welfare when they embark on export-subsidization programs. Governments A and B thus have strong incentive to form a trade agreement, in which they prohibit the use of export subsidies. Such an agreement would generate a terms-of-trade gain for exporting countries, corresponding to the increased national profits that would be enjoyed on exports.

Once again, though, it is important to consider the impact of such an agreement on consumers as well. Clearly, an agreement to prohibit export subsidies would raise the world price and thereby hurt consumers in country C. Indeed, if a trade agreement were formed with the goal of maximizing global welfare (i.e., the joint welfare of governments A, B, and C), then the agreement would feature a floor on export subsidies rather than a ceiling. This is because the market is initially distorted, with too little output.

The Brander–Spencer model of strategic export subsidies provides a possible interpretation for why governments may be tempted to offer unilateral export subsidies, while allowing that governments maximize national welfare.[114] The theory also explains why governments of exporting countries might gain from

---

[114] The prediction that the optimal unilateral export policy is an export subsidy may fail when other oligopoly models are considered or when other market structures are considered. See Eaton and Grossman (1986) for a model with price competition and differentiated products, in which the optimal unilateral export policy is an export tariff. See Brander (1995) for a survey of the strategic-trade literature.

an agreement to restrict the use of export subsidies. But in this model such an agreement would again lower consumer – and world – welfare.

Summarizing, whether governments have political–economic preferences and export markets are perfectly competitive or governments maximize national welfare and export markets are imperfectly competitive, governments of exporting countries may have an incentive in the absence of a trade agreement to offer export subsidies; furthermore, governments of exporting countries may also have incentive to form an agreement that prohibits the use of export subsidies. Such an agreement would harm consumer welfare in importing countries. In the described models, such an agreement would also lead to a reduction in total government welfare.

We now return to an issue raised at the beginning of this Section: the differing treatments of import tariffs and export subsidies in the WTO would seem to suggest that the economic case for disciplines on export subsidies must be stronger than that for import tariffs. Our discussion above confirms that this conclusion does not follow from the competing-exporter extensions of the terms-of-trade theory of trade agreements. Indeed, if anything, this theory suggests that export subsidies should be treated with *greater* leniency than import tariffs. Accordingly, the treatment of export subsidies in the SCM Agreement is somewhat puzzling from the perspective of this theory.

Further Considerations in Competing-Exporters Models   It is important to emphasize that the competing-exporters models presented above make a number of strong assumptions and thus may ignore important considerations. Here, we highlight and discuss a few of these omitted considerations.

First, in the competing-exporters models described above, the importing country does not have an import-competing industry. If there were an import-competing industry in country C, and if government C had political–economic preferences such that it weighed heavily the well-being of its import-competing industry, then it is possible that export subsidies offered by governments A and B would lead to a welfare loss for government C. To see the point, let us suppose that country C imposes a small import tariff, so that we may distinguish between the terms-of-trade and local-price effects for country C of the export subsidies that governments A and B provide. Export subsidies generate a reduction in the local price in country C as well as a terms-of-trade gain for country C. For government C, it is possible that the welfare gain of a terms-of-trade improvement may be smaller than the welfare loss of diminished import-competing profits that accompanies a fall in the local price. In this case, export subsidies would generate a negative international externality for government C, on balance.

This is certainly a valid point, but it also has a couple of limitations. One limitation is that the government of an importing country can experience an overall welfare loss from foreign export subsidies that improve its terms of trade only if it has bound its import tariff at a level that is sufficiently far below its optimal unilateral tariff.[115] A second limitation is that the importing government has the option of responding to export subsidies by imposing a countervailing duty. If the countervailing duty is set so as to offset the export subsidies and restore the local price in the importing country to its original (pre-subsidy) level, then the government of the importing country must gain. Simply, following the introduction of a countervailing duty of this kind, the importing country maintains its original local price and enjoys a terms-of-trade gain. The importing country's terms-of-trade gain takes the form of an increase in tariff revenue.

A second omitted consideration is that the competing-exporter models do not include all of the welfare costs that are associated with export subsidies. For example, export subsidies may distort the allocation of production across firms and possibly divert production from more efficient firms to less efficient firms. Also, in some cases, preexisting market distortions may be exacerbated rather than diminished by the use of export subsidies. A further potential welfare cost is that a program of export subsidization may encourage wasteful rent-seeking behavior.

All of these welfare costs are potentially important, and we do not intend to minimize their significance. We do have two comments, however. One comment is that similar welfare costs are associated with the use of import tariffs; thus, it is not clear that these additional welfare costs offer an interpretation for a more aggressive treatment in the WTO of export subsidies than of import tariffs. A further comment is that we take the view that a role for a trade agreement arises if it enables governments to achieve mutual gains in welfare relative to the welfare that they would enjoy in the absence of a trade agreement. This orientation directs our attention to the international externalities that are associated with trade policies and also to the possibility that a trade agreement may enable a government to make commitments to its private sector. From this perspective, the various potential welfare costs of export subsidies provide insight into the purpose and design of a trade agreement insofar as governments are unable to address these costs without a trade agreement.

A third omitted consideration is that a prohibition of export subsidies may make negotiated market-access concessions more secure and predictable, and thereby increase the willingness of governments to exchange reciprocal tariff concessions in the first place.[116] The value to a government of a reciprocal exchange of tariff concessions is the additional access that its exporters enjoy to the foreign market. Negotiations leading to reciprocal tariff liberalization are thus more likely to succeed when the rules of the broader trade agreement work

---

[115] A government must gain when it sets its import tariff at the unilaterally optimal level and then enjoys a terms-of-trade gain as a consequence of changes in the trade policies of other governments. For a formal demonstration, see Bagwell and Staiger (2002, p. 192).
[116] For additional discussion of this possibility, see Sykes (2005, 2010).

to increase the security of negotiated market-access concessions. An export subsidy offered by a country with competing exporters could undermine the market access that a government obtained in a previous negotiation. While the immediate effect of an export subsidy might be beneficial to the government of the importing country, it is conceivable that even this government could lose if the potential for export subsidies served to undermine reciprocal tariff liberalization in the first instance. Our discussion here is broadly related to our comments above about the benefits of rules that limit "concession erosion." Relatedly, and in line with our discussion above concerning the benefits of "tariffication," we note that the potential for governments to use export subsidies may also undermine tariff negotiations, by expanding the set of trade-policy instruments and making the outcomes of tariff negotiations less predictable.

The possible negative effect on tariff-liberalization negotiations of a permissive stance toward export subsidies is potentially important and has not received adequate attention in the economics literature. Accepting that such a negative effect may exist, one might still ask whether the appropriate legal response is a blanket prohibition on export subsidies. A different approach, for example, might adopt a less absolutist stance toward export subsidies but encourage governments to file nonviolation complaints when their negotiated access to a market is nullified or impaired by the introduction of an export subsidy offered by a third party.[117] This approach may be challenging to implement, however, as it requires measurement of the market access lost as a consequence of the export subsidy received by foreign exporters.

The fourth and final omitted consideration that we will mention concerns fairness.[118] While any government can impose an import tariff, governments may differ significantly with regard to their ability to finance export subsidies. Countries with well-functioning systems of taxation or with the capacity to borrow at attractive rates have the ability to raise funds in order to finance an export-subsidization program. For other countries, however, the social cost of funds may be so high as to make an export-subsidization program practically infeasible. This consideration suggests one possible interpretation of a system that

[117] See Bagwell and Mavroidis (2010) for further discussion of this approach. See Bagwell and Staiger (2010b) for a formal analysis of the role of nonviolation complaints when a government negotiates with different partners over time.
[118] As we describe more fully in the text, this consideration seems to be present in arguments that call for the elimination of rich-country agricultural export subsidies on the grounds that farmers from poor agricultural exporting countries cannot expect similar help from their governments. We observe, though, that if trade agreements were expected more generally to serve governments that exhibited internationally interdependent utility functions of this kind, where one government cares directly about welfare of the citizens of another country, then the entire structure of the trade agreement – and whether it could even be called a "trade" agreement – would likely be vastly different than what we see in the WTO/GATT.

treats export subsidies more aggressively than import tariffs. At the same time, the same countries that find export subsidization infeasible may benefit when export subsidies are given to some of the goods that they import, and so it is again not obvious that a blanket prohibition on export subsidies is the optimal response.

Export Subsidies and Firm-Delocation Effects The competing-exporters model with imperfect competition highlights the role that export subsidies may play in "shifting profits" across exporting countries. In our discussion of imperfect competition in Section 3.2 of this study, we note that trade policies can also have "firm-delocation" effects. We now discuss a model with firm-delocation effects that offers a partial interpretation of WTO disciplines on export subsidies.

Following Venables (1985), we may imagine a two-country model with two-way trade in a single homogeneous good. In this model, the government of each country selects an import policy and an export policy. After the policies are set, firms endogenously locate in the domestic and foreign markets. Once the number of firms in each market is determined, each firm decides on a quantity of output to sell in its home-country market and also a quantity of output to export to the market in the other country. In addition to the marginal costs of production, a firm must incur a per-unit transport cost on exported units. In each market, the price is then determined to equate consumer demand with the total supply for that market. A further assumption is that the markets are "segmented," which means that the price in one market responds to supply and demand conditions in that market and is otherwise free to vary independently of the price in the other market.[119] An important feature of this model is that entry is endogenous; thus, this model captures the manner in which trade policies might affect the entry decisions of firms into domestic and foreign markets, where competition in these markets is imperfect and takes the form of quantity or "Cournot" competition as just described. In this model, if a government raises its import tariff or export subsidy, then it encourages entry into the domestic market and exit from the foreign market. In this way, such policies "delocate" firms from the foreign country to the home country. We can thus refer to this model as the "Cournot delocation model" of trade policy.

As Venables (1985) shows, in the Cournot delocation model, free trade is not an optimal unilateral trade policy for a government that maximizes national welfare. Indeed, if all trade policies in both countries are initially set at free trade, then a government generates a welfare gain for its country when it introduces

---

[119] By contrast, in an "integrated" market, the possibility of arbitrage ensures that any price difference across markets equals the total trade cost (i.e., the sum of any trade taxes and the transport cost). The monopolistic competition model explored by Venables (1987) and discussed previously assumes that markets are integrated.

a small import tariff and also when it introduces a small export subsidy. These policies, however, generate welfare losses in the other country. When demand and cost functions take linear forms, Bagwell and Staiger (2009c) characterize the optimal unilateral or "Nash" policies for governments. They find that optimal unilateral policies entail the use of both import and export tariffs. Thus, while a small export subsidy may generate a welfare gain for the subsidizing country when all other trade policies are set at free trade, an export subsidy is not used when both countries select their import and export policies without restriction. A further finding is that free trade in import and export policies is efficient in the linear Cournot delocation model.

Together, these findings suggest a potential interpretation of the evolution of WTO/GATT subsidy rules. In particular, the model suggests that governments would have unilateral incentive to use export subsidies only once import tariffs have been negotiated to low levels that approximate free trade. With import tariffs bound at low levels, each government has an incentive to use an export subsidy as the preferred means of engineering firm delocation. As free trade is an efficient outcome in the linear Cournot delocation model, the governments could achieve mutual gains when import tariffs are bound at low levels if they were to cap – and even prohibit – the use of export subsidies. This story fits well with the fact that prohibition on export subsidies found in the SCM Agreement of the WTO followed several GATT rounds of significant reductions in import tariffs. At the same time, the model also predicts that governments would benefit by reaching an agreement in which they prohibit import tariffs, and so it does not provide an interpretation for why WTO rules treat export subsidies in a more aggressive manner than import tariffs.

The linear Cournot delocation model offers a partial rationalization for WTO export subsidy rules. The model explains why governments might seek to cap and even prohibit export subsidies, once import tariffs have been negotiated to a sufficiently low level; however, it does not explain why export subsidies are treated more aggressively than import tariffs. It is also important to emphasize that this model does not apply to all markets. In particular, the model posits that firms have market power and engage in Cournot competition and that markets are segmented. Each of these assumptions is strong. One implication of these assumptions is that two-way trade occurs in a homogeneous good; thus, in markets without trade of this kind, the model may not apply. Additionally, governments in this model are focused on the long run. A government chooses its trade policies with a view as to their effects on the entry and exit decisions of firms, which in turn determine prices and thus consumer welfare in the domestic country. Governments focused on the short-run effects of trade policy may be more interested in transitional profit-shifting effects that occur en route to the new long-run equilibrium. Despite these limitations, the model may capture aspects of the reasoning of those who are attentive to the firm-delocation effects of export subsidies and recommend a prohibition of export subsidies on this basis.

3.6.2.2 *Export tariffs*

We return now to our standard economic model, in which two (large) countries trade two goods and supply is generated by perfectly competitive industries. In this model, if a government maximizes national welfare, then as we note above the optimal unilateral export policy for the government is an export tariff. In practice, though, while export tariffs are sometimes observed, they are not frequently observed. What accounts for the infrequent use of export tariffs?

One possible answer to this question is that governments do not maximize national welfare. As we explain above, when a government has political–economic preferences and puts extra weight on the well-being of its export industry, then the optimal unilateral policy for the government may be an export subsidy. A second potential answer is also apparent in our discussion above. Specifically, even if governments maximize national welfare, if the export industry is oligopolistic, then in some cases the optimal unilateral export policy is an export subsidy. Export subsidies may also be attractive for governments in the presence of other market imperfections. For instance, the optimal unilateral export policy for a government may be an export subsidy when foreign consumers are uninformed about the quality of the domestic export good, or when firms face common uncertainty about the profitability of exporting to a foreign market. Finally, while governments do not often impose taxes on exports, they may nevertheless achieve a comparable restriction on export volumes through other means. We note in particular that many countries, including the United States, have domestic laws that adopt a relatively permissive stance toward export cartels. An effective export cartel achieves a restriction in export volume, just as does an export tariff, and retains the associated monopoly rents as profit (rather than as tariff revenue).

For the standard economic model with two goods, two countries and perfectly competitive industries, we mention above that an increase in a country's export subsidy has the same effect on local and world prices as would an equivalent reduction in that country's import tariff. Building on this point, we see that any negotiated reduction in a country's import tariff could be "undone" by an equivalent decrease in that country's export subsidy (or by an equivalent increase in that country's export tariff). An import-tariff reduction triggers a terms-of-trade loss and causes the local price of the import good to fall relative to the local price of the export good, while an export-subsidy reduction generates a terms-of-trade gain and makes the local price of the import good rise relative to the local price of the export good. As Ethier (2004) argues, if the terms-of-trade theory is correct, then negotiations that focus on reductions in import tariffs may be ineffective unless the agreement also prevents governments from undoing the effects of their import-policy concessions with offsetting changes in their export policies. Since governments are not restricted from using export tariffs in the WTO, Ethier questions the relevance of the terms-of-trade approach to trade agreements.

Ethier's argument builds from a famous principle known as "Lerner symmetry." This principle holds that a government only needs $n-1$ trade-policy instruments when n goods are traded. In our discussion above, we focus on the simple case of two goods. With $n = 2$ in that case, it follows that a government needs only one trade-policy instrument. As our discussion above indicates, that instrument could be an import instrument or an export instrument. In this context, a trade agreement that restricts import tariffs while imposing no restrictions on export tariffs or subsidies has, in effect, not restricted governments' abilities to manipulate local and world prices. The two-good model offers a simple and useful framework within which to develop a range of ideas; however, this model is somewhat special with regard to its prediction that a country's import and export tariffs are completely interchangeable. If instead the two countries traded $n >$ 2 goods in total, and each government bound its import tariffs through negotiations, then the remaining export instruments available to each government would in general not enable the government to undo the economic effects of its import-tariff bindings. Interesting future work might consider multi-good models in more detail and explore the degree to which export-policy adjustments might be used to undo some of the economic effects that are associated with import-tariff negotiations.[120]

3.7 The Case Law on Export Policies

3.7.1 Export Subsidies

The most prominent feature of WTO law on export subsidies, following the entry into force of the SCMs Agreement, is the general prohibition on them. This prohibition completes a lengthy process during which the rules on export subsidies have been steadily tightened. At the inception of GATT, the only restraints on subsidies involved a little-enforced reporting requirement in Article XVI, and the

---

[120] In this regard, notice also that in the two-good model where Ethier's (2004) critique has full force, Lerner Symmetry implies that both the local- and world-price effects of an import tariff can be replicated by an export tax, as we have observed. But this implies that *all* economic effects of a negotiated binding on the import tariff could be undone by adjustments in the export tax if the export tax were not also constrained, not just the terms-of-trade effects; and so this critique would apply not just to the terms-of-trade theory, but equally to any theory of trade agreements that claims that such agreements have economic value to the member governments.

authority for importing nations to use countervailing duties under Article VI (an authority which, by the way, was employed relatively infrequently). Some limits on export subsidies were introduced into Article XVI by the 1955 review and by the Tokyo Round Code, but accepted by only a portion of the membership as noted earlier. The outright prohibition of export subsidies throughout the system (excepting agriculture under the peace clause) was not imposed until the end of the Uruguay Round.

An important question is: Why are export subsidies prohibited, and is the prohibition sound as a policy matter? Unlike the WTO/GATT treatment of other border instruments that we have considered in this study, the WTO prohibition of export subsidies presents a puzzle for economic theory, as we have detailed in Section 3.6. In particular, using the terms-of-trade theory of trade agreements, we find that it is possible to provide a partial interpretation of the evolution of WTO/GATT subsidy rules from the perspective of the terms-of-trade theory, but this interpretation can only account for some of the salient features of the treatment of export subsidies that we observe, and it arises only under conditions that are quite special. More generally, we suggest that from the perspective of the terms-of-trade theory, the prohibition of export subsidies is puzzling. Accordingly, our answer to the second part of this question is that there is reason to be skeptical about the soundness of the WTO/GATT prohibition of export subsidies as a policy matter. Regarding the first part of this question, we have described in Section 3.6 how according to the terms-of-trade theory it is no mystery that exporting governments would support agreements to limit export subsidies. Therefore, in answer to the first part of this question, we conjecture that efforts to use the WTO/GATT as a means to restrict export subsidies may represent a victory for governments of exporting countries that comes at the expense of importing-country – and global – government welfare.[121]

With these caveats in mind, in the remainder of this Section, we consider some of the more important issues that arise in the implementation of the prohibition on export subsidies.

---

[121] Our discussion here has abstracted from political–economy forces in import-competing sectors to emphasize how such forces in export sectors can provide a reason for governments to subsidize their exports. But our conclusions about the treatment of export subsidies in trade agreements remains valid in the presence of import-competing political–economy pressures provided that importing governments are permitted to respond to export subsidies with import tariffs to offset the impacts of these export subsidies on the local prices in their markets if they so desire. Hence, while our discussion leads to the conclusion that the WTO/GATT prohibition on export subsidies is puzzling, it is important to be clear that allowable *importer-country* responses to export subsidies such as countervailing duties do not present a puzzle from the perspective of the terms-of-trade theory.

Financial Contribution and Benefit As with all "subsidies," an export subsidy arises only if a government makes a "financial contribution" that provides a "benefit." SCMs Article 1. In most cases these requirements are easily met, but at times issues of interpretation can arise.

Suppose, for example, that a government borrows money at 4% per annum, and lends to private firms for export financing at 5% – does the fact that the program makes money for the government insulate it from attack as a subsidy? It might be argued that under these circumstances the government has made no "financial contribution," or that no government "benefit" is being conferred. In *Canada–Aircraft*,[122] however, the Appellate Body rejected this line of thinking in holding that the provision of funding is a "financial contribution" and that a "benefit" arises if the government program affords better terms to the recipient than are available in the market. The decision reinforced the long-standing practice under GATT to the effect that subsidies disciplines focus not on the cost of a program to the government, but on its benefits to recipients.[123]

The existence of a benefit to the recipient is necessary but not sufficient for a subsidy to arise. For example, in the long-running softwood lumber dispute between the United States and Canada, the United States took the position that log export restrictions imposed by Canada – which had the effect of depressing log prices in Canada and thus conferring a competitive advantage on Canadian lumber processors – confer a countervailable subsidy. An unappealed Panel Report held, however, that no subsidy existed because the government provided no "financial contribution" to Canadian processors.[124] In that case, of course, any subsidy would have been a domestic rather than export subsidy, but a similar issue can arise with regard to allegations of export subsidization. For example, if a government intervenes in currency markets to reduce the price of its currency, could that be deemed an export subsidy when no "financial contribution" has been made to an exporting firm?[125] Likewise, consider a case in which exported goods are exempted from compliance with regulations that apply to similar goods destined for the domestic market. It seems clear that no "subsidy" would exist there given the "financial contribution" requirement.

Another difficult issue under WTO subsidies law, which has arisen in the context of export-subsidies disputes, concerns the issue of when government

---

[122] *Canada – Measures Affecting the Export of Civilian Aircraft*, WT/DS70/AB/R, Appellate Body Report adopted August 20, 1999, paras. 149–161.

[123] Note the special rules in SCMs Annex I, items (j) and (k), regarding "export credit guarantee or insurance programmes" and "export credits," both of which make reference to the costs of such programs to the government.

[124] *United States – Measures Treating Exports Restraints as Subsidies*, WT/DS194/R, Panel Report adopted August 23, 2001.

[125] Other issues arise here as well, such as the proper interpretation of the specificity requirement.

tax policy results in a "financial contribution" by way of a government forego-
ing "revenue that is otherwise due." (see SCMs Art. 1.) *United States–Foreign
Sales Corporations* (FSC) raises the issue squarely. In that case, the Appellate
Body determined that the United States conferred a prohibited export subsidy
by reducing the taxation of income from export sales transactions engaged in by
certain foreign subsidiaries of U.S. companies relative to the taxation of other
income (such as investment income) earned by those same foreign subsidiaries.
Yet, the Appellate Body also noted that the United States was under no obligation to tax the foreign income of U.S. subsidiaries at all, and could have chosen
not to do so without running afoul of the SCMs Agreement.[126] Thus, a complete
exemption from taxation for income earned by the foreign subsidiaries at issue
would be unproblematic under WTO law, while a partial exemption is illegal,
even though the former would seem to confer a greater benefit than the latter.
The case illustrates a more general and fundamental problem with the notion
of a tax subsidy. When one firm pays less tax than another (or some activities of
a firm pay less tax than other activities, as in the FSC case), is the firm that pays
a lower tax "subsidized," or is the firm that pays the higher tax simply "taxed" at a
higher rate? In other words, which tax rate applies as the benchmark for deciding
whether revenue "otherwise due" has been forgone?

Distinguishing Domestic and Export Subsidies – The Illustrative List In
domestic subsidies cases, often difficult issues arise as to whether the subsidy
is "specific" under WTO law. If the subsidy is an export subsidy, however, it is
automatically "specific" and subject to discipline (indeed, prohibited).

As an aid to the identification of export subsidies, Annex I to the SCMs Agreement reflects the current version of the "illustrative list" of export subsidies first
devised by a 1960 GATT working party. The list makes clear that export subsidies
can be conferred through mechanisms other than direct bounties for exportation. Examples include preferential prices for government-supplied goods and
services used to produce exports, preferential internal transport charges on
goods for exportation, tax exemptions for export earnings or export production, and programs that offer preferential currency conversion rates on foreign
exchange derived from export earnings.

Although the characterization of a program as an export subsidy is often
straightforward, subtle issues can arise, many of which have never been fully
resolved. For example, footnote 4 to the SCMs Agreement provides that a subsidy
can be "contingent" on export performance in a *de facto* sense. The mere fact that
a company is engaged in export trade is not enough to make every subsidy that

---

[126] *United States – Tax Treatment for "Foreign Sales Corporations,"* WT/DS108/AB/R, Appellate Body Report adopted March 20, 2000.

it receives into an export subsidy according to the note, but what sort of circumstances would justify a finding of *de facto* export contingency? In the compliance review in *Canada–Civilian Aircraft*, Brazil argued that Canada's revised financing program was an export subsidy because it "specifically targeted" Canada's regional aircraft industry due to its "high export orientation." In other words, the claim was that even if subsidies to Canadian aircraft manufacturers were not formally contingent on or limited to exports, the subsidies were motivated by the fact that the Canadian industry exported much of its output. The Appellate Body held, however, that "the fact that an industrial sector has a high export orientation is not, by itself, sufficient to preclude that sector from being expressly identified as an eligible or privileged recipient of subsidies."[127] The decision nevertheless leaves open the question of what does constitute *de facto* export contingency.

It is also important to bear in mind that the list in Annex I is illustrative and not exhaustive, and that programs may confer export subsidies even if they are not of the types specifically described in the Annex. In *Canada–Autos*, Canada had a system in place whereby automobile manufacturers could import vehicles for sale in Canada duty free if they met certain requirements with respect to their domestic production of automobiles. Among these were certain "ratio requirements," whereunder companies could only import vehicles duty free as long as the ratio of their domestic production of vehicles to their total sales of vehicles exceeded a specified threshold. The logical implication of this system was that the more vehicles a company produced in Canada and exported, the more vehicles it could import duty free (for sale in Canada). The Appellate Body found that the import-duty exemption was a financial contribution in the form of the forgone revenue, and that it was contingent on export performance and therefore a prohibited subsidy.[128]

Tax Rebates and Duty Drawbacks   GATT Article VI provides that no product shall be subject to a countervailing duty "by reason of the exemption of such product from duties or taxes borne by the like product when destined for consumption in the country of origin or exportation, or by reason of the refund of such duties or taxes." Thus, goods for export can be exempted from domestic taxes and duties "borne by" the like product when it is sold in the home market. This exemption from countervailing duties has evolved into a general understanding that these tax and duty exemptions (or refunds) do not confer subsidies at all.

The question then becomes, what taxes and duties are "borne by" the like product? The general understanding on such issues is embodied in Annex I to

---

[127] WT/DS70/AB/RW, Appellate Body Report adopted August 4, 2000, para. 49.
[128] WT/DS139 and 142/AB/R, Appellate Body Report adopted June 19, 2000.

the SCMs Agreement. Under item (e), an export subsidy is conferred by the exemption, remission, or deferral of "direct taxes or social welfare charges paid or payable by industrial or commercial enterprises." By implication, such direct taxes are not "borne by" the like product destined for the home market even if they are paid by producers of the product. Direct taxes include such items as income taxes, property taxes, and payroll taxes. Item (f) likewise provides that an export subsidy arises when the tax base for the computation of such taxes is affected by "special deductions directly related to exports or export performance."

By contrast, items (g) – (i) implicitly define the tax and duty rebates or exemptions that do *not* confer export subsidies. Item (g) says that an export subsidy arises from the remission or exemption of *indirect taxes* on exports *in excess of* those levied on like products sold in the home market. In other words, no export subsidy arises when exports are exempted from or receive a remission of indirect taxes that are paid on the like product sold at home as long as the exemption or remission does not exceed the amount of those taxes. Indirect taxes are defined as all taxes other than direct taxes and import charges, and include sales taxes, excise taxes, transfer taxes, and various others. Item (h) goes on to provide that an exemption or a remission of "prior stage cumulative indirect taxes" on exports is an export subsidy *unless* those taxes are levied on inputs "consumed in" the production of the exported product, in which case the exemption or remission is not an export subsidy. Finally, item (i) concerns the remission or drawback of import duties paid on inputs that are consumed in the production of the exported product – once again, such remissions do not confer an export subsidy as long as they do not exceed the duties paid on the inputs consumed.

The upshot of this system is that exports may be exempted from indirect taxes paid on like products sold in the home market, and may be exempted from indirect taxes and import charges paid on inputs into the exported product that are physically consumed in its production. Exemptions from direct taxes, however, are impermissible.

Thus, for example, exported products may be exempted from value-added taxes that would otherwise be payable when they are purchased, or such taxes may later be refunded to the purchaser. A nation that relies on value-added taxes for much of its revenue, therefore, can ensure that exports are not so taxed. A nation that relies heavily on income and payroll taxes to raise much of its revenue, by contrast, will not be able to provide associated tax exemptions for exports. The wisdom and consequences of such an arrangement have long been a source of controversy.

Remedies In general, the issues covered by the GATT provisions relating to subsidies and by the SCMs Agreement are subject to the ordinary principles of

WTO dispute settlement in the Dispute Settlement Understanding (DSU), sup-plemented by the "unilateral" option of countervailing duties against subsidized imports that cause or threaten material injury to import-competing firms. We will not address these general remedial provisions in this study, but note two issues of particular relevance to export subsidies.

First, suppose that a government grants a nonrecurring export subsidy, say, for the construction of a manufacturing facility that will produce exported goods. The subsidy is ruled to be a prohibited export subsidy, and thus a recommen-dation is issued to the effect that the subsidizing member "withdraw" the sub-sidy pursuant to SCMs Article 4.7. What is required for "withdrawal?" Ordinar-ily under WTO law, members are required to cease offending practices within a "reasonable period," but there is no obligation to "undo" what has occurred in the past. This feature of WTO dispute resolution raises a number of puzzles that apply in all types of cases. But these puzzles are particularly acute where, as hypothesized here, no ongoing practice exists that a violator can cease. One WTO Panel responded to this situation by ruling that an obligation existed on the part of the company that had received the subsidy to repay it.[129]

The second issue concerns the nature of the countermeasures allowed if a member fails to comply with adopted dispute recommendations within a rea-sonable period. The ordinary countermeasures under Article 22.4 of the DSU consist of the withdrawal of concessions or other obligations "equivalent to the level of nullification or impairment." Thus, in the usual case, a crude effort is made to limit the trade impact of countermeasures to a level more or less equivalent to the trade impact of the violation. Under SCMs Article 4.10, how-ever, the aggrieved nation is permitted to take "appropriate countermeasures" against prohibited subsidies, although accompanying footnote 9 provides that such countermeasures should not be "disproportionate." The dispute process has responded predictably to this difference in language, concluding that coun-termeasures against prohibited export subsidies are not restricted to be "equiv-alent to the level of nullification or impairment." One option in this regard has been to allow countermeasures in an amount based on the value of the subsidy, rather than the magnitude of its trade impact. See generally *Canada–Civilian Air-craft* and *United States–FSC*, noted earlier. The more recent arbitral decision in *United States – Subsidies on Upland Cotton*,[130] however, concluded that counter-measures should be linked to the trade harm done to the complainant even in a prohibited-subsidies case.

---

[129] See *Australia – Subsidies Provided to Producers and Exporters of Automotive Leather – Recourse to Article 21.5 of the DSU by the United States*, WT/DS126/RW, adopted February 11, 2000.

[130] *Recourse to Arbitration by the United States under Article 22.6 of the DSU and Article 4.11 of the SCM Agreement*, WT/DS267/ARB/1, August 31, 2009.

3.7.2 Export Tariffs

The only WTO litigation involving export taxes is the dispute in *China–Raw Materials*.[131] China agreed in its Accession Protocol to abolish export duties except on products listed in Annex 6, and to obey the ceilings on the duties applicable to such products set out in Annex 6. The Panel and the Appellate Body found that China had violated these commitments with respect to a number of mineral exports. For the most part, the legal analysis of the claim that the export taxes have exceeded any permitted levels is straightforward – the question is whether China has reserved its rights to impose export taxes on the goods in question in Annex 6 and, if so, whether total export duties exceed the ceiling in Annex 6.

The harder issue in the case, as relates to export taxes, is whether China can invoke an exception under GATT Article XX to justify a breach of its commitments on export taxes. The Panel and the Appellate Body held not, essentially suggesting that the language of the specific commitments on export taxes, and their context, excludes any intent of the parties to allow China to invoke Article XX.

The case does illustrate the fact that export taxes can create problematic international externalities from the standpoint of terms-of-trade theory, particularly when the exporter in question has substantial market power over the relevant product (as China well may with respect to certain mineral exports). The fact that WTO members insisted on limiting China's use of export taxes provides some further evidence that terms-of-trade considerations are important drivers of trade agreements.

At the same time, we may ask why restrictions on export tariffs are of so little importance within the system. Our discussion from Section 3.6 suggests that in large part the answer to this question may simply derive from the fact that export tariffs are not frequently employed by governments, and so a central need for constraining them through international agreement is lacking. This, of course, begs the question why export taxes are not more frequently observed, and we have suggested above that the answer may in part come from the presence of important political–economy forces and/or market imperfections that make export subsidies rather than taxes attractive to governments, and in part from the more subtle forms (e.g., export cartels) that export-tax-like policies may take when governments do in fact employ them. And finally, there is the related issue of whether a lack of restraints on export tariffs could pose a serious problem for the ability of WTO/GATT tariff bindings to offer meaningful market-access commitments, and we suggest in light of the multitude of tariff bindings negotiated by the typical WTO member that this is unlikely.

---

[131] *China – Measures Related to the Exportation of Various Raw Materials*, WT/DS394, 395, and 398/R and AB/R, adopted February 22, 2012.

3.8 Conclusion

In this study we analyze the treatment of border instruments in the WTO/GATT system from both a legal and economic perspective and with both positive and normative goals. From a positive perspective, we draw on the economic theory of international trade and relevant aspects of economic history to explain the legal treatment of border instruments in the WTO/GATT system as it has evolved over time. From a normative perspective, we build on an economic understanding of the function of the various legal disciplines to critique elements of the treaty text and the case law.

Our legal analysis provides a general overview of the WTO obligations that the study addresses, along with aspects of the case law that raise interesting economic issues. It serves as the basis for a series of questions in each subject area to which the economic analysis might be directed.

Our economic analysis provides an overview of the economics of international trade agreements. We organize our discussion around three topics: the purpose of trade agreements, the design of WTO/GATT, and the treatment of export policies.

With regard to the purpose of trade agreements, we argue that trade agreements can be mutually beneficial to governments when international externalities are associated with trade-policy selections or when governments seek a means of making credible commitments to their private sectors. Most economic research has focused on the international-externality rationale for trade agreements. In this context, research in economics also highlights the terms-of-trade externality as the primary international externality that provides a rationale for trade agreements. We discuss the terms-of-trade theory of trade agreements and its practical relevance. We also consider the extension of this theory to markets with imperfect competition and other international externalities.

In our discussion of the design of WTO/GATT, we argue that the terms-of-trade theory of trade agreements provides an interpretation of negotiations that generate reciprocal liberalization of tariffs, where those negotiations result in tariff bindings. We also discuss and interpret provisions in WTO/GATT for renegotiation that proceeds according to the principle of reciprocity. After developing perspectives on the reasons that trade liberalization occurs gradually, through rounds of negotiation over time, we use the terms-of-trade theory of trade agreements to interpret and evaluate the principle of nondiscrimination. We argue that the principles of reciprocity and nondiscrimination together have many desirable effects and may account for much of the success that WTO/GATT member governments have had in negotiating trade liberalization over time. Finally, we interpret and evaluate as well the benefits of tariffs over quotas in an international trading system.

Our third topic is export policies. We consider two-country models, and we also extend the analysis to allow for a three-country model so that the effects of export subsidies on competing exporters from other countries can be considered. Allowing for both perfectly and imperfectly competitive markets structures, we report a set of findings that reveal a tension between economic theory and the treatment of export subsidies in the WTO. In light of this tension, we describe some further considerations that are not included in the economic models, and we also describe a recent theory that emphasizes the firm-delocation effects of export subsidies and that offers a partial interpretation of the treatment of export subsidies in the WTO. We also consider export tariffs and discuss potential reasons that they are not more often used.

On the whole, our discussion suggests that the economic rationale for a trade agreement like the WTO/GATT is solid. In the absence of a trade agreement, governments would have incentive to engage in beggar-thy-neighbor policies in which they shift the costs of their policy choices onto one another, with the end result being an inefficient set of trade policies leading to too little trade volume. Emphasizing in its design the principles of reciprocity and nondiscrimination, the WTO/GATT system is well-constructed to help governments achieve mutually advantageous (i.e., more efficient) trade-policy outcomes. We note, though, that not all features of the WTO/GATT system are easily interpreted within the context of the economic theory that we discuss.

REFERENCES

Amador M, Bagwell K. 2011. The theory of optimal delegation with an application to tariff caps. Mimeogr., Stanford Univ.

Antras P, Staiger RW. 2008. Offshoring and the role of trade agreements. NBER Working Paper No. 14285.

Bagwell K. 2008. Remedies in the WTO: an economic perspective. In *The WTO: Governance, Dispute Settlement & Developing Countries*, eds. Janow ME, Donaldson VJ, Yanovich A. Huntington, New York: Juris Publishing.

Bagwell K, Mavroidis PC. 2010. Too much, too little...too late? In *Law and Economics of Contingent Protection in International Trade*, eds. Bagwell K, Bermann GA, Mavroidis PC. Cambridge Univ. Press.

Bagwell K, Staiger RW. 1999. An economic theory of GATT. *American Economic Review* 89: 215–248.

Bagwell K, Staiger RW. 2001. Strategic trade, competitive industries and agricultural trade disputes. *Economics and Politics* 13: 113–128.

Bagwell K, Staiger RW. 2002. *The Economics of the World Trading System*. Cambridge, MA: The MIT Press.

Bagwell K, Staiger RW. 2005a. Enforcement, private political pressure and the GATT/WTO escape clause. *The Journal of Legal Studies* 34: 471–513.

Bagwell K, Staiger RW. 2005b. Multilateral trade negotiations, bilateral opportunism and the rules of GATT/WTO. *Journal of International Economics* 67: 268–294.

Bagwell K, Staiger RW. 2009a. Delocation and trade agreements in imperfectly competitive markets. NBER Working Paper Number 15444.

Bagwell K, Staiger RW. 2009b. Profit shifting and trade agreements in imperfectly competitive markets. NBER Working Paper Number 14803.

Bagwell K, Staiger RW. 2009c. The economics of trade agreements in the linear cournot delocation model. NBER Working Paper Number 15492.

Bagwell K, Staiger RW. 2010a. The WTO: theory and practice. *Annual Review of Economics*.

Bagwell K, Staiger RW. 2010b. Backward stealing and forward manipulation in the WTO. *Journal of International Economics* 82: 49–62.

Bagwell K, Staiger RW. 2011, What do trade negotiators negotiate about? Empirical evidence from the World Trade Organization. *American Economic Review* 101: 1238–1273.

Bagwell K, Sykes AO. 2004. Chile – price band system and safeguard measures relating to certain agricultural products. *World Trade Review* 3: 507–528.

Bhagwati J. 1965. On the equivalence of tariffs and quota. In *Trade, Growth and the Balance of Payments*, ed. R.E. Baldwin et al. Chicago: Rand-McNally.

Bhagwati J. 1991. *The world trading system at risk*. Princeton: Princeton Univ. Press.

Bown C. 2004. Trade policy under the GATT/WTO: empirical evidence of the equal treatment rule. *Canadian Journal of Economics* 37: 678–720.

Brander JA. 1995. Strategic trade policy. In *Handbook of International Economics, Volume 3*, eds. Grossman GM, Rogoff K. Amsterdam: North Holland.

Brander JA, Spencer BJ. 1981. Tariffs and the extraction of foreign monopoly rents under potential entry. *Canadian Journal of Economics* 14: 371–389.

Brander JA, Spencer BJ. 1984a. Trade warfare: tariffs and cartels. *Journal of International Economics* 16: 227–242.

Brander JA, Spencer BJ. 1984b. Tariff protection and imperfect competition. In *Monopolistic Competition and International Trade*, ed. Kierzkowski. Oxford: Clarendon Press.

Brander JA, Spencer BJ. 1985. Export subsidies and international market share rivalry. *Journal of International Economics* 18: 83–100.

Broda C, Limao N, Weinstein D. 2008. Optimal tariffs and market power: the evidence. *American Economic Review* 98: 2032–2065.

Eaton J, Grossman GM. 1986. Optimal trade and industrial policy under oligopoly. *Quarterly Journal of Economics* 51: 383–406.

Eicher T.S., Henn C. 2011. In search of WTO trade effects: Preferential trade agreements promote trade strongly, but unevenly. *Journal of International Economics* 83: 137–153.

Ethier W. 2004. Political externalities, nondiscrimination, and a multilateral world. *Review of International Economics* 12: 303–320.

Freund C, Orenelas E. 2010. Regional trade agreements. *Annual Review of Economics* 2(1): 139–166.

Gardner RN. 1956. *Sterling-Dollar Diplomacy: Anglo-American Collaboration in the Reconstruction of Multilateral Trade*. Oxford: Clarendon Press.

General Agreement on Tariffs and Trade. 1949. "The Attack on Trade Barriers: A Progress Report on the Operation of the GATT, January 1948-August 1949." Geneva: GATT.

Goldberg PK, Knetter MM. 1997. Goods prices and exchange rates: what have we learned? *Journal of Economic Literature* 35: 1244–1272.

Grossman GM, Sykes AO. 2005. A Preference for Development: The Law and Economics of GSP, *World Trade Review* 4: 41–68.

Horn H, Maggi G, Staiger RW. 2010. Trade agreements as endogenously incomplete contracts. *American Economic Review* 101: 394–419.

Irwin D, Mavroidis PC, Sykes AO. 2008. *The Genesis of the GATT.* Cambridge: Cambridge Univ. Press.

Jackson JH. 1969. *World Trade and the Law of the GATT.* Indianapolis: Bobbs-Merrill.

Jackson JH, Davey WJ, Sykes AO. 2008. *Legal Problems of International Economic Relations* 5th ed. Minneapolis: Thomson-West.

Johnson HG. 1953–1954. Optimum tariffs and retaliation. *Review of Economic Studies* 21: 142–153.

Karacaovali B, Limao N. 2008. The clash of liberalizations: preferential vs. multilateral trade liberalization in the European Union. *Journal of International Economics* 74: 299–327.

Limao N. 2006. Preferential trade agreements as stumbling blocks for multilateral trade liberalization: evidence for the U.S. *American Economic Review* 96: 896–914.

Limao N. 2007. Are preferential trade agreements with non-trade objectives a stumbling block for multilateral liberalization? *Review of Economic Studies* 74: 821–855.

Ludema RD, Mayda AM. 2007. The free-riding effect of the mfn clause: evidence across countries. Mimeogr. Johns-Hopkins Univ.

Ludema RD, Mayda AM. 2009. Do countries free ride on mfn? *Journal of International Economics* 77: 137–150.

Maggi G, Rodriguez-Clare A. 2007. A political-economy theory of trade agreements. *American Economic Review* 97: 1374–1406.

Mavroidis PC. 2005. *The General Agreement on Tariffs and Trade: A Commentary.* Oxford: Oxford Univ. Press.

Mavroidis PC. 2011. Always look at the bright side on non-delivery: WTO and preferential trade agreements, Yesterday and Today. *World Trade Review* 10: 375–387.

Mill JS. 1844. *Essays on Some Unsettled Questions of Political Economy.* London: Parker.

Ossa R. 2011. A 'new-trade' theory of GATT/WTO negotiations. *Journal of Political Economy* 119: 122–152.

Regan DH. 2006. What are trade agreements for?: two conflicting stories told by economists, with a lesson for lawyers. *Journal of International Economic Law* 9: 951–988.

Schatz AW. 1970. The Anglo-American Trade Agreement and Cordell Hull's search for peace 1936–1938. *Journal of American History* 57: 85–103.

Schwartz WF, Sykes AO. 1997. The economics of the most-favored-nation clause. In *Economic Dimensions in International Law: Comparative and Empirical Perspectives*, eds. Bhandani JS, Sykes AO. Cambridge: Cambridge Univ. Press.

Shirono K. 2004. Are WTO tariff negotiations reciprocal? An analysis of tariff liberalization. Mimeogr., Columbia Univ.

Subramanian A, Wei S-J. 2007. The WTO promotes trade, strongly but unevenly. *Journal of International Economics* 72: 151–175.

Sykes AO. 2005. The economics of WTO rules on subsidies and countervailing measures. In *The World Trade Organization: Legal, Economic and Political Analysis. Vol. II*, eds. Appleton A, Macrory P, Plummer M. Springer-Verlag.

Sykes AO. 2010. The questionable case for subsidies regulation: a comparative perspective. *Journal of Legal Analysis* 2: 473–523.

Torrens R. 1844. *The Budget: On Commercial Policy and Colonial Policy.* London: Smith, Elder.

U.S. Tariff Commission. 1948. Operation of the Trade Agreements Program, July 1934 to April 1948, Part 1. Summary. Washington, DC: Government Printing Office.

Venables A. 1985. Trade and trade policy with imperfect competition: the case of identical products and free entry. *Journal of International Economics* 19: 1–20.

Venables A. 1987. Trade and trade policy with differentiated products: a chamberlinian-ricardian model. *Economic Journal* 97: 700–717.

Viner J. 1950. *The customs union issue.* New York: Carnegie Endowment for International Peace.

GENE M. GROSSMAN, HENRIK HORN, AND PETROS C. MAVROIDIS

4 National Treatment

4.1 Introduction

The purpose of the study is to propose interpretations of the National Treatment (NT) provision included in Art. III GATT, unbound by case-law interpretations of this provision. To make such proposals, we need to understand the role of the provision in the agreement. To this end, we first examine in Section 4.2 the negotiating record relevant to the rationale for the enactment of this provision, as well as the manner in which case law has understood it. In the same Section, we also discuss the role of NT in the General Agreement on Tariffs and Trade (GATT) from the perspective of economic theory. Having established the purpose of NT, we discuss in Section 4.3 the manner in which this provision has been implemented in case law: that is, here we focus on the understanding of the key terms implementing the purpose of NT by GATT and World Trade Organization (WTO) adjudicating bodies. At the end of this Section we provide a critical assessment of the case law. In light of our dissatisfaction with the case-law interpretations of some key terms, we present in Section 4.4 our preferred interpretation of NT.

The main findings of this study could be summarized as follows: we believe that case law, economic theory, and the negotiating record point in the same direction concerning the purpose of the provision: NT is meant to outlaw protectionist use of domestic instruments. It is often unclear whether case-law interpretations of the key terms of this provision promote, if at all, the purpose of the provision. This seems to be largely explained by the absence of a coherent

We would like to thank in particular Steve Charnovitz, Meredith Crowley, Bernard Hoekman, John Ragosta, Donald Regan, and Alan Sykes, for many extremely useful comments. We are also grateful for very helpful comments on previous drafts from Bill Davey, Rob Howse, Michael Trebilcock, Michael Traynor, Evan Wallach, other advisers to the project participating in presentations of the study, the ALI Council, and participants in a seminar at the Tilburg Law and Economics Center, Tilburg University.

methodology, based on both legal and economic thinking. This is the gap that this study aims to fill.

The reason for relying on legal analysis for an evaluation of a provision of the GATT needs no motivation in this context. But why also base the study in economics? There are several reasons why the working and appropriate design of Art. III GATT cannot be adequately addressed without economic analysis.[1]

A first reason derives from the fact that in order to determine how Art. III GATT should be interpreted (and possibly redrafted), it is crucial to take into consideration the rationale for the provision, and hence also the rationale for the agreement as a whole. We will discuss below the possible purpose of the agreement in much more detail, let us here just quote the preamble to the GATT:[2]

> ...Recognizing that their relations in the field of trade and economic endeavour should be conducted with a view to raising standards of living, ensuring full employment and a large and steadily growing volume of real income and effective demand, developing the full use of the resources of the world and expanding the production and exchange of goods. ...[3]

The stated *purposes* of the GATT are thus all of inherently economic nature.

A second reason why economic analysis is needed as part of the evaluation is the fact that the extent to which the agreement achieves these policy objectives depends on how the regulations it imposes affect the working of markets. This interaction is of course an intrinsically economic issue.

Hence, the objectives of the GATT and the mechanisms through which the regulation it imposes achieve these objectives, are of inherent economic nature. An analysis of Art. III GATT that relied solely on a traditional legal (i.e., legalistic) perspective would not adequately reflect the importance and the meaning of the objectives. Economic analysis is thus an essential component when examining the question of how Art. III GATT should be interpreted.

How this should be done is far from being obvious: economic theory rarely provides concrete guidance for the design of regulations. In the case of Art. III GATT, matters are worse, since there is hardly any economic research on the appropriate design of a NT-provision. Also, to the extent that theory does provide

[1] Note the difference between necessary and sufficient conditions.

[2] The preamble to the *Agreement Establishing the World Trade Organization* goes a step further, adding objectives related to the environment and sustainable development:

> *Recognizing* that their relations in the field of trade and economic endeavour should be conducted with a view to raising standards of living, ensuring full employment and a large and steadily growing volume of real income and effective demand, and expanding the production of and trade in goods and services, while allowing for the optimal use of the world's resources in accordance with the objective of sustainable development, seeking both to protect and preserve the environment and to enhance the means for doing so in a manner consistent with their respective needs and concerns at different levels of economic development, ...

[3] One should not neglect that according to Art. 31 of the *Vienna Convention on the Law of Treaties* (VCLT), recourse to the object and purpose of a treaty is compulsory, leaving the interpreter with no discretion as to its relevance.

suggestions for the treatment of domestic instruments in a trade agreement, the suggested treatment has very little resemblance to the structure of Art. III GATT, and it is therefore difficult to draw any concrete inferences. Consequently, we are forced to rely on our subjective judgment when drawing on economic theory for the interpretation of Art. III GATT.

In this section, we concentrate on the study of Art. III.2 GATT dealing with fiscal instruments.

4.1.1 The Text of Art. III GATT

The full text of Art. III GATT and its Interpretative Notes are reproduced here:

Article III*
National Treatment on Internal Taxation and Regulation

1. The contracting parties recognize that internal taxes and other internal charges, and laws, regulations and requirements affecting the internal sale, offering for sale, purchase, transportation, distribution or use of products, and internal quantitative regulations requiring the mixture, processing or use of products in specified amounts or proportions, should not be applied to imported or domestic products so as to afford protection to domestic production.*

2. The products of the territory of any contracting party imported into the territory of any other contracting party shall not be subject, directly or indirectly, to internal taxes or other internal charges of any kind in excess of those applied, directly or indirectly, to like domestic products. Moreover, no contracting party shall otherwise apply internal taxes or other internal charges to imported or domestic products in a manner contrary to the principles set forth in paragraph 1.*

3. With respect to any existing internal tax which is inconsistent with the provisions of paragraph 2, but which is specifically authorized under a trade agreement, in force on April 10, 1947, in which the import duty on the taxed product is bound against increase, the contracting party imposing the tax shall be free to postpone the application of the provisions of paragraph 2 to such tax until such time as it can obtain release from the obligations of such trade agreement in order to permit the increase of such duty to the extent necessary to compensate for the elimination of the protective element of the tax.

4. The products of the territory of any contracting party imported into the territory of any other contracting party shall be accorded treatment no less favourable than that accorded to like products of national origin in respect of all laws, regulations and requirements affecting their internal sale, offering for sale, purchase, transportation, distribution or use. The provisions of this paragraph shall not prevent the application of differential

internal transportation charges which are based exclusively on the economic operation of the means of transport and not on the nationality of the product.

5. No contracting party shall establish or maintain any internal quantitative regulation relating to the mixture, processing or use of products in specified amounts or proportions which requires, directly or indirectly, that any specified amount or proportion of any product which is the subject of the regulation must be supplied from domestic sources. Moreover, no contracting party shall otherwise apply internal quantitative regulations in a manner contrary to the principles set forth in paragraph 1.*

6. The provisions of paragraph 5 shall not apply to any internal quantitative regulation in force in the territory of any contracting party on July 1, 1939, April 10, 1947, or March 24, 1948, at the option of that contracting party; *Provided* that any such regulation which is contrary to the provisions of paragraph 5 shall not be modified to the detriment of imports and shall be treated as a customs duty for the purpose of negotiation.

7. No internal quantitative regulation relating to the mixture, processing or use of products in specified amounts or proportions shall be applied in such a manner as to allocate any such amount or proportion among external sources of supply.

8. (a) The provisions of this Article shall not apply to laws, regulations or requirements governing the procurement by governmental agencies of products purchased for governmental purposes and not with a view to commercial resale or with a view to use in the production of goods for commercial sale.

   (b) The provisions of this Article shall not prevent the payment of subsidies exclusively to domestic producers, including payments to domestic producers derived from the proceeds of internal taxes or charges applied consistently with the provisions of this Article and subsidies effected through governmental purchases of domestic products.

9. The contracting parties recognize that internal maximum price control measures, even though conforming to the other provisions of this Article, can have effects prejudicial to the interests of contracting parties supplying imported products. Accordingly, contracting parties applying such measures shall take account of the interests of exporting contracting parties with a view to avoiding to the fullest practicable extent such prejudicial effects.

10. The provisions of this Article shall not prevent any contracting party from establishing or maintaining internal quantitative regulations relating to exposed cinematograph films and meeting the requirements of Article IV.

To this there are the following ad notes.

Ad Article III

Any internal tax or other internal charge, or any law, regulation or requirement of the kind referred to in paragraph 1 which applies to an imported
product and to the like domestic product and is collected or enforced in the
case of the imported product at the time or point of importation, is nevertheless to be regarded as an internal tax or other internal charge, or a
law, regulation or requirement of the kind referred to in paragraph 1, and
is accordingly subject to the provisions of Article III.

Ad Paragraph 1

The application of paragraph 1 to internal taxes imposed by local governments and authorities with the territory of a contracting party is subject
to the provisions of the final paragraph of Article XXIV. The term "reasonable measures" in the last-mentioned paragraph would not require, for
example, the repeal of existing national legislation authorizing local governments to impose internal taxes which, although technically inconsistent with the letter of Article III, are not in fact inconsistent with its spirit,
if such repeal would result in a serious financial hardship for the local governments or authorities concerned. With regard to taxation by local governments or authorities which is inconsistent with both the letter and spirit
of Article III, the term "reasonable measures" would permit a contracting party to eliminate the inconsistent taxation gradually over a transition
period, if abrupt action would create serious administrative and financial
difficulties.

Ad Paragraph 2

A tax conforming to the requirements of the first sentence of paragraph
2 would be considered to be inconsistent with the provisions of the second
sentence only in cases where competition was involved between, on the one
hand, the taxed product and, on the other hand, a directly competitive or
substitutable product which was not similarly taxed.

Ad Paragraph 5

Regulations consistent with the provisions of the first sentence of paragraph
5 shall not be considered to be contrary to the provisions of the second sentence in any case in which all of the products subject to the regulations are
produced domestically in substantial quantities. A regulation cannot be justified as being consistent with the provisions of the second sentence on the
ground that the proportion or amount allocated to each of the products
which are the subject of the regulation constitutes an equitable relationship
between imported and domestic products.

4.1.2 Art. III GATT 1947, Art. III GATT 1994

The text reproduced above is from the GATT 1947, that is, the original GATT. The GATT 1994 is not the same agreement that was signed in 1947. The latter was substantially modified through the negotiations during the *Uruguay Round* during which it was agreed to add to the original text all decisions adopted by the GATT contracting parties since 1947. So, although the original text has not been modified, some GATT practice has been incorporated into the text of the GATT as a result of the successful conclusion of the *Uruguay Round*. WTO Members are nowadays bound by the GATT 1994 which comprises the following elements:

(a) the provisions in the General Agreement on Tariffs and Trade, dated 30 October 1947, annexed to the Final Act Adopted at the Conclusion of the Second Session of the Preparatory Committee of the United Nations Conference on Trade and Employment (excluding the Protocol of Provisional Application), as rectified, amended or modified by the terms of legal instruments which have entered into force before the date of entry into force of the WTO Agreement;

(b) the provisions of the legal instruments set forth below that have entered into force under the GATT 1947 before the date of entry into force of the WTO Agreement:

(i) protocols and certifications relating to tariff concessions;

(ii) protocols of accession (excluding the provisions (*a*) concerning provisional application and withdrawal of provisional application and (*b*) providing that Part II of GATT 1947 shall be applied provisionally to the fullest extent not inconsistent with legislation existing on the date of the Protocol);

(iii) decisions on waivers granted under Article XXV of GATT 1947 and still in force on the date of entry into force of the WTO Agreement[4];

(iv) other decisions of the CONTRACTING PARTIES to GATT 1947;

(c) the Understandings set forth below:

(i) Understanding on the Interpretation of Article II:1(b) of the General Agreement on Tariffs and Trade 1994;

(ii) Understanding on the Interpretation of Article XVII of the General Agreement on Tariffs and Trade 1994;

---

[4] The waivers covered by this provision are listed in footnote 7 on pages 11 and 12 in Part II of document MTN/FA of 15 December 1993 and in MTN/FA/Corr.6 of 21 March 1994. The Ministerial Conference shall establish at its first session a revised list of waivers covered by this provision that adds any waivers granted under GATT 1947 after 15 December 1993 and before the date of entry into force of the WTO Agreement, and deletes the waivers which will have expired by that time.

(iii) Understanding on Balance-of-Payments Provisions of the General Agreement on Tariffs and Trade 1994;

(iv) Understanding on the Interpretation of Article XXIV of the General Agreement on Tariffs and Trade 1994;

(v) Understanding in Respect of Waivers of Obligations under the General Agreement on Tariffs and Trade 1994;

(vi) Understanding on the Interpretation of Article XXVIII of the General Agreement on Tariffs and Trade 1994; and

(d) the Marrakesh Protocol to GATT 1994.

The term "other decisions of the CONTRACTING PARTIES to GATT 1947" featured in Art. 1(b)(iv) GATT 1994 is relevant for the purpose of our exercise: depending on its purview, the substantive content of Art. III GATT 1947 might have been modified. The term has been the subject matter of adjudication. As will be explained *infra*, GATT/WTO dispute-settlement reports do not come under the term "other decisions of the CONTRACTING PARTIES to GATT 1947," but the *Working Party report on Border Tax Adjustments*, which relates to the coverage of Art. III GATT, should be understood as an "other decision."

4.2 The Rationale for NT

In this section we will seek to highlight the purpose of NT from three different angles: the negotiating record, the case law, and economic theory.

4.2.1 The Rationale for NT in Negotiating History

This section discusses the negotiating record of Art. III GATT in order to unveil the purpose of the provision as perceived by its drafters, and thus the spirit behind the terms it contains.[5] As will be made clear, the words chosen to express the NT discipline are often wanting even in the view of the negotiators; it is no wonder the Art. III GATT case law has had a difficult time to define a clear benchmark for acceptable behavior, and a methodology that would resolve disputes coming under its purview in a more or less predictable manner.

The study of the negotiating record of the NT provision points to two conclusions:

(a)   This provision was thought as an anti-circumvention device, that is, as a means to safeguard the value of tariff concessions that would be exchanged in the first multilateral negotiation in Geneva (1948);

---

[5] In this Section, we provide a broader account of issues than necessary to discuss the rationale for NT in the negotiating record. The history of the negotiation of Art. III GATT is comprehensively discussed in Charnovitz (1994), and Jackson (1969).

(b) With the exception of a few specific domestic instruments that have explicitly been exempted from coverage in the body of the provision, NT was meant to cover all domestic instruments, whether of fiscal or nonfiscal nature.

These two conclusions seem solid in the light of the negotiating record that will be cited in what follows. There are further good reasons to believe that negotiators aimed at outlawing practices that either had the effect of conferring an advantage on domestic production, and/or were intentionally designed to do so: besides the actual words that were incorporated in the final text, a number of hypothetical examples that were used as basis for illuminating the parameters of this obligation, as well as various statements by participating delegates, point in this direction. The negotiating record also reveals the dissatisfaction of the framers of the Agreement with some of the terms that found their way into Art. III GATT: for example, the term *like products* was chosen *faute de mieux*, and it had been agreed to re-discuss it under the auspices of the planned International Trade Organization; this organization will be briefly described below.

4.2.1.1 *The Forum and Context of Negotiation*

The original GATT entered into force on January 1, 1948, at the end of a speedy negotiation that lasted less than a year. We will briefly describe in what follows the evolution of the drafting during these negotiations. As a background, we start with a broad overview of the developments.

Following a proposal for an International Conference on Trade and Employment at its first session on February 18, 1946, the United Nations (UN) Economic and Social Council (ECOSOC) established the *Preparatory Committee* charged with the task of drafting a convention for international trade.[6] Its members were: Australia, Belgium, Brazil, Canada, Chile, China, Cuba, Czechoslovakia, France, India, Lebanon, Luxembourg, the Netherlands, New Zealand, Norway, South Africa, the Union of Soviet Socialist Republics (USSR),[7] the United States, and the United Kingdom. At its second session (May 31, 1946), the ECOSOC announced

---

[6] See E/PC/T/117 Rev. 1 of July 9, 1947 at p. 1. See on this score, Curzon (1965), Dam (1970), Irwin et al. (2008), Jackson (1969), Hudec (1975), and Wilcox (1949).

[7] The USSR declined to participate. This is how Irwin *et al.* (2008, p. 72) discuss this decision: "In Moscow, George Kennen of the U.S. State Department requested a meeting to discuss Soviet participation in the upcoming conference. Soviet officials never granted this request and never responded one way or another to the U.S. invitation, despite the fact that their delegates had participated in the UN Economic and Social Council discussion of the resolution-on-trade conference and voted for resolution. The State Department was skeptical that the Soviet Union, given the state monopoly control on foreign trade, could participate in a useful way in the tariff negotiations. Still, despite the lack of response from Soviet officials, the State Department decided to include the USSR on the list of countries with which it intended to negotiate, leaving the door open for their participation (FRUS 1946, I, 1354–1355). The U.S. Embassy in Moscow cabled back with this message: "We have noted with interest several recent reports from London of conversations with Soviet officials

that the necessary arrangements were in place for the *Preparatory Committee* to convene its first meeting in London on October 15, 1946.[8] The London negotiations went on until November 20, 1946,[9] and were also attended by countries that were members of the UN but not of the *Preparatory Committee*,[10] by UN specialized agencies,[11] by other international organizations,[12] and by nongovernmental organizations.[13] The *Preparatory Committee* held two meetings (sessions):

(a) from October 15, 1946, to November 20, 1946, in London (first session);
(b) from April 10, 1947, to October 30, 1947, in Geneva (second session), where the GATT text that entered into force on January 1, 1948, was definitively agreed.

In between, from January 20, 1947, to February 25, 1947, the *Drafting Committee*, an organ appointed by the *Preparatory Committee*, met in New York and

giving various explanations why Soviet Government does not participate in many international meetings, particularly ITO. Reasons given for nonparticipation range from lack of personnel to Soviet preoccupation with questions of security. While there may be some modicum of truth in these arguments, we believe that in regard to such institutions as the International [i.e., World] Bank, ITO and PICAO [i.e., Provisional International Civil Aviation Organization], the principal, if not the only, reason the Russians do not join is that they do not wish to. Kremlin insistence on keeping its independence of action in world affairs has even on occasion been frankly expressed by certain responsible Soviet officials, and, in any event, is self-evident in every aspect of Soviet policy in action." Furthermore, the cable added, for the Soviets "to join any organization which would require them to give statistics on national income, international trade, balance of payments and gold production, would imply a complete reversal of a basic and scrupulously maintained Soviet policy of state secrecy in such matters. On the other hand, whenever they stand to gain something concrete by participation in an international organ or run the risk of losing something important by failure so to do, they appear to find no difficulty in effecting such participation (UNRRA, telecommunications, whaling). It would appear unreal, therefore, in the absence of concrete evidence to the contrary, to base any policy on the belief that Russians actually desire to join such organs as ITO but are precluded because of personnel or other administrative considerations" (FRUS 1946, I, 1355–1356)."

[8] See E/PC/T/33 on p. 3. See on this score, Robbins (1971).
[9] See E/PC/T/117 Rev. 1 of July 9, 1947 at p. 1.
[10] Colombia, Denmark, Mexico, Peru, Poland, and Syria sent observers to both the first and the second session of the *Preparatory Committee*; Colombia, and Mexico, to the *Drafting Committee* (which became operational during the *New York Conference*, see infra); Afghanistan, Argentina, Ecuador, Egypt, Greece, Iran, Saudi Arabia, Sweden, Syria, Turkey, Uruguay, Venezuela, and Yugoslavia sent representatives to the second session of the *Preparatory Committee*. Note that the Syrian delegates were representing the Syro-Lebanese customs union, see E/PC/T/117 Rev. 1 of July 9, 1947 at p. 2.
[11] The International Labor Office (ILO), and the Food and Agriculture Organization (FAO), see E/PC/T/117 Rev. 1 of July 9, 1947 at p. 2.
[12] The International Bank for Reconstruction and Development (World Bank, WB), and the International Monetary Fund (IMF), see E/PC/T/117 Rev. 1 of July 9, 1947 at p. 2.
[13] The American Federation of Labor (AFL), the International Chamber of Commerce (ICC), the International Co-operative Alliance (ICA), the World Federation of Trade Unions, and the International Federation of Agricultural Producers, see E/PC/T/117 Rev. 1 of July 9, 1947 at p. 2.

prepared the first comprehensive draft of the GATT. The *Preparatory Committee*
established the following working committees:

(a) Committee I: *Employment and Economic Activity;*
(b) Committee II: *General Commercial Policy;*
(c) Committee III: *Restrictive Business Practices;*
(d) Committee IV: *Inter-governmental Commodity Arrangements;*
(e) Committee V: *Administration and Organization.*

Committee II is our main interest because under its aegis the first draft GATT
articles, including the NT provision, were prepared. Committee II established
a series of Sub-committees which were requested to report to it their findings:
chief among them, the *Technical Subcommittee*, which dealt with a number of
provisions appearing in the GATT, ranging from customs valuation to NT. Participation to the *Technical Subcommittee* was open to delegates for all the countries
represented on the *Preparatory Committee*. Delegates of six different nationali-
ties acted as *rapporteurs*, Leddy (U.S.), who is credited with the drafting of the
first GATT text, being one of them.

The *Preparatory Committee* did not start negotiating from a clean slate:
the U.S. proposal to establish an International Trade Organization (ITO) served
as the basis for the negotiations (the *Suggested Charter*). In anticipation of the
London Conference, the U.S. government prepared a *Suggested Charter* for the
ITO in September 1946. This was a U.S. initiative, but very much the product of
extensive consultations between the U.S. and UK governments.[14] The *Suggested
Charter* was divided into seven chapters: I Purposes; II Membership; III Employment provisions; IV General Commercial Policy; V Restrictive business practices;
VI Inter-governmental commodity arrangements; VII Organization. NT figured
in Chapter IV. The NT provision included in the *Suggested Charter* was the first
multilateral attempt to introduce NT-type of provisions in a treaty, but not the
first NT provision in general: the U.S. Tariff Act of 1930, as well as bilateral agreements that the United States had signed with Canada (1938), Mexico (1942), and
Uruguay (1942), contained similar clauses.[15] These provisions provided an inspi-
ration to the drafting of the NT provision that was included in the *Suggested
Charter*, and the drafting of the eventual GATT NT provision.

The text that entered into force on January 1, 1948, is not the current Art.
III GATT: it underwent one final transformation during the *Havana Conference*
in 1948, where negotiators aimed at streamlining the language used, but also to
leave little room for doubt as to the function of this provision within the overall
GATT architecture.

[14] Compare the views of Meade (1990), and Miller (2000) on this score.
[15] See Jackson (1967) at p. 314.

4.2.1.2 *The Transformation of NT*

During the negotiations, NT underwent a series of changes.

4.2.1.2.1 The GATT, an (Independent) Part of the ITO. The decision to dissociate the drafting of the GATT from the drafting of the wider ITO Charter was taken during the *London Conference,* but in the beginning the *raison d'être* of the *London Conference* was the negotiation of the ITO.[16] It became increasingly clear to the negotiators, however, that a less ambitious project would keep the ball rolling and probably also provide the impetus for subsequent negotiations on the more ambitious endeavor.[17] The idea was to start with a multilateral exchange of tariff concessions rather than with a comprehensive Charter regulating each and every facet of international trade. At that point, the GATT (or, more generally, a tariff agreement) would become necessary in order to safeguard the value of tariff concessions made during the negotiations.[18] The actual *ambit* of the GATT was nevertheless not definitively agreed at the *London Conference.*[19] Quoting from negotiating documents, Jackson (1969, p. 43) states that it was agreed that the GATT would include "such other provisions as may be appropriate." NT was considered to be a key element of this less ambitious project, which became the GATT.

4.2.1.2.2 NT in the Various Drafts

4.2.1.2.2.1 *NT in the London Conference.* The NT provision was Art. 15 of the *London Draft.* The text of the *Suggested Charter* underwent a few changes in London.[20] The negotiations, which took place within *Committee II,* initially focused on internal taxes, which were distinguished from customs tariffs in that they were decided unilaterally by every state and were applied to both domestic and foreign products.[21] Eventually, the negotiators moved to other areas of internal regulation of nonfiscal nature.

The negotiators early on recognized the impossibility to draft a perfect regulation of domestic instruments. This is how the Chairman of the Technical Subcommittee in charge of preparing the draft provision on National Treatment (NT)

---

[16] See on this score, Hart (1995), Wilgress (1967), and Zeiler (1999).

[17] See Hart (1998), Irwin (1996), and Irwin *et al.* (2008).

[18] The term *tariff concession,* which has customarily been used in the GATT-context and continues to be used in the WTO-era, does not make much economic sense: states make a concession to themselves as well since, at least those that cannot affect terms of trade, gain from trade liberalization. It does, nevertheless, make good legal sense, since it signals the transfer of sovereignty associated with the tariff promise: absent such transfer, trading nations would be free to increase or decrease tariff protection to their liking; through tariff concessions, they concede their sovereignty in this respect to the international plane.

[19] See on this score, Jackson (1969, pp. 42ff.).

[20] See E/PC/T/C.6/65.   [21] See E/PC/T/C.II/2.

during the London meeting of the Preparatory Committee understood the function of the group he was heading:

> Whatever we do here, we shall never be able to cover every contingency and
> possibility in a draft. Economic life is too varied for that, and there are all
> kinds of questions which are bound to arise later on. The important thing is
> that once we have this agreement laid down we have to act in the spirit of it.
> There is no doubt there will be certain difficulties, but if we are able to cover
> 75 or 80 or 85 per cent of them I think it will be sufficient.[22]

At the suggestion of the U.S. delegation, the negotiations were entrusted to a
group of experts, in light of the technical nature of the issues at stake: a subcommittee (*Technical Subcommittee*) was created to this effect where delegates of all
participants were invited to participate.[23] The negotiations were inconclusive,
however, and the *London Draft* postponed consideration of this item.[24] Nevertheless, considerable progress was made in London:

First, discussions were held regarding the overall *purpose* of this provision.
The views of many delegations on this score were later synthesized at the *Technical Subcommittee*-level. In the words of the French delegate, the NT provision
should outlaw disguised restriction of trade through internal taxes;[25] in similar vein, the delegate of Benelux argued that the provision was meant to protect the value of tariff concessions by eliminating indirect protection of domestic
production;[26] the report of the *Technical Subcommittee* ultimately held that the
purpose of NT should be to avoid undoing the tariff promise through either fiscal
or nonfiscal domestic instruments.[27]

Second, negotiations focused on the *coverage* of the NT obligation. There was
an implicit consensus that negotiations should not focus on a positive (which
instruments should be included) list, but rather on a negative (which instruments should be excluded) list, since it was understood that the value of tariff
promise *could* be undone by a very large number of domestic instruments. In
an effort to underscore the wide coverage of NT, the UK delegation proposed
the introduction of the term "*indirectly*" so as to ensure that *any* domestic measure, without mentioning them explicitly one by one, should be in principle covered by this discipline. The UK proposal was unopposed, suggesting a consensus
across the participants to opt for the widest possible coverage for this provision.
Some instruments were explicitly mentioned: the widespread use of local content measures (including mixing requirements) probably explains why negotiators felt necessary to *explicitly* outlaw their use (in current Art. III.5 GATT).[28]

---

[22] See E/PC/T/C.II/PRO/PV/7.   [23] See E/PC/T/C.II/3 at pp. 13–15.
[24] See E/PC/T/33 at p. 28.   [25] See E/P/C.II/12 at p. 2.
[26] See E/P/C.II/32 at pp. 1 and 2.   [27] See E/P/C.II/54 and 54 Rev. 1.
[28] For example, New Zealand had in place a number of local content measures involving
tobacco and wool that it sought to exempt from the coverage of NT (E/PC/T/C.II/28 at

National delegations also tabled various proposals for carve-outs, some of which were accepted and found their way into the final text, and some that did not: government procurement, subsidies, and films belong to the first category.

Government procurement is the one area where there was consensus that it should be left out of the coverage of NT. Political economy-type of reasons were advanced some time explicitly and some time in a concealed manner to defend this policy choice.[29]

The U.S. delegation, in line with the beliefs of the New Dealers, was eager to make room for subsidies (which would become for all practical purposes obsolete if they were to be covered by NT). In the words of Harry Hawkins, a U.S. negotiator:[30]

...subsidies kept prices down and demand up. They were expansionist rather than contractionist measures.[31]

Hawkins defended the choice to seek to target the use of tariffs and quantitative restrictions (QRs) that were harmful to trade rather than to focus on disciplining subsidies;[32] in the U.S. delegation's view, direct subsidies to producers were not harmful to international trade for the reason explained above in the quoted passage. The U.S. delegation was prepared however, to distinguish between domestic and export subsidies, and it was not opposed to condemning the export subsidies that were in its view considered harmful to international trade.[33] Canada

p. 2). The overwhelming majority of delegations were opposed to the continuation of similar measures, see E/P/C.II/54 and Rev. 1.

[29] See the lengthy discussions reflected in E/PC/T/C.II/PRO/PV/7. The UK and French delegations made proposals to this effect (see E/P/C.II/11 at p. 1 and E/P/C.II/12 at p. 1 respectively); Cuba proposed for a more limited exception that would cover only military procurement, which was eventually rejected (E/P/C.II/15 at p. 1), while Czechoslovakia agreed with the carve out but wished all foreigners to be treated on an MFN basis in national procurement markets (E/P/C.II/24 at p. 1). The advent of the Government Procurement Agreement (GPA) in the *Tokyo Round*, and its modern reincarnation as a plurilateral agreement during the *Uruguay Round* have set aside any arguments that have persisted to the effect that the proposal by Czechoslovakia had survived and government procurement had to be MFNed. Government procurement is, of course, nowadays exempted from the coverage of NT by virtue of Art. III.8 GATT.

[30] Hawkins later taught at Tufts University. See Irwin *et al.* (2008) for information about the *vitae* of the key delegates.

[31] See E/PC/T/C.II/37 at p. 8.

[32] It is probably true that negotiations focused on border measures since there was ignorance regarding the ambit and bite of domestic measures that were anyway nonobservable because of the high tariffs (customs duties) and QRs in place. There was some discussion of nontariff barriers in the literature; as exemplified by Bidwell (1939). The prevailing feeling among the negotiators was, however, that the bite of nontariff barriers was blurred by the high tariffs applied during that time. Baldwin's (1970) parable of the tide reflected this point. See also Hawkins (1951).

[33] See E/PC/T/C.II/3 at pp. 2–3.

agreed with the U.S. delegation,[34] and so did the UK delegation, which explicitly accepted the bifurcation between domestic and export subsidies.[35] The U.S. position was not totally unopposed though: both Brazil,[36] and Australia argued in favor of special treatment of subsidies, pointing to their adverse effects on foreign competitors.[37]

The UK delegation should be credited with the carve out regarding films.[38] In the words of Shackle (the UK delegate), it was axiomatic (sic) that film be exempted from the NT discipline, since it was not strictly an economic matter: it involved cultural and other aspects of national life.[39] The UK found support in the New Zealand delegation: New Zealand had in place the *film hire tax*, a domestic tax that discriminated between domestic and foreign films, and also between UK films and other foreign films which were treated worse than imported films of British origin.[40] To this effect, it was the UK delegation that initially proposed (what later became Art. IV GATT) the exclusion of films from the coverage of Art. 15 of the *London Draft*. In the words of the UK delegate (Mr. Rhydderch):

> ...he would prefer a note to the Article to say it did not apply to films. There were cultural, as well as commercial, considerations to be taken into account in the case of films.[41]

This is probably one of the first expressions in favor of a *cultural exception* in the post-war world trading system.

There were proposals regarding the treatment of other domestic instruments: for example, Brazil tabled a proposal aimed at explicitly addressing navigation port dues,[42] and New Zealand wished to exempt some of its measures regarding domestic tobacco and wool. All proposals other than those concerning the treatment of government procurement, subsidies, and films were defeated.

---

[34] *Idem* at p. 9. Compare Hart (1995), and (1998), and also Brown (1950) who gives a detailed account regarding the U.S. position with respect to farm subsidies.

[35] *Idem* at p. 10.   [36] *Idem* at p. 9.

[37] *Idem* at p. 10. See Capling (2001). Subsidies are currently exempted from the coverage of NT by virtue of Art. III.8 GATT. They are being regulated in a separate agreement (*Agreement on Subsidies and Countervailing Measures*, SCM) that was negotiated during the *Uruguay Round*.

[38] In the current GATT text, films are treated in Art. IV and explicitly acknowledged as exception to Art. III GATT which now reflects the NT discipline.

[39] See E/PC/T/C.II/55 at p. 8. See also E/PC/T/C.II/11 at p. 1 where the UK delegation explicitly admitted that their film quota in place was inconsistent with NT.

[40] See E/PC/T/C.II/28 at p. 1.

[41] See E/PC/T/C.II/E.14 of November 4, 1946 at p. 5. Incidentally, the UK position was supported by Czechoslovakia, France (later, an ardent supporter of the "cultural exception"), New Zealand, and Portugal).

[42] See E/PC/T/C.II/37 at p. 14.

Third, we observe the beginning of a discussion regarding the *parameters of the legal test* for consistency with the NT discipline. India, for example, wanted to ensure that discriminatory taxation for the *sole purpose* of raising revenue should be acceptable. It seems as if India was implicitly advancing the understanding that NT should be concerned only with measures that *intentionally* were aiming at protecting domestic production, and not with measures which unintentionally did so.[43] By the same token, Norway expressed its wish to be allowed to vary domestic taxes for the purpose of achieving a uniform price across products (domestic and foreign) sold in its market.[44] Although the objective of NT was clear in the negotiators' minds,[45] no provision equivalent to the current Art. III.1 GATT was included in the *London Draft;* recall that this provision condemns any domestic regulation (of fiscal or nonfiscal character) that operates so as to afford protection. It was left for later to explicitly state that such should be the objective of this provision.

There was nevertheless substantial discussion regarding the terms that would be used to express the (undefined) test for consistency. The text prepared by the *Technical Subcommittee* refers to similar or identical products when it discusses the treatment of non fiscal instruments, and simply contains a prohibition not to use taxes so as to afford protection, without any reference to either similar or identical products.[46] Eventually, the term "*similar*" gave way to "*like*" during the New York Conference, probably in order to underscore the parallelism in the obligations assumed under MFN and NT; there was already some discussion in London as to the appropriateness of this term to express the agreed purpose of NT, and we observe a general dissatisfaction with the choice which was due to two main factors:

  (a) on the one hand, it was felt that the term was obscure, and that it would be necessary for the ITO to try to clarify at a subsequent stage. The idea was that a *Definitions Section* should be subsequently negotiated that would, *inter alia,* include an agreed definition of this term;[47]
  (b) on the other, it was felt that, since the *Suggested Charter* contained references to *like products* only,[48] with no reference at all to competitive

---

[43] See E/PC/T/C.II/54 Rev. 1.   [44] See E/PC/T/C.6/97 at p. 7.

[45] See, for example, the French proposal where, in application of the French doctrine of *abus de droit,* France requested the insertion of a paragraph to the effect that "The members undertake not to institute or maintain internal taxes on the products of other member-countries the object of which might be a disguised form of protection for national production." This is one of the first statements to the effect that the national-treatment obligation would operate as an anti-circumvention provision: ITO Members should not circumvent through internal taxes their obligations with respect to tariff treatment of foreign products. Producer welfare would thus be legally protected through tariffs only.

[46] See E/PC/T/C.II/54.   [47] See E/PC/T/C.II/54 at pp. 36–38.

[48] See the *Suggested Charter,* at p. 4.

products, what is now known as directly competitive or substitutable products (DCS), something should be done to address cases where a domestic tax on imported coffee was higher than that imposed on domestic chicory.[49] In the words of the Dutch delegate, Mr. Van den Berg, the additional paragraph that was being negotiated during the *London Conference*, and that dealt with competitive products aimed "to guard against the more concealed types of discriminatory taxation."[50]

Fourth, there was acknowledgement of the fact that *federal structures* might have a hard time enforcing NT. Roux (France) acknowledged that there are many issues to discuss regarding how much federal governments can do to force the hand of states.[51] It was felt that this issue extended beyond the coverage of NT. As a result, it was removed from the NT agenda, and eventually became the current Art. XXIV.12 GATT.

4.2.1.2.2.2 *NT in the New York (Lake Success) Conference.* In Lake Success it was not the *Preparatory Committee*, but the *Drafting Committee* that was in session. The mandate of the *Drafting Committee* was supposed to be limited to streamlining agreed upon terms and concepts. With respect to NT, nonetheless, it was thought that more than mere streamlining was necessary in light of the number of issues that were left undecided during the *London Conference*. NT was further negotiated under the aegis of the Subcommittee dealing with Arts. 15-23, with the participation of delegates from the United States, France, the United Kingdom, the Netherlands, Belgium, Australia, and Czechoslovakia.[52]

Two days into the negotiations, the U.S. delegation submitted its first proposal concerning a redrafting of Art. 15 of the *London Draft*.[53] Negotiations were smooth,[54] probably because it became gradually clear that the GATT would not contain any *detailed* obligations concerning domestic instruments, other than

---

[49] See E/PC/T/C.II/W.2 at pp. 5ff. In the words of Leddy (U.S.) wheat was like to wheat only, and not to other cereals. Leddy made his comments in the context of discussions regarding the ambit of MFN and not NT. It was feared however, that had this attitude been exported to NT as well, the overall purpose of NT would be severely undermined, see E/PC/T/C.II/65 at p. 2.

[50] *Idem.* The level of sophistication of the arguments made is remarkable. See, for example, an exchange between Mr. Morton (Australia) and Mr. Johnson (U.S.) on the legality of some Australian mixing requirements and preferential tariff rates, see E/PC/T/C.II/W.2 at p. 7.

[51] See E.PC/T/C.II/55 at p. 2.   [52] See E/PC/T/C.6/4.

[53] See E/PC/T/C.6/6 of January 22, 1947.

[54] It is New Zealand only that objected to the redraft insisting for some sort of arrangement that would take care of its *film hire tax*, see E/PC/T/C.6/8 of January 23, 1947. The *film hire tax*, however, was a delayed customs duty levied at the point where the real value of the film had become apparent. The New Zealand delegate eventually conceded that this imposition could form the subject matter of tariff negotiations under Art. 24 of the *London Draft*. New Zealand was not, at the time, producing films, other than educational and newsreels, see E/PC/T/C.6/55/Rev. 1 at pp. 7–8.

the obligation not to discriminate.[55] There are various reasons that mandated this approach:

(a) more detailed provisions regarding (some) domestic instruments would be included in the ITO Charter, the advent of which would supersede the GATT. The GATT was conceived as some sort of regulatory minimum necessary to ensure that tariff concessions would not be circumvented. To this effect, an obligation not to discriminate was considered an adequate insurance policy against the danger of circumvention;

(b) it was at least the U.S. view, that nontariff barriers (NTBs) should not matter much;[56]

(c) many NTBs were simply not known to negotiators since they were "hidden" behind high tariffs. It was thus quite rational to first address tariff barriers before moving to discuss in a more elaborate manner NTBs.

The corresponding provision in the *London Draft* underwent some changes without altering its rationale or basic design.[57] With respect to internal measures of non fiscal nature, South Africa proposed the insertion of the terms "*laws, regulations and requirements*" that denoted a wide coverage of this provision, since it reduced the potential for circumvention.[58] As already mentioned *supra*, the term *identical or similar products* gave way to the term *like products*.[59] India continued to insist on a carve-out for taxation "strictly for the purposes of raising revenue," but this proposal was not accepted.[60]

The final redraft of NT was not unanimously accepted. It was decided, however, to leave it to dissidents to consider whether they would maintain their objections: Cuba wanted an exemption for protection of infant-industry purposes; India's desired carve-out regarded, as mentioned above, the possibility to tax discriminate in order to raise government revenue; Norway requested a carve-out in order to be in a position to tax discriminate, if necessary, to maintain uniform prices for a given product in its domestic market.[61] Two texts (albeit with a lot of bracketed language which denoted lack of agreement) were prepared during the New York Conference: one for the GATT, and one for the ITO Charter. The NT provision figured in both, was identical and became Art. II of the *New York* GATT Draft, and Art. 15 of the *New York* Draft ITO Charter.

---

[55] See E/PC/T/C.6/67 at p. 1.   [56] See Proposals, pp. 2ff.

[57] See E/PC/T/C.6/55 at pp. 2ff.

[58] See E/PC/T/C.6/55 at p. 3. It was argued by South Africa that laws could refer only to *formal* laws in some domestic legal contexts and thus, were NT to be limited to such acts only, the possibility for circumventing it through *informal* laws (such as, for example, administrative acts) would be open.

[59] Id.   [60] See E/PC/T/C.6/W.19 of January 24, 1947.

[61] See E/PC/T/C.6/55/Rev. 1 at pp. 3ff.

4.2.1.2.2.3 *NT in the Geneva Conference*. During the negotiations, it was once again made clear that there was no room for preferential internal taxes, such as those previously practiced in some parts of the world (New Zealand, the United States).[62] As a result, a definitive end was put to these requests. China wanted to limit the NT obligation to taxes (fiscal measures) only, but this attempt was thwarted by others.[63]

On the other hand, key terms such as *like products* which had been provisionally accepted *faute de mieux* continued to provoke a lot of discussion: Brazil mentioned the existence of a Committee (*Comisão de Similares*) that they had established to deal with determinations of like products precisely because the term was hard to define. It was felt that some similar action should be undertaken at the multilateral level as well. It was decided, however, not to overburden the GATT negotiations with similar tasks. Since the GATT would eventually come under the aegis of the ITO, and the ITO would possess sufficient institutional structure, it was decided to leave it to the ITO

...later on to establish a jurisprudence on the meaning of this term.[64]

Following a U.S. proposal to this effect, the obligation of NT was extended to cover not only *like*, but also *directly competitive or substitutable* (DCS) products,[65] the intent being to ensure that, in the absence of domestic production of like products, taxes could not be used to favor domestic DCS products.[66] The original idea was quite different from the current text: the DCS-discipline would come into play only when the regulating state had *no substantial* production of the *like* product; in this case, the regulating state could neither introduce new, nor increase old taxes so as to afford protection to its domestic DCS products. In contrast, were the regulating state to have substantial domestic production, it could legitimately treat DCS products in different manner, as long as it did not treat its products any better than the imported like products. Moreover, it was possible to maintain existing internal taxes that afforded protection to DCS products, in cases in which there was no substantial production of the like product, subject to negotiations for their elimination or reduction (Art. 17).[67]

The UK delegation continued to think of films not only as economic, but as cultural goods as well. The continued support of Chile, Czechoslovakia, New Zealand, and now India, Norway, and South Africa, left only the U.S. delegation opposing the UK view. The United States saw no reason to treat films differently from other goods; in the view of its delegates, the preference of the audience

[62] See E/PS/T/W/179 at p. 3.
[63] See E/PC/T/W/181 at p. 3. In China's view, hence, there should be no NT obligation with respect to regulatory (nonfiscal) domestic instruments.
[64] See E/PC/T/A/PV/40(1) at p. 14.   [65] See E/PC/T/W7150 at p. 5.
[66] See E/PC/T/174 at p. 6.   [67] See E/PC/T/186.

should determine the trade in films.[68] It was clear, nonetheless, that the U.S. delegation was fighting a losing battle on this issue.[69]

Finally, during the Geneva Conference, the provision expanded and the current Art. III.8 GATT was introduced in order to ensure that subsidies and government procurement were not coming under the coverage of NT.[70]

4.2.1.2.2.4 NT in the Havana Conference. The *Havana Conference* on Cuba during the first months of 1948 is the first multilateral conference after the entry into force of the GATT. The main mandate of the negotiators was to discuss the Draft ITO Charter.[71] At the same time, however, some important GATT provisions were also discussed and important clarifications/amendments were agreed upon. NT is one of the provisions that underwent substantial redrafting during this conference.[72] Although its basic structure was not put into question, negotiators added clarity to a text that had left, as we saw, many of them unsatisfied:

(a) It is now made clearer than ever before, through the introduction of what is now Art. III.1 GATT, that the intention of the drafters was that domestic instruments should not be used as a means of protection;[73]

(b) A series of *Interpretative Notes* were agreed which clarify a number of issues regarding the ambit of NT;[74]

(c) An outright elimination of all taxes that protect domestic DCS in the absence of substantial production of domestic like products was agreed;[75]

(d) Some clarification regarding mixing regulations was also agreed: regulations consistent with the first sentence of (what is now) Art. III.5 GATT shall not be considered to be contrary to the second sentence in any case in which all of the products subject to the regulation are produced domestically in substantial quantities.[76]

The records of the *Havana Conference* further reveal some interesting discussions whereby negotiators advance specific examples to demonstrate their understanding of the various terms used. Although the legal relevance of such examples specifically mentioned in the negotiating documents is limited, some

---

[68] See E/PC/T/W/181 pp. 7–8.

[69] As already discussed, eventually, a separate provision applicable only to films and justifying an exception to national treatment would be agreed to in subsequent negotiations (the current Art. IV GATT).

[70] See E/CONF.2/C.3/A/W/W.49.   [71] See Toye (2003).

[72] It figures as Art. 18 in the *Havana Conference* Draft.

[73] See E/CONF.2/C.3/A/W.47.

[74] See E/CONF.2/C.3/A/W.49. For example, it was agreed that domestic measures enforced at the border should be considered to be covered by the NT discipline, and not by the discipline regarding QRs (Art. XI GATT).

[75] See E/CONF.2/C.3/A/W/52 at p. 8.   [76] See E/CONF.2/C.3/A/W.47 at p. 5.

of them bear mention: for example, the final text provided for the outright elimination of taxes protecting DCS products irrespective whether there was substantial production of the domestic like product; it was stated, nevertheless, that,
an internal law that might help a domestic product (say, butter), but which hits
equally imported and domestic oleomargarine (a DCS product), does not violate
NT, if domestic production of oleomargarine is substantial.[77] More generally, we
read that a tax that is uniformly applicable to a considerable number of products
which conformed to (what is now) Art. III.2, first sentence (like products) would
also conform to Art. III.2, second sentence (DCS products).[78] Similar opinions
expressed provide further support to the view that the underlying intent of the
negotiators was to outlaw protectionist intent.

During the *Havana Conference*, it was also felt that the language chosen
might be *too* encompassing and that delimitations of the coverage were thus,
in order. For instance, according to the *Havana Report* (p. 61):

> ...neither income taxes nor import duties fall within the scope of Art 18 (of
> the Havana Charter – Art III of the GATT) which is concerned solely with
> internal taxes on goods.[79]

If at all, this language seems to suggest that at least *some* fiscal instruments (like
income duties) were meant to be left outside the coverage of NT. As we will see in
Section 4.3.2.2, this issue was re-discussed in the context of the *Working Party on
Border Tax Adjustments* where negotiators did not manage to write an exhaustive
list regarding the coverage of this provision.

The *Havana Conference* signals the end of the negotiation on NT: Art. III
GATT has remained unchanged since the last negotiations in the early months
of 1948 in Havana.

4.2.1.3 *Summarizing the Negotiating Record*

The negotiating record can be summarized as follows.

First, the study of the negotiating record of Art. III GATT shows that there was
a consensus view regarding the function of this provision: it was considered to
be necessary to safeguard the value of exchanged concessions. Absent an insurance policy to this effect, it was thought that participants would lose the incentive to continue engaging in trade liberalization, since the value of tariff concessions that they had extracted (and for which they had paid a price in terms of
themselves making tariff concessions in return) could be easily undone through
subsequent (to the international negotiation) unilateral action conferring an

---

[77] See *Havana Reports* at pp. 61–67.   [78] See *Havana Reports* pp. 62ff.
[79] See § 12 of the Annex to the Working Party report on *Border Tax Adjustments, op cit.*, citing
the *Havana Conference*.

advantage to the domestic product. NT was thought of as the insurance policy against this eventuality.

Second, the negotiators explicitly acknowledged that they had to be content with an incomplete NT provision, in light of the number of instruments that qualify as domestic instruments, and their ever changing form. They thus knowingly left the provision to be gradually "completed" through subsequent adjudication (and, eventually, renegotiation).

Third, there was a consensus view that in principle all domestic instruments but those explicitly excluded from the coverage of the provision should observe the NT discipline.

Fourth, it was commonly understood that certain key terms, such as *like products*, were not specific enough, but it was agreed that the ITO would at a later stage give these terms more precision. The failure to launch the ITO hence meant that today's judge has less guidance when dealing with cases coming under the ambit of Art. III GATT than was originally intended.

Finally, there is some, admittedly inconclusive, evidence that negotiators wanted to outlaw practices that were either intentionally protectionist, had a protectionist effect, or both.[80]

4.2.2 The Rationale for NT in Case Law

Recall that the negotiating record[81] suggests that the obligation to accord NT serves one purpose: prevention of *concession erosion*, that is, that tariff concessions made to trading partners should not be eroded through (subsequent) favorable treatment of domestic goods by means of domestic instruments; what is, for example, the value of a 5% import duty on imported cars if they are burdened with a 100% consumption tax whereas domestic cars are exempted from consumption tax altogether?

There has been repeated institutional acknowledgment of this rationale in case law. By means of illustration, we observe that a note by the GATT Secretariat summarizing the meetings of the *Working Party on Border Tax Adjustments* on 18 to 20 June 1968 captures this point in the following terms:

> In the case of Article III, the rules were designed to safeguard tariff concessions[82]

The AB, in its report on *Japan – Alcoholic Beverages II*, confirmed this understanding of NT. As we will see in more detail *infra*, the AB dealt in this case with

---

[80] See C.3/A White Paper of 26 January 1948 (suggested by the Subcommittee) at p. 3 (on file at the WTO Library).

[81] See the discussion in Section 4.1.

[82] See GATT Doc. L/3039 of 11 July 1968, GATT Doc L/3464, adopted on 2 December 1970, GATT Doc BISD 18S/97ff.

a Japanese scheme that was taxing alcoholic drinks that were predominantly produced in Japan less onerously (in *ad valorem* terms) than drinks produced abroad. It went on to find that the Japanese scheme was GATT-inconsistent. The starting point of its analysis was its understanding for the rationale for Art. III GATT, which it stated in the following terms (p. 16):

> ...The broad and fundamental purpose of Article III is to avoid protectionism in the application of internal tax and regulatory measures. More specifically, the purpose of Article III 'is to ensure that internal measures not be applied to imported or domestic products so as to afford protection to domestic production.' Toward this end, Article III obliges Members of the WTO to provide equality of competitive conditions for imported products in relation to domestic products.

This statement has been reproduced almost verbatim in each and every dispute that subsequently dealt with Art. III GATT. More on this in Section 4.4 where we discuss the case law.

4.2.3 The Rationale for NT from the Perspective of Economics

The previous Section sought to shed light on the motive for the drafters of the GATT to include a NT provision in the agreement. This Section considers the role of NT from the perspective of economics, and in particular, the economic literature on trade agreements.

It is a deeply rooted notion among economists that there are significant potential gains from international trade. These gains stem from a variety of sources: for instance, they originate from exploitation of comparative advantages stemming from differences in access to technology, in endowments of factors of production, or in preferences; there are gains stemming from increased competition and from better exploitation of economies of scale; gains can be derived from more product variety in consumption and production, etc. It is also clear that when governments determine their policies unconstrained by international obligations, they are prone to restrict imports. A theory of trade agreements requires an explanation of why national decisionmakers do not unilaterally ensure that these potential gains from trade are reaped. Indeed, if governments did not have such "protectionist" preferences, there would not be any role for a NT provision to play.

Most theories of trade agreements build on the notion that when making unilateral decisions concerning trade (and other) policies, national decisionmakers disregard the adverse impact these policies have on trading partners – there are in this sense negative *international externalities* from unilaterally pursued policies. The general purpose of trade agreements is to make countries "internalize" these external effects. This "international externalities" perspective will be adopted also here, even though we will say a few words towards the end of this Section about the main alternative – and in most respects complementary – view.[83]

In order to specify the nature of these international externalities, we must specify the objectives – the "preferences" – of the decisionmakers that bring the agreement about. Broadly speaking, the preferences describe how decisionmakers rank different possible outcomes of their interaction. Significant efforts have been spent by economists and political scientists to understand the nature of the preferences that are expressed through political decisionmaking. But for much of what follows, we can skirt the thorny issues concerning the nature of these preferences, by adopting an agnostic position. We will assume that the policies of relevance from an NT point of view are determined by a single rational decisionmaker – the "government." The preferences of this government are hence the economic/political trade-offs that the country would be willing to make in the interaction with the governments representing trading partners. For the most part we do not need to take a stand on the more precise nature of these preferences, or the political constraints under which it operates. We will see the purpose of our exercise in Section 4.4 as identifying interpretations of Art. III GATT that would enhance the efficiency of the agreement – that is, enhance the extent to which it achieves the objectives of Member country governments of reaping gains from trade.

The structure of the rest of this overview is as follows. Section 4.2.3.1 highlights some basic aspects of the main economic approach to understanding the purpose of trade agreements; the reader is referred to the accompanying study *Why the WTO? An Introduction to the Economics of Trade Agreements* for a more extensive discussion. Section 4.2.3.2 describes the role of NT in this framework, and discusses some of the likely pros and cons of such a clause. Section 4.2.3.3 offers a brief comment on NT building on an alternative view of the role of trade agreements. Section 4.2.3.4 summarizes.

4.2.3.1 *The Purpose and Structure of Trade Agreements*

Section 4.2.3.1.1 provides a very brief discussion of the complex issues involved in formulating the preferences of national decisionmakers. The subsection can be omitted without interrupting the flow of the reading.

4.2.3.1.1 A Digression on Policy Objectives. Trade negotiations are conducted by officials appointed by their national governments. To predict the outcome of a negotiation, and to interpret the meaning of the language of the agreement, we need to understand the objectives of these negotiators. Whose preferences do they represent? How do they evaluate and rank alternative proposals? And

---

[83] See, e.g., Bagwell and Staiger (2002), and Staiger (1995), for reviews of the literature.

what guides the voting behavior of legislators, who in most cases must ratify the product of any negotiation? These are difficult questions that have perplexed economists and political scientists for decades.

It is tempting to argue that negotiators in a democracy represent the aggregate preferences of society. But how do we aggregate individuals' preferences? How much weight do the views of a particular person receive? Should we weigh individuals equally in some sense? If so, how do we deal with the fact that the intensity of an individual's preferences is a personal matter and impossible to compare to that of another? Suppose citizen 1 in country A would very much like a trade agreement with some given terms, but is less enthusiastic about another agreement. Meanwhile, citizen 2 has the opposite ordering. What are the preferences of society?

Perhaps the simplest approach would be to assume that each government seeks to maximize its country's national income, i.e., the sum of the incomes of all of its citizens. However, it is difficult to justify national income as the appropriate government objective either descriptively or prescriptively. As a description of government objectives, simple income measures are suspect because they neglect citizens' concerns about the prices of the goods they buy, the insecurity they feel about potential disruptions to their income flows, the conditions under which they work, the quality of their environment, and so on. As a prescription, the measures suffer from these same omissions and moreover imply a lack of societal concern about the distribution of income.

A more common approach begins with the notion of a social welfare function. Social welfare is intended to measure overall societal well-being, a worthy objective for governments if not always the one they pursue. A non-paternal social welfare function is one that reflects only the citizen's own evaluation of their happiness and well-being. A paternalistic social welfare function can assess an individual's plight in a given situation differently than she would herself. In either case, the social welfare function must impose some scheme for aggregating individuals' well-being. Should they simply be summed and, if so, in what units should they be measured? If summing seems inappropriate, what weights should be applied to different individuals and what is the implicit evaluation of inequality in outcomes?

The assumption that governments maximize a measure of social welfare has the advantage of flexibility. In principle, the social welfare function can accommodate any considerations that the analyst deems appropriate. The analyst need not take a stand a priori on what are valid concerns for members of society or how these concerns ought to be weighed or compared. Of course, in the application of this approach, the analyst adopts an objective function with particular arguments and so implicitly imposes restrictions on the validity and importance of alternative concerns. Unfortunately, there is little to guide the choice of the social welfare function; essentially, the governments' objectives under this approach must come from outside the analysis.

An alternative approach to specifying the governments' objective function begins with an appreciation of political interactions. In this approach, the governments' objectives are induced by the political regime. Government officials, like private agents, are assumed to pursue their own well-being (or "utility") subject to constraints. Their utilities might reflect a taste for power or a pure desire to "do good," in addition to private concerns about material goods and perhaps the perquisites of office. After specifying the objectives of the political agents, the analyst must model the political interactions: What is the assumed electoral system? What are the voting rules, the political institutions, the role of campaign contributions, and the behavior of voters? Given the analyst's model of the political system, and the assumed interactions between political players, the government's objectives in its trade negotiations can be derived as a political outcome. That is, the electoral system, political institutions, and rules of the political game determine, among other things, the identities of the elected leaders and the policy positions they take.

This "political-economy" approach to government objectives recognizes, for example, that elected officials might pursue more strongly the interests of some constituents than others. The favored constituencies might be residents of swing districts, voters for whom trade policy is the most salient issue, or groups with ample resources to contribute to campaign financing. In any case, it is no longer clear, or even expected, that the government will pursue the aggregate and socially-just welfare of society.

The political-economy approach also has shortcomings. First, the approach relies on the modeling of political interactions. The more explicit are the government preferences used in the analysis, the more dependent are the predictions about trade negotiations on the plausibility and reliability of the assumed political model. Second, the induced government objective function need not be stable over time. Changes in the identities of the elected leaders may change the preferences of trade negotiators; changes in political institutions in the negotiating countries almost certainly will do so. This makes it difficult to render interpretations or predictions about trade agreements without detailed information about the state of politics in all the participating countries at the time of their discussions. Third, and perhaps most troubling, the governments' preferences may be jointly determined with the outcome of the trade negotiations. For example, if changes in trade policy strengthen some groups in society and weaken others, it will be impossible to know the governments' preferences without knowing what trade policies prevail, and of course, impossible to predict the trade policies without knowing the preferences of the negotiating agents. In such circumstances, governments' preferences must be treated as endogenous, and predictions about the results of trade negotiations must be made jointly with predictions about political outcomes.

Arguably, the political-economy approach is the more useful for answering positive questions, whereas the social-welfare approach may hold appeal for addressing normative issues. In the category of positive questions, we would include predictions about the outcomes of trade negotiations and matters of interpretation of existing agreements. For these, an understanding of the political circumstances seems unavoidable. In particular, matters of interpretation require us to consider what the negotiators were trying to achieve when drafting the agreement. Their intentions surely are conditioned on their actual politically-induced preferences, and not on some ethically-defensible preferences that they might have held in some best-of-all-possible worlds. In contrast, normative questions are fundamentally about what ought to be – how should the WTO contract be structured to achieve some specific goal. Here, the analyst may be justified, depending on the circumstances of the analysis, in ascribing "social" preferences that are his or her own, or that come from outside the analysis.

4.2.3.1.2 Externalities from Unilateral Decisionmaking. The international externalities approach to trade agreements rests on two main assumptions. The first is that countries are economically entwined such that decisions by one government have noticeable effects on the welfare of other governments. The second central assumption is that when governments make unilateral decisions, they are only concerned about their consequences for various national interests (for instance, domestic firms and consumers), while the consequences for trading partners are of no direct concern. The international externalities from unilateral decisionmaking stem from the combination of these circumstances. The externalities could be positive; for instance, when deciding in how much to invest in medical research, governments may put less weight on the value of resulting medical advances for people in other countries. But for many policies, the externalities from unilateral decisionmaking are negative. This is particularly true of policies that seek to enhance the competitive position of domestic products relative to foreign firms.

The existence of externalities implies that the outcome of the interaction between governments does not bring the parties as much benefit as it could – the outcome is in economic jargon "inefficient." Broadly speaking, a situation is efficient if it is not possible to improve the well-being of any economic agent, without reducing the well-being of some other agent. Henceforth, we will use the notion of efficiency to capture the extent to which pursued policies allow governments to achieve their objectives. It should be emphasized that this efficiency notion uses *government* preferences as the yardstick.[84] More exactly, we will say that a policy is (politically) efficient if the gain that any change would yield to

---

[84] The notion employed here should be distinguished from the more conventional economic concept of "economic (or market) efficiency" which refers to the extent to which a market allocation maximizes social welfare.

some governments could not suffice to compensate the governments that lose from the change; that is, we adopt a Kaldor-Hicks type of efficiency concept.

The distinguishing feature of unilateral decisionmaking – that is, when governments make their decisions without coordinating with other governments – is thus that it gives rise to international externalities that cause the outcome to be inefficient. It would, therefore, in principle be possible to change these policies, and in each case let the exporting country compensate the importing country's government for the loss resulting from the reduction of its trade barriers. However, trade agreements use a different means of achieving something similar, which is to let the compensation take the form of reciprocal market access. That is, trade agreements can be seen as means to *reciprocally reduce trade barriers that governments would not pursue if they were to bear the full global costs of their policies.*

4.2.3.1.2.1 *Externalities Can Be Internalized through Negotiations.* The basic role of a trade agreement is to determine tariff levels through negotiations rather than through unilateral decisionmaking.[85] The exchange of offers and counteroffers during the bargaining over the tariffs may effectively present governments with the externality costs of their border barriers. For instance, if countries A and B negotiate their respective measures X and Y, B might offer A to change policy Y against a certain change by A in policy X. Government A can choose to continue pursuing the same policy X, but it has now become sensitized to the internationally experienced cost of this policy, in terms of the forgone change by B in policy Y. As a matter of theory, provided a number of special conditions are fulfilled, the negotiated outcome will be (internationally) efficient, and this is also assumed in most of the trade agreement literature.

4.2.3.1.2.2 *What Is Efficient Depends on Government Preferences.* The defining feature of an efficient situation is that it is impossible to rearrange policies such that some government gains without causing losses to other governments. It follows that the preferences of governments determines what is an efficient policy outcome. For instance, if governments seek to maximize national income, and markets are characterized by perfect competition, no scale economies, etc., efficiency requires free trade. But more generally it is by no means necessary that free trade is efficient. For instance, tariffs redistribute income from consumers of the imported products to local producers of these (or similar) goods, and the government may find such redistribution desirable, and for various reasons hard to

---

[85] We here for simplicity treat a trade agreement as a once-and-for-all negotiated agreement on tariff levels. But economic theory highlights a number of more complex aspects of actual trade agreements, such as the role of bindings on other border instruments, the role of repeated negotiations, and the reasons for negotiated tariff ceilings rather than levels.

achieve through other means. It may, therefore, be part of a (politically) efficient international arrangement that Members maintain tariffs.

4.2.3.1.2.3 *Desirable and Undesirable Border Protection.* Section 4.4 will distinguish between two notions of "protection." First, the term can be used in the same sense as the term "shield," that is, as referring to a change in the competitive conditions to the benefit of domestic producers. Tariffs always protect in this sense. As just mentioned, an efficient agreement can feature positive tariffs, and it can hence be efficient despite protecting in this sense. Second, "protection" is also often used to refer to a policy that causes negative international externalities. For instance, a tariff that exceeds the efficient negotiated level would have such a property. To capture the protective effect of tariffs without taking a stand on whether they are efficient or not, we will say below that they "shield from competition," whereas we will reserve the terms "protectionist" and "protectionism" to denote the pursuit of inefficient policies. As will be highlighted further in Section 4.4.1, the GATT uses the term protection in both these senses.

4.2.3.1.3 The Incompleteness of Trade Agreements. Border instruments are likely to be the instruments *par preference* for countries seeking to restrict trade, since they are targeted at trade, and are relatively easy to handle administratively. But many domestic policy instruments can be used for similar purposes as border instruments, and some instruments with more or less identical effects. For instance, sales taxes imposed specifically on imports are largely import tariffs by another name. If a trade agreement restricted the use of border instruments only, governments might instead resort to domestic instruments for the same purposes, if possible. The agreement must, therefore, constrain also the use of domestic instruments.

    The inclusion of domestic instruments severely complicates a problem that exists already with regard to border instruments. First, there are an extremely large number of different domestic policy instruments with trade impact. These instruments are typically used for purposes that the members would agree to be legitimate, but they could also be employed for the purpose of protectionism. The agreement hence has to be sensitive to the underlying policy rationale – to be able to "sort the wheat from the chaff" – for an extremely large number of domestic policies.

    Second, there is a need to make the restrictions imposed on domestic policies responsive to changes in the underlying economic/political environment. One possibility would be that the agreement specified for each Member the policies to be pursued in each and every situation that the Member might find itself in, that is, that the agreement is "state-contingent" in economic jargon.[86] But of

---

[86] An alternative means of achieving a politically efficient state contingency would be to leave discretion to the importing country government over its domestic instruments, but to have in place a mechanism that ensured that the governments face appropriate incentives from

course, with the agreement intended to be in place for an extended period of time, there would be a huge number of such different economic/political situations that would call for different policy responses.

Needless to say, it would require an enormously complex agreement to separately bind all domestic instruments with trade effects in a state contingent fashion. To the extent it would be conceptually feasible at all, the costs of negotiating and drawing up such a grand contract would be huge, and would most likely dominate the gains it would bring. Indeed, it would amount to central planning at a global scale. Trade agreements are for these (and probably also other) reasons therefore much less complex – they are contractually "incomplete."

As an illustration of the difficulty facing negotiators, let us here quote again the Chairman of the Technical Sub-committee in charge of preparing the draft provision on National Treatment (NT) during the London meeting of the Preparatory Committee:[87]

> Whatever we do here, we shall never be able to cover every contingency and possibility in a draft. Economic life is too varied for that, and there are all kinds of questions which are bound to arise later on. The important thing is that once we have this agreement laid down we have to act in the spirit of it. There is no doubt there will be certain difficulties, but if we are able to cover 75 or 80 or 85 per cent of them I think it will be sufficient.

Contractual incompleteness can take many forms.[88] For instance, undertakings in the agreement may not be conditioned on changes in the economic/political environment – they are "rigid." In other instances the agreement is silent on particular issues, leaving "discretion" to individual governments to determine the policies unilaterally. Provisions may also be vaguely formulated, postponing to future adjudication or negotiations the clarification of the exact nature of the undertakings. The GATT exhibits all these forms of incompleteness, albeit sometimes in less clean form than described here. For instance, border (trade) instruments are rigidly bound: import and export quotas are forbidden and thus set at their free trade levels; import tariffs are legal, but tariff levels are negotiated, and the agreed-upon levels are then bound; export subsidies are illegal. But while the bindings of tariffs are rigid in the sense of not being explicitly conditioned on say the level of imports, there are still a number of ways in which the tariffs can be adjusted ex post tariff negotiations. For instance, temporary safeguards can be unilaterally imposed, it is possible to temporarily increase tariffs in case of severe macroeconomic disturbances, and renegotiations are possible.

---

an efficiency point of view when unilaterally determining its domestic policies. A dispute-settlement mechanism would be a natural part of such a mechanism.

[87] Document E/PC/T/C.II/PRO/PV/7.

[88] The reasoning in the remainder of this Section draws partly on Horn, Maggi, and Staiger (2010).

Another example of the incompleteness of the GATT is the fact that it leaves domestic instruments at the discretion of Members. As noted, there are strong reasons to believe that governments have incentives to use such discretion for protectionist purposes, as a substitute for the border instruments that have been bound. The first line of defense against such behavior in most trade agreements is some form of NT provision.

4.2.3.2 *The Role of NT: To Filter Out Protectionist Policies*

The basic idea of the NT provision is deceptively simple: since inefficiencies from the use of domestic instruments stem from less favorable treatment of imported products, countries should not be allowed to treat domestic products better than foreign products solely by virtue of their different origins. While persuasive at a general level, the practical implementation of this simple idea is far from trivial.

As emphasized above, the basic problem facing the treatment of domestic instruments in a trade agreement is the need for it to be responsive to the nature of the national regulations it affects. The fact that a regulation imposes costs on trading partners is not sufficient to show that the measure is inefficient. It is, therefore, highly desirable that the regulation of domestic instruments primarily filters out only those instances where differential treatment is (internationally) inefficient.

A fundamental practical problem for this filtering is the fact that it *depends on the preferences* of the Members whether a policy is efficient or not. For instance, it may be efficient to restrict imports of a product when its environmental impact in the importing country is of concern to the importing country government, while it would not be efficient if the government were oblivious to such consequences. However, it is often very difficult to observe directly the preferences of governments, and hence the true rationale for policies that are pursued. Indeed, if it were possible to observe these motives, a NT provision would not be needed in the first place: it could then be replaced by a simple yet powerful general dictum not to pursue any inefficient policy.[89,90]

4.2.3.2.1 The Efficacy of NT for Given Tariff Levels.
Having discussed the rationale for NT, we briefly turn to the question of its likely efficacy at preventing inefficient use of domestic policies, drawing on the meager economic literature on the role of NT in trade agreements. This literature is still in its infancy, and can at most help identify some likely positive as well as negative features of the provision. The literature for the most part considers a simplistic form of NT, what

---

[89] Such a policy would in principle just be an extreme case of negative integration, while its outcome would be an extreme case of positive integration.

[90] The problem would be exactly the same if the measure were to be evaluated under an exceptions clause such as Art. XX GATT.

we will refer to as a "rigid" NT rule, according to which members of the trade agreement must not treat a foreign product differently than competing domestic products, *regardless* of any policy motives possibly advanced as rationale for the differentiation. There exists thus hardly any economic analysis that highlights the role of NT as a "filtering device."

The literature has identified several mechanisms through which NT may affect the welfare of the parties, even if rigidly imposed so that no differential treatment is allowed of imported and domestic products even if efficient. We will in this Section consider effects that appear also for given tariffs.

Consider first some possible beneficial aspects of a rigid NT rule.

A *first* observation is that the direct impact of a rigid NT rule is indeed to constrain the incentive to use domestic instruments for protectionism, since any disadvantage imposed on imported products must also be imposed on domestic products.

Second, this chilling effect on the incentives to use domestic instruments for protectionism comes at a relatively limited contractual cost, since negotiators do not have to agree on a huge number of specific domestic policies, but only need to agree on a principle that requires a few lines of legal text. Furthermore, once such a principle is established and accepted, it does not need to be renegotiated in subsequent rounds of tariff negotiations.

Third, as discussed above, for bindings of domestic policy instruments to be fully efficient they would need to be state-contingent, conditioning the prescribed policy levels on all relevant circumstances that would affect their optimal levels. But such a complete contract scenario would be enormously costly. A rigid NT rule allows for a similar adjustment to exogenous circumstances, but in a very different, and from a contracting cost point of view much cheaper, way: by leaving discretion over the common treatment of imported and domestic products to importing country governments, it escapes the need for the parties to determine the level for these instruments for long swathes of time, as would be the case if this had to be done in a negotiation round. Instead, the importing country government can unilaterally respond to changes in the economic environment whenever it likes. NT hence has the virtue of limiting the possibility to use domestic instruments for protectionist purposes, while at the same time preserving a certain degree of freedom to respond to unforeseen events.

Turn next to the negative side of NT, still for constant tariffs. There are several fundamental reasons to believe that NT (applied as a rigid rule or not) will not be panacea for achieving full efficiency. To illustrate why, consider an example of taxation. A *first* limitation is that NT only applies in situations where the tax on a domestic product is lower than the tax on a competing imported product. This restriction would be hard to understand in a full information context, but can be seen as a partial remedy to an informational problem, since it tends to focus attention to cases where the likelihood of protectionism is likely to be higher. Consequently, it does not have any bite in situations where the domestic product is taxed higher than the imported product, but where this difference in taxation should be even larger. Nor can it enforce higher taxation of the domestic product in situations where it is taxed lower at the outset, it can maximally enforce equal taxation.

To illustrate, suppose that a domestic and a foreign product are identical in all respects, except for that the domestic product gives rise to environmental damage in the importing country. Suppose further that the efficient tax on imports is $t_I = 0\%$ and that the efficient tax on the domestic product is $t_D = 40\%$. If the importing country were to set, say, $t_D = 20\%$ and $t_I = 10\%$, NT could have no impact, despite the fact that these taxes are not efficient.

A *second* limitation to the efficacy of the NT provision is the fact that the decision over the common tax $t_D = t_I$ will be made unilaterally by the importing country, and will thus likely give rise to international externalities. To illustrate, modify the example above so that both products are equally damaging to the environment, with efficiency requiring taxes $t_D = t_I = 5\%$, The importing country may unilaterally prefer $t_D = 0\%$ and $t_I = 20\%$ absent NT. But forced to set uniform taxes, it might balance the benefits from taxing the imported product against the costs of the taxation of the domestic product, by setting an inefficient common tax $t_D = t_I = 10\%$.[91] This would be a higher level than would be called for from the point of view of combating the environmental problem. But the resulting distortion would be worthwhile from the importing country government's point of view, since the government puts a value on the restraining effect on imports. More generally, whenever the policy decision neglects foreign interests, there are almost always alternative policies that are more efficient internationally.

This example reflects a more general asymmetry between the treatment of border instruments and domestic instruments from an efficiency point of view. There is a presumption that the negotiations over the bindings of border instruments will (at least under certain circumstances) lead to efficient outcomes. In the case of domestic instruments however, there is no presumption that NT-compatible tax levels will be efficient.

4.2.3.2.2 The Interaction between Tariffs and Taxes. As argued in Section 4.2.2, the purpose of NT is to prevent tariff concessions from being undermined through subsequent opportunistic use of domestic instruments, in order to provide incentives for countries to make such concessions. It is therefore essential to take into consideration the interplay between tariff setting and subsequent unilateral determination of domestic instruments. The literature has

---

[91] We are here disregarding the possibility that trade agreements may serve as a commitment device; this possibility will be discussed briefly in Section 4.4.

so far concentrated on the interplay with tax setting, so we concentrate on this case.[92]

First, as repeatedly stressed in the above, it may be desirable from an (international) efficiency point of view to allow for higher taxation of imported products. It may therefore seem inevitable that a NT rule that does not allow for such differential treatment must be inefficient when it is desirable to tax imported products higher than domestic products. While there is something to this argument, some caution is needed. The reason is that the argument implicitly rests on the assumption of constant tariffs. But what matters for the market access of imported products is not only domestic taxation, but the total taxation these products face. For instance, in the case where the domestic instrument perfectly substitutes for the tariff, as with a sales tax on the imported product, what matters for imports is the sum of the tariff and the sales tax.

To illustrate, consider a case where because of an environmental hazard from imports, efficiency requires that the total taxation of the imported product exceeds that on the domestic product. It is clear that if such an environmental hazard were to appear unexpectedly after import tariffs have been agreed upon, an inability to impose a higher tax on imported products would be costly. On the other hand, if the environmental hazard is known at the time of tariff negotiations, and is taken into account by trade negotiators, the tariff on this product can fully reflect the adverse environmental impact, even if taxes are set equally, and the rigid NT rule hence is respected.

This example illustrates two related points. First, in order to assess the cost of an inflexible imposition of NT it is necessary to take tariff setting into account. Second, the cost of this inflexibility can be mitigated (and may in theory at least be dominated by the gains), provided that trade negotiators take into consideration the noncommercial effects of their tariff agreement.

Second, it was emphasized above that at the core of the rationale for NT is an informational problem: the need for the provision stems from the fact that government preferences are not easily observable. But very little work has been done to date on informational aspects of NT. One of the few steps in this direction (Horn (2009)) suggests a reason why NT primarily restrains governments with, from an efficiency point of view, legitimate reasons for imposing higher taxes on imported products than on competing domestic products.

Consider the following illustrative example. An importing country government can have two different motives to impose a higher tax on imports than on domestic competing products: all governments have the standard protectionist motive, and some governments face local environmental problems stemming from the transportation or consumption of the imported product. Outsider observers cannot tell whether a higher tax on an imported product is motivated

---

by one or both of these motives. In economic jargon, we can thus think of the governments as being of two "types" – those that have only protectionist motives for differential taxation, and those that have both protectionist and environmental motives – and governments' types are unknown.

Now note two features: First, since an environmentally affected government faces the same protectionist motives as the other type of government, its unilaterally optimal tax differential will be larger than if only protectionism motivated the tax setting, since the environmental problem adds a reason for taxing the imported products higher. Second, if the negotiated tariff is sufficiently high, there is no need to use domestic taxes to achieve any of these objectives. The importing country can set the same tax rate (perhaps equal to zero), and can achieve both its protectionist and a possible environmental target in a NT-compatible fashion through the tariff.

As the tariff is gradually lowered from this level however, it becomes increasingly likely that there is not enough of a difference in total taxation between the imported and the domestic product. The government to first experience this problem is the government that faces the environmental problems from imports, since it has stronger incentives to maintain a large tax differential than the government that is solely motivated by the protectionism. The environmentally affected type of government type will hence be the first to switch to lower taxation of the domestic product, and thus come under NT. In this sense, as trade is liberalized, *NT first affects those governments that desire high total taxation of the imported product not only for protectionist reasons, but also for environmental* reasons. NT in this sense starts to bind from the wrong side of the spectrum of government types.

Of course, this feature of NT may be immaterial if the adjudication process flawlessly determines whether countries have been exposed to environmental hazards of sufficiently severe nature for it to be in the global interest to let these countries continue with their differential taxation. But if there are, e.g., litigation costs, or adjudicating bodies occasionally commit judicial mistakes, this aspect may take on significance.

4.2.3.2.3 The Nature of the Costs of Judicial Errors.
Because of the difficulties in assessing the true nature of domestic measures, adjudicating bodies are bound to make mistakes. These can broadly speaking take one of two forms. One possible mistake is to permit measures that should be declared illegal. The cost of such mistakes are borne by the affected trading partner, and will at least partly take the form of reduced profits of exporters, and consequent losses of income for other interests associated with the exporting firms.

The other type of mistake is to outlaw measures that should be allowed. Considering the nature of the values that domestic regulations may seek to protect, such as human health and the environment, it may appear as if the costs from judicial mistakes in the form of erroneous impositions of an inflexible dictum not to set lower taxes on domestic products may be particularly severe. While there is something to this argument, it does not seem to be entirely correct.[93]

To see why, consider the case where imports are associated with a severe health hazard; for instance, it has just been discovered that asbestos constitutes a severe danger to human health. With the tariff on an asbestos-containing product bound, efficiency might require to let the importing country set a higher domestic tax on the imported product, since consumers who are oblivious to the dangers of asbestos would otherwise purchase the cheaper asbestos-containing product. But suppose the adjudicator erroneously declares the measure to violate NT. In such case, despite the constraint imposed by NT, the importing country is still not forced to accept health damage from the consumption of the imported product: *it can still set the common tax level high enough to completely choke off imports.*[94] This will be optimal for the government to do if the health hazard is severe enough.

The point illustrated through this example is hence that a rigid application of NT always leaves the importing country with the possibility to shut out imports completely. The cost of the judicial mistake is in such an instance not in the form of reduced human health (other than possibly indirectly through, e.g., reduced national income). The cost takes instead the form of lost domestic consumer and producer welfare, since domestic production must face the same prohibitive taxes as imports. Health effects might instead arise in situations where the hazard is less severe, and where consequently it is not worthwhile for the government to completely shut out imports.

4.2.3.3 *An Alternative View of the Role of Trade Agreements*

The theory laid out above sees trade agreements as means to limit international externalities from unilateral policymaking. An alternative view of the purpose of trade agreements builds on the notion that absent an agreement, each government pursues policies that are *not* in its own long-run interest. In particular, because of previous actions by private interests, a government may find itself in a situation where it finds it optimal to behave in a more protectionist fashion than it would normally prefer to do; for instance, a government may find it necessary to bail out a domestic industry that has put itself in dire straits in expectation of a bail-out. A commitment to a trade agreement may make it more costly for a government to give in to such a request. This may in turn induce private interests not to behave so as to put the government in this position in the first place, knowing that the commitment to the trade agreement will prevent the government from pursuing the policies the private interests would like to see. The difference between this approach and the international externalities approach is thus that a trade agreement in this view solves a domestic

---

[93] The reasoning here builds on Horn (2009).
[94] We disregard the possibility of a nonviolation complaint.

political problem, rather than an international problem. The international dimension of the interaction concerns only the enforcement – the trade agreement provides a commitment possibility.

In what follows, we will rely on an international externalities approach, partly since it is used by all economic studies of the role of NT that we are aware of, and partly since it seems to explain certain features of Art. III GATT better than the commitment approach. It seems that if the main purpose of trade agreements were to commit governments to liberal trade, agreements would have been drafted differently. Indeed, a main feature of the DSU is that it limits the possibility for enforcement of concessions.[95] This is by no means to deny the fact that agreements may also serve other purposes, for instance, to help governments to commit to certain policies at the international plane so as to preempt requests by lobbies to follow a particular policy.

4.2.3.4 *Summary of the Rationale of NT from an Economic Perspective*

The main observations to stem from the discussion of the role of NT from the perspective of economics are the following:

(a) The purpose of trade agreements is to limit the extent to which governments expose trading partners to negative externalities from their unilateral policy decisions.
(b) The role of NT is to reduce the externalities that follow from the fact that it is infeasible for governments to bind domestic instruments.
(c) NT is likely to constrain the use of domestic instruments for protectionist purposes, but there are a number of reasons why NT will not achieve full efficiency, including the fact that unilaterally set NT-compatible (i.e., common) tax levels will not be internationally efficient.
(d) The evaluation of the efficiency of a contested measure, whether it amounts to "protectionism," requires information concerning government preferences.

4.3 The Implementation of NT in Case Law

4.3.1 The Case Law Regarding Art. III GATT

In Section 4.3, we discuss the completion of Art. III GATT through case law since 1948. The main conclusions that stem from this study are as follows:

(a) Case law is not consistent in its interpretation of several core concepts in the provision;

---

[95] For instance, it puts an upper bound on the magnitude of counter-measures that can be legally imposed, and it can retard the implementation of counter-measures by several years by requesting the case to be reviewed by both a panel and the AB, and this despite the fact compensation is not possible.

(b) Case law is often highly uninformative concerning the reasoning behind determinations. The fears of the negotiators regarding the (in)appropriateness of some of the terms used in the body of this provision have been confirmed: case law has not managed to pin them down in one measurable dimension and, as a result, there is still considerable uncertainty regarding the understanding of terms such as "*like products*" and "*less favorable treatment.*" This is probably due to the fact that, in line with the overall attitude especially of the AB, case law has privileged a textualist, a-contextual understanding of the various terms appearing in the body of Art.III GATT and deprived them of their connecting thread, the objective of this provision which is embedded in the first paragraph of Art. III GATT. References to the objectives of this provision have been selective and self-contained, in the sense that they have not informed the interpretation of the key terms appearing in the body of Art. III GATT.

(c) Overall, it is unclear to what extent case law interpretations have implemented the purpose of NT.

Recall that Art. III GATT requests from WTO Members not to afford protection to domestic production through their domestic instruments; in other words, once (imported) goods have paid their ticket to entry (e.g., tariff) into a market, they cannot be subjected to any burden that the domestic products with which they are competing are not subjected to; as a result, all protection through border instruments in the GATT is a matter of negotiation and can take one form only: tariff protection. Art. III GATT does not enumerate one by one the domestic instruments to which it applies, except for local content requirements that are explicitly mentioned in Art. III.5 GATT. Two instruments (government procurement, subsidies) are explicitly omitted, and all the remaining instruments (irrespective whether of fiscal or nonfiscal nature) are, in principle, covered.

Recall further that the GATT does not impose any common policies on WTO Members; they remain free to unilaterally define their fiscal, competition, public-health, environment, etc. policies in any manner they deem it appropriate. What matters is that, at the stage when they regulate, they do not discriminate against imported products. The GATT is thus a *negative integration* scheme. Put differently, Art. III GATT seeks to equate conditions of competition *within* and not *across* markets.

The remaining part of this section is divided as follows: Section 4.3.2 discusses the rationale for NT as it has been explained in case law, and the case-law interpretation of the various terms appearing in the provision; Section 4.3.3 discusses the exceptions to NT; in Section 4.3.4, we revert to the critique that has been voiced against the manner in which case law has interpreted NT: this section, although not exhaustive, reproduces the quintessence of the critique voiced so far. Section 4.3.5 briefly concludes the analysis of the case-law implementation of Art. III GATT.

4.3.2 The Legal Discipline

In theory, the argument could be made that *all* instruments affecting trade come under the purview of Art. III GATT. This view finds ample support in the text of the provision, which explicitly excludes two instruments only from its coverage, and has been endorsed, as we will see in more detail *infra*, in case law. The fact, however, that all domestic instruments are, in principle, covered by the NT provision does not mean that all of them can be *legally* used by the importing state and imposed on imported products: for example, the text of Art. III.2 GATT leaves little doubt that a domestic (say consumption) tax is covered by its disciplines and a WTO Member has an *obligation* not to impose on imported goods a tax higher than it imposes on domestic *like* goods. This obligation nonetheless is predicated on a *right* to apply consumption taxes to domestic and imported goods. This right does not originate in the GATT. In fact, the GATT framers did not spend anytime discussing this issue. They took it for granted that the GATT contracting parties (now, WTO Members) are all well-defined jurisdictional entities and will behave in line with the (public international law) rules governing allocation of jurisdiction.[96] These rules, nonetheless, are far from clear: one distinguishes between the *nationality*-principle (whereby a state regulates behavior of its nationals wherever committed), and the *territoriality*-principle (whereby a state regulates behavior which either occurs in, or has an effect on home soil).[97] Whereas it is clear in public international law that, in case of conflict between the two, it is the *territoriality*-principle that prevails, it is unclear what happens if a transaction affects more than one jurisdiction. In principle, more than one jurisdiction could decide this issue; this is so, for a number of reasons: first, it is nowhere stated that a quantification of effects is an appropriate tool in this context, and consequently it cannot be excluded that, in practice, even minimal effects might confer jurisdiction; second, it could be the case that the importance two states attach to a particular effect differs (state A is not very risk averse and hence does not mind if acid rain hits it one day, whereas state B is quite risk averse and wants to avoid even a couple of drops); third, it is unclear whether effects must be tangible, physical effects, or whether 'moral' effects (such as for example, distress in country A caused by the fact that country B practices child labor, even if such products are not being exported to A), also confer jurisdiction. As a result, it is not unheard of that, in practice, a transaction is often submitted to various jurisdictions with the resulting burden in terms of transaction costs,

[96] See Horn and Mavroidis (2008).
[97] There are other bases conferring jurisdiction: there is for example, universal jurisdiction; it covers however, specific transactions. The two bases mentioned here are the default bases applicable whenever another, more specific rule does not kick in, see various contributions in Meessen (1996) on this score.

and that disputes arise regarding the question who is competent to regulate a particular transaction.

4.3.2.1 *Which Measures Come under the Scope of NT?*

The precise boundary between border and domestic instruments is unclear, and has been a recurring theme in case law. With regard to domestic instruments, Art. III.1 GATT stipulates an extremely broad coverage by referring to

> ...internal taxes and other internal charges, and laws, regulations and requirements....

having the effect of

> ...affecting the internal sale, offering for sale, purchase, transportation, distribution or use of products, and internal quantitative regulations requiring the mixture, processing or use of products in specified amounts or proportions....

The same broad approach is continued in Art. III.2 GATT, which states that exports of a Member shall not be subject,

> ...*directly or indirectly*, to internal taxes or other internal charges *of any kind* in excess of those applied, *directly or indirectly*, to like domestic products.... [emphasis added]

Similarly, Art. III.4 requests no less favorable treatment of imported products with respect to

> ...all laws, regulations and requirements affecting their internal sale, offering for sale, purchase, transportation, distribution or use.

There are two exceptions to this approach:

(a) Art. III.5 GATT explicitly outlaws *local content* requirements: all measures whereby a government privileges goods containing a set amount of domestic added value are outlawed. This prohibition has been further underscored through the advent of the TRIMs Agreement which contains an illustrative list of such measures. No other domestic instruments (other than local content requirements), are explicitly prohibited by Art. III GATT;

(b) two measures are explicitly *exempted* from the NT obligation by virtue of Art. III.8 GATT: producer subsidies, and government procurement. Hence, with respect to these measures, WTO Members can behave unconstrained by the NT obligation.

The wording that the framers privileged was quite wide: the term *directly or indirectly* in Art III.2 GATT were inserted at the initiative of the UK delegate, and replaced the terms *in connection with* previously used.[98] It was felt that limits to the discretion of the regulating state were in order. At Havana, for example, it was recorded that:

> ...neither income taxes nor import duties fall within the scope of Art 18 (of the Havana Charter – Art III of the GATT) which is concerned solely with internal taxes on goods.[99]

The preparatory work thus suggests that the intent of the negotiators was to exclude at least some taxes from the coverage of this provision, even though the wording they agreed upon gives the opposite impression. It should be recalled however, as pointed out above, that the intention was to renegotiate some of the key terms of Art. III GATT in the ITO. This renegotiation never took place however, nor did GATT Members renegotiate the provision in subsequent GATT rounds. The failure of the ITO did lead to one attempt to clarify the ambit of Art. III GATT – the creation of the *Working Party on Border Tax Adjustments*. Some clarification with respect to the coverage of NT was provided through the negotiations in this context, although no full agreement was achieved regarding the coverage, but as we will argue below, the outcome did not resolve the core issues concerning the interpretation of the provision. We discuss this further in Section 4.3.2.2.

There is probably less ambiguity with respect to internal measures of nonfiscal nature. Art. III.4 GATT covers all internal laws, regulations and requirements *affecting* imported products. The term *affecting* suggests a will to cast the net widely. This view is also supported by the fact that there is no negotiating record indicating that specific transactions were intended to be excluded.[100]

We now leave the letter of the law and its negotiating history, to turn to the case law. Case law has further clarified that NT covers transactions relating to both bound (i.e., goods on which a tariff concession has been concluded) and unbound items as well. The AB left no doubt in this regard (*Japan – Alcoholic Beverages II*, p. 17):

> ...The Article III national treatment obligation is a general prohibition on the use of internal taxes and other internal regulatory measures so as to

---

[98] See § 13 of the annex to the Working Party report on *Border Tax Adjustments* (GATT Doc. BISD 18S/87ff).

[99] See § 12 of the annex to the working party report on *Border Tax Adjustments, op cit.*

[100] See on this score, Irwin *et al.* (2008). This is not to suggest that NT can *equally* meaningfully apply to *all* domestic policies/measures. Its application on substantive (as opposed to procedural) antitrust laws is, for example, problematic: a WTO Member which accepts a merger between two domestic companies and, subsequently, rejects a merger between a foreign and a domestic company operating all four in the same relevant product market has not necessarily violated NT; moving from say six to five or from five to four companies in a market involves different considerations (*inter alia*, because the degree of concentration as measured in Herfindhal-Hirschmann Index terms will be different).

afford protection to domestic production. This obligation clearly extends also to products not bound under Article II.

Note that domestic measures enforced at the border come, according to the *Interpretative Note ad Art III of the GATT*, under the purview of Art. III GATT. Thus, a sales ban which is enforced at the border (and could be viewed as a trade embargo) will still be considered to be a sales ban (and, consequently, come under the purview of Art. III GATT, and *not* that of Art. XI GATT).

Finally, GATT panels and WTO adjudicating bodies have consistently held that not only *de jure*, but also *de facto* discrimination is covered by Art. III GATT.[101]

4.3.2.2 *The Right to Regulate*

As mentioned above, the GATT contracting parties did not spend any time during the negotiation of the GATT discussing the right to regulate for example, the level of customs duties or domestic taxes. One can thus reasonably assume that they took it for granted that the default rules governing the permissible jurisdictional reach of national legislation would be applicable in the trading context as well.

The default rules do solve some problems, but not others.[102] One deficiency is that the *default rules* do not exclude the possibility of *concurrent* exercise of jurisdiction (that is, cases where more than one sovereignty is awarded jurisdiction over a transaction and exercises its right to regulate it). Disputes concerning cases where countries concurrently exercising jurisdiction impose different forms of regulation often find their way to courts and arbitral tribunals, if one (some of them) dispute the right of others to regulate the particular transaction. The GATT contracting parties entertained a discussion on this issue subsequent to the entry into force of the GATT in the above-mentioned *Working Party on Border Tax Adjustments*. This Working Party was not intended to discuss all issues associated with jurisdictional reach. In fact, its origins were much humbler: some GATT contracting parties felt that the GATT was not neutral towards the basic properties of a domestic fiscal system and was not treating in even-handed manner direct and indirect taxation. By attempting to determine which fiscal instruments could (and could not) be adjusted at the border by either the importing or the exporting state, this Working Party provided nevertheless, a partial response

---

[101] In the former case, imported and domestic products are treated differently solely by virtue of their different origins. *De facto* discrimination is less well-defined. It arises in situations where domestic and foreign goods are subject to the same policy rule, and in this respect are treated identically. But due to differences in the characteristics of the two products the application of the policy rules results in differential treatment, even though there is no regulatory motive for this other than protectionism.

[102] For a concise description, see Horn and Mavroidis (2008).

to the question which fiscal instruments can a particular jurisdiction lawfully employ.[103]

The Working Party did not manage to reach a total solution, as we will see in more detail infra. Consequently, disagreements on the permissible jurisdictional reach would have to be submitted to adjudication. However, at the time of writing, there has not been one single case where a WTO adjudicating body was requested to directly address the core jurisdictional issue: how are the rights to regulate distributed among WTO Members. Indirectly, nonetheless, WTO adjudicating bodies did provide scarce evidence regarding their understanding of this issue. They have not managed though, to complete the contract in this regard. For example, in *US–Shrimp*, the AB did state that the United States should have shown a "nexus" between its interest to regulate and the transaction at hand, but the AB did not specify the precise meaning of this concept, nor did the AB explain what the implications would be if parties on both sides of the dispute could demonstrate a nexus. We tend to believe that the AB is mindful of the jurisdictional issue as prerequisite for lawful exercise of jurisdiction but we still lack a test that explains in concrete terms how to discern lawful exercise jurisdiction.

4.3.2.3 *Fiscal Measures*

Art. III.2 GATT reads:

> The products of the territory of any contracting party imported into the territory of any other contracting party shall not be subject, directly or indirectly, to internal taxes or other internal charges of any kind in excess of those applied, directly or indirectly, to like domestic products. Moreover, no contracting party shall otherwise apply internal taxes or other internal charges to imported or domestic products in a manner contrary to the principles set forth in paragraph 1.

The *Interpretative Note ad Art. III.2 of the GATT* reads:

> A tax conforming to the requirements of the first sentence of paragraph 2 would be considered to be inconsistent with the provisions of the second sentence only in cases where competition was involved between, on the one hand, the taxed product and, on the other hand, a directly competitive or substitutable product which was not similarly taxed.

Art. III.1 GATT (to which Art. III.2 GATT refers) reads:

> The Members recognize that internal taxes and other internal charges, and laws, regulations and requirements affecting the internal sale, offering for sale, purchase, transportation, distribution or use of products, and internal

---

[103] An origin principle is often taken to mean that the taxation of a traded product is determined by the exporting country, while the importing country is assumed to set the tax on the product under the destination principle. However, the issue of origin versus destination principle is in principle separate from the allocation of the jurisdiction.

quantitative regulations requiring the mixture, processing or use of products in specified amounts or proportions, should not be applied to imported or domestic products so as to afford protection to domestic production.

Therefore, a complaining party can choose between two possible routes. One is to argue that:

(a) the domestic and the foreign products are *like*; and
(b) the latter is taxed *in excess* of the former.

The other is to claim that:

(a) the two products are *directly competitive or substitutable* (DCS);
(b) the two products are *not similarly taxed*; and that
(c) the dissimilar taxation is *applied so as to afford protection* (ASATAP) to domestic production.

Central to the scope of NT is the adjudicating bodies' interpretation of the italicized terms.

4.3.2.3.1 The Working Party Report on Border Tax Adjustments. The adoption of the report by the *Working Party (WP) on Border tax Adjustments* (BTAs)[104] was preceded by intermediate reports that remain unpublished[105] and that reflect the earlier discussions among the members of the WP.

The WP was asked to discuss which border tax adjustments were permissible by exporting and importing GATT contracting parties: could for example, the importing state lawfully adjust (lower) payroll taxes imposed by the exporting state? Could it adjust sales taxes? Conversely, could the exporting state exempt from domestic sales taxation exported products without running the risk of being accused for violating Art. XVI GATT? In short, how much regulatory authority do the exporting and importing states have when taxing traded goods?

4.3.2.3.1.1 *The Findings in the Working Party Final Report.* The negotiators agreed on the so–called *destination principle*, which was understood to circumscribe the taxes that can be lawfully adjusted. Section 4 of the final report of the WP explains this principle in the following terms:

> ...which enable exported products to be relieved of some or all of the tax charged in the exporting country in respect of similar domestic products sold to consumers on the home market and which enable imported products sold to consumers to be charged with some or all of the tax charged in the importing country in respect of similar domestic products.

---

[104] Art. II.2 GATT provides the legal basis for border tax adjustments since it explicitly provides that tax adjustments are lawful provided that they meet the requirements of Art. III GATT. It does not, however, explain whether adjustments can be lawfully made on all or only on some taxes.

[105] GATT Docs. L/3138 and L/3190.

Taxation could thus, in principle, be adjusted by both the importing and the exporting state: the key was that if the destination of the good was a market other than the market where the good had been produced either the exporter or the importer could adjust the level of taxation imposed when the same good were sold in the market where it had been produced. The GATT contracting parties had before them a rather detailed document that explained how adjustment took place across various countries practicing it (GATT Doc. L/3389), and that served as background information.

The GATT contracting parties reached agreement on *some* measures, but failed to do so on many others. The extent of their agreement is reflected in the following paragraph:

> ...the Working Party concluded that there was convergence of views to the effect that taxes directly levied on products were eligible for tax adjustment. Examples of such taxes comprised specific excise duties, sales taxes and cascade taxes and the tax on value added. It was agreed that the TVA, regardless of its technical construction (fractioned collection), was equivalent in this respect to a tax levied directly – a retail or sales tax. Furthermore, the Working Party concluded that there was convergence of views to the effect that certain taxes that were not directly levied on products were not eligible for tax adjustment. Examples of such taxes comprised social security charges whether on employers or employees and payroll taxes.[106]

The GATT contracting parties also agreed to provide information if requested, regarding the reasons for, and the calculation of, any tax adjustment (§ 17 of the final report):

> It was generally agreed that countries adjusting taxes should, at all times, be prepared, if requested, to account for the reasons for adjustment, for the methods used, for the amount of compensation and to furnish proof thereof.[107]

There was also agreement between negotiators that some taxes, such as *cascade taxes*,[108] were eligible for adjustment, the modalities for adjusting were not clear though (§ 16 of the final report):

> The Working Party noted that there were some taxes which, while generally considered eligible for adjustment, presented a problem because of the difficulty in some cases of calculating exactly the amount of compensation. Examples of such difficulties were encountered in cascade taxes. For adjustment, countries operating cascade systems usually resorted to calculating average rates of rebate for categories of products rather than calculating the

---

[106] See § 14 of the final report.

[107] On the allocation of burden of proof in GATT/WTO, see Horn and Mavroidis (2009).

[108] A *cascade tax* is a *turnover tax* which is applied in every stage of the production process.

actual tax levied on a particular product. It was noted, however, that most cascade tax systems were to be replaced by TVA systems, and that therefore the area in which such problems occurred was diminishing. Other examples included composite goods which, on export, contained ingredients for which the Working Party agreed in principle it was administratively sensible and sufficiently accurate to rebate by average rates for a given class of goods.

There was a divergence of views regarding the eligibility for adjustment of *taxes occultes* and some other taxes such as *property taxes*. The scarcity of complaints with respect to either of these two taxes however, persuaded negotiators to stop negotiating on them (§ 15 of the final report):

> The Working Party noted that there was a divergence of views with regard to the eligibility for adjustment of certain categories of tax and that these could be sub-divided into
>
> (*a*) "Taxes occultes" which the OECD defined as consumption taxes on capital equipment, auxiliary materials and services used in the transportation and production of other taxable goods. Taxes on advertising, energy, machinery and transport were among the more important taxes which might be involved. It appeared that adjustment was not normally made for taxes occultes except in countries having a cascade tax;
>
> (*b*) Certain other taxes, such as property taxes, stamp duties and registration duties ... which are not generally considered eligible for tax adjustment. Most countries do not make adjustments for such taxes, but a few do as a few do for the payroll taxes and employers' social security charges referred to in the last sentence of paragraph 14.
>
> It was generally felt that while this area of taxation was unclear, its importance – as indicated by the scarcity of complaints reported in connexion with adjustment of taxes occultes – was not such as to justify further examination.

The Working Party did not manage to resolve all ambiguities and disagreements regarding tax adjustability: for instance, no agreement with respect to *tax occultes* was possible; moreover, besides the agreement on the two outer sides of the continuum (consumption taxes on the one hand, property taxes on the other) this Working Party did not manage to design a legal test that would guide future practice with respect to the adjustability (or not) of domestic instruments.

4.3.2.3.1.2 *The Legal Significance of the Working Party Final Report.*[109] The report of the Working Party on BTAs was adopted by the GATT CONTRACTING

---

[109] This Section relies heavily on Mavroidis (2007).

PARTIES, the GATT-organ that had the authority to do so.[110] The legal value of similar acts is addressed in GATT (as it has been amended following the successful conclusion of the *Uruguay Round*) albeit in unclear terms: there is doubt whether the Working Party report should qualify as a decision by the CONTRACTING PARTIES, and thus come under the purview of Art. 1(b)(iv) GATT 1994, or whether it should be considered as part of the GATT *acquis*, and then come under the purview of Art. XVI of the *Agreement Establishing the WTO*. But no matter how it is classified, the WP report will have legal significance: if however, it comes under the former it should be regarded as *binding* on all WTO Members, whereas if it comes under the latter it should be regarded as merely creating *legitimate expectations* across WTO Members to the effect that WTO practice will be guided by its content.

Recall that the GATT 1994 is not content-wise the same agreement as GATT 1947. The latter was substantially modified through the negotiations during the *Uruguay Round* during which it was agreed to add to the original text all decisions adopted by the GATT CONTRACTING PARTIES since 1947. The GATT 1994 (as the new GATT is known) comprises a series of decisions by the GATT CONTRACTING PARTIES aiming at clarifying the original text.

Among the instruments included, Art. 1(b)(iv) GATT 1994 mentions "other decisions" of the CONTRACTING PARTIES. The meaning of this term is unclear. The panel report on *Japan–Alcoholic Beverages II* addressed the issue of whether GATT panel reports that had been adopted by way of a decision of the GATT CONTRACTING PARTIES are in fact "decisions" of the CONTRACTING PARTIES to GATT 1947 within the meaning of Art. 1(b)(iv) GATT 1994. The panel was of the view that adopted panel reports had the status of any *other decision* of the CONTRACTING PARTIES. Consequently, the panel held that adopted panel reports form an integral part of GATT 1994 as they are "other decisions of the Contracting Parties to GATT 1947" within the meaning of Art. 1(b)(iv) of GATT 1994." (§ 6.10). The Appellate Body (AB) disagreed with the panel, and held that the "decision" to adopt a panel report is not a "decision" within the meaning of Art. 1(b)(iv) GATT 1994, although it did acknowledge that adopted reports are "an important part of the GATT *acquis*." (p. 15). The term "GATT *acquis*" is a creation of the AB, which only clarified the meaning of this concept subsequently in *US – Shrimp (Art. 21.5 – Malaysia)*. We quote from §§ 108–109:

> In this respect, we note that in our Report in *Japan – Taxes on Alcoholic Beverages*, we stated that:
>
> 'Adopted Panel Reports are an important part of the GATT acquis. They are often considered by subsequent panels. They create legitimate expectations among WTO Members, and, therefore,

should be taken into account where they are relevant to any dispute.'

This reasoning applies to adopted Appellate Body Reports as well. Thus, in taking into account the reasoning in an adopted Appellate Body Report – a Report, moreover, that was directly relevant to the Panel's disposition of the issues before it – the Panel did not err. The Panel was correct in using our findings as a tool for its own reasoning. Further, we see no indication that, in doing so, the Panel limited itself merely to examining the new measure from the perspective of the recommendations and rulings of the DSB.'

Hence, it turns out that what the AB meant by the term *acquis* was the legitimate expectations of WTO Members to see that the relevant prior case law will duly be taken into account in future disputes, even though there is no *legal* obligation to follow the findings and conclusions of GATT panels that had previously dealt with the same issue. This issue arose again in the context of the dispute that led to the panel report on *US–FSC*, where the panel was of the view that *decisions* to adopt reports should come under Art. XVI of the *Agreement Establishing the WTO* (WTO Agreement). Such decisions are not legally binding on subsequent panels. Nevertheless, they are not totally irrelevant from a pure legal perspective either. Art. XVI WTO Agreement reads:

...the WTO shall be guided by the decisions, procedures and customary practices followed by the CONTRACTING PARTIES to GATT 1947.

Consequently, the legal effect of adopted GATT reports is to provide "guidance." On appeal, the AB in its report on *US–FSC* followed a rather convoluted reasoning even though it ended up ultimately following the panel's conclusion (§§ 108–115).

Previous decisions by GATT panels are usually referred to as support for findings already reached. This trend is observable in WTO practice. In light of this discussion, it seems that the better arguments lie with the view that the Working Party report should come under Art. 1(b)(iv) GATT 1994: the Working Party was not convened to adjudicate on a dispute between two GATT contracting parties;[111] it was requested to discuss the treatment of tax adjustments at the GATT-wide level. In subsequent practice, a number of WTO panel and AB reports have referred to this report, without however, classifying it either as part and parcel of Art. 1(b)(iv) GATT 1994 or under Art. XVI WTO Agreement.[112] But, as already argued, even if one takes the view that it should be considered to be part of the GATT *acquis*, it would still retain legal value as explained above. The fact that it has been often cited in WTO case law leaves little room for doubt that recourse

[111] Although the term WP was often reserved to what is now always referred to as a GATT panel, that is, an adjudicating body.
[112] See, for example, the panel and AB report on *Japan–Alcoholic Beverages II*.

to it will be made again if, for example, the question whether payroll taxes can be adjusted comes up. Consequently, at the very least, we should understand Art. III GATT as excluding from adjustment by the importing state some taxes such as payroll taxes.[113]

4.3.2.3.2 DCS Products.[114] The AB in its report on *Korea–Alcoholic Beverages* held that *like* products are a sub-set of *DCS* products: if two products are like, they are, by definition, *DCS* as well (§ 118):

> 'Like' products are a subset of directly competitive or substitutable products: all like products are, by definition, directly competitive or substitutable products, whereas not all 'directly competitive or substitutable' products are 'like'.

It follows that case law regarding the definition of *DCS* is *ipso facto* relevant for the interpretation of the term *like* products.

The AB in its report on *Japan–Alcoholic Beverages II* provided its understanding of DCS products. This dispute arose because of a Japanese taxation scheme which, while on its face neutral, subjected *predominantly* Western products to a heavier taxation than predominantly Japanese products: as a result, *sochu* (an alcoholic beverage predominantly produced in Japan) was subjected to less burdensome taxation than, *inter alia*, whisky (an alcoholic beverage predominantly produced in Europe and the United States). Europe and the United States protested arguing that the products at hand were at least *DCS*, if not *like*, products. The panel had already accepted that all of the products concerned (with the exception of vodka that was deemed to be *like* product to *sochu*) were DCS products. The AB upheld the panel's findings in this regard. In its view:

(a) physical characteristics;
(b) common end-uses; and
(c) tariff classification

are appropriate elements to take into account when defining whether two products are *DCS*. Importantly, upholding the panel's findings in this regard, the AB made it clear that the test to define whether two products are DCS is in the marketplace, in the sense that, it is *consumers* who will ultimately decide whether two products are indeed in competition with each other. To this effect,

---

[113] To some extent this report is consonant with the default rules regulating allocation of jurisdiction: whereas sales taxes should be prescribed by the country where a sale takes place, payroll taxes should be prescribed by countries where production takes place.

[114] We start with the interpretation of the term DCS products because, as we will see, case law has clarified that DCS is a necessary but not sufficient property of like products.

econometric indicators (for instance, the *cross-price elasticity*)[115] are relevant to define whether two products are indeed in competition with each other. The European Community had submitted some consumer surveys to this effect, suggesting that Japanese consumers in the absence of discriminatory taxation would be prepared to substitute a host of Western drinks for *sochu* (p. 25):

> In this case, the Panel emphasized the need to look not only at such matters as physical characteristics, common end-uses, and tariff classifications, but also at the 'market place.' This seems appropriate. The GATT 1994 is a commercial agreement, and the WTO is concerned, after all, with markets. It does not seem inappropriate to look at competition in the relevant markets as one among a number of means of identifying the broader category of products that might be described as 'directly competitive or substitutable'.

> Nor does it seem inappropriate to examine elasticity of substitution as one means of examining those relevant markets. The Panel did not say that cross-price elasticity of demand is '*the* decisive criterion' (footnote omitted) for determining whether products are directly competitive or substitutable. The Panel stated the following:

> In the Panel's view, the decisive criterion in order to determine whether two products are directly competitive or substitutable is whether they have common end-uses, *inter alia*, as shown by elasticity of substitution.

> We agree. And, we find the Panel's legal analysis of whether the products are 'directly competitive or substitutable products' in paragraphs 6.28–6.32 of the Panel Report to be correct. (italics and emphasis in the original)

In *Korea–Alcoholic Beverages*, the AB kept the same test for defining whether two products are DCS, reducing, however, econometric indicators to be but one of several possible avenues to show that a DCS-relationship between two products exists. In this case, the facts were similar to those in *Japan–Alcoholic Beverages II*: beverages predominantly produced in Korea (*soju*) were hit by a substantially lower tax burden than their counterparts which were predominantly produced in the European Community, Canada, and the United States (vodka, whisky, etc). The European Community, Canada, and the United States complained, arguing that the Korean regime was GATT-inconsistent. Korea argued that its system could not be held to be GATT-inconsistent since, the products concerned were not *DCS* in the first place: the price of (diluted) *soju*[116]

---

[115] The cross-price elasticity of demand provides information about the demand relationship between two products, by capturing how a price increase for one product increases the demand for another product. (Formally, it is defined as the percentage change in quantity demanded of some good X divided by the percentage change in price for good Y). Adjudicating bodies have not so far provided any guidance on what values of the cross-price elasticity would normally be necessary for two products to be considered DCS.

[116] The price of non-diluted *soju* was substantially higher.

was a small fraction of the price of the Western drinks at hand, claiming thus that changes in the price of *soju* would not lead its consumers to consumption of Western drinks. Consequently, following the analysis in *Japan–Alcoholic Beverages*, and the relevance of econometric indicators in deciding whether two products are DCS, Korea argued that with respect to (diluted) *soju* at least no claim under Art. III.2 GATT could be sustained.

Complaining parties claimed that the fact that the western drinks hit by higher taxation were in DCS-relationship with a similar drink (*sochu*) in a similar market (Japan) provided enough evidence that *soju* as well was DCS product to the same drinks. The panel essentially upheld the complaining parties' view, holding that the products were indeed in a DCS relationship: only a reading of the AB report on *Japan–Alcoholic Beverages II* whereby cross-price elasticity would be elevated to *the* decisive criterion conferring DCS status, would lead the panel to rule otherwise; such a reading of Art. III.2 GATT, however, was in the panel's eyes unwarranted. The absence of systematic information concerning consumer purchasing behavior thus did not prevent the panel from finding that the two products were like in the eyes of Korean consumers. The AB upheld the panel's findings without any modification in this regard. It thereby explicitly reduced the importance of econometric indicators, claiming that it is but one of the various ways to show that two products are in DCS-relationship. The AB did not explain itself as to which other ways are available. It did however mention several factors that it took into account in order to confirm that *soju* and the western drinks were indeed in a *DCS* relationship. Price was not one of them (§§ 114 ff. and especially 133–134, 135–138):

1. Potential Competition

...In our view, the word 'substitutable' indicates that the requisite relationship *may* exist between products that are not, at a given moment, considered by consumers to be substitutes but which are, nonetheless, *capable* of being substituted for one another....

2. Expectations

As we have said, the object and purpose of Article III is the maintenance of equality of competitive conditions for imported and domestic products.

3. 'Trade Effects' Test

...the Panel stated that if a particular degree of competition had to be shown in quantitative terms, that would be similar to requiring proof that a tax measure has a particular impact on trade. It considered such an approach akin to a 'type of trade effects test'.

We do not consider the Panel's reasoning on this point to be flawed.

4. Nature of Competition

The Panel considered that in analyzing whether products are 'directly competitive or substitutable,' the focus should be on the *nature* of competition and not on its *quantity*.... For the reasons set above, we share the Panel's reluctance to rely unduly on quantitative analyses of the competitive relationship. In our view, an approach that focused solely on the quantitative overlap of competition would, in essence, make cross-price elasticity *the* decisive criterion in determining whether products are 'directly competitive or substitutable'. We do not, therefore, consider that the Panel's use of the term 'nature of competition' is questionable.

5. Evidence from the Japanese Market

...It seems to us that evidence from other markets may be pertinent to the examination of the market at issue, particularly when demand on that market has been influenced by regulatory barriers to trade or to competition. Clearly, not every other market will be relevant to the market at issue. But if another market displays characteristics similar to the market at issue, then evidence of consumer demand in that other market may have some relevance to the market at issue. This, however, can only be determined on a case-by-case basis, taking account of all relevant facts. (emphasis in the original)[117]

The AB report on *Korea – Taxes on Alcoholic Beverages* represents the state of the art as far as the definition of DCS products is concerned in WTO case law. It is, hence, now accepted that:

(a) two products will be *DCS* if they are viewed as such by consumers (that is, the test is in the marketplace);
(b) recourse to econometric indicators is not *passage obligé*: a *DCS*-relationship can also be established through recourse to criteria such as physical characteristics, end uses, consumer preferences.

These criteria have been consistently referred to in subsequent case law.[118]

---

[117] In the case at hand, the argument was made that demand in Korea was *latent* because of the regulatory barriers that impeded access for Western drinks. It did not however, beyond the generic references in the passage included above, refer specifically to these barriers. Hence, evidence from third-country markets was necessary to establish whether *soju* and a series of Western beverages were indeed *DCS* products. Korea pointed out that the price of *shochu* was higher than that of *soju*, and closer to that of the Western drinks. Note also that there have not been any *serious* challenges regarding likeness in subsequent case law.

[118] Sharing the same tariff classification is not a necessary criterion to decide whether two products are *DCS*. It has been used, however, in order to decide whether two products are

4.3.2.3.3 Applied So as to Afford Protection (ASATAP). Art. III.2 GATT makes it clear that taxation of two *DCS* products is GATT-inconsistent, if it operates in a manner that is not consistent with Art. III.1 GATT; recall that Art. III.1 GATT outlaws domestic instruments that operate so as to afford protection (ASATAP) to domestic production. The *Interpretative Note ad Art III of the GATT* (to which Art. III.2 GATT refers) further explains that taxation operates ASATAP if a pair of products is not similarly taxed: it does, in other terms offer (at least) one instance where taxation across DCS products operates ASATAP, that is, the case of dissimilar taxation.

Two interrelated interpretative questions arise in this context:

(a) how should we understand the terms "*not similarly taxed*" appearing in the *Interpretative Note ad Art III of the GATT*?
(b) does *any* dissimilar taxation suffice for a tax scheme to operate ASATAP?

The AB addressed these issues in various reports. In its report on *Japan–Alcoholic Beverages II*, it held that, with respect to *like* products, taxation in excess should be understood as an instance of a measure operating ASATAP precisely because the imported product was taxed higher than the domestic like good (in other words, taxation in excess equals ASATAP as far as like goods are concerned); consequently, a complainant who has established that taxation on imported products is in excess of that on domestic *like* products, does not have to *also* establish that the measure at hand operates ASATAP (pp. 18–19):

> Article III:1 informs Article III:2, first sentence, by establishing that if imported products are taxed in excess of like domestic products, then that tax measure is inconsistent with Article III. Article III:2, first sentence does not refer specifically to Article III:1. There is no specific invocation in this first sentence of the general principle in Article III:1 that admonishes Members of the WTO not to apply measures so as to afford protection. This omission must have some meaning. We believe the meaning is simply that the presence of a protective application need not be established separately from the specific requirements that are included in the first sentence in order to show that a tax measure is inconsistent with the general principle set out in the first sentence. However, this does not mean that the general principle of Article III:1 does not apply to this sentence. To the contrary, we believe the first sentence of Article III:2 is, in effect, an application of this general principle. The ordinary meaning of the words of Article III:2, first sentence leads inevitably to this conclusion. Read in their context and in the light of the overall object and purpose of the *WTO Agreement*, the words of the first sentence require an examination of the conformity of an internal tax

---

like (as we will see *infra*). Since *like* products in case law are a sub-set of *DCS* products, it is reasonable to assume that this criterion is *relevant* (albeit *not necessary*) to decide whether two products are *DCS*.

measure with Article III by determining, first, whether the taxed imported and domestic products are 'like' and, second, whether the taxes applied to the imported products are 'in excess of' those applied to the like domestic products. If the imported and domestic products are 'like products,' and if the taxes applied to the imported products are 'in excess of' those applied to the like domestic products, then the measure is inconsistent with Article III:2, first sentence. (italics in the original)[119]

With regard to *DCS* products, nevertheless, a similar reading was rejected (p. 27):

Unlike that of Article III:2, first sentence, the language of Article III:2, second sentence, specifically invokes Article III:1. The significance of this distinction lies in the fact that whereas Article III:1 acts implicitly in addressing the two issues that must be considered in applying the first sentence, it acts explicitly as an entirely separate issue that must be addressed along with two other issues that are raised in applying the second sentence. Giving full meaning to the text and to its context, three separate issues must be addressed to determine whether an internal tax measure is inconsistent with Article III:2, second sentence. These three issues are whether:

(1) the imported products and the domestic products are '*directly competitive or substitutable products' which are in competition with each other*;

(2) the directly competitive or substitutable imported and domestic products are '*not similarly taxed*'; and

(3) the dissimilar taxation of the directly competitive or substitutable imported domestic products is '*applied...so as to afford protection to domestic production.*' (emphasis in the original)

Hence, in the AB's view, Art III.1 GATT is relevant for the *whole* of Art. III.2 GATT, but its impact on the interpretation of the first sentence (dealing with like products) is not symmetric to its impact on the second sentence (dealing with DCS products):

(a) with respect to like products, taxation in excess of the imported like product *ipso facto* amounts to a violation of the ASATAP requirement;

(b) whereas with respect to *DCS* products, establishment of taxation in excess of the imported product is a *necessary*, but not *sufficient* condition for finding that a measure operates so as to afford protection.

Case law responded to the question what else, beyond differential taxation, the complainant needs to demonstrate in order to satisfy that a tax scheme operates ASATAP to the domestic DCS product in a series of reports.

---

[119] As we will see *infra, any* tax differential, even if infinitesimal, satisfies the *in excess* criterion.

In its report on *Japan–Alcoholic Beverages II* considered the distinction between *in excess*, on the one hand, and ASATAP, on the other, in the following terms (pp. 29–32):

> In the *1987 Japan – Alcohol* case, the panel subsumed its discussion of the issue of 'not similarly taxed' within its examination of the separate issue of 'so as to afford protection':
>
> > ... whereas under the first sentence of Article III:2 the tax on the imported product and the tax on the like domestic product had to be equal in effect, Article III:1 and 2, second sentence, prohibited only the application of internal taxes to imported or domestic products in a manner 'so as to afford protection to domestic production.' The Panel was of the view that also small tax differences could influence the competitive relationship between directly competing distilled liquors, but the existence of protective taxation could be established only in the light of the particular circumstances of each case and there could be a *de minimis* level below which a tax difference ceased to have the protective effect prohibited by Article III:2, second sentence.
>
> To detect whether the taxation was protective, the panel in the 1987 case examined a number of factors that it concluded were 'sufficient evidence of fiscal distortions of the competitive relationship between imported distilled liquors and domestic shochu affording protection to the domestic production of shochu.' These factors included the considerably lower specific tax rates on shochu than on imported directly competitive or substitutable products; the imposition of high *ad valorem* taxes on imported alcoholic beverages and the absence of *ad valorem* taxes on shochu; the fact that shochu was almost exclusively produced in Japan and that the lower taxation of shochu did 'afford protection to domestic production'; and the mutual substitutability of these distilled liquors. The panel in the 1987 case concluded that the application of considerably lower internal taxes by Japan on shochu than on other directly competitive or substitutable distilled liquors had trade-distorting effects affording protection to domestic production of shochu contrary to Article III:1 and 2, second sentence.
>
> As in that case, we believe that an examination in any case of whether dissimilar taxation has been applied so as to afford protection requires a comprehensive and objective analysis of the structure and application of the measure in question on domestic as compared to imported products. We believe it is possible to examine objectively the underlying criteria used in a particular tax measure, its structure, and its overall application to ascertain whether it is applied in a way that affords protection to domestic products.
>
> Although it is true that the aim of a measure may not be easily ascertained, nevertheless its protective application can most often be discerned from the

design, the architecture, and the revealing structure of a measure. The very magnitude of the dissimilar taxation in a particular case may be evidence of such a protective application, as the Panel rightly concluded in this case. Most often, there will be other factors to be considered as well. In conducting this inquiry, panels should give full consideration to all the relevant facts and all the relevant circumstances in any given case.

In this respect, we note and agree with the panel's acknowledgment in the *1987 Japan – Alcohol* Report:

> ...that Article III:2 does not prescribe the use of any specific method or system of taxation.... there could be objective reasons proper to the tax in question which could justify or necessitate differences in the system of taxation for imported and for domestic products. The Panel found that it could also be compatible with Article III:2 to allow two different methods of calculation of price for tax purposes. Since Article III:2 prohibited only discriminatory or protective tax burdens on imported products, what mattered was, in the view of the Panel, whether the application of the different taxation methods actually had a discriminatory or protective effect against imported products.

We have reviewed the Panel's reasoning in this case as well as its conclusions on the issue of 'so as to afford protection' in paragraphs 6.33–6.35 of the Panel Report. We find cause for thorough examination. The Panel began in paragraph 6.33 by describing its approach as follows:

> ...if directly competitive or substitutable products are not 'similarly taxed,' and if it were found that the tax favors domestic products, then protection would be afforded to such products, and Article III:2, second sentence, is violated.

This statement of the reasoning required under Article III:2, second sentence is correct.

However, the Panel went on to note:

> ...for it to conclude that dissimilar taxation afforded protection, it would be sufficient for it to find that the dissimilarity in taxation is not *de minimis*.... the Panel took the view that 'similarly taxed' is the appropriate benchmark in order to determine whether a violation of Article III:2, second sentence, has occurred as opposed to 'in excess of' that constitutes the appropriate benchmark to determine whether a violation of Article III:2, first sentence, has occurred.

In paragraph 6.34, the Panel added:

(i) The benchmark in Article III:2, second sentence, is whether internal taxes operate as to afford protection to domestic production, a term which has been further interpreted in the Interpretative Note ad Article III:2, paragraph 2, to mean dissimilar taxation of domestic and foreign directly competitive or substitutable products.

And, furthermore, in its conclusions, in paragraph 7.1(ii), the Panel concluded that:

(ii) Shochu, whisky, brandy, rum, gin, genever, and liqueurs are directly competitive or substitutable products and Japan, by not taxing them similarly, is in violation of its obligation under Article III:2, second sentence, of the General Agreement on Tariffs and Trade 1994.

Thus, having stated the correct legal approach to apply with respect to Article III:2, second sentence, the Panel then equated dissimilar taxation above a *de minimis* level with the separate and distinct requirement of demonstrating that the tax measure 'affords protection to domestic production.' As previously stated, a finding that 'directly competitive or substitutable products' are 'not similarly taxed' is necessary to find a violation of Article III:2, second sentence. Yet this is not enough. The dissimilar taxation must be more than *de minimis*. It may be so much more that it will be clear from that very differential that the dissimilar taxation was applied 'so as to afford protection.' In some cases, that may be enough to show a violation. In this case, the Panel concluded that it was enough. Yet in other cases, there may be other factors that will be just as relevant or more relevant to demonstrating that the dissimilar taxation at issue was applied 'so as to afford protection.' In any case, the three issues that must be addressed in determining whether there is such a violation must be addressed clearly and separately in each case and on a case-by-case basis. And, in every case, a careful, objective analysis, must be done of each and all relevant facts and all the relevant circumstances in order to determine 'the existence of protective taxation.' Although the Panel blurred its legal reasoning in this respect, nevertheless we conclude that it reasoned correctly that in this case, the Liquor Tax Law is not in compliance with Article III:2. As the Panel did, we note that:

> ...the combination of customs duties and internal taxation in Japan has the following impact: on the one hand, it makes it difficult for foreign-produced shochu to penetrate the Japanese market and, on the other, it does not guarantee equality of competitive conditions between shochu and the rest of <white = and <brown = spirits. Thus, through a combination of high import duties and differentiated internal taxes, Japan manages to 'isolate' domestically produced shochu from foreign competition, be it foreign produced shochu or any other of the mentioned white and brown spirits. (italics in the original)

In *Korea – Taxes on Alcoholic Beverages*, the AB almost *verbatim* reproduced this view (§ 150):

> Although it is true that the aim of a measure may not be easily ascertained, nevertheless its protective application can most often be discerned from the design, the architecture, and the revealing structure of a measure. The very magnitude of the dissimilar taxation in a particular case may be evidence of such protective application...Most often, there will be other factors to be considered as well.

In *Chile–Alcoholic Beverages*, the AB had the opportunity to apply this test in a particular case. In this case, the AB was asked to pronounce on the consistency of the Chilean tax system for alcoholic beverages with the GATT: the scheme distinguished between two categories of alcoholic beverages, using alcoholic content as the distinguishing criterion: below 35° and above 39°.[120] The complaining party (European Community) had argued that many western products of slightly more than 39° were DCS products to Chilean products of less than 35°, and, that the tax differential operated ASATAP. In the view of exporters of "western" alcoholic drinks, the Chilean tax regime favored predominantly locally produced alcoholic beverages (some categories of *pisco*). Chile responded that its scheme did not condition the payment of the higher tax on the origin of the product, and, moreover, that in the 39° and above tax category the majority of the products hit by high taxation were domestic. As a result, in Chile's view, no protection could result from such a taxation scheme (§ 58).

The AB condemned the Chilean fiscal scheme. It first held that the tax differential (27% and 47%) across the two categories of lower and higher alcoholic content drinks was more than *de minimis* (§§ 44ff).

The AB then asked the question whether the dissimilar taxation supported the conclusion that it was ASATAP to the domestic product. In this context, it repeated and clarified the test it had developed to decide whether such was the case. Although the quoted passage is quite lengthy, we believe it deserves to be cited since it sheds precious light on the manner in which the AB understands the ASATAP test in case of differential taxation across two DCS products (§§ 62–66):

> ....The *subjective* intentions inhabiting the minds of individual legislators or regulators do not bear upon the inquiry, if only because they are not accessible to treaty interpreters. It does not follow, however, that the statutory purposes or objectives – that is, the purpose or objectives of a Member's legislature and government as a whole – to the extent that they are given

---

[120] All cases discussed so far are cases of alleged *de facto* discrimination.

objective expression in the statute itself, are not pertinent. To the contrary, as we also stated in *Japan – Alcoholic Beverages*:

> Although it is true that the aim of a measure may not be easily ascertained, nevertheless its protective application can most often be discerned from the *design*, the *architecture*, and the revealing *structure* of a measure. (emphasis added)

We turn, therefore, to the design, the architecture and the structure of the New Chilean System itself. That system taxes *all* alcoholic beverages with an alcohol content of 35° or below on a linear basis, at a fixed rate of 27 per cent *ad valorem*. Thereafter, the rate of taxation increases steeply, by 4 percentage points for every additional degree of alcohol content, until a maximum rate of 47 per cent *ad valorem* is reached. This fixed tax rate of 47 per cent applies, once more on a linear basis, to *all* beverages with an alcohol content in excess of 39°, irrespective of how much in excess of 39° the alcohol content of the beverage is.

We note, furthermore, that, according to the Panel, approximately 75 per cent of all domestic production has an alcohol content of 35° or less and is, therefore, taxed at the lowest rate of 27 per cent *ad valorem*. [footnote omitted] Moreover, according to figures supplied to the Panel by Chile, approximately *half* of all domestic production has an alcohol content of 35° and is, therefore, located on the line of the progression of the tax at the point *immediately before* the steep increase in tax rates from 27 per cent *ad valorem*. The start of the highest tax bracket, with a rate of 47 per cent *ad valorem*, coincides with the point at which most imported beverages are found. Indeed, according to the Panel, that tax bracket contains approximately 95 per cent of all directly competitive or substitutable imports. [footnote omitted]

Although the tax rates increase steeply for beverages with an alcohol content of more than 35° and up to 39°, there are, in fact, very few beverages on the Chilean market, either domestic or imported, with an alcohol content of between 35° and 39°. [footnote: Chile's response to Question 1 of the Panel, 26 November 1998. These figures indicate that approximately 5 per cent of all distilled alcoholic beverages have an alcohol content in this range. At the oral hearing, Chile confirmed that very few beverages have an alcohol content of between 35° and 39°.] The graduation of the rates for beverages with an alcohol content of between 35° and 39° does not, therefore, serve to tax distilled alcoholic beverages on a progressive basis. Indeed, the steeply graduated progression of the tax rates between 35° and 39° alcohol content seems anomalous and at odds with the otherwise linear nature of the tax system. With the exception of the progression of rates between 35° and 39° alcohol content, this system simply applies one of two fixed rates of taxation, either 27 per cent *ad valorem* or 47 per cent *ad valorem,* each of which applies to distilled alcoholic beverages with a broad range of alcohol content, that is, 27 per cent for beverages with an alcoholic content of *up to 35°* and 47 per cent for beverages with an alcohol content of *more than 39°.*

In practice, therefore, the New Chilean System will operate largely as if there were only two tax brackets: the first applying a rate of 27 per cent *ad valorem* which ends at the point at which most domestic beverages, by volume, are found, and the second applying a rate of 47 per cent *ad valorem* which begins at the point at which most imports, by volume, are found. The magnitude of the difference between these two rates is also considerable. The absolute difference of 20 percentage points between the two rates represents a 74 per cent increase in the lowest rate of 27 per cent *ad valorem.* Accordingly, examination of the design, architecture and structure of the New Chilean System tends to reveal that the application of dissimilar taxation of directly competitive or substitutable products will "afford protection to domestic production." (italics and emphasis in the original)

Note that the AB agreed that, as a matter of fact, most of the alcoholic drinks hit by the higher taxation were of Chilean origin. However, it dismissed the relevance of this observation for the interpretation of the ASATAP requirement in the following terms (§ 67):

This fact does not, however, by itself outweigh the other relevant factors, which tend to reveal the protective application of the New Chilean System. The relative proportion of domestic versus imported products within a particular fiscal category is not, in and of itself, decisive of the appropriate characterization of the total impact of the New Chilean system under Article III:2, second sentence, of the GATT 1994. This provision, as noted earlier, provides for equality of competitive conditions of *all* directly competitive or substitutable imported products, in relation to domestic products, and not simply, as Chile argues, those imported products within a particular fiscal category. The cumulative consequence of the New Chilean System is, as the Panel found, that approximately 75 percent of all domestic production of the distilled alcoholic beverages at issue will be located in the fiscal category with the lowest tax rate, whereas approximately 95 percent of the directly competitive or substitutable imported products will be found in the fiscal category subject to the highest tax rate. (emphasis in the original)

It should also be noted that the AB does not compare in absolute terms the size of the domestic production that is being hit by the higher tax to the absolute volume of imports being hit by the tax – it only compares proportions. But what if the domestic industry, despite representing a relatively small share of the total domestic industry, were much larger than imports, and therefore carried most of the burden of the tax? Could this not be interpreted to mean that the tax distinction serves some other purpose than protectionism, a purpose that deserves to be taken into consideration in the evaluation of the measure? Chile argued that domestic producers were carrying most of the tax burden in the high tax category. In the view of the AB, however, this was not enough to establish that the legislation at hand did not operate ASATAP; in the view of the AB, the purpose of Art. III GATT is to establish equality of competitive conditions with respect to all DCS products. Since, in the AB's view, drinks slightly above and slightly below 39° are DCS products, and since some western drinks above 39° were hit harder than some domestic drinks containing alcohol below 39°, the Chilean tax scheme operated ASATAP.

Chile offered a more 'regulatory' defense as well in an effort to justify the tax differential (§ 69):

> Before the Panel, Chile stated that the New Chilean System pursued four different objectives: "(1) maintaining revenue collection; (2) eliminating type distinctions [such] as [those which] were found in Japan and Korea; (3) discouraging alcohol consumption; and (4) minimizing the potentially regressive aspects of the reform of the tax system

The AB was not persuaded (§ 71):

> The conclusion of protective application reached by the Panel becomes very difficult to resist, in the absence of countervailing explanations by Chile. The mere statement of the four objectives pursued by Chile does not constitute effective rebuttal on the part of Chile.

It follows that in this case the AB confirmed and clarified the basic approach that a 20 percent tax differential may satisfy the 'not similarly taxed' requirement; in this case it is the sharp tax differential across the two categories of alcoholic drinks (the lower category being predominantly of national origin, the higher of foreign origin) that reveal the protective character of the legislation. The fact that *de facto* it is domestic goods that bear the bulk of the tax burden in the higher-taxation category was judged immaterial since neither effects nor intent is relevant in the context of Art. III GATT.

4.3.2.3.4 Like Products. Recall that, for a complainant to demonstrate a violation of Art. III.2 GATT, first sentence, it will have to demonstrate that:

(a) the domestic and the foreign products are *like*; and
(b) the latter is taxed *in excess* of the former.

The term *like products* has been interpreted in many GATT/WTO panels, and not always in consistent manner. GATT case law evidences two trends:

(a) there are a number of cases that follow a marketplace test: *likeness* is defined by reference to consumers' reactions;[121]

(b) there are two cases which reveal a willingness to take into account regulatory intent when establishing likeness among domestic and foreign products.

Let us start with the former. The *Working Party on Border Tax Adjustments*[122] established four criteria to define *likeness* (§ 18):

(a) the properties, nature and quality of the products;

(b) the end-uses of the products;

(c) consumers' tastes and habits – more comprehensively termed consumers' perceptions and behavior – in respect of the products; and

(d) the tariff classification of the products.

It did not assign a particular weight on each of them. Relying on these four criteria, the panel report on *Japan–Alcoholic Beverages I* held that, alcoholic beverages (§ 5.6):

> ...should be considered as 'like products' in terms of Article III:2 in view of their similar properties, end-uses and usually uniform classification in tariff nomenclatures.

The two reported cases that dismissed marketplace as the relevant criterion to decide on likeness are the panel reports on *US–Malt Beverages* and on *US–Taxes on Automobiles* ('*Gas Guzzler*', as it is widely known).[123]

In *US – Malt Beverages*, the panel defines *likeness* in § 5.25:

> Consequently, in determining whether two products subject to different treatment are like products, it is necessary to consider whether such product differentiation is being made 'so as to afford protection to domestic production'. While the analysis of 'like products' in terms of Article III:2 must take into consideration this objective of Article III, the Panel wished to emphasize that such an analysis would be without prejudice to the 'like product' concepts in other provisions of the General Agreement, which might have different objectives and which might therefore also require different interpretations.

---

[121] So far, there is not one single case where supply-substitutability has been accounted for when defining likeness or *DCS* relationship.

[122] See GATT Doc L/3464, adopted on 2 December 1970, GATT Doc. BISD 18S/97.

[123] This report remains unadopted and is, hence, of limited legal value. In fact, as we will see *infra*, it was totally rejected by a subsequent WTO panel dealing with the same issue.

In *US–Taxes on Automobiles*,[124] the panel had the opportunity to elaborate further on this proposition by introducing the so-called *aims and effects* test (§§ 5.7 and 5.10):

> In order to determine this issue, the Panel examined the object and purpose of paragraphs 2 and 4 of Article III in the context of the article as a whole and the General Agreement.
>
> …
>
> The Panel then proceeded to examine more closely the meaning of the phrase 'so as to afford protection.' The Panel noted that the term 'so as to' suggested both aim and effect. Thus the phrase 'so as to afford protection' called for an analysis of elements including the aim of the measure and the resulting effects. A measure could be said to have the *aim* of affording protection if an analysis of the circumstances in which it was adopted, in particular an analysis of the instruments available to the contracting party to achieve the declared domestic policy goal, demonstrated that a change in competitive opportunities in favour of domestic products was a desired outcome and not merely an incidental consequence of the pursuit of a legitimate policy goal. A measure could be said to have the *effect* of affording protection to domestic production if it accorded greater competitive opportunities to domestic products than to imported products. The effect of a measure in terms of trade flows was not relevant for the purposes of Article III, since a change in the volume or proportion of imports could be due to many factors other than government measures. (emphasis in the original)

According to this view, consequently, likeness will not be defined by reference to prevailing perceptions in the marketplace about the products concerned but, instead, by reference to the regulatory aims pursued by the intervening government.

In *Japan–Alcoholic Beverages II*, the panel explicitly rejected for various reasons (ranging from the insurmountable burden that such a test would impose on the complainant to the fact that adoption of the test would lead Art. XX GATT to redundancy) the relevance of the *aims and effects* test (§§ 6.15–6.19). The AB endorsed the panel's approach (pp. 16ff.).

In the same report, the AB (pp. 19ff.) ruled that the term *like products* should be defined by reference to the marketplace. The AB did not *explicitly* hold in this report that for two products to be like they have to be DCS. It did so, however, in

---

[124] In this case, the European Community challenged the consistency of the U.S. tax scheme applicable to cars, according to which, the total fleet of a producer would be taken into account in order to decide on the tax that would be imposed. Producers with a fleet that consisted of large cubism cars (gas guzzlers) would suffer most, as a result. Many European producers belonged to this category. The U.S. regime was apparently enacted at a time when those suffering most were U.S. producers, in an effort to dissuade consumers eager to buy such cars from buying them.

a subsequent report that we mentioned above, in its report on *Korea–Alcoholic Beverages* (§ 118). In *Japan–Alcoholic Beverages II*, the AB did state explicitly that the term *like products* invites a narrow reading, that is, a reading narrower than DCS, and that customs classification is relevant to establish likeness, beyond the criteria traditionally used to establish DCS relationship. In this often-quoted passage, the AB held that:

> The concept of 'likeness' is a relative one that evokes the image of an accordion. The accordion of 'likeness' stretches and squeezes in different places as different provisions of the WTO Agreement are applied. The width of the accordion in any one of those places must be determined by the particular provision in which the term 'like' is encountered as well as by the context and the circumstances that prevail in any given case to which that provision may apply. We believe that, in Article III:2, first sentence of the GATT 1994, the accordion of 'likeness' is meant to be narrowly squeezed.

However, not just any customs classification can assist in the definition of likeness. A necessary condition is that the classification be precise (pp. 23–24):

> If sufficiently detailed, tariff classification can be a helpful sign of product similarity.
>
> ...
>
> It is true that there are numerous tariff bindings which are in fact extremely precise with regard to product description and which, therefore, can provide significant guidance as to the identification of 'like products.'

This would *usually* be the case with respect to six-digit classifications. Four-digit classifications are usually uninformative, and eight-digit classifications are a matter of national definition, and not of worldwide acceptance.

We can conclude that case law in its totality suggests that two products will be like if they are DCS *and* if they share a detailed (six digit for the overwhelming majority of cases) tariff classification.

4.3.2.3.5 Taxation in Excess. The AB has stated that even a *minimal* tax differential suffices to satisfy the in-excess criterion. In *Japan–Alcoholic Beverages II*, the AB relevantly held (p. 23):

> Even the smallest amount of 'excess' is too much. 'The prohibition of discriminatory taxes in Article III:2, first sentence, is not conditional on a 'trade effects test' nor is it qualified by a *de minimis* standard. (italics in the original)

This approach is very much in line with the GATT panel report on *US–Superfund*: a mere arithmetic difference suffices for a demonstration of violation of the *in excess* requirement.

4.3.2.4 *Nonfiscal Instruments*

Art. III.4 GATT deals with domestic nonfiscal instruments. The list of such instruments is endless as per our discussion *supra* on incomplete contracting, covering areas such as public health, environmental protection, human rights, antitrust, and consumer protection. Irrespective of the precise subject matter, a complainant aiming to establish that this provision has been violated, will according to Art. III.4 GATT have to demonstrate that:

(a) with respect to a law, regulation, or requirement;
(b) affecting internal sale, offer for sale, purchase, transportation, distribution, or use;
(c) a foreign good is afforded in comparison to a domestic like good;
(d) less favorable treatment.

4.3.2.4.1 Laws, Regulations, or Requirements. GATT/WTO case law has understood the term 'laws, regulations and requirements' featured in Art. III.4 GATT as equivalent to the term 'measure' featured in Art. XXIII.1b GATT, and Art. XI GATT. Case law under these provisions has consistently used the term 'measure' in a broad manner.[125] The same should consequently hold true in the context of Art. III.4 GATT as well; indeed, so far we have witnessed no case where a WTO adjudicating body has rejected a claim because the complainant failed to show that a 'law, regulation or requirement' was being challenged. The inclusion of the term 'requirements' definitely supports this construction: it was meant to ensure that the provision is not restricted to formal laws only.

The next question is to what extent a measure is attributed to a government, since the GATT does not regulate private behavior. WTO case law has addressed attribution in the context of Art. III.4 GATT in parallel with the approach followed in the context of Art. XI GATT: not only acts of governments, but also acts of private parties can be challenged under Art. III.4 GATT, provided that they can be attributed to a government.[126] We read in the Panel report on *US–FSC* (§ 10.376):

> A literal reading of the words *all laws, regulations and requirements* in Article III:4 could suggest that they may have a narrower scope than the word *measure* in Article XXIII:1(b). However, whether or not these words should be given as broad a construction as the word measure, in view of the broad interpretation assigned to them in the cases cited above, we shall assume for the purposes of our present analysis that they should be interpreted as

---

[125] See, for example, the Panel report on *Japan–Trade in Semiconductors*, discussed in Section 3.3.2, which has been cited in every single case dealing with Art. XI GATT ever since. See also the Panel report on *Japan–Film* (Kodak/Fuji) on this score.

[126] Note that attribution is a nonissue in the context of Art. III.2 GATT: fiscal measures can only be imposed by governments, or by nongovernmental organs, following delegation of authority by governments.

encompassing a similarly broad range of government action and action by private parties that may be assimilated to government action. In this connection, we consider that our previous discussion of GATT cases on administrative guidance in relation to what may constitute a 'measure' under Article XXIII:1(b), specifically the panel reports on *Japan – Semi-conductors and Japan – Agricultural Products*, is equally applicable to the definitional scope of 'all laws, regulations and requirements' in Article III:4. (italics and emphasis in the original)

It follows that government behavior that is channeled through private actors can be challenged under Art. III.4 GATT. This observation might have practical import in the field of antitrust where, following government authorization, private practices that might restrain trade could come under the purview of Art. III.4 GATT.

4.3.2.4.2 Affecting Sale, Offering for Sale. This term has been interpreted to cover measures that not only actually, but also *potentially* and/or *indirectly* affect trade. The AB report on *US–FSC* confirmed the wide interpretation of the term 'affecting' (§§ 208–210):

> ...the word 'affecting' assists in defining the types of measure that must conform to the obligation not to accord 'less favourable treatment' to like imported products, which is set out in Article III:4.

> The word 'affecting' serves a similar function in Article I:1 of the *General Agreement on Trade in Services* (the 'GATS'), where it also defines the types of measure that are subject to the disciplines set forth elsewhere in the GATS but does not, in itself, impose any obligation....

> In view of the similar function of the identical word, 'affecting', in Article III:4 of the GATT 1994, we also interpret this word, in this provision, as having a 'broad scope of application." (italics in the original)

There is not one single case where a challenged measure failed to meet the 'affecting' requirement.

4.3.2.4.3 Like Products in Art. III.4 GATT. Art. III.4 GATT does not distinguish between like and DCS products, in contrast to Art. III.2 GATT. The question hence arises whether the term like should have the same meaning across the two paragraphs. The AB decided that this should not be the case, as we detail in what follows. In its report on *EC–Asbestos*, the WTOP adjudicating bodies were called to pronounce on the GATT-consistency of a French ban on the sales of asbestos-containing construction material. The sales ban was nondiscriminatory, that is, it applied irrespective of the origin of the asbestos-containing construction material. France's prohibition (administrative decree) of sales of asbestos-containing construction material was based on scientific evidence: the *chrysotile fibers* in the asbestos in the imported product was a known carcinogen. But Canada argued that construction material containing chrysotile fibers was a like product to construction material containing *PCG fibers*, the corresponding asbestos-free substance in the domestically produced construction material. Construction material containing PCG fibers was being legally sold in France. Canada argued that by allowing sales of the material containing PGG fibers but not chrysotile fibers, the French ban accorded the Canadian good less favorable treatment than that accorded to the French-like good.[127]

The Panel had decided that the two products were indeed like since the end uses of the two products were the same. The differential treatment of the two products meant that France was according imported products less favorable treatment than that accorded to domestic like products. Consequently, Art. III.4 GATT was violated. The Panel therefore moved to examine the French (or rather EU) defense under Art. XX GATT.

The AB first addressed the issue whether asbestos-containing and asbestos-free materials were like products. In order to respond to this question, the AB as a first step held that the term like products in Art. III.4 GATT should be interpreted in light of the over-arching purpose of Art. III GATT: absent parallelism in the coverage across paragraphs III.2 and III.4 GATT, WTO Members would be incurring obligations of different scope with respect to fiscal and nonfiscal instruments; this view was not in the eyes of the AB supported by the negotiating record. The AB consequently held that the term like products in Art. III.4 of the GATT should be understood as covering products that are in competitive relationship with one another. It explicitly accepted a wide coverage of the term like products (wider than that of the corresponding term featured in Art. III.2 GATT), but not wider than the combined coverage of the terms like and DCS coming under the purview of Art. III.2 GATT (§§ 98–100).

Then, the AB reversed the Panel's findings with respect to likeness. In its view, the Panel should have examined all four criteria mentioned in the WP on BTAs (border tax adjustments) to confer likeness and not just end uses. Had it done so, the Panel would in the AB's view have observed the differences in physical characteristics between the two products. In the AB's view, the composition of a product is very much part of the physical-characteristics analysis. Chrysotile fibers and PCG fibers are not the same: the first are carcinogenic, whereas the latter are not. The health hazard would in the AB's view most likely have led ultimate consumers of construction material to avoid purchase material containing chrysotile fibers, had it been marketed. Professional buyers of construction material, who would often not be exposed themselves to the health risk, but

[127] See the discussion of the AB report in Horn and Weiler (2007), which forms the basis for the analysis here.

would take such reactions into account, would therefore purchase less of such material. Based on such reasoning, the AB found the two products to be unlike (§§ 101–154). The finding of non-likeness was hence based on the AB's assessment of the construction companies' assessment of how the latter would be affected, through the market mechanism, of the assessment of their customers of differences in risk.

The AB effectively held that the presence of health risk in asbestos containing-construction material only raised a presumption that the two products were unlike, increasing the burden of proof for Canada. *In casu*, Canada did not rebut this presumption and consequently lost the case.[128]

The *EC–Asbestos* dispute hence contains a novelty from a burden-of-proof point of view. When making its likeness determination, the AB did not rely on studies or information concerning actual buyer behavior, the AB uses instead its own interpretation of what buyers would reasonably do, if facing a choice between the two products (§ 122):

> In this case especially, we are also persuaded that evidence relating to consumers' tastes and habits would establish that the health risks associated with chrysotile asbestos fibres influence consumers' behaviour with respect to the different fibres at issue. We observe that, as regards *chrysotile asbestos and PCG fibres*, the consumer of the fibres is a *manufacturer* who incorporates the fibres into another product, such as cement-based products or brake linings. We do not wish to speculate on what the evidence regarding these consumers would have indicated; rather, we wish to highlight that consumers' tastes and habits regarding *fibres*, even in the case of commercial parties, such as manufacturers, are very likely to be shaped by the health risks associated with a product which is known to be highly carcinogenic. A manufacturer cannot, for instance, ignore the preferences of the ultimate consumer of its products. If the risks posed by a particular product are sufficiently great, the ultimate consumer may simply cease to buy that product. This would, undoubtedly, affect a manufacturer's decisions in the marketplace. Moreover, in the case of products posing risks to human health, we think it likely that manufacturers' decisions will be influenced by other factors, such as the potential civil liability that might flow from marketing products posing a health risk to the ultimate consumer, or the additional costs associated with safety procedures required to use such products in the manufacturing process. (§ 122, italics in the original, underlining added)

---

[128] In a separate but concurring opinion, an unnamed member of the AB held the view, that the scientific proof cited in this case was sufficient to conclude that the two products were unlike. One way to understand the need for a separate opinion is probably that, in this member's eyes, the difference in physical characteristics, and the ensuing consumers' reaction, does not merely raise a presumption, but amounts to a home run: Canada could never rebut such evidence.

In the preceding recital to the above-quoted passage, the AB had however, noted:

> Furthermore, in a case such as this, where the fibres are physically very different, a panel *cannot* conclude that they are "like products" if it *does not examine* evidence relating to consumers' tastes and habits ... (italics in original).

Still, the AB did not think it was necessary to look for market evidence when deciding on the likeness of the products concerned. So the test for likeness is a market test in name only, since it is the hypothetical reactions of a reasonable consumer that will define, according to this test, whether two products are like.[129] In other words, the AB here effectively reduced the probative value of quantitative evidence.

This finding in the report raises a number of issues:

(a) if as the AB asserts, consumers would treat the two products as like, what was then the need for France to impose the sales ban in the first place? Arguably, France imposed the measure precisely because consumers would treat the two goods as substitutes. The axiomatic distinction that the AB drew is probably not supported by facts;[130]

(b) this is not to say that France should have lost this case. On the contrary, France produced highly credible scientific evidence of the health hazard from exposure to asbestos. In our view, the question before the AB should have been whether France's measures afforded less favorable treatment to the imported goods, an issue that we discuss in what immediately follows.[131]

4.3.2.4.4 Less Favorable Treatment. The function of this requirement has occupied a number of reports, and in particular the question regarding the relationship between less favorable treatment (LFT) and the ASATAP-requirement

---

[129] The AB found additional support for its overall finding in the fact that chrysotile fibers and PCG fibers do not share the same tariff classification, and, also, in the fact that scientific evidence was cited in support of the carcinogenic nature of chrysotile fibers.

[130] Lydgate (2011) reaches similar conclusions.

[131] The report received mixed reactions in doctrine. On one end of the spectrum, Yavitz (2002) criticizes this case law for not interpreting the key terms in this provision in a manner that would honor its agreed function, that is, to avoid that WTO Members use nonfiscal instruments so as to afford advantages to their domestic production. In contrast, Howse and Tuerk (2001) agree with the basis of the reasoning of the AB report, and disagree vehemently with the Panel approach. The authors defend a comprehensive discrimination test that should take place within the four corners of Art. III GATT (instead of moving the discussion to Art. XX GATT). They thus see the AB report as a positive step in this direction. These and other views are not necessarily mutually inconsistent, since their focus is on different parts of the report.

which appears in Art. III.1, and III.2 GATT. In *EC–Bananas III*, the AB held that:

> Article III:4 does not specifically refer to Article III:1. Therefore, a determination of whether there has been a violation of Article III:4 does *not* require a separate consideration of whether a measure afford[s] protection to domestic production. (emphasis in the original)

In its report on *EC–Asbestos*, the AB explicitly held that LFT echoes the principle set forth in Art. III.1 GATT: WTO Members should not use domestic measures so as to afford protection to domestic production (§ 100):

> The term 'less favourable treatment' expresses the general principle, in Article III:1, that internal regulations 'should not be applied … so as to afford protection to domestic production.' If there is 'less favourable treatment' of the group of 'like' imported products, there is, conversely, 'protection' of the group of 'like' domestic products. However, a Member may draw distinctions between products which have been found to be 'like,' without, for this reason alone, according to the group of 'like' *imported* products 'less favourable treatment' than that accorded to the group of 'like' *domestic* products. (emphasis in the original)

Two consequences stem from the quoted passages:

(a) the complainant who is asked to show LFT, does not have to also show that a law is ASATAP;
(b) distinctions can be drawn between like goods without necessarily violating Art. III.4 GATT.

The natural questions to follow are: What needs to be shown besides differential treatment? And who should carry the burden of proof? This is an area where case law has not progressed smoothly and coherently.

The AB report on *Korea–Various Measures on Beef* was the first report that discussed in detail the nuts and bolts of the LFT test. This dispute, between Korea on the one hand, and a host of beef exporters on the other, concerned the distribution of beef in the Korean market. Korea had enacted a law whereby traders at the retail level could sell either domestic or imported beef but not both; this was denoted the "dual retail system." The complainants argued that as a result of this system, there were only 5000 points of sale for imported beef, compared to over 45,000 points of sale for domestic beef. Since this made it more difficult to sell imported than domestic beef, the dual retail system therefore violated Art. III.4 GATT. Korea pointed to the fact that it had in place an import quota for beef, the legality of which was not put into question during the proceedings: indeed, Korea had invoked the balance-of-payments provisions of the GATT to impose a quota on the import of beef, and complainants had not questioned the legitimacy of this action. Korea added that the quota had been absorbed all years when the system was in place, with one exception only: following the financial crisis in 1997, when overall consumption (of both domestic and foreign beef) fell dramatically. Hence, in Korea's view complainants suffered trade damage only one year.

Korea also argued before the Panel that the dual retail system was not discriminatory, in light of the fact that traders were free to choose whether they would sell domestic or foreign beef, and that there was no legal compulsion obliging them to choose one category of beef over the other; they could further subsequently switch at no cost from selling beef of one origin to selling the other.[132] Korea claimed that a legislation that provides equality of competitive conditions passes the test of consistency with Art. III GATT, even if some trade effects might look harmful to exporters; it was effectively arguing that the complainants cannot on the one hand claim that trade effects are immaterial, and on the other, base their complaint on trade effects.[133] The Panel rejected all of Korea's claims, and found in favor of the complainants.

On appeal, the AB held that this system, although formally nondiscriminatory, still modified the conditions of competition to the detriment of the imported product, and found Korea's practices to be inconsistent with Art. III.4 GATT since it afforded LFT to imported like products. The modification of conditions of competition was evident, in the AB's view, by the fact that fewer retailers decided to sell imported beef (§§ 143–151). The AB accepted that the choice to distribute domestic or imported beef was in the hands of private retailers. In a rather cryptic passage it held that LFT resulted from Korea's decision not to stick to the prior regime (§ 146):

> We are aware that the dramatic reduction in number of retail outlets for imported beef followed from the decisions of individual retailers who could choose freely to sell the domestic product or the imported product. The legal necessity of making a choice was, however, imposed by the measure itself. The restricted nature of that choice should be noted. The choice given to the meat retailers was *not* an option between remaining with the pre-existing unified distribution set-up or going to a dual retail system. The choice was limited to selling domestic beef only or imported beef only. Thus, the reduction of access to normal retail channels is, in legal contemplation, the effect of that measure. In these circumstances, the intervention

---

[132] Korea did not contest before the Panel the assertion of complainants that domestic and imported beef were like goods.

[133] Korea also made claims under Art. XX GATT, and argued that the system was in place in order to combat tax fraud: traders had the incentive to sell imported beef for domestic, in light of the very substantial price-differential between imported and domestic beef (the latter being substantially more expensive than the former).

of some element of private choice does not relieve Korea of responsibility under the GATT 1994 for the resulting establishment of competitive conditions less favourable for the imported product than for the domestic product. (emphasis in the original)

The AB was quick to highlight what it had not been prejudging through its decision (§ 149):

It may finally be useful to indicate, however broadly, what we are *not* saying in reaching our above conclusion. We are *not* holding that a dual or parallel distribution system that is *not* imposed directly or indirectly by law or governmental regulation, but is rather solely the result of private entrepreneurs acting on their own calculations of comparative costs and benefits of differentiated distribution systems, is unlawful under Article III:4 of the GATT 1994. What is addressed by Article III:4 is merely the *governmental* intervention that affects the conditions under which like goods, domestic and imported, compete in the market within a Member's territory. (emphasis in the original)

So, the AB did not go so far as to outlaw exclusivity contracts signed between suppliers and retailers. Arguably, exclusivity contracts, assuming market power in the upstream (or even, in some legal orders, in the downstream) market, will be judged illegal under many national antitrust statutes, unless they have benefited from antitrust exemption. Is a government anti-trust exemption sufficient for the AB to outlaw similar practices? The AB did not provide a comprehensive response to this question, although it did note that purely private contracts that provide for exclusivity have not been outlawed as a result of this report.

This case raises many questions casting serious doubt on the intellectual legitimacy of the AB's reasoning:

(a) What exactly is the LFT here? Is it the fact that imported beef was previously being sold through the same channel as domestic beef, or is it the fact that only 5000 outlets sell imported beef whereas 45,000 outlets sell domestic beef? It cannot be the former, since the same requirement was imposed on domestic beef (it cannot be sold through the same channels as imported beef), hence no LFT results from this modification of conditions of competition. It cannot be the latter either since trade effects, so says consistent case law, are immaterial. Or are they?

(b) If trade effects do matter, how can we judge whether availability of imported beef in 5000 as opposed to 45,000 outlets operates to the detriment of imported beef unless if we have information about the sales volumes in these outlets as well as the sales volumes in the policy-unconstrained case?

(c) What exactly is the detriment to imported beef when the quota was absorbed all the years that it was in place except for one when indeed extraordinary circumstances (by any reasonable account) occurred? We should add here that it cannot be that the modification of conditions of competition *per se* constitutes a GATT violation: the GATT is a negative integration contract and trading partners retain the right to design and modify their laws as they find appropriate, as long as they observe the basic nondiscrimination obligation. Hence, it is the notion that the modification of conditions of competition is to the detriment of imported goods that must form the basis of the AB judgment; and

(d) Since LFT equals ASATAP, should not the AB inquire into the design, structure, and architecture of the law? Well, it did so in the context of Art. XX GATT and did not cast doubt on the Korean justification that it was done for consumer-protection purposes: Korean beef sold at a much higher price than imported beef, and Korea argued that the dual retail system (along with other measures) were meant to guarantee that traders would not fraudulently sell imported beef as Korean. The acceptance by the AB of this reasoning leads to the question of how does the design, structure, and architecture of the measure support a finding of LFT?[134]

Without explicitly deviating from this case law, the AB in fact reversed it in a subsequent case: In its report on *Dominican Republic–Import and Sale of Cigarettes*, the AB upheld the Panel's rejection of Honduras's claim under Art. III.4 GATT. It agreed with the Panel that a detrimental effect of a measure (the measure here was a bond requirement, under which cigarette importers had to post a bond to ensure payment of taxes) on a given imported product does not necessarily imply that the measure accords less favorable treatment to imports, if the effect is explained by factors unrelated to the foreign origin of the product; in this case, the factor explaining the treatment was the market share of the importer, in the sense that the level of the bond requirement depended on the market share that the importer (or the domestic producer) attained in the Dominican Republic market (§ 96):

The Appellate Body indicated in *Korea – Various Measures on Beef* that imported products are treated less favorably than like products if a measure

---

[134] In §§ 172ff. of its report, the AB held that Korea had violated its obligations under Art. XX(d) GATT not because the measure was not authentically pursuing consumer protection, but because it was unnecessary, in the sense more trade-restrictive than necessary. We discuss this aspect of the report in Section 4.4. Suffice, nonetheless, to mention here that there is no necessity requirement in Art. III GATT: if the measure did indeed modify conditions of competition to the detriment of imported goods (a highly doubtful proposition for the reasons mentioned above), and was not origin-based (as the Panel and the AB accepted), then it should have passed the test of consistency under Art. III GATT as the AB report on *Dominican Republic–Import and Sale of Cigarettes* that we discuss infra has held.

modifies the conditions of competition in the relevant *market to the detriment of imported products*. However, the existence of a detrimental effect on a given imported product resulting from a measure does not necessarily imply that this measure accords less favorable treatment to imports if the detrimental effect is explained by factors or circumstances unrelated to the foreign origin of the product, such as the market share of the importer in this case. In this specific case, the mere demonstration that the per-unit cost of the bond requirement for imported cigarettes was higher than for some domestic cigarettes during a particular period is not, in our view, *sufficient* to establish "less favourable treatment" under Article III:4 of the GATT 1994. Indeed, the difference between the per-unit costs of the bond requirement alleged by Honduras is explained by the fact that the importer of Honduran cigarettes has a smaller market share than two domestic producers (the per-unit cost of the bond requirement being the result of dividing the cost of the bond by the number of cigarettes sold on the Dominican Republic market). In this case, the difference between the per-unit costs of the bond requirement alleged by Honduras does not depend on the foreign origin of the imported cigarettes. Therefore, in our view, the Panel was correct in dismissing the argument that the bond requirement accords less favorable treatment to imported cigarettes because the per-unit cost of the bond was higher for the importer of Honduran cigarettes than for two domestic producers. (italics and emphasis in the original)

The argument here differed from the approach in *Korea–Various Measures of Beef*, where the principle laid down was that a measure afforded LFT if the detrimental effect for imported goods was a function of their origin. The AB did not explain the exact nature of the test that determines whether the detriment is due to the origin of goods (or not). In this case, it found in favor of the defendant because on its face the law did not link the level of bond requirements to anything other than market share. There is thus a marked difference between the two reports: a measure that operates to the detriment of imported goods is in violation of Art. III.4 GATT in the world of *Korea–Various Measures of Beef*; this is not necessarily the case in the world of *Dominican Republic–Import and Sale of Cigarettes*: if the measure is justified on reasons other than the origin of the goods then, even in presence of detrimental effects to imported goods, it will pass muster under Art. III.4 GATT.

In a similar vein, the AB held in its report on *US–FSC* (Article 21.5–EC) in § 215:

The examination of whether a measure involves "less favourable treatment" of imported products within the meaning of Article III:4 of the GATT 1994 must be grounded in close scrutiny of the "fundamental thrust and effect of the measure itself". This examination cannot rest on simple assertion, but must be founded on a careful analysis of the contested measure and of its implications in the marketplace. At the same time, however, the examination need not be based on the *actual effects* of the contested measure in the marketplace. (emphasis in the original)

Yet, in a more recent case, we see no mention to the AB report on *Dominican Republic–Import and Sale of Cigarettes*. In *Thailand–Cigarettes*, the AB was asked to pronounce on the consistency of a Thai tax measure with Art. III.4 GATT. Thailand had argued before the Panel and the AB that its measures were not origin-related and hence not in violation of Art. III.4 GATT. In § 126 of its report, the AB discusses LFT referring time and again to *Korea–Various Measures on Beef* and avoiding any reference to *Dominican Republic–Import and Sale of Cigarettes*. To make things even more confusing on this front, in *US–Clove Cigarettes*, a Panel report released in September 2011, the Panel discusses the LFT requirement exclusively in light of the findings of the AB report on *Dominican Republic–Import and Sale of Cigarettes* (pp. 79ff.). This Panel report was issued months after the AB report on *Thailand–Cigarettes*, and it is quite legitimate to suspect that its authors were fully aware of its content. The only fitting conclusion here is that WTO adjudicating bodies are still struggling with the test that should be applied in order to decide whether the LFT requirement has been established or not.

4.3.2.4.5 No Effects and No Intent Either? The Standard of Review. Note that in all cases discussed so far, the complainants were not asked to produce evidence regarding harmful effects resulting from the violation of Art. III GATT. A violation of Art. III GATT can, in other words, be established irrespective whether it has produced harmful trade effects to imported goods. Case law, at least in its original form went one step further: it did not request from the complaining party to demonstrate protectionist intent either. A complainant arguing a case under Art. III GATT would thus be requested to show that:

(a) either an imported product was taxed in excess of a domestic like product;
(b) or an imported product was taxed differently than a domestic DCS product, in the sense that the taxation operates ASATAP to the domestic DCS product;
(c) or a domestic nonfiscal scheme affords, to an imported product, treatment less favorable than that afforded to a domestic like product.

In none of these three scenarios would the complaining party be *required* to demonstrate harmful trade effects or protectionist intent. This point was made clear in a GATT case, the panel report on *US–Superfund*. The United States had been taxing imported petroleum products slightly higher than its domestic counterpart. When the measure was challenged before the GATT dispute-settlement process, the U.S. response was that the difference was so minimal that it could not reasonably have an impact on the prices in the U.S. market. The products concerned by the U.S. taxation scheme were *like* products, a point conceded by the United States, which did not, however, advance any defense other than the absence of impact on the prices.

The GATT panel dismissed the U.S. argument. In its view, the fact that the effects on the market were negligible was a nonissue: Art. III GATT should be constructed and understood as a mechanism protecting legitimate expectations as to the quality of competitive conditions (§ 5.1.9):

> ...Article III:2, first sentence, cannot be interpreted to protect expectations on export volumes; *it protects expectations on the competitive relationship between imported and domestic products.* A change in the competitive relationship contrary to that provision must consequently be regarded <u>ipso facto</u> as a nullification or impairment of benefits accruing under the General Agreement. A demonstration that a measure inconsistent with Article III:2, first sentence, has no or insignificant effects would therefore in the view of the Panel not be a sufficient demonstration that the benefits accruing under that provision had not been nullified or impaired even if such a rebuttal were in principle permitted. (underlining in the original; emphasis added)

So this report concluded that there is no need to show trade effects in order to establish a violation of Art. III.2 GATT when two like products have been treated differently.[135]

The holding in this report did not change at all over the years as far as the absence of need to demonstrate trade effects is concerned: if at all, subsequent panel and AB reports expanded its coverage and held that there is no need to show trade effects when DCS products are concerned, or when nonfiscal measures are at stake.

The AB in its report on *Japan–Alcoholic Beverages II* reproduced this idea in the following terms (p. 16):

> ...it is irrelevant that 'the trade effects' of the tax differential between imported and domestic products, as reflected in the volumes of imports, are insignificant or even non-existent; Article III protects expectations not of any particular trade volume but rather of the equal competitive relationship between imported and domestic products.

---

[135] The panel did not explain its position any further. Probably what it had in mind is that prices fluctuate and a small tax differential can become quite big in the future. What it did, however, explicitly state is that trading partners expect a certain kind of behavior by the other GATT contracting parties, and that there should be no need to check the outcome of a particular behavior that is not accepted in the treaty language negotiated. A violation establishes a *prima facie* case that is clearly rebuttable as *per* the DSU (and before, in the GATT years, as *per* Art. XXIII.2 GATT), although as yet no respondent has made the rebuttal successfully.

Consequently, in this report the AB extended the irrelevance of a trade-effects test to cases where *DCS* products are involved. Recall that, with the exception of the pair vodka, *shochu*, all other products were, in the AB's view, *DCS* products.

We detect a similar attitude in the context of Art. III.4 GATT. The AB clarified, in its report on *US–FSC*, that, in parallel with its case law under Art. III.2 GATT, for a complainant successfully to absolve its burden of proof and demonstrate that the group of imported products have been afforded LFT than the group of domestic like products, there is no obligation to show trade effects (§ 215):

> The examination of whether a measure involves 'less favourable treatment' of imported products within the meaning of Article III:4 of the GATT 1994 must be grounded in close scrutiny of the 'fundamental thrust and effect of the measure itself.' This examination cannot rest on simple assertion, but must be founded on a careful analysis of the contested measure and of its implications in the marketplace. At the same time, however, the examination need not be based on the *actual effects* of the contested measure in the marketplace. (emphasis in the original)

Following this line of thinking, the AB condemned an EC scheme that provided traders with an incentive to trade EC goods at the expense of imported like products, even in the absence of any tangible evidence suggesting that there was a quantified trade impact stemming from this measure (§§ 213–214 of the AB report on *EC–Bananas III*). By the same token, the panel, in its report on *Canada–Wheat Exports and Grain Imports*, found that a routine authorization scheme was GATT-inconsistent simply because it was not being imposed on domestic products (§ 6.193). The fact that the scheme was not onerous at all (§ 6.193), that economic operators were familiar with it (§ 6.197), that in the past authorization had always been granted (§ 6.200), that the agency at hand had enough discretion to always grant authorization (§ 6.203), that there was an institutional possibility to obtain advance authorization (§ 6.207), that a more attractive, than the authorization scheme, alternative was available to foreign products (§ 6.213) were not reason enough for the panel to change its mind on this issue.[136]

The relevance of an intent test is a slightly different story. A couple of GATT panel reports (*US–Malt Beverages*, and *US–Taxes on Automobiles*) held, as we

---

[136] WTO Members might have to quantify the effects of a trade measure they have successfully challenged, at a later stage of the proceedings: assuming no compliance has occurred and the complainant requests authorization to impose counter-measures, it will have to quantify the trade damage it suffered, in light of the obligation enshrined in Art 22.4 of the DSU, that the overall level of counter-measures should not exceed that of the trade damage incurred.

saw *supra*, that intent matters in the context of analysis under Art. III GATT. WTO panels explicitly overruled this approach. WTO panels did not, nevertheless, totally exclude the relevance of an intent test: case law has time and again stated that the *subjective* intent of the legislator does not matter, leaving thus room for the relevance of *objective* intent. As we will see, in what immediately follows, the substantive content of the two terms has not, alas, been clarified in case law.

In *Japan–Alcoholic Beverages II*, the AB distinguishes between *subjective* intent and the purpose of a regulatory intervention, as disclosed by *objective* features of the design of the measure. The former is irrelevant when it comes to establishing an Art. III.2 of the GATT violation; the latter could be relevant (p. 27):

> This third inquiry under Article III:2, second sentence, must determine whether 'directly competitive or substitutable products' are 'not similarly taxed' in a way that affords protection. This is not an issue of intent. It is not necessary for a panel to sort through the many reasons legislators and regulators often have for what they do and weigh the relative significance of those reasons to establish legislative or regulatory intent. If the measure is applied to imported or domestic products so as to afford protection to domestic production, then it does not matter that there may not have been any desire to engage in protectionism in the minds of the legislators or the regulators who imposed the measure. It is irrelevant that protectionism was not an intended objective if the particular tax measure in question is nevertheless, to echo Article III:1, '*applied* to imported or domestic products so as to afford protection to domestic production.' This is an issue of how the measure in question is *applied*.
>
> ...
>
> As in that case, we believe that an examination in any case of whether dissimilar taxation has been applied so as to afford protection requires a comprehensive and objective analysis of the structure and application of the measure in question on domestic as compared to imported products. We believe it is possible to examine objectively the underlying criteria used in a particular tax measure, its structure, and its overall application to ascertain whether it is applied in a way that affords protection to domestic products. (emphasis in the original)

In the same report as well as in *Chile–Alcoholic Beverages*, the AB went one step further: it brought *objective regulatory purpose*, that is, the purpose as revealed through the design and architecture of the measure, within the analysis of the ASATAP criterion. At the same time, however, it continued to explicitly reject a *subjective* intent test. Moreover, it did not establish any criteria as to how it will evaluate the objective regulatory purpose, other than referring to the design and the architecture of the measure at hand. It discussed summarily the four regulatory objectives advanced as justification of the measure by Chile, and it explicitly rejected the relevance of the necessity criterion when evaluating a claim under Art III of the GATT (§§ 71–72):

> We recall once more that, in *Japan – Alcoholic Beverages*, we declined to adopt an approach to the issue of "so as to afford protection" that attempts to examine "the many reasons legislators and regulators often have for what they do." We called for examination of the design, architecture and structure of a tax measure precisely to permit identification of a measure's objectives or purposes as revealed or objectified in the measure itself. Thus, we consider that a measure's purposes, objectively manifested in the design, architecture and structure of the measure, *are* intensely pertinent to the task of evaluating whether or not that measure is applied so as to afford protection to domestic production. In the present appeal, Chile's explanations concerning the structure of the New Chilean System – including, in particular, the truncated nature of the line of progression of tax rates, which effectively consists of two levels (27 per cent *ad valorem* and 47 per cent *ad valorem*) separated by only 4 degrees of alcohol content – might have been helpful in understanding what *prima facie* appear to be anomalies in the progression of tax rates. The conclusion of protective application reached by the Panel becomes very difficult to resist, in the absence of countervailing explanations by Chile. The mere statement of the four objectives pursued by Chile does not constitute effective rebuttal on the part of Chile.
>
> At the same time, we agree with Chile that it would be inappropriate, under Article III:2, second sentence, of the GATT 1994, to examine whether the tax measure is *necessary* for achieving its stated objectives or purposes. The Panel did use the word "necessary" in this part of its reasoning. Nevertheless, we do not read the Panel Report as showing that the Panel did, in fact, conduct an examination of whether the measure is necessary to achieve its stated objectives. It appears to us that the Panel did no more than try to relate the observable structural features of the measure with its declared purposes, a task that is unavoidable in appraising the application of the measure as protective or not of domestic production. (emphasis in the original)

Regulatory intent can, consequently, be an issue in the limited case where two products are DCS, *and* the tax differential is not large enough, keeping in mind that case law has not provided a quantitative benchmark to decide what large actually means.

Case law regarding the relevance of *objective* intent when the consistency of a fiscal measure with the GATT is being challenged, can usefully be summed up as follows:

(a) there is a threshold issue: not *any* tax differential is ASATAP; the tax differential must be more than *de minimis*. We do not know, however, what exactly constitutes *de minimis*, since case law did not provide a quantitative estimate in this regard. We do know, nonetheless, that mere arithmetic difference satisfies the *in excess* requirement, but not the *de minimis* requirement. Consequently, when dealing with claims regarding DCS products, if a WTO adjudicating body reaches the conclusion that a tax differential is less than *de minimis*, it will reject the complaint;[137]

(b) assuming that the *de minimis* criterion has been satisfied, if the tax differential is *substantial*, then it will suffice, in and of itself, to establish a violation of Art. III.2 GATT. Once again, WTO adjudicating bodies have not provided an arithmetic benchmark. In *Chile–Alcoholic Beverages*, nevertheless, a 20 percent tax differential between two *DCS* products was judged *substantial*. There has been no case so far where a tax differential was judged more than *de minimis* but less than *substantial*; and

(c) if a tax differential is more than *de minimis* but less than *substantial*, then an inconsistency with Art. III.2 GATT can be established only through recourse to other factors as well.[138]

Now, of course, one might legitimately wonder whether in practice inquiries into the *objective* intent will be necessary: indeed, a government that wishes to confer an advantage to its domestic production will, in all likelihood opt for substantial tax differentials assuming that this term covers cases where the tax differential affects prices. One will be hard pressed to find cases where, given protectionist intent, governments will opt for small tax differentials that might not affect prices at all.

Finally note that case law has clarified that the *objective* intent will be revealed through the design and the architecture of the measure challenged, but it has not explained in what way it differs from *subjective* intent. Indeed, in the absence of explanation, one might legitimately ask the question whether the distinction between *objective* and *subjective* intent is meaningful at all.

4.3.2.5 *Allocation of the Burden of Proof*

As conventional, we divide the *burden of proof* into the *burden of production* (who must bring forward evidence?), and the *burden of persuasion* (how much

---

[137] Hence, infinitesimal tax differentials will satisfy the *in excess* – but not the *ASATAP* – criterion.

[138] This is a theoretical possibility that has been flagged by the AB. So far, as noted above, no such case has been submitted to WTO adjudication.

evidence is necessary for the burden to shift to the other party?). The GATT does not explicitly address this central issue, but it has been dealt with in case law.

Consider first the burden of production. The allocation of burden of proof is not explicitly addressed in the DSU. Panels however, have consistently made references to general maxims of law regulating this issue; even when they did not refer to them explicitly, they addressed the issue in a manner consistent with those maxims. By virtue of the maxim *actori incumbit probatio*, it is for the party making a claim to provide the necessary evidence that the claim holds. This maxim is the direct consequence of another maxim, *in dubio mitius*, which essentially means that there should be a presumption of legality of the challenged measure. If the law distinguishes between a rule and an exception, then legal orders follow the maxim *quicunque exceptio invokat ejudem probare debet*: the party invoking the exception carries the burden of proof to demonstrate compliance with the conditions reflected in the exception. In this case, there is a presumption of illegality since the party invoking an exception has by definition broken the rule; that is the legal canon for which the presumption of legality has been agreed.

The situation in case law is somewhat confusing, but essentially follows these two maxims.[139] There is no doubt that Art. III GATT is a rule and not an exception to a rule. As a result, the burden of production of proof stays with the complainant. The next question is, how much proof must the complainant contribute for the burden to shift to the other party? This takes us straight into the discussion regarding the burden of persuasion.

Let us next turn to the burden of persuasion. It is by now clear, that the complainant, in general (that is, not only in Art. III GATT cases) need not provide full proof that its claim holds; a *prima facie* case suffices. What exactly constitutes a *prima facie* case is difficult to specify: there is discrepancy across panel reports but, in general, some sort of reasonableness standard seems to emerge. Assuming a *prima facie* case has been made, the burden will shift to the other party which will aim at refuting the evidence against it. Absent effective *refutation* of *prima facie*, the complainant will prevail. Note that the defendant will prevail even in the case of *equipoise* between its own evidence and that provided by the complainant.

WTO adjudicating bodies will not shift the burden of proof from one party to the other depending on whether a *prima facie* case has been made; dispute adjudication in the WTO is nothing like a game of tennis where the ball has to fly above the net for the other party to respond: they will typically request from both parties to provide all evidence they wish to submit, and they will make their

---

[139] In three cases (*EC–Sardines, EC–Hormones, EC–Tariff Preferences*) where the text of the agreement clearly indicates that we are dealing with an exception, case law still assigned the burden of production of proof with the complaining party. None of these cases is a GATT case though.

judgment whether a *prima facie* case has been made against this background, that is, by reviewing all of the evidence submitted before them. In this vein, we note that the panel, in its report on *Turkey–Rice*, summing up prior case law, held that it would not request from the defendant to respond only after the complainant had successfully made a *prima facie* case; rather, it would decide whether a *prima facie* case had been made on the basis of the totality of evidence brought by the parties to the dispute. There is not one single case so far that does not evidence this approach.

4.3.2.5.1 Making a *Prima Facie* Case. This requirement was first introduced by the AB in its report on *US–Wool Shirts and Blouses*. It has been cited in practically all disputes ever since when a burden of proof issue arose (§ 14):

> It is a generally accepted canon of evidence in civil law, common law, and, in fact, most jurisdictions, that the burden of proof rests upon the party, whether complaining or defending, who asserts the affirmative of a particular claim or defense. If that party adduces sufficient evidence to raise a presumption that what is claimed is true, the burden then shifts to the other party, who will fail unless it adduces sufficient evidence to rebut the presumption.

This passage provides only an indication as to the burden of *persuasion*; making a *prima facie* case is shorthand for observing the burden of persuasion. In subsequent cases, panels have used the term "to make a *prima facie* case" as equivalent to the obligation to "*raise a presumption*" that what is claimed is true (*US–Stainless Steel* at § 6.2). *Raising a presumption* is not a self-interpreting term either and, as a result, the question of the quantum of proof needed to discharge the obligation of burden of persuasion can be evaluated only on a case-by-case basis in WTO jurisprudence. Nevertheless, *raising a presumption* cannot amount to providing full proof by any reasonable understanding of this term. So it seems that what matters is that panels are satisfied that enough proof has been submitted regarding a particular claim and that the submitted proof, absent counter proof, could reasonably lead to the conclusion the complainant should prevail.[140]

The panel on *Mexico–Taxes on Soft Drinks* ruled that the duty of the complainant to make a *prima facie* case is not affected by the defendant's decision not to challenge the claims and arguments made. In the case at hand, Mexico had chosen not to raise any defense in some of the claims advanced by the United States. The panel implicitly held that Mexico's inaction did not amount to admission that the United States had made a *prima facie* case (§§ 8.16ff.). The

---

[140] A claim is the identification of a factual situation and the ensuing breach of a legal rule: by imposing a quota on imports of widgets, country X acts inconsistently with its obligations under Art. XI GATT.

panel went on and examined to what extent, in its view and in absence of a Mexican response, such was indeed the case.

4.3.2.5.2 Refuting a *Prima Facie* Case. In theory, assuming a presumption that a claim holds has been raised, the burden of proof will shift to the other party which will have to effectively refute the presumption: the panel report on *Thailand–H-Beams* for example, requests (§ 7.49) from Thailand to provide "effective refutation" against Poland's *prima facie* case. In practice, nonetheless, as already noted, WTO adjudicating bodies do not raise a flag anytime a presumption has been created; rather, WTO adjudicating bodies will make a global evaluation based on what has been pleaded before them by the parties to the dispute. As the AB noted in its report on *Korea–Dairy* there is:

> ...no provision in the DSU ... that requires a panel to make an explicit ruling on whether the complainant has established a *prima facie* case of violation before a panel may proceed to examine the respondent's defence and evidence. (§ 145 italics in the original)

Consequently, the issue whether a party has indeed established a *prima facie* case, and/or the adjunct issue whether the *prima facie* case was effectively refuted will form an integral part of the general evaluation by the panel. This does not mean however, that panels cannot, at the end of the process decide that the complainant did not make a *prima facie* case (see, for example, *India–Autos* §§ 7.231–7.233). That is, the fact that the defendant has attempted to rebut a claim presented by the complainant does not *necessarily* mean that, in the panel's view, the complainant has established a presumption.

(c) Equipoise
The panel, in its report on *US–1916 Act (EC)* concluded that evidence submitted by the complainant and the defendant was in *equipoise*. It then asked itself what the legal consequence of this finding should be. It held that, in such cases, the advantage rests with the party responding to the claim (§ 6.58):

> If, after having applied the above methodology, we could not reach certainty as to the most appropriate court interpretation, i.e. if the evidence remains in equipoise, we shall follow the interpretation that favours the party against which the claim has been made, considering that the claimant did not convincingly support its claim.

4.3.2.5.3 Art. III GATT Case Law.[141] In *Japan–Alcoholic Beverages II*, the complainant provided econometric evidence (based on consumer surveys) that the

---

[141] In line with the approach in this paper, we will limit our observations to the leading, in our view of course, cases.

products in question were DCS. It also pointed to the fact that the defendant had not invoked any rationale for the tax differential across the various products. The defendant claimed that there was some policy rationale which was, however, discarded by the panel (and the AB) since it was considered to be an *ex post facto* justification: the Japanese law providing for the tax differential across sochu and a series of western drinks did not contain any policy justification for the differential treatment of the various drinks coming under its purview.

In *Korea–Alcoholic Beverages*, the complainant provided evidence from the Japanese market regarding the relationship between the products in question arguing, inter alia, that the two markets (Japan, Korea) were highly comparable. However, as facts make it clear, western drinks did exist in the Korean market, the tax differential notwithstanding. The defendant claimed that the price differential between soju and the predominantly western drinks was such that Korean consumers would never treat interchangeably (at least diluted) soju and the western drinks involved. Nevertheless, neither the panel nor the AB explained why such evidence could not have been appropriately taken into consideration; they discussed evidence from the Japanese market without adequately explaining why evidence from the Korean market did not fit the bill. The panel and the AB further rejected the claims by Korea arguing that recourse to econometric indicators is not the only way in which likeness can be established. In the AB's view, two products would be considered like to the extent that they share physical characteristics, and end uses and consumers perceive them as such even if a price difference between the two exists.

In *Chile–Alcoholic Beverages*, the complainants provided evidence to the effect that some western drinks were being taxed substantially higher than some foreign drinks although the difference in alcoholic content was minimal. They submitted as evidence the Chilean law which contained sharp tax differentials across alcoholic drinks with various alcoholic contents. The defendant responded that it was Chilean producers of alcoholic drinks that were shouldering the majority of the tax burden in the higher category and provided evidence to this effect. Still the AB held that on balance the evidence submitted by Chile did not detract from the fact that imported goods were being taxed more onerously than domestic like/DCS products.

In *EC–Asbestos*, the complainant argued that the two products (construction material with and without asbestos) were like products and that the French measure was treating imported goods less favorably than their domestic counterparts. The defendant replied that the measure was based on scientific evidence pointing to the health hazards stemming from exposure to asbestos containing construction material. The panel and the AB reached divergent conclusions: in the panel's view the evidence submitted was not sufficient to show that the products were unlike. So it held that Canada won its claim under Art. III GATT, but it went on to find for the defendant under Art. XX GATT. In the AB's view, the evidence submitted supported a conclusion that the two products were unlike, because of consumers' perceptions regarding the health hazard associated with the imported goods.

In *Korea–Various Measures on Beef*, the complainants submitted evidence to the effect that, following the introduction of the dual retail system, most traders opted for selling domestic rather than imported beef. Korea responded arguing that this was only normal in light of the fact that a legitimate import quota was in place as a result of which total imports amounted to less than 10 percent of the total consumption. Korea also submitted evidence to the effect that the import quota had always been absorbed except for the years of the financial crisis when consumption was heavily reduced (with respect to consumption beef as well). The panel and the AB rejected Korea's arguments finding that the measure had modified conditions of competition to the detriment of imported goods since fewer stores were now carrying imported beef; they did not deem the evidence on absorption of quota to be relevant since, in their view, the standard of review under Art. III GATT does not require analysis of trade effects. They further found against Korea under Art. XX GATT holding that while this measure was genuinely aiming at consumers' protection, it was unnecessary since it was overly restrictive of trade.

In *Dominican Republic–Import and Sale of Cigarettes*, the complainant presented evidence regarding the bond requirement that imported cigarettes had to pay arguing that it was in excess of the similar burden on domestic like goods. The defendant did not dispute that occasionally this would be the case. It did, however, claim that the payable amount was a function of the size of the market of the producer involved in the transaction and, consequently, it was not linked to the foreign origin of the goods. The AB sided with the defendant stating that, to the extent that the regulator can point to a ground for adopting a measure other than the origin of goods, a measure will pass the test of consistency with Art. III GATT (even if occasionally it produces a negative trade outcome for imported goods).

There is little to disagree with the AB's attitude on the *original* assignment concerning burden of production. For the rest, however, the AB's attitude is hard to discern:

(a) In name, the AB suggests that neither the regulatory intent nor trade effects will be taken into account: but in *Korea–Various Measures on Beef* the AB does in a way look at effects; how can it rule that conditions of competition have been modified to the *detriment* of importing goods without taking into account that there are fewer stores now (than before) selling imported beef?

(b) By the same token, in *Dominican Republic–Import and Sale of Cigarettes*, the AB held that origin must not be the rationale for law, otherwise a measure will run afoul of Art. III GATT. How different is that from saying that the intent of the regulator cannot be to punish imported goods because of their origin? In the same context, in *Chile–Alcoholic Beverages* the AB attempts a difficult-to-understand distinction between objective (as opposed to subjective?) intent;

It is clear by now that panels and the AB will not turn the green light on every time the complainant has adduced enough proof to switch the burden to the other party. Unless, however, the standard of review, that is, all issues regarding burden of production and burden of persuasion, becomes clear, both parties might be disadvantaged when preparing themselves for adjudication at the WTO.

4.3.3 Exceptions to NT

A WTO Member that has been found to be in violation of its obligations under Art. III GATT can still exonerate itself from liability by invoking one of the exceptions mentioned in the GATT. To this effect, however, the regulating WTO Member will carry the burden of proof to show that its measures, although in violation of Art. III GATT, are not GATT-inconsistent. We are not concerned here with temporary deviations, such as for example, a waiver, but rather with permanent exceptions that is, legal grounds that justify departures from NT without imposing any time constraints.

4.3.3.1 *Art. IV GATT: Film*

The letter and the negotiating history of Art. IV GATT make it clear that WTO Members can treat domestic cinematographic film better than foreign.[142] To this effect, they can, for example, establish screen quotas and thus, treat imported films less favorably than domestic films that might run quota free. From a pure legal perspective though, film quotas should not be treated as exceptions to NT, but rather as *lex specialis* to this provision. This is so since, otherwise, the burden of proof would have to shift to the country imposing the film quota. Art. XX GATT entitled 'General Exceptions' is prima facie an exception to Art. IV GATT as well, and it is in this context that the WTO Member imposing a film quota will be requested to defend it, that is, only assuming that the complainant had previously successfully challenged the consistency of a measure with Art. IV GATT.

So far, there have been no cases adjudicated under Art. IV GATT.

4.3.3.2 *Art. XX GATT: General Exceptions*

The title of this provision leaves no doubt that it was intended to be an exception to, in principle, all GATT provisions. Case law has confirmed that Art. XX GATT is an exception to NT: an appropriate illustration is offered by the

---

[142] Deciding on the origin of films might be a quixotic test. This is not, however, an issue for the purposes of this work.

aforementioned report on *Korea–Various Measures on Beef*, it was a domestic instrument of nonfiscal nature (*dual retail system*) that was judged to be inconsistent with Art. III GATT; Korea attempted (unsuccessfully) to justify it through recourse to Art. XX GATT: both the panel and the AB examined the consistency of the challenged measure with Art. XX GATT, in accordance with Korea's claims.

4.3.3.3 *Art. XXI GATT: Security Exception*

The security exception is, like Art. XX GATT, an exception to, in principle, all GATT provisions. There has been no case law so far regarding domestic instruments in this context; indeed, there has been no case law at all under this provision since the inception of the WTO: the European Community attempted to challenge the consistency of the US *Helms Burton Act* with the WTO rules, but requested suspension of the panel established to this effect before it issued its report, and did not request that it reconvene within the statutory deadlines. As a result, the panel's authority lapsed (Art. 12.12 DSU). During the GATT years, one case was actually litigated: in *US–Nicaraguan Trade*, a rather idiosyncratic GATT panel, since it was clear that the final report was not going to be implemented anyway. In this case, the measures at stake were border measures (two-way embargo).[143] Still, there should be no doubt that a WTO Member can legitimately depart from NT if this is necessary to safeguard its national security: the wording of this provision leaves no room for doubt in this regard. It pertinently reads:

> *Nothing* in this Agreement shall be construed
>
> …
>
> (b) to prevent any contracting party from taking *any* action which it considers necessary for the protection of its essential security interests. (emphasis added)

4.3.4 Critique of the Case Law

In what follows, we provide an overview of the debate and the critique expressed in the doctrine concerning the application of Art. III GATT in specific instances by the WTO adjudicating bodies, as well as the overall understanding of this provision by the WTO adjudicating bodies.[144]

A significant part of the criticism regarding the case-law approach to Art. III GATT borrows from doctrinal work on the understanding of Art. III GATT, and

---

[143] See Mavroidis (2007) at pp. 322ff.
[144] Hundreds of papers have directly or indirectly discussed either specific applications of Art. III GATT or the WTO judges' overall understanding of this provision. We thus have to be selective in our description of the literature.

on the role it is called to play within the world trading system. The question that many authors have asked concerns the limits that NT places on the regulatory authority of WTO Members. There are, of course, many variations regarding this basic question. Almost unanimously the doctrine condemns the tendency in (at least some) case law to base its findings in the perception that the terms of Art. III GATT should be understood in a contextual manner, without *adequate* regard to the *role* that NT has been committed to play by the GATT framers. Voices in the doctrine have not condemned the institutional architecture of the GATT or the drafting of Art. III GATT: critique has centered on the understanding of this provision by GATT/WTO adjudicating bodies.

There is still scarce analysis of NT in economics, and in particular of the NT case law. The same largely applies to the law-and-economics literature. It is illustrative that the two volumes coedited by Bhagwati and Hudec (1996), while containing many interesting contributions addressing the harmonization of domestic policies, did not contain any paper specifically addressing NT.[145]

We first present a summary of the general critique, that is, papers which do not discuss specific case law but rather the general approach of GATT/WTO panels when dealing with disputes coming under the purview of Art. III GATT (including a normative discussion, that is, the manner in which GATT/WTO panels *should* – rather than *do* – understand this provision). We then discuss critiques against specific reports by GATT/WTO panels.

We divide the doctrinal discussion into four parts: papers dealing with the *mandate and coverage* of NT, its *legal nature*, the *standard of review* that GATT/WTO panels do and/or should apply across cases, and finally the *understanding of specific terms* appearing in the body of Art. III GATT.

The mandate and coverage of NT: In a series of papers and books authored alone or with coauthors, Jackson (1989, 1998, 2003, 2006) explains the changing role of domestic regulation in a world where border instruments are becoming less and less meaningful.[146] Jackson recognizes the problems posed by the extension of NT to cover cases of *de facto* discrimination, but argues that, unless construed this way (that is, to encompass *de facto* discrimination as well), this provision would be easily circumvented. The extension of the ambit of NT to cover cases of *de facto* discrimination is thus a necessary evil; adjudicating bodies then face the task of devising the appropriate test to ensure that in such cases they will be punishing only discriminatory (origin-wise) behavior and nothing else.

Staiger and Sykes (2011) deal with the limits of the current draft of Art. III GATT. They observe that WTO rules and disputes center on complaints about excessively stringent regulations. Employing the international externalities

---

[145] See Bhagwati and Hudec (1996).
[146] Jackson (1969) provided the first comprehensive assessment of the negotiation of this provision.

(terms-of-trade) framework for the modeling of trade agreements, they show how large nations may have an incentive to impose discriminatory product standards against imported goods once border instruments are constrained, and how inefficiently stringent standards may emerge under certain circumstances even if regulatory discrimination is prohibited. They then assess the WTO legal framework in light of their results, arguing that it does a reasonably thorough job of policing regulatory discrimination, but that it does relatively little to address excessive nondiscriminatory regulations.

The legal nature of NT: Surprisingly this area has not attracted a lot of interest. Petersmann (2002) is probably the only paper that squarely addresses this issue. He does not put into question the historic role for Art. III GATT. However, he does question its continued legitimacy in today's world. In Petersmann's view, the nondiscrimination principle in Art. III GATT should be understood as a 'constitutional' provision (using this term to denote hierarchy across the various GATT provisions) and should be anchored in human rights, that is, it should be interpreted in light of jurisprudence in the field of protection of human rights.

The standard of review: A number of papers have dealt with the *aims and effects* test and this should not come as surprise: in GATT/WTO, total reversals of case law are quite rare. Moreover, explicit over-turnings are even less frequent. Yet this is what happened, as we saw supra, in the context of disputes relating to Art. III GATT: the very first case that was adjudicated under the WTO (*Japan–Taxes on Alcoholic Beverages*) explicitly rejected the standard of review employed in the last GATT case that came under the purview of this provision (*US–Taxes on Automobiles*).

There are authors who have taken an unambiguous stance in favor of reinstating the *aims and effects* test (or a version of this test that would essentially ask the question what is the regulatory intent of the challenged measure and would subject the ultimate decision regarding violation on the response to this question). Hudec is one of many authors who devoted considerable efforts analyzing the standard of review that should be applied in cases dealing with Art. III GATT. Hudec (1988, 1998, 2000) explains the shortcomings of an Art. III test that disregards protective intent: in Hudec's view, this can cause GATT/WTO judges to strike down domestic measures that should be considered legitimate. Hudec's criticism has been echoed by many other scholars.

Howse and Regan (2000) agree that intent should matter, and take a stance in favor of an *aims and effects* test à la *US–Taxes on Automobiles*. They mentioned the relevance of PPMs (process and production methods) when defining like products, arguing that, for example, environment-friendly and -unfriendly products should not be treated as like goods.

Building on his work with Howse, Regan (2002, 2003) has argued that the judge should inquire into the legislative intent in order to decide whether a measure is consistent with Art. III GATT: only measures pursued with the intent to protect should be judged GATT-inconsistent. Regan maintains, like others as well, that *de facto* the WTO judge does inquire into intent. At a principle level, he does not take distance from the *aims and effect* test as applied in GATT case law.

Roessler (1996) takes the view that panels have only paid lip service to the overarching purpose of Art. III GATT, that is, to combat protectionism. Consequently, in his view, domestic measures that serve a purpose other than protectionism should be exonerated from liability under Art. III GATT. To ensure that this indeed the case, Roessler calls for an understanding of the term *like products* that would be inspired by the regulatory objective pursued. Roessler also takes issue with the standard of review adopted by adjudicating bodies: in his view, recourse to Art. XX GATT is no panacea since this provision includes only an exhaustive list of justifying grounds whereas there are arguably many more potential policy goals that a society might legitimately wish to achieve. He thus argues in favor of a refocus of the nondiscrimination test as embedded in Art. III GATT.

Charnovitz (2002) expresses disagreement with the manner in which WTO adjudicating bodies have, by applying an erroneous standard of review that does not inquire into the intent of the challenged measure, *de facto* subjected the pursuit of social preferences (often pursued in nondiscriminatory terms) to trade concerns. This goes against the negotiating intent (that Charnovitz has explored in this and other work), and undoes the balance of rights and obligations as struck by the WTO Members during negotiations.

Porges and Trachtman (2003) use a legal-realist methodology and hypothesize that tribunals will, when examining domestic regulation under Art. III GATT, always look at *aim and effects* (no matter what they say). The authors then review the post-*Japan–Alcoholic Beverages* case law to prove that, indeed, tribunals have looked at aim and effects. This paper shows that the category of *de facto* discrimination cannot be determined except through a judicial evaluation of the *aim and effects* of domestic measures – discrimination is not otherwise a coherent concept.

There are also papers that do not espouse the *aims and effects* test. Davey and Pauwelyn (2000) express some dissatisfaction with the test applied by WTO adjudicating bodies in the context of Art. III GATT, and argue for the introduction of a discriminatory-effect test that should be introduced in order to decide for example, whether a tax has been imposed in excess. To them, the decisive question that panels and the AB should always ask when dealing with claims under the NT provision should be: is there discriminatory impact related to origin?

In similar vein, DiMascio and Pauwelyn (2008) look at both the negotiating work and the case-law understanding of Art. III GATT and conclude that it serves a dual purpose: to protect tariff concessions and to prevent protectionism. They lament, nonetheless, the manner in which WTO adjudicating bodies have applied this principle in concrete cases. They argue that WTO panels and the AB have had recourse to 'cyclical' interpretations of this provision, moving from inquiries into the regulatory intent to marketplace tests and back, without always paying attention to its overarching objective. They conclude that, as a result, we still lack a compass against which we can judge the consistency of domestic instruments with the GATT.

Verhoosel (2002) and Bartels (2009) have advanced more or less the same argument: they call for the application of an 'integrated necessity test' (the term first coined by Verhoosel) whereby the WTO adjudicator will decide whether *de facto* discrimination has occurred by engaging in a two-prong test: first ask whether a measure specifically affects imported products, and if the response to this question is affirmative, then check whether the measure is necessary to achieve a legitimate policy goal.

A number of papers argue in favor of an economics-informed standard of review. There are differences, sometimes important, across these papers which typically reject the *aims and effects* test as applied in case law but do not necessarily reject an inquiry into the regulatory intent of the challenged measure. In fact, some of them explicitly call for this to happen.

Sykes (1999) observes that a wide array of policy instruments can protect domestic firms against foreign competition. Regulatory measures that raise the costs of foreign firms relative to domestic firms are exceptionally wasteful protectionist devices however, with deadweight costs that can greatly exceed those of traditional protectionist instruments such as tariffs and quotas. He examines the welfare economics of regulatory protectionism, and undertakes a related political–economy analysis of the national and international legal systems that must confront it, including the WTO, the NAFTA, the European Union, and the U.S. federal system. Sykes explains why regulatory measures that serve no purpose other than to protect domestic firms against foreign competition will generally be prohibited in politically sophisticated trade agreements, even when other instruments of protection are to a degree permissible. He further suggests why regulatory measures that serve honest, nonprotectionist objectives will be permissible in sophisticated trade agreements even though their regulatory benefits may be small and their adverse effect on trade may be great – that is, he explains why trade agreements generally do not authorize "balancing analysis" akin to that undertaken in certain dormant Commerce Clause cases under U.S. law.

Horn and Mavroidis (2004) point to the relevance of regulatory intent but disagree with the *aims and effects* test. But since intent normally is difficult to determine directly, adjudicating bodies have to seek recourse to indirect evidence, as is frequently done in legal practice. Trade effects may be one such indicator.

Palmeter (1993, 1999) argues that WTO Members do not, by signing the WTO agreement, usurp each other's sovereignty; they agree only to limit the exercise of their own sovereignty when they believe that such limitation is to their advantage. It is this understanding of trade agreements that should inform the role that the NT provision is called to play. He further makes the point that the earlier negative reaction of environmentalists to GATT rulings (such as *US–Tuna/Dolphin*), although probably grounded in solid arguments, was disproportionate: after all, it is not the text of the GATT that is a threat to environmental protection, but one application of it. Gains from trade liberalization on the other hand, can help finance environmental protection. The attention of adjudicating bodies should be shifted towards honoring the objective of the NT provision: in his view, when discussing the *Tuna/Dolphin* litigation, the GATT is quite explicit that WTO Members may impose nondiscriminatory environmental standards. It is when standards imposed on trading partners are more onerous than those imposed on the regulator that the NT provision is being violated.

Trebilcock and Fishbein (2007) take the view that if every attempt by governments to pursue domestic policy objectives is subjected to the imperative to facilitate imports, then regulatory autonomy would have been seriously impaired. In their view, this is not the appropriate standard of review to apply in cases dealing with NT. The authors believe that WTO adjudicating bodies have not managed to successfully distinguish cases of legitimate exercise of regulatory autonomy from cases of regulatory protectionism, precisely because of their incapacity to design the proper standard of review to be applied in similar cases.

Ortino (2003) does not espouse an economics-based approach but does point to similar observations. In his view, the lack of methodology by WTO adjudicating bodies has resulted in lack of coherence across cases. This author finds it difficult to decipher the standard of review that WTO adjudicating bodies have employed, arguing that, while it is clear that they have rejected the *aims and effects* test, it still remains unclear what they have replaced it with. In his view, the quasi mechanistic application of the *Vienna Convention on the Law of Treaties* is probably an important contributing factor to the situation he describes: the insistence of adjudicating bodies on a contextual understanding of key terms has had an involuntary by-product, that is, the non advent of a methodology to deal with Art. III cases.

The understanding of specific terms: Recall our discussion supra, that some of the terms were chosen *faute de mieux*, and that there was even an in-principle understanding that some key terms (*like products*) would have to be renegotiated following the advent of the ITO.

The view has been expressed that it is never too late to address any deficiencies in this respect through legislative action: Bronckers and McNelis (2000) are of the view that, in light of the experience so far, it is probably too risky to leave it to adjudicating bodies to continue interpreting terms such as *like products*. They argue that it would be wiser to legislate further (in an effort to attempt to complete the contract to the extent possible) and preempt judicial action by clarifying this concept.

Others believe, without explicitly addressing the issue of legislative inter-ference, that these terms could be clarified through adjudication. What these papers have in common is that they all argue for a contextual interpretation of the key terms, that is, an interpretation that would take into account the leg-islative objectives and the committed instruments to attain them. Horn and Mavroidis (2004) argue for a clear market-based interpretation of the terms *like* and *DCS products*. They also argue however, for an understanding of terms such as ASATAP and LFT whereby the key question would be whether the contested measure is indeed protectionist or not, that is, whether the rationale for regula-tory differentiation reflects the origin of the good.

Giri and Trebilcock (2005) agree with this understanding of the terms *like* and *DCS products*. With respect to the terms ASATAP and LFT, they argue that the question WTO adjudicating bodies should ask is whether the equality of com-petitive conditions across domestic and foreign products has been affected as a result of the challenged regulatory intervention.

In the same vein, Melloni (2005) agrees with the view espoused by adjudi-cating bodies that the NT provision is there to guarantee that no recourse will be made to regulatory protectionism. In his view, however, this test has been misapplied largely because the WTO adjudicating bodies (and more especially the AB) have refused to entertain any analysis grounded on economics. In his view, recourse to simple econometric indicators such as cross-price elasticity for example, would greatly reduce the current uncertainty regarding the under-standing of terms such as *DCS* and / or *like products*.

Dunoff (2009) discusses how WTO Members can through domestic instru-ments advance social goals, paying particular attention to cases where the regu-lating government acts as purchaser. He points to the difficulties that might arise in this context as a result of the manner in which WTO adjudicating bodies have understood the key terms that appear in the body of Art. III GATT.

Choi (2003) discusses exhaustively all of the case law until 2003. Her main conclusion is that the key term in the NT provision, *like products*, has been inter-preted inconsistently. She pleads for an interpretation in line with the overall WTO aims, that is, trade liberalization that takes sufficient account of the neg-ative integration model established by the GATT.

A number of authors have criticized specific applications of the NT provi-sion in WTO disputes. Mattoo and Subramanian (1998) have argued that the panel ruling on *US–Taxes on Automobiles* has certain important implications. The manner in which Art. III GATT has been interpreted and applied tilted the balance heavily in favor of regulatory freedom, diluting the disciplines of Art. III GATT, which is one of the keystones in the construction of the GATT system. Two factors contributed to this dilution: first, very high standards are set for estab-lishing that origin-neutral measures are protectionist; and second, the incon-sistent or selective application of measures by a government is not given due consideration in determining whether the national-treatment obligation is violated. The combination of these two factors could make it difficult to establish that origin-neutral measures are inconsistent with Art. III GATT.

The report on *Chile–Alcoholic Beverages* has provoked substantial criticism. Ehring (2002) asks the pertinent question how many transactions should be affected for a scheme like the Chilean to be found inconsistent with NT? Would it suffice that one unit of account only (say one bottle of European whisky) be discriminated against for a violation of NT to occur, even if all other European exports to the Chilean market are treated in a nondiscriminatory manner? This author's criticism stems from his dissatisfaction with the AB's decision to totally neglect the fact that Chilean pisco was carrying the overwhelming majority of the tax burden in the higher-taxed category of alcoholic drinks, and not western drinks.

Horn and Mavroidis (2004) do not agree with the methodology the AB used in its report on *Korea–Alcoholic Beverages* to define whether the products concerned were like/DCS. In particular, in their view, the AB does not seem to recognize that the characteristics it refers to assess the extent of consumer likeness – end-uses, physical characteristics, etc. – are reflected in a cross-price elasticity estimation. In the authors' view, statistical analysis should be the primary method of establishing consumer preferences for the products at stake. These other indicators are imperfect substitutes to employ in cases where there is not enough data, or its quality is too poor, to undertake statistical analysis. In contrast, the AB seemed to view neither of the two approaches as being conceptually superior.

Charnovitz (1996) takes issue with the *Japan–Alcoholic Beverages* panel's rejection of the aim-and-effect test. Noting first how two GATT panels had interpreted Art. III.2 GATT, the first sentence "narrowly in order to reduce interference with national tax sovereignty," Charnovitz warned that the decision "has important implications for the autonomy of national governments" and explained that with the door to Art. III GATT closed, environmental regulations will be reviewed under the restrictive rules of Art. XX GATT. After the Appellate Body upheld the panel, Charnovitz wrote again to criticize the abandonment of the aim-and-effect test. Charnovitz (1997) noted that the new broader interpretation of like product "could spell trouble for policy-based taxes." He also suggested that Art. III GATT "may be even more important" than Art. XX GATT because no environmental defense under Art. XX GATT had succeeded (at the time of his writing, that is, before the AB report on *US–Shrimp*).

The AB report on *EC–Asbestos* has also provoked a number of reactions. In general, the environmental community took a favorable stance since it seemingly opened the door to PPM-based distinctions that the environmental community has been arguing in favor of for years. Horn and Weiler (2007), however, point to a number of weaknesses they see in the report. The authors are puzzled by the fact that the AB first expresses its intention to look for market evidence regarding consumers' reactions to asbestos-containing and asbestos-free construction material, only to reverse itself in the next paragraph and decide the issue of likeness in the absence of market evidence. They find the AB's reasoning to be based on a rather optimistic (or naïve) view of the working of the market, where for instance the threat of future liability would deter buyers from using dangerous construction materials. A number of arguments in their view instead suggest that the market should be expected to work very poorly in the case of a product with the presumed characteristics of asbestos-containing products. Indeed, the regulation might be needed exactly because buyers would not take the differences in hazards into account. But if so, the products are not like, contrary to the argument by the AB.

According to Mavroidis (2007), in *EC–Asbestos*, the AB *de facto* adopted a "reasonable consumer" test, speculating a fully informed consumer's likely purchasing behavior. This approach is problematic for a number of reasons: first, if manufacturers, as the AB contends, were indeed anticipating consumers' reactions, then they would not be producing asbestos-containing products either; as a result, there would be no need for regulation in the first place. Manufacturers stopped producing asbestos-containing construction material, not because of consumers' reactions, but because of the statutory prohibition to produce; second, if all that was needed was to inform buyers, in all likelihood, France would have financed an information campaign, and it would not have enacted a statutory prohibition on sales of asbestos-containing products. The government was probably worried that private parties would in any event impose health externalities on the society, and this is what prompted the prohibition; third, *some* manufacturers at least do produce such products and *some* consumers continue to buy them. They are located in Canada and not in France. Are they unreasonable, the author asks. Assuming that the risk associated with the consumption of such goods is, relatively speaking, low, and the price difference between asbestos-containing and asbestos-free products substantial, a country might think it makes good sense to allow for the production of both products, tax production/consumption of the former, and finance research to combat associated health hazards. This is not to suggest that France should have lost that case. In Mavroidis's (2007) opinion, France should have won anyway: its victory, however, should, in this author's view, have come under the *less favorable treatment* analysis.

Yavitz (2002) appreciates that the AB aimed at removing some of the strain that prior case law had caused on domestic regulators by interpreting key terms in Art. III.4 GATT in a mechanical, acontextual manner. Yavitz criticizes prior (to *EC–Asbestos*) case law for avoiding to interpret the key terms in this provision in a manner that would honor the agreed function of this provision, that is, to avoid that WTO Members use nonfiscal instruments so as to afford advantages to their domestic production.

In similar vein, Howse and Tuerk (2001) agree with the basis of the reasoning of the AB report, and disagree vehemently with the panel approach. The authors defend a comprehensive discrimination test that should take place within the four corners of Art. III GATT (instead of moving the discussion to Art. XX GATT). They thus see the AB report as a positive step in this direction.

4.3.5 Concluding Remarks

We will not attempt to summarize the critique of the case law in the literature. But our impression is that this critique points to the fact that adjudicating bodies have interpreted Art. III GATT lacking a conceptual framework (basically, an economic theory) for the role of Art. III GATT in the agreement. It also seems that WTO adjudicating bodies have been more concerned not to allow measures that are protectionist, than to avoid accepting measures that are not protectionist. But as of *EC–Asbestos* the AB appears to have adopted a different attitude: reading between the lines, in this dispute the AB seemed more concerned not to make the error of striking down the legislation mistakenly. Also, in the subsequent case *Dominican Republic–Import of Cigarettes* the AB states that the term *less favourable treatment* must be understood as condoning differential treatment across like products if the rationale for differentiation is not protectionism. These are both steps toward a different approach to Art. III GATT. But the AB has still failed on a crucial point – to provide a conceptual framework for defining protectionism for the purpose of Art. III GATT. One of the purposes with the analysis to follow is to contribute toward this end.

4.4 How Should NT Be Interpreted?

We initiated the analysis above by examining the negotiating record of Art. III GATT. It was argued that the basic purpose of the GATT, as it appears from the negotiating record, was to liberalize trade, while at the same time preserving as much discretion for Members to pursue their domestic policy objectives as possible – hence the choice of negative integration as the *modus operandi* of the GATT. Indeed, a number of countries held the view that the ITO had gone too far in disciplining certain policies such as employment and the GATT formula (negative integration) was far more acceptable.

The following Section (Section 4.2) recapitulated some basic observations in the economic theory literature on the role of NT. It started from the observation that an inherent feature of domestic policy instruments is that they can be used both for protectionism, and for purposes that would be in the collective interest of GATT Members to allow. Ideally, the GATT should disallow the former but not the latter. The problem is, of course, that it is difficult to assess whether a particular measure is desirable or not from an international perspective, since this depends on the preferences of the regulating Member, as well as those of other Members, and these preferences are not directly observable. It was also noted that the fact that a measure harms trade partners is *not* sufficient to make it undesirable: oftentimes the benefit to the regulating country may dominate the harm to trade partners. The role of NT is then to sort the wheat from the chaff, that is, to prevent countries from pursuing internationally inefficient (beggar-thy-neighbor) policies, while allowing measures that countries generally view as legitimate. Members will, of course, be harmed when NT restricts them from pursuing the domestic policies they would prefer to pursue. But they will also benefit from the imposition of NT as exporters. Since NT prevents measures that are internationally inefficient, NT increases the total "size of the pie" to be shared among members of the trade agreement, and unless countries are highly asymmetric, they all share the net gains.

Section 2 also presented the main features of the case law, as well as the scholarly critique, which led us to conclude that adjudicating bodies have failed to honor the agreed rationale for Art. III GATT, by not providing a contextual interpretation of the terms appearing in the text of the provision:

- While the basic purpose of Art. III GATT is to prevent domestic instruments from being "applied so as to afford protection," "protection" has not been defined in satisfactory manner in case law.
- Case law has further failed to clearly define central concepts such as "like" and "DCS" products. Adjudicating bodies have, during the WTO era, interpreted these notions as reflecting the market relationship between imported and domestic products, but during the GATT era also devised different, and arguably internally inconsistent, understanding of these terms.[147]

There is undeniably a need for a more coherent approach to interpreting Art. III GATT since the understanding of this provision is central in the functioning of the GATT since it covers all domestic policies (instruments) hinging on the interpretation of the terms mentioned above. In particular, there is a need for a conceptual framework that can be applied across Art. III GATT disputes, making outcomes more consistent with the rationale of the provision, and for this reason, more predictable. In Section 4.4.1, we will suggest two alternative approaches to interpreting Art. III GATT that we believe would serve such a purpose. Both

---

[147] Indeed, even the very recent AB report on *Philippines–Distilled Spirits* is unclear in this respect: it advances first an interpretation of likeness to the effect that the competitive relationship among two products must be more intense than in case of DCS products, only to return to the relevance of HS classification (which does not necessarily reflect intense competitive relationship) a few paragraphs later.

approaches rest on the idea that an examination of the legality of a domestic measure requires an evaluation of the extent to which the measure constitutes protectionism. The main difference between the approaches is the context in which this evaluation will be performed. According to one approach, the evaluation is done primarily in connection with the determination of whether the contested measure violates Art. III GATT. According to the other approach the evaluation is instead performed if and when an Art. XX GATT exception is sought.

The choice of approach would be immaterial if they were to yield the same adjudicated outcomes; "possibly" since there might be other aspects than the outcome that matters, such as legal fees. But as we will argue in Section 4.4.2, the two approaches would often yield different outcomes. This raises the question of which of the two approaches is to be preferred. Section 4.4.3 will discuss pros and cons of the two interpretations in light of the differences between them that were identified in Section 4.4.2. It will be argued that it is preferable to evaluate protectionism in the context of Art. III GATT. In Section 4.4.4, we will deal in more detail with the preferred approach. Section 4.4.5 revisits the leading cases from the perspective of the proposed interpretation. Our findings will be condensed into "Principles," presented in the concluding Section 4.5. Finally, an appendix lists all Art. III GATT disputes since 1947.

4.4.1 Two Approaches to Evaluate Protection

The two interpretations to be proposed are both compatible with the economic view of NT and they are both consistent with the legal text as well. Hence, both approaches start from the notion that the general objective of the regulation of domestic instruments in the GATT is to limit the use of domestic instruments for protectionism, while at the same time allowing legitimate use of such instruments, even if this causes adverse consequences for trading partners by shielding import-competing products from foreign competition.

Broadly speaking, "Interpretation XX" largely continues the approach pursued in case law until recently: for a violation of Art. III GATT it suffices that there is potential for disparate effects in the sense that imported goods might be burdened more than domestic goods with which they compete. The alternative approach, "Interpretation III" requires that the measure is internationally inefficient, that is, that it can be said to constitute protectionism, in a sense to be made more precise below. Interpretation XX undertakes the evaluation of the protection as part of the determination of whether an Art. XX GATT exception can be granted (assuming that respondents request such exceptions if found to violate Art. III), and accepts as nonprotectionist only measures coming under the aegis of Art. XX GATT. According to Interpretation III, the evaluation is performed as part of the determination of whether Art. III GATT is violated and grounds

Gene M. Grossman, Henrik Horn, and Petros C. Mavroidis

beyond those reflected in Art. XX GATT could serve as basis to conclude that a measure is not protectionist. Put differently, Interpretation XX sees Art. III GATT as a net with fine meshes, and uses Art. XX GATT to evaluate what in the catch should be thrown back to sea. Interpretation III instead lets Art. III GATT take a more select catch, but one that for the most part is meant to be kept. The choice between the two interpretations would be (with the caveat mentioned) immaterial if the measures that are found to violate Art. III GATT according to Interpretation XX – measures that protect in the sense of shielding from competition – are also invariably protectionist, and thus internationally inefficient. However, as will be argued in Section 4.4.2, the outcomes of the two approaches are likely to differ.

One might legitimately ask how come Art. III GATT can be read in two so different ways? The term "protection" is nowhere defined in the GATT: as noted, there is no list of explicitly permitted and explicated prohibited policies, the GATT is "incomplete" in this way. Moreover, the term "protection," which appears in both Arts. III.1 and XX GATT, is used in the GATT with two different meanings. It is occasionally used to mean "to shield from competition," without any value judgment attached as to whether this is desirable or not. In other instances, it is used to denote illegitimate measures, i.e., in our terminology protectionist, or internationally inefficient, measures. This dual meaning of "protection" is reflected in the text of the GATT. For instance, when using the phrase "so as to afford protection" concerning government mandated or operated monopolies, Art. II.4 states that

> ... such a monopoly should not ... operate so as to afford protection on the average in excess of the amount of protection provided for in that Schedule.

Hence, a certain degree of "protection" is legitimate – the protection provided for in the Schedule – while any additional "protection" is illegal.[148]

It is clear that when Art. III.1 GATT sets the sight on domestic policy measures that are "applied so as to afford protection," it refers to an undesirable form of "protection." But it is also clear from negotiating history of the GATT, and from the general construction of the agreement, that the purpose of the GATT is not to prevent countries from persecuting all policies that protect in the sense of shielding import-competing firms from competition. This would effectively require positive discrimination of imported goods, since these could not face higher taxation in cases where they would be taxed higher, had they been domestic products (for instance, due to their environmental properties). A critical feature of the regulation of domestic instruments in the GATT is hence that, among all measures with protective effects, it manages to filter out only those that are harmful to the Membership, whereas measures that are detrimental to

---

[148] Economic theory would suggest that the legitimacy of the protection provided by the measures that are bound in the Schedule stems from the fact that it has been *negotiated*.

the parties' common joint interest are allowed. Interpretation III is based on the idea that Art. III GATT should *only* capture measures that are undesirable in this sense, and that the protectionism test should hence be performed under this provision.

We now turn to a more detailed description of the two Interpretations, focusing in particular on the more novel Interpretation III, starting with the more conventional Interpretation XX.

4.4.1.1 *Interpretation XX*

To reach Art. XX GATT the complainant must have first established a violation of a GATT provision, in our discussion, Art. III GATT. WTO Members can justify violations of obligations assumed under the GATT through recourse to one of the grounds mentioned in Art. XX GATT. This list covers a variety of policy objectives, ranging from the protection of public health to conservation of natural resources. The provision was modeled after the corresponding provision included in the 1927 *International Convention for the Abolition of Import and Export Prohibitions and Restrictions* (World Economic Conference of 1927), the first multilateral attempt to liberalize international trade.[149]

Art. XX GATT opens with the sentence:

> Subject to the requirement that such measures are not applied in a manner which would constitute a means of arbitrary or unjustifiable discrimination between countries where the same conditions prevail, or a disguised restriction on international trade, nothing in this Agreement shall be construed to prevent the adoption or enforcement by any contracting party of measures:
> ...

The words "nothing in this agreement" leaves no doubt that the legislator's intent was that all grounds mentioned in this provision "trump" the trade liberalizing obligations in the rest of the GATT. Art. XX GATT thus provides a hierarchy between trade commitments and (national) social preferences: public morals, protection of human health, and all the other grounds mentioned in the body of this provision are more important than trade commitments. Trade thus is not elevated to the supreme common value that all WTO Members must observe at any cost. This understanding of GATT commitments is, of course, perfectly consistent with the negative-integration character of the GATT.[150]

At the same time, it does not suffice that a WTO Member simply invokes a ground mentioned in the body of this provision in order to lawfully violate its trade commitments. Two types of restrictions are imposed. First, the *actual purpose* of a contested measure must be to achieve one of the listed objectives. This

---

[149] On the content of the negotiations, and the reasons for the nonratification of the final text, see Charnovitz (1991), and Irwin *et al.* (2008).

[150] See the corresponding discussion in Section 4.3.

is ensured by the qualifiers concerning the measure not being an "arbitrary or unjustifiable discrimination" or "disguised restriction on international trade," in order to qualify for an exception. Second, there are some restrictions imposed on the *means* by which the objectives are achieved. For instance, measures that protect public morals, or human, animal, or plant life or health must be "necessary."

There may have been some disagreement as to the ambit of the provision during the negotiations. It seems that what the UK negotiator (one of the architects of this provision) had in mind was to include a provision which would operate as exception to import and export restrictions only, and not to internal measures:

> The undertakings in Chapter IV of this Charter relating to import and export restrictions shall not be construed to prevent the adoption or enforcement by any member of measures for the following purposes, provided that they are not applied in such a manner as to constitute a means of arbitrary discrimination between countries where the same conditions prevail, or a disguised restriction of international trade.[151]

It is unclear how widespread this view was. But GATT/WTO case law has by now accepted that recourse to Art. XX GATT can be made in order to justify violations assumed with respect to both trade and domestic instruments. An example of the former is offered by the GATT Panel on *Thailand–Cigarettes*: in this case, the United States challenged the consistency of the *Thai Tobacco Act* of 1966 with Art. XI GATT. According to this law,

> the importation . . . of tobacco is prohibited except by license of the Director–General (§63).

The *Thai Tobacco Act* of 1966 defined tobacco to include cigarettes. There was no dispute between the parties that the measure at hand constituted a quota in the sense of Art. XI GATT (§§ 21, 65); Thailand attempted to justify the quota in place by invoking, *inter alia*, Art. XX(b) GATT (§§ 72ff.). An example of how case law has accepted the applicability of Art. XX GATT to domestic instruments is offered in the report on *EC–Asbestos*, where the AB held that Art XX GATT could serve as legal basis to justify domestic measures that had been previously found to be inconsistent with Art. III GATT (§ 115).[152] The Panel on *China–Raw Materials* confirmed prior case law to the effect that Art. XX GATT could also serve as an exception to obligations assumed under a Protocol of Accession; nevertheless, this would be the case only if there is explicit or even implicit reference to this provision in the relevant protocol (§§ 7.158–7.160).

---

[151] E/PC/T/C.II/50, pp. 7ff.; E/PC/T/C.II/54, pp. 32ff.
[152] For confirmation, see the AB report on *Korea–Various Measures on Beef* §§ 152 ff.

The AB has constructed Art. XX GATT akin to a two-tier test. For example, assuming a WTO Member invokes Art. XX(b) GATT in order to justify an import embargo on toxic waste (which is considered to be harmful to human health), the WTO adjudicating body will first examine whether such a measure is necessary to achieve the stated objective (protection of human health), that is, whether the measure at hand conforms with the requirement included in Art. XX(b) GATT, before it examines whether the measure has also been applied in a manner consistent with the *chapeau* of the GATT. Both obligations must be met for a measure to be judged GATT-consistent, as the AB stated in its report on *US–Gasoline* (p. 22):

> In order that the justifying protection of Article XX may be extended to it, the measure at issue must not only come under one or another of the particular exceptions – paragraphs (a) to (j) – listed under Article XX; it must also satisfy the requirements imposed by the opening clauses of Article XX. The analysis is, in other words, two-tiered: first, provisional justification by reason of characterization of the measure under XX(g); second, further appraisal of the same measure under the introductory clauses of Article XX.

The AB in its report on *US–Shrimp* expressed the view that it is the language of the chapeau that makes it clear that all exceptions appearing in Art. XX GATT are limited and conditional (§ 157). The AB, in its report on *Brazil–Retreaded Tyres*, eliminated any doubts on this score (§ 139).

Case law has consistently held, by virtue of the maxim that the party invoking an exception carries the associated burden of proof (*quicunque exceptio invokat ejusdem probare debet*), that the party invoking Art. XX GATT carries the burden of proof to demonstrate that it has met its requirements. The AB, citing prior case law to this effect (*US–Gasoline*, pp. 22–23; *US–Wool Shirts and Blouses*, pp. 15–16; *US–FSC (Article 21.5–EC)*, § 133) has confirmed this view in its report on *US–Gambling* (§ 309).

The AB, in its report on *Korea–Various Measures on Beef*, clarified that its judicial review has to be confined to the means used to achieve a particular objective, and cannot extend to an examination of the ends themselves (§ 176). Over the years, the AB made it clear that it would be more deferential when human health was at stake, and less so when WTO Members were pursuing other regulatory objectives mentioned in the body of Art. XX GATT. In its report on *EC–Asbestos*, the AB confirmed that this was indeed the case (§ 172).

Against this description of core features of the text and case law of Art. XX GATT, let us now turn to our first suggested interpretation of how Art. III GATT can be interpreted – denoted Interpretation XX – which largely continues the case-law approach. Interpretation XX hence stipulates that Art. III GATT is violated if an imported and a domestic product are "like" in the sense of being in a highly competitive relationship, and that the imported product is directly or indirectly taxed "in excess" of the domestic product.[153] There would also be an Art. III GATT violation if the products are in a DCS-relationship, meaning that they are in competition albeit in less fierce competition than in the case of like products, provided that the products are "not similarly taxed."

The focus in Interpretation XX is hence on the degree of competition between the imported and domestically produced goods, and the magnitude of the tax difference. If products are like, but not necessarily policy-like (a concept we explain in more detail infra) – perhaps approaching perfect substitutes – then any price differential due to differential taxation has the potential to have a significant impact on imports. As products become less substitutable, and cross the line into DCS, a small price differential due to differential taxation may have small effects on imports and be appropriately ignored. But a significant tax differential may be presumed to have a nontrivial impact on imports.

It should be stressed again that the extent to which products are like and/or DCS does not reflect possible differences between the products from a policy point of view. Similarly, the evaluation of whether the taxation of the imported product is "in excess" or that the products are "not similarly taxed," does not take into consideration any policy rationale for a tax distinction. Both like and DCS products hence measure the same qualitative feature of the market situation – the extent of competition between the products – with like referring to situations with more intense competition.

An application of Interpretation XX would not mean that business should continue as usual in the case law, however. Until *Philippines–Distilled Spirits* (a report issued in January 2012) likeness was not necessarily confined to goods with high substitutability between them. And even there, as we stated supra, it is questionable whether the HS-classification is irrelevant to define likeness since the AB does mention it as a relevant criterion a few paragraphs later. Recall that for example, vodka and sochu share the same tariff classification at the six-digit HS level, and would yet by many consumers be viewed as far from perfectly substitutable.

4.4.1.2 *Interpretation III*

The regulation of fiscal instruments in Art. III GATT combines a general statement in Art. III.1 GATT with two specific restrictions in Art. III.2 GATT on the permissible difference in the level of taxation of imported and domestic products (and for fiscal instruments more generally). Interpretation III understands Arts. III.1 and III.2 GATT as jointly imposing a prohibition on protectionist measures, but on protectionist measures only. There are several ways in which the text could be read to harbor such an interpretation.

---

[153] As stated, although not a very clear pronouncement to this effect, the AB report on *Philippines–Distilled Spirits* seems to side with this approach.

A first possibility would be to interpret Art. III.1 GATT as imposing a substantive restriction, requiring a demonstration that a measure is "applied so as to afford protection," in order to establish a violation of Art. III GATT.

A second possibility would be to interpret the terms "in excess" concerning like products, and "not similarly taxed" concerning DCS products to reflect the rationale for any differences in absolute levels: for instance, an imported and a domestic product could then be viewed as being similarly taxed, even if they are burdened with different amounts of environmental taxation, provided that they differ in environmental impacts.

Interpretation III relies on yet another way of requiring a meaningful protectionism test under Art. III GATT, which is to interpret the notion of *like products* to reflect not only market likeness, but also *likeness from a policy point of view*. In what follows we will explain how such an interpretation is compatible with the text, and the associated interpretation of the requirement for DCS products.

4.4.1.2.1 Like Products. Interpretation III, as well as Interpretation XX, follows the case law by interpreting "in excess" in Art. III.2 GATT, first sentence, as requesting that there should be no difference at all in tax burden in case of "like" products (a mere arithmetic difference suffices according to case law to satisfy this criterion, *US–Superfund*). But which product pairs are "like"? A distinguishing feature of Interpretation III is that it interprets products to be like if *there is no legitimate reason for imposing different tax burdens*, where legitimacy is evaluated from the point of view of the combined interests of the governments of the exporting and importing countries. Somewhat loosely put, two competing (we will return to this aspect below) products are "like" if an efficient agreement between the governments would stipulate identical taxes. Interpretation III hence requires that for products to be *like* for the purpose of Art. III.2 GATT:

- products would be competitive if they had equal opportunities of market access (they are "market-like"); and
- an internationally efficient agreement would entail no tax differential (they are "policy-like").

Note two crucial features of this understanding of the ambit of Art. III.2 GATT:

First, Art. III.2 GATT, first sentence, plays the fundamental role for the whole regulation of fiscal instruments of *defining the level of ambition* for the combat of internationally inefficient use of domestic fiscal instruments in the GATT.[154] It achieves this by specifying a necessary and sufficient condition for a fiscal measure not to constitute illegal protection in a case of particular importance: where

---

[154] It does so also in another respect, following from our interpretation of "in excess" as any strictly positive tax difference, which is that it specifies the acceptable tax difference for like products to be 0%. This might seem as a natural number to choose, but the provision could in principle allow a 10% difference, say.

there is *no* efficiency rationale for treating highly competitive products differently. Put differently, Art. III.1 GATT sets the sight on (undesirable) protectionist use of domestic instruments, but does not specify what precisely defines protection. Art. III.2 GATT, first sentence, specifies exactly what constitutes the border between protectionism and nonprotectionism in one special case – where there is no (international) efficiency reason to allow differential taxation. For such a situation Art. III.2 GATT, first sentence, stipulates that it *suffices* for nonprotectionist behavior that each unit of the imported product does not carry a heavier fiscal burden than does each unit of the competing domestic product.

Second, the level of ambition that is laid down in Art. III.2 GATT, first sentence, is limited in that it does *not* explicitly or implicitly request from Members to pursue policies that are internationally efficient. As explained in Section 4.2, it should be expected that when Members unilaterally decide on a common tax level for domestic and imported products, they will disregard the interests of their trade partners, thus exposing them to international externalities. Consequently, *Art. III GATT-consistent taxation is likely to be internationally inefficient, even in the case of like products.* Put differently, Art. III.2 GATT, first sentence, does not require that the importing country refrain from measures that give rise to international externalities, only *not to use differential taxation* to this end and/or effect (we will discuss aims versus effects below).[155]

4.4.1.2.2 DCS Products. We next turn to Art. III.2 GATT, second sentence, and the Ad Article III Interpretative Note.[156] The latter explicitly refers to product pairs that are defined in terms of the extent to which they are in competition, i.e., in terms of the degree of market likeness, through the notion of "directly competitive or substitutable." But it does not solely refer to this criterion. According to Interpretation III, the second sentence of Art. III.2 GATT requests that imported products for such product pairs should respect the principles of nonprotectionism embedded in Art. III.1 GATT, as given some precision through Art. III.2 GATT, first sentence. But while III.2 GATT, first sentence, pertains to situations where there is no efficiency basis to treat products differently, *the second sentence of*

---

[155] The following statement by Harry Johnson was not made in the context of a discussion of NT, but seems relevant here nevertheless:

> ...the principle of non-discrimination has no basis whatsoever in the theoretical argument for the benefits of a liberal international trade order in general, or in any rational economic theory of the bargaining process in particular. [Johnson (1976), p. 18]

[156] As a comment on the origin of the DCS notion, let us just recall from Section 4.2 that the negotiating history suggests that the DCS category was added because some negotiators felt that the value of tariff concessions would be too limited in case government behavior was not regulated for a wider set of circumstances than those involving like products, since the latter required that products fall under the same tariff heading in the predecessor to the Harmonized System, the tariff classification scheme being used at the time.

Art. III.2 GATT addresses the situation where there is an efficiency rationale for yielding imported and domestic market-like products different policy treatment.

As repeatedly mentioned above, there are situations in which it is desirable to allow an imported product to be burdened with a higher tax or fiscal duty than a competing domestic product. But the importing country obviously cannot be given a free reign to tax domestic and imported competing products differently. According to Interpretation III, Art. III.2 GATT, second sentence pertains to those instances where a higher tax on the imported product would be allowed, but where the particular tax difference is excessive. In contrast to the case of like products, it is not possible to specify exactly the property of the tax pairs that make them permissible. This is what explains the reference back to Art. III.1 GATT, which lays down a principle for how large the tax difference might be – it must not amount to undesirable protection.

The question then arises: what criterion should be used to evaluate whether a higher tax on an imported product than on a competing domestic product is acceptable?

From a theory point of view, the ideal would be to reject any tax pair other than the pair that maximizes the joint welfare of the two parties (or even better, the global membership). However, such an approach would request much more cooperation from the importing country than it agreed to when entering the GATT. The (negative integration) spirit of the regulation of domestic instruments in the GATT allows Members freedom to determine their domestic policies, subject "only" to the proviso that they are not "applied so as to afford protection." The meaning of protection is, generally speaking, not clear, but as explained above, the first sentence of Art. III.2 defines exactly what is required in the special case of a policy- and market-like product to behave in a nonprotectionist fashion, which is not to tax the imported product higher than the domestic product. Since this provision refers to situations where there is no ground for tax differentials, the requirements for DCS products (where there are grounds for tax differentials) should be less strict.

To facilitate the discussion, we use the example of an importing country that levies a higher "environmental" tax on an imported product than on a competing domestic product, claiming that this is reasonable in order to achieve some emissions level that we denote E. It is clear that each unit of the imported product is emitting more of the harmful substance (E) than does the corresponding domestic product, so there is a case from an environmental point of view to tax the imported product higher. The case hence clearly concerns a pair of DCS rather than a pair of like pair products. What is not clear, however, is whether the taxation scheme, which levies 40% on an imported good, and 0% on a competing domestically produced good, should be considered legal.

The fundamental problem is that, in principle, there are many tax pairs that could achieve the emissions level E. It might, for instance, be possible to achieve

E by completely shutting out the imported product, by taxing it much higher than the domestic product. Alternatively, one could levy the same tax on both products, but set this common tax level high enough to achieve the target. There will also be tax pairs in between these extremes that will achieve the particular target. *Which* tax pair among all those that can achieve the emissions target should be considered legal? And could we, for example, envisage a situation where more than one tax pair is considered legal? And if yes, what criteria should be fulfilled for this to be the case?

Let us here recall that the basic problem that the agreement seeks to address stems from the fact that when countries set their policies unilaterally, they have no direct concern for the interests of their trading partners. This is the source of the protectionism that the agreement seeks to limit. Hence, when looking for acceptable tax pairs, it would be desirable to consider the consequences for the *joint* welfare of the parties, rather than the welfare for the importing country only. There are different ways in which this could be done.

One possibility would be to argue as follows. The gist of Art. III.2 GATT is to request equal taxation of closely competing imported and domestically produced goods, while at the same time acknowledging that there will be occasions where equal taxation is not warranted. Differences in tax rates should then be permitted if, and only if, the gain to the importing country government from pursuing the differential taxation (rather than imposing a uniform tax), is large enough that the importing country could in principle compensate the exporting country for the adverse effects it is being exposed to as a result of the differential taxation and still benefit from pursuing its regulatory objective.[157] It should be emphasized that the idea is not that the importing country actually compensates the exporter in the industry at stake. Instead, with countries sometimes in the role of exporters and sometimes in the role of importers, there is a common interest in an NT-regime that allows differential taxation if and only if it increases aggregate welfare. What a Member might lose as an exporter, is then more than compensated for by what it might gain as a regulating importer in another industry. The logic is here exactly the same as in the case of reciprocal tariff liberalization: the reduction in tariffs hurts the importing country government, but benefits the exporting country government more. The compensation for the import country government comes in the form of increased exports in other sectors, and due to the fact that overall there is too little trade at the outset, this gain will be larger than the loss on the import side.

For instance, suppose in the example above the importing country government taxes the imported product at 40% and the domestic product at 0% in order to achieve the environmental emissions target E. Assume also that if forced to set equal taxes, the importing country would set 8% on both products. The criterion

---

[157] That is, the differentiation is desirable in the Kaldor-Hicks sense.

for accepting the (40%, 0%) pair would then be that it yields higher welfare for the countries combined than does the pair (8%, 8%).

This approach would hence accept the pair (40%, 0%) provided that the importing country government could *in principle* compensate the exporting Member government for the cost the latter is exposed to as a result of facing the pair (40%, 0%) rather than the pair (8%, 8%). Compensation would be possible, and the measure would be legal, only if the gains to the importing Member from addressing the environmental problem were sufficiently significant.[158]

Note that this criterion pays no attention to the alleged rationale for the regulation nor to the desirability (or lack thereof) of the emissions target level (E). All it cares about is whether the joint welfare of the parties is higher with the pair (40%, 0%) than with the pair (8%, 8%). But the objective might still play a role in the evaluation of the gains from the differential taxation.

Another possibility could be to accept the alleged purpose for the differential taxation – the emissions target E – and still condition the acceptance of the measure on achieving the target in a reasonable manner from a joint welfare point of view. As with the previous alternative, this approach would take into consideration the possibility that it is desirable also from an international point of view to let the importing country tax the imported product higher than the domestic product, but in contrast to the previous alternative, the importing country would not do the protectionist calculation unilaterally, since it would have to take into account the costs for the exporting country. Suppose, for example, that the court concludes that a 20% tax on the imported product and a 15% tax on the domestic product would be the most efficient manner of achieving the emissions target E.

It would then be possible for the court to reject any pair of taxes, where the tax on the imported product is higher than on the tax on the domestic product, other than the taxes 20% and 15%. The difference between this approach and the previous one is hence that whereas in the previous case the evaluation seeks to determine whether the challenged taxation is better than equal taxation (assumed to result in a common tax of 8%) regardless of its purpose, the evaluation here asks whether the stated objective of having emissions at the level E is achieved in an efficient manner.

Yet another possibility would be to follow the previous approach in accepting the emissions target E, and to determine that taxes 20% and 15% would be efficient means to reach the target E; but rather than rejecting any other differential taxes than those two, it would be determined that a 5 percentage point

[158] To avoid misunderstandings, it is not suggested that this compensation should take a monetary form, but normally to come from the reciprocal nature of undertakings. If countries are highly asymmetric, so that some countries cannot be fully compensated for allowing its trading partners to differentiate their domestic taxation, the proposed solution is still desirable from the point of view of maximizing the size of the "pie," but may give rise to distributional problems between countries.

difference in taxation is what is maximally legitimate. The importing country could then set say 25% on the imported product and 20% on the domestic product, if it so wanted. In light of the possible uncertainty regarding calculations, providing for a leeway might be one way to reduce pressure on regulators and adjudicators alike.

All three approaches have their pros and cons. They all have a certain logic from an economic point of view, in that they build on some form of efficiency notion. But none of them implements the ideal criterion that we discussed above. The first approach goes the furthest in this direction, but the contested pair of taxes is in this approach only compared with the common tax level that the country would set if unable to differentiate in its taxation (which is not fully efficient since we are in the case of DCS products). The contested pair is not compared with all other possible pairs of taxes (which would be required to ensure full international efficiency). It hence imposes only a limited form of efficiency-restriction. In the second approach, the comparison is with an efficient tax pair, but only in the limited sense of being the tax pair that best achieves the emissions target E. This aspect pertains to the third approach as well. The third approach further suffers from the weakness that if the importing country were to choose any other tax pair with a 5 percentage point difference, the target E would be over- or undershot, which would cast doubt on the relevance of the calculation based on E in the first place. Suppose, for instance, that with the adjusted taxes, the resulting emissions level is E' < E. The question could then be raised whether a 5 percentage point tax difference is part of the optimal way for the parties to achieve E'.

On the other hand, while the second, and in particular the third, approach is less attractive from an economic point of view, they are more consonant with the text of Art. III GATT, because of their focus on whether tax *differentials* afford protection. The third approach in particular seems more in line with a negative integration mode than the previous two approaches – the unilaterally determined policy target E is accepted – and it operates by defining legality in terms of the degree of deviation from the equal taxation benchmark. We will therefore view it as the main candidate for how to more specifically understand Interpretation III.

4.4.2 The Difference in Outcome with the Two Approaches

The choice between the Interpretations III and XX would (or at least could) be immaterial if they accepted and rejected the same domestic policy measures. This Section will argue that this will not be the case. Instead, *Interpretation XX is likely to impose a more restrictive regime on domestic measures compared to Interpretation III.* Following Interpretation XX, Art. III GATT is insensitive to whether a measure is pursued for legitimate purposes, as long as it protects domestic production in the sense that it shields domestic goods from competition from imported products. Hence, a measure that provokes this outcome will only be justified through recourse to Art. XX GATT. This would not matter if the test is the same under both provisions. But the test for protectionism that is performed under Art. XX GATT is more demanding than the test performed under Art. III GATT, for at least two reasons.[159] First, as explained in more detail in Section 4.4.2.1, Art. XX GATT imposes certain requirements that must be met for a measure, otherwise inconsistent with Art. III GATT, to be exonerated from liability under GATT rules. Second, as discussed in Section 4.4.2.2, the two interpretations have different implications for the allocation of the burden of proof. Interpretation III requires the complainant to establish that a contested measure affords protection. With Interpretation XX, the burden will be much lighter for the complainant however, if the respondent requests an Art. XX exception. In the resulting protectionism test, it is instead the respondent who will have to show that a measure that shields a domestic product from import competition is not "disguised protection" (or undesirable protection, that is, protectionism in our terminology), in order to be allowed to continue pursuing a contested measure. This difference will contribute to make Interpretation XX a more stringent regime for the domestic instruments protectionism test is what makes it a more stringent regime.

The fact that Interpretation XX imposes a more stringent regime for the domestic measures would seem welcome if the measures that would be exposed to this additional restrictiveness would all be protectionist. But as Section 4.4.2.3 will explain, there is no presumption that the measures caught under Art. III GATT following Interpretation XX will all be protectionist.

4.4.2.1 *Interpretation XX Imposes Additional Restrictions for Measures Not to Constitute Illegal Protection*

One difference between a protectionism test performed under Art. III GATT and under Art. XX GATT, is that Art. XX (and hence Interpretation XX) imposes some conditions for measures to be granted an exception that have no counterpart in Art. III GATT. These additional restrictions stem from two sources.

The first additional hurdle to pass in order to be granted an exception under Art. XX GATT, is that the measure at hand must seek to *achieve one of the policy objectives listed in the body of Art. XX GATT*. This list of justifications has in case law – reasonably in our view, in light of the wording – been interpreted as closed: in the absence of a legislative acknowledgment that the list is indicative, it is not possible to invoke grounds not explicitly appearing in this list. Considering the

---

[159] There could be a difference between the two Interpretations even if the tests were the same, if they could lead to judicial errors. With Interpretation III, if the respondent loses in the test performed under Art. III GATT, the respondent can seek an Art. XX GATT exception, in which case the same test would be performed twice, making it more likely that the contested measure would be allowed.

fact that Art. III GATT applies to an extremely broad range of government measures, and thus may have very significant impact on the possibility for governments to pursue unilateral policies, the exhaustive nature of the list of objectives embedded in Art. XX GATT might have important consequences on the overall ambit of obligations assumed upon accession to the WTO.

Second, Art. XX GATT does not simply specify a list of policy objectives that serve as a blanket basis for exceptions from undertakings in the rest of the GATT, provided they are not disguised protection. It also qualifies the grounds for several of those exceptions, by *imposing requirements on how the listed objectives should be achieved.* In particular, in order to be eligible for some of the grounds for exceptions, the measures employed must be "necessary." For instance, Art. XX(b) GATT provides an exception possibility for measures "necessary" to protect human, animal, and plant life or health. The case law has interpreted this concept to require that no less trade restrictive alternative can achieve the same regulatory objective, more recently with the specification that the alternative measure should be "reasonably available."[160]

4.4.2.2 *The Evidentiary Burden Falls Heavier on the Complainant with Interpretation XX*

The GATT does not explicitly regulate the burden of proof. The current practice has instead been developed in case law. Case law has endorsed the *in dubio mitius* principle, according to which WTO Members' actions should be presumed legitimate, unless challenged and proven inconsistent before a WTO panel (and/or the AB, as the case may be). This principle hence imposes the original burden of production of proof on the complainant. Assuming the complainant produces sufficient evidence to raise a presumption (an undefined notion in case law), the burden shifts to the other party. Conversely, the respondent has the burden of proof to establish eligibility for an Art. XX GATT exception.

As a consequence of these well-established evidentiary standards, Interpretations III and XX will differ in the extent to which it will fall on the complainant to provide evidence of illegal protection, as per Interpretation III, or on the regulating country to defend its practices, as advocated by Interpretation XX. In either case the demonstration will involve providing evidence of the objective of the contested measure – that is, information concerning the policy preferences of the regulating country. In a hypothetical situation of perfect information, it would be immaterial whether the burden is put on one party or the other, except that the distribution of the costs for judicial process might differ. But it may be important in situations where the true rationales for pursued policies are not known before the dispute-settlement proceedings, as is typically the case in this

---

[160] See Sykes (2003).

context. As argued in Section 4.2, at the heart of the rationale for Art. III GATT is an information problem; as explained, if there were easily available information concerning the true motives for regulations, it would be possible to contract these more directly, in which case there would not be any need for Art. III GATT in the first place, at least not as we know it.

4.4.2.3 *The Nature of Measures That Are Market-Like But Not Policy-Like*

As we have argued in the above, Interpretation XX will impose a more demanding protectionism test than Interpretation III. This would be desirable, if all these measures were known to be protectionist. After all, it may reflect outright protectionism if a higher fiscal burden is imposed on an imported product than on a competing domestic product. But there can be no *presumption* that the measures caught under Art. III GATT following Interpretation XX will be protectionist, however. On the contrary, such differences in fiscal burdens may reflect the *governments' pursuit of some of the fundamental roles that economic theory identifies as grounds for social-welfare-increasing government market interventions.*

To see why, recall that one of the main efficiency-enhancing motives for government intervention identified by economic theory is to *eliminate negative externalities* between economic decisionmakers, such as consumers and producers. The distinguishing feature of such externalities is that their adverse impact for other consumers and producers is disregarded by those who cause them. A standard example is a negative environmental consumption externality, which arises when buyers disregard the adverse environmental impact of their consumption, treating polluting products as interchangeable with cleaner products. It is very easy to point to real-world examples of such behavior. For example, consumers may disregard the environmental impact that arises when products are scrapped, and will therefore not pay extra for more environmentally friendly product designs, unless forced to. Or, buyers of automobiles disregard the fact that their brakes emit asbestos into the air, since each buyer's emissions have negligible impact on the buyer's personal health (in contrast to the combined emissions from automobiles). Or, construction companies may not take into consideration when buying construction material whether it will expose residents, or future demolition workers, to asbestos. A central, efficiency-enhancing role for governments is to combat such negative externalities by, for example, inducing buyers of polluting products to shift their purchases toward cleaner products.

Another rationale for government intervention might be informational problems. For instance, consumers may not be aware of differences in the safety of products, or may not take such information sufficiently into account in their consumption decisions, in the view of the government. Progressive taxation of beverages according to their alcohol content is occasionally motivated by such concerns (there are also other concerns, as the Art. III GATT case law has revealed).

Both of the above types of situations provide reasons for government intervention that are legitimate from an economic efficiency point of view. Indeed, they constitute two of the main rationales that economic theory identifies for government intervention.[161] The distinguishing feature of these situations is precisely that consumers do *not* necessarily (very often for good reasons) distinguish between the products, that is, that *the products are market-like but not policy-like*. Indeed, environmental regulations are to a large extent predicated on the fact that market likeness *differs* from policy likeness, and it is exactly *because of the market likeness* that there is a need for government intervention.

The need for governments to remedy the above type of problems is obviously not confined to situations where only domestic products are involved, but may also exist in case of imports. Hence, a necessary condition in order for a trade agreement to be efficient is that in situations where imported products are associated with more pronounced negative externalities than those stemming from competing domestic products, importing country governments are allowed to levy higher taxes per unit of consumption or production on the imported products. Such taxation would violate Art. III GATT according to Interpretation XX, however. In contrast, the basic idea underlying Interpretation III is that such measures should not by automaticity be understood to run afoul of Art. III GATT. By including policy likeness in the definition of like and DCS, Interpretation III ensures that a test for protectionism is undertaken under Art. III GATT. Consequently, internationally desirable higher taxation of imports must seek exceptions through the more demanding Art. XX GATT test.[162]

To conclude, the main difference in terms of the measures that violate Art. III GATT under the two approaches, is that measures that put a heavier fiscal burden on imported products than on competing domestic products, will be exposed to a more demanding protectionism test following Interpretation XX compared to Interpretation III. This stricter test will be applied to purely protectionist measures. But it will also be applied to measures that are *legitimate* from an international perspective, despite imposing a higher fiscal burden on imports, measures that would be compatible with Art. III GATT according to Interpretation III.

[161] Other rationales are that markets are imperfectly competitive, that the laissez/faire income distribution is undesirable, and "non-economic" policy objectives (national security, for instance).

[162] Recapitulating from above, following Interpretation III, measures that buyers treat interchangeably but that differ from a policy perspective, will be viewed as DCS, since there is a policy rationale for taxing them differently. The issue will instead be whether the magnitude of the tax differential is justified. If too large from an international perspective, the measure will be illegal, if not too large it will be acceptable.

4.4.3 Which Interpretation Is Preferable?

Section 4.4.2 showed that Interpretation XX will impose a stricter protectionism test than Interpretation III. Is this desirable, or does it unduly restrict the freedom for WTO Members to choose domestic policies? In this Section, we explain why we believe that, on balance, Interpretation III is to be preferred, even if there are arguments pointing in the opposite direction.

In the discussion to follow, we will for analytical purposes distinguish between the consequences of the choice of interpretation for the expected adjudicated outcome of disputes, and for governments' policy decisions, such as the choice of domestic policy measures, and tariff concessions. Sections 4.4.3.1–4.4.3.3 will discuss the former type of effects. Sections 4.4.3.1 and 4.4.3.2 will focus on the desirability of the additional restrictions that Art. XX GATT imposes compared to Art. III GATT (as per the discussion in Section 4.4.2.1), and Section 4.4.3.3 will focus on the difference in the allocation of the burden of proof between the two interpretations (as per the discussion in Section 4.4.2.2). The benchmark for evaluating the two interpretations will here be the extent to which the NT provision manages to sort the wheat from the chaff: does it allow Members to achieve legitimate domestic policy objectives, while at the same time prevent them from using domestic measures for protectionist reasons?

The effects of choice of interpretation for expected adjudicated outcomes of disputes are relatively clear. But as emphasized in Sections 4.2 and 4.3, the overriding purpose of NT is to provide incentives for Members to increase trade, while still allowing them to use domestic instruments for legitimate policy purposes. The effects on tariff and trade liberalization are harder to determine, however. Section 4.4.3.4 will more briefly highlight such policy effects of the choice of interpretation, and discuss their desirability.

4.4.3.1 *The List of Permissible Objectives in Art. XX GATT*

As highlighted in Section 4.4.2.1, Art. XX GATT contains a closed list of policy objectives that may serve as a ground for an exception from other obligations in the GATT. A first question is whether this list was intended to describe not only the policy objectives that can serve as grounds for an exception from, e.g., Art. III GATT, but also as a *complete description of all permissible grounds for imposing heavier financial burdens on imported products than on competing domestic products*, as would be maintained according to Interpretation XX.

In our view, it does not seem plausible that Art. XX GATT was drafted with this role in mind. It rather appears as if it was meant to serve as a safety valve, as an assurance that despite efforts to ensure that core regulatory values would not be infringed upon, nothing in the agreement would do so.[163] This view of the

---

[163] See Irwin et al. (2008).

original rationale for Art. XX GATT is consistent with the view of the GATT as a negative integration scheme, in which domestic policies will be defined unilaterally and only to the extent that they exhibit international externalities will tend to be regulated through Art. III GATT (as well as the Most-Favored-Nation Provision in Art. I GATT, which also applies to domestic instruments, by virtue of Art. I.1). This view of Art. XX GATT speaks against letting the list define the set of situations in which it would be permissible to treat imported products less favorably than competing domestic products, that is, against Interpretation XX.

A second and related issue is whether the closed list should, by any reasonable benchmark, be regarded as complete, in light of Members' policy preferences. It is fairly easy to come up with examples of common measures that might find it difficult to qualify as exceptions under Art. XX GATT, if their consistency with the GATT is challenged. For example, a WTO Member distinguishing between "ordinary" and "luxury" items in such a manner as to indirectly tax an imported product higher than a competing domestic product, will have a hard time finding justification under Art. XX GATT. Another example would be domestic taxation that treats products originating from small and medium enterprises more favorably than products of "bigger" players.[164] According to current case law for a violation of Art. III GATT, it suffices in both instances that just one imported product is taxed heavier than its domestic counterpart. The defendant would have then a hard time justifying its measures under Art. XX GATT since no exception enlisted in Art. XX GATT corresponds to the examples provided for here. Yet another policy would be the promotion of culture.[165] These examples of real-world policy objectives that would normally find it hard to find defense under Art. XX GATT suggests that the list in Art. XX GATT is not complete from the point of view of Member preferences, and thus that Interpretation III is preferable in this regard.

But there are counterarguments. A first argument is that the list in Art. XX(a) GATT includes the reference to measures that are "necessary to protect public morals." This interpretation of this basis for exceptions is unclear, and negotiating history supports a narrow reading.[166] It can be noted, nevertheless, that in GATS, the negotiators opted for the most encompassing expression of the notion of "public order" (Art. XIV GATS), according to which *any* regulatory intervention is presumably done to serve public order. Were adjudicating bodies to interpret

---

[164] The EU promotion of small and medium-sized enterprises may exemplify such a policy.

[165] It can be argued that in several of these examples it would be easy to suggest alternative means of achieving the same policy objectives, but without running afoul of Art. III GATT. We will discuss the question of whether the GATT imposes restrictions on the means by which Members can achieve legitimate regulatory objectives in the next subsection.

[166] Based on the negotiating record, Feddersen (1998) argues that the term "public morals" was not perceived to be equivalent to "public order." Charnovitz (1998) does not exclude a more wide understanding of the term without, however, disputing the evidence provided by Feddersen.

Art. XX GATT in a similar fashion, the closed nature of the list in Art. XX GATT would not be a severe constraint on the possibility to pursue nonprotectionist unilateral policies.

Secondly, it can be noted that the GATT membership has not seen the need to expand the list of exceptions in Art. XX GATT over its 60-year history. It is also noteworthy that there has been no dispute so far where a WTO Member found it impossible to fit a tax differential under one of the grounds mentioned in Art. XX GATT. Of course, it could be the case that WTO Members have preferred not to legislate fearing that their legislation would be struck down as a result of the current construction of Arts. III and XX GATT. We do not have sufficient information to conclusively decide on this point. However, at the very least it can be concluded that the track record does not suggest that the closed list feature of Art. XX GATT has so far unduly constrained Members (by providing an unacceptably short list of permissible policy objectives). Indeed, had this been the case, one would have expected much more movement toward change or amendment to loosen the grip of GATT on domestic regulation.[167] To the contrary, the clear trend in the history of GATT has been to expand the obligations imposed on national regulators through the technical barriers agreements.

Thirdly, it may possibly be argued that the closed-list feature is actually desirable, in that absent this limitation on the domain of possible exceptions to Art. III GATT, the door would be open to questionable policy rationales. This raises the more general issue of whether the GATT restricts the freedom of Members to pursue policy objectives beyond prohibiting protectionist policies. Interpretation III and XX are based on different views on this issue, as will be discussed later in this Section.

To conclude, Interpretations III and XX are supported by two rather different views on the closed-list feature of Art. XX GATT. Interpretation III is based on the notion that the provision was never intended to serve as a definition of the set of policy objectives that could justify a less favorable treatment of imported products. Interpretation XX finds support mainly in the practical experiences with the legislation. In our view, the former arguments weigh significantly heavier, however, in particular when formulating principles for the design of the regulation of domestic instruments.

4.4.3.2 The Additional Requirements Imposed by Art. XX GATT

The body of Art. XX GATT contains some qualifiers for the eligibility for exceptions that have no counterpart in Art. III GATT, as pointed out in Section 4.4.2.1. In particular, it requests, with respect to some of the grounds mentioned in the list at least, that the contested measure be "necessary" to achieve the stated

[167] On the other hand, amendments occur only seldom in the WTO, see Kennedy (2010).

objective. The presence of such qualifiers raises the central issue of whether the GATT should be generally construed as requesting Members not to use policy instruments that impose different burdens on domestic and imported competing products, when instruments with more symmetric effects are somehow available. And if so, what should be meant by "available"? For instance, if the purpose of a luxury tax is to redistribute income from the rich to the poor, there might be other instruments, such as income taxation, that can be used to this end, and that possibly treat imported and domestic products more equally. Similarly, if the goal of the different taxation of goods of small and large enterprises is to subsidize small business, a government could tax all goods uniformly and pay subsidies to small business without violating the NT provisions by virtue of Art. III.8(b) GATT, which exempts from NT the payment of subsidies to domestic producers (but possibly at the risk of facing, e.g., a countervailing duty). Is it a purpose of the GATT to discipline Members in this sense? Interpretations III and XX are supported by different views on this important issue.

Interpretation III is based on the view that the GATT framers did not conceive the GATT as an instrument for deregulation or for efficient domestic regulation, but rather for nondiscrimination, where the disciplining of domestic instruments served one purpose only: to ensure that the value of tariff concessions would not be impaired through their discriminatory use.

Interpretation XX takes a rather different view, seeing the additional disciplines imposed by Art. XX GATT as both valuable and intentional, fearing that the disciplines would be lost in an open-ended evaluation of protection under Art. III GATT, since regulations can often be designed in multiple ways to achieve the same objective. To take an example: a measure regulating acceptable levels of pollution created by automobiles might require that all automobiles use a catalytic converter to reduce emissions. But perhaps some automakers can achieve the same emissions target more cheaply by shifting to a different technology, like hybrid propulsion. If such manufacturers are foreign, regulators may nevertheless require that all manufacturers use catalytic converters simply because they have no regard for the burden imposed on foreigners, even if the regulators' objectives are legitimately related to environmental protection, or worse, as a means for protectionism. The necessity test, together with the chapeau of Art. XX GATT make it impossible for the regulator to be indifferent to international externalities since the measure chosen must be the least burdensome on international trade.[168]

[168] In *US–Shrimp*, the AB requested from the United States to be flexible and accept in its market not only shrimps fished with TEDs (turtle excluding devices, a U.S. technology that guaranteed a low incidental take of life of sea turtles when fishing shrimps) but also shrimps fished with other technology as long as the rate of accidental take of life of sea turtles was comparable to that of TEDs.

This raises the general question of how far WTO Members should be requested to go in order to minimize adverse trade effects from domestic policies, in order to be eligible for an Art. XX GATT exception? Case law has more recently added a "reasonably available" qualification to the "least trade restrictive" interpretation of *necessary* in Art. XX.b GATT. Even so though, Art. XX GATT imposes an extra discipline on regulators (when compared to Art. III GATT) by requesting that measures are not only nondiscriminatory but further the least restrictive means: a proxy (necessity) is thus elevated to a positive obligation. The upside is that an appropriate proxy to detect protectionism (or absence thereof) becomes part of the legal test for consistency with the GATT; the downside is it might lead to "regulatory chill," definitely not part of the objectives the GATT was meant to pursue.

Art. 3.2 DSU clearly states that it is not for the interpreter to undo the balance of rights and obligations as struck by the framers of the WTO. So, even if desirable to do so, the interpreter should stop short of imposing its own rationality thus relegating negotiating intent to second-order consideration.

4.4.3.3 *The Allocation of the Burden of Proof*

As explained in Section 4.2, NT basically solves an informational problem – the lack of information for adjudicators concerning factual circumstances of the cases they are to adjudicate, and in particular with regard to government motives for contested regulation. Due to these informational problems, the design of the rules for the burden of proof will be important. In order to determine which interpretation is better in this regard, we will draw on the law-and-economics literature, focusing on two of the main themes in this literature. We thus start by analyzing how the possibility of judicial mistakes affects the desirable choice between Interpretations III and XX, and then turn to how this choice may contribute to the extraction of the parties' private information considering the circumstances that lead to the imposition of the contested measure.[169]

A first fundamental aspect that is highlighted in the literature is the impact of the allocation of the burden of proof for the occurrence of *judicial mistakes*. Generally speaking, the allocation of the burden of proof needs to balance the costs of false positive findings of violations ("Type I errors") against the costs of erroneous acquittals ("Type II errors"). In the present context, it seems plausible that what is at stake for the complainant, is market access in its export market. For the respondent, what is at stake is instead the possibility to use domestic instruments for protectionism, or for legitimate purposes, as the case may be. The allocation of the burden of proof, therefore, needs to weigh the cost of erroneously

---

[169] A third consideration pointed to in the literature is the desire to minimize legal costs. This may not be a prime concern to developed WTO Members, but may be of considerable importance to poorer Members. It is not clear how the desirable choice between Interpretations III and XX would be affected by such a consideration, however.

denying an exporter the market access it should legitimately have, against the cost of denying a regulating country the possibility to pursue legitimate regulatory policies. The cost of the latter type of mistake, which would force the regulating country to levy a higher fiscal burden on the domestic product than it would otherwise do, will partly take the form of reduced sales for its import-competing industry. But, it may also suffer a cost if the prohibition of its measure induces a lower level of ambition with regard to the policy objective it was pursuing.

It is hard to say anything definitive about the relative costs of Type I and Type II errors. But a number of considerations would suggest that *in dubio* it is probably preferable to err on the side of commercial rather than public-order objectives. First, it is clear that WTO Members have explicitly recognized that certain regulatory objectives are more important than commercial export interests, the chapeau of Art. XX GATT being an example. Second, Type I errors might comport negative implications for the institution itself: it is one thing for a panel to keep a dubious health policy in place and impose a trade cost on those trading with the country imposing it; it is yet another to strike down a health policy on dubious grounds and provoke a disease as a result.

A second theme in the law-and-economics literature on the burden of proof is the notion that it may be desirable to lay the burden on the party that is *better informed* concerning the contested issue; this may stem from the fact that the other party simply does not have access to information, or can only provide the information at a higher cost. By laying the burden of production on the better informed party, information that would otherwise not be available will be presented (or the information will be made available at lower cost). In the present context, the importing country is likely to be better informed concerning the reasons for the contested measure. The above reasoning would hence speak in favor of evaluating protection under Art. XX GATT, since the importing country would then bear most of the evidentiary burden. This would also be natural given the fact that a fundamental obstacle to the implementation of NT is lack of information concerning the government preferences that leads to the regulation.

To conclude, the choice between Interpretations III and XX should partly be influenced by the implications of the choice for the allocation of the burden of proof. The literature here points to a number of factors. One fundamental factor is the cost of judicial mistakes of different types; from this perspective, Interpretation III seems preferable. Another factor is the extent to which private information is extracted; Interpretation XX seems to perform better in this respect.

4.4.3.4 *Consequences for Trade Liberalization*

The discussion of the pros and cons of the Interpretations III and XX has thus far focused on how it would affect the outcome of adjudication, but has for analytical reasons disregarded implications for Members' policy choices. But the design of the adjudication mechanism will likely affect a whole range of government decisions, such as whether to invest resources in investigating domestic measures pursued by trading partners, whether to bring complaints, whether to request the establishment of panels, whether to appeal, etc. By affecting the likelihood of winning different types of claims, the choice of interpretation is likely to affect all these decisions.

What is of particular interest in this regard is whether Interpretation III or XX is more conducive to tariff liberalization, since a main purpose of NT is to support trade liberalization, while allowing governments to pursue legitimate domestic policies as they like (as emphasized in Sections 4.2 and 4.3).

What matters for trade liberalization is the combined effect of changes in tariffs and in the levels of domestic-trade-impeding instruments. We can here point to several mechanisms through which trade liberalization will be affected.

First, governments are typically unwilling to curb their discretion when it comes to regulation affecting their domestic market. They are therefore likely to respond to the imposition of stricter NT regimes for domestic instruments by maintaining higher tariffs, so as to ensure some policy space. The less restrictive Interpretation III may for this reason allow more tariff reductions than Interpretation XX.

Second, in order for countries to find it meaningful, and be willing, to make tariff concessions in the first place, it is necessary that they do not expect their trading partners to undercut the concessions they have given through opportunistic changes in the domestic policies. The stricter regime of Interpretation XX is likely to be better from this point of view. It is not possible to say, however, whether the combined effect will be to make Interpretation III or XX more conducive to reduced tariffs.

Third, trade liberalization requires not only tariff reductions, but also that domestic instruments are not used to fully offset the tariff concessions that countries have promised. Interpretation XX will be more efficient in preventing protectionist responses through domestic measures.[170]

There is also a broader aspect to take into consideration here, which is the *legitimacy* of the WTO more generally, since this affects the general willingness of countries to participate in the process of trade liberalization. We believe that Interpretation XX may be more problematic in this regard, since it puts on the regulating country the burden of proof to establish that contested measures are not disguised protection. According to Interpretation XX, a government would hence almost by automaticity violate one of the two fundamental nondiscrimination principles underlying the GATT/WTO if it were to intervene against regulatory problems that are particularly associated with imported goods. We believe

---

[170] Recall also, from the discussion in Section 4.3, that even if countries do not differentiate in domestic taxation, they can still respond to tariff reductions by increasing the common level of taxation, in order to at least partly dampen the effect of the tariff liberalization.

that Interpretation XX may, for this reason, be seen as imposing a more intrusive legal regime than what is politically desirable.

To illustrate, consider the case of environmental policies. For instance, suppose an imported car pollutes the air more than does a competing domestically produced car, per unit of gasoline consumed. An environmental policy that imposes a tax in proportion to the fuel consumption of cars would thus impose a higher fiscal burden on the imported product. It would then be very simple for the exporting WTO Member to establish a violation of Art. III GATT. According to Interpretation XX, the regulating country would then face the burden to defend the environmental policy before a panel and possibly the AB, having to prove that the taxation is not disguised protection, and that it fulfills the requirements in the body of Art. XX GATT. The latter may or may not be simple, depending on the precise ground in Art. XX GATT that is called upon. But to establish that the measure is not disguised protection may be more onerous.

Even if it would often be straightforward to defend such measures, we believe that Members would still be unwilling to let there be a presumption that environmental measures of this kind violate one of the two core nondiscrimination principles in the WTO.[171] The same issue would arise for all public-health measures that do not come under the purview of the *Agreement on the Application of Sanitary and Phytosanitary Measures* (SPS): the regulating state would have to show why the measure is necessary, despite the fact (according to Interpretation III) that all it promised when acceding to the WTO was not to discriminate.

In sum, above we pointed to several counteracting mechanisms for how the choice between Interpretations III and XX will affect trade liberalization, but it does not seem possible to say anything conclusive about their net effect. We believe, however, that a major consideration for longer-run trade liberalization is the legitimacy of the WTO among Members. It would politically and legally violate the spirit of the GATT if governments would have to request exceptions for obviously legitimate policies, and in particular when they are denied such exceptions. This is, in our view, a major drawback of Interpretation XX.

4.4.3.5 *Concluding Discussion*

Section 4.4.1 sketched out two different approaches to interpret the regulation of fiscal instruments in Art. III GATT. In Sections 4.4.2 and 4.4.3, we discussed the merits of the two approaches, paying particular attention to their

---

[171] See Horn and Weiler (2007) for a similar argument regarding the AB's determination in the *EC–Asbestos* dispute. They find it plausible that the AB simply could not accept the panel's approach of classifying the asbestos ban as violating one of the pillars of the WTO – NT – in light of the popular support of the measure, and perhaps also their own belief in its desirability.

implications for exercising the right to regulate at the national level and we linked this discussion to the overarching purpose that Art. III GATT was designed to serve. More specifically, Section 4.4.3.1 concluded that the list of legitimate grounds in Art. XX GATT should not be construed as a complete list of all permissible grounds for differential tax treatment of competing imported and domestic products, and pointed to the example of policy objectives that would be difficult to find acceptance for under Art. XX GATT. Section 4.4.3.2 discussed the various requirements imposed by Art. XX GATT, such as the "necessity" requirements for certain policy objectives. The Section concluded that the GATT should not be construed as requiring "good governance," and that what is required from WTO Members is that they refrain from adopting some obviously beggar-thy-neighbor policies where they impose on imported goods a burden higher than that imposed on their domestic counterparts. On balance, these aspects point quite strongly in favor of Interpretation III.

Section 4.4.3.3 examined the desirable distribution of the burden of proof, highlighting two aspects. First, the fact that respondents are likely to have better access to information concerning the motives for regulations suggests that the evidentiary burden should be put on respondents, as it is under Interpretation XX. Second, there is a significant likelihood that judges will make mistakes, imperfectly informed as they are about the circumstances that have led to the disputes they adjudicate. To the extent that Members are more troubled when adjudicators erroneously strike down legitimate domestic regulations than when they erroneously allow protectionist measures – which we believe typically is the case – Interpretation III is preferable.

In our view, the analysis of Sections 4.4.3.1–4.4.3.3 of how the choice of interpretation is likely to affect the outcome of adjudication, speaks in favor of Interpretation III, although there are some arguments to the contrary. But as emphasized in Sections 4.2 and 4.3, a basic rationale for a NT provision is to induce countries to liberalize trade. We identified several differences between the interpretations in this regard. We finally took a broader perspective, highlighting the consequences of the choice of interpretation for the "legitimacy" of the WTO, an admittedly amorphous concept. We here concluded that a serious drawback of Interpretation XX is that it is likely to be perceived as too severely restricting the "policy space" that WTO Members want to retain with regard to domestic policies. Based on the above, we conclude that Interpretation III is preferable. But we acknowledge that this decision is not only based on a strict legal and economic analysis, but also on our intuition.

A final consideration for the choice between evaluating protection under Art. III and XX GATT, is the consistency with existing practice. Changing practice comes at a cost, but so does, of course also, the continuation of a bad practice. It is actually difficult to determine where the case law currently stands with regard to the choice of whether to evaluate protection under Art. III or XX GATT. One thing is for sure though: case law slowly moves towards an interpretation of Art. III GATT where the complainant will have to show that a measure that seemingly (e.g., because of potential trade effects) imposes a higher cost on imported goods is also linked to the origin of the good: first, in *EC–Asbestos*, the AB "widened" the understanding of likeness; then, in *Dominican Republic–Import and Sale of Cigarettes*, the AB confirmed that "mechanical," acontextual understandings of the key terms appearing in Art. III GATT are a thing of the past. It thus appears as if the AB has embarked on a quest for a meaningful protectionism test. Interpretation III is very much in line with this attitude.

4.4.4 Further Remarks on Interpretation III

Above we proposed two modes of interpreting the nexus of Arts. III and XX GATT, one more in line with the earlier case law, and one more novel. We identified the differences between the two interpretations, and discussed their pros and cons. We concluded that Interpretation III is to be preferred. This Section will offer a number of further reflections, further comments on, in particular, the proposed Interpretation III.

4.4.4.1 *The Relevance of Art. III.1 GATT*

It is sometimes argued that Art. III.1 GATT is hortatory and that the legally binding language concerning fiscal instruments is contained in Art. III.2 GATT. However, absence of legally binding language does not lead to irrelevance: Art. III.1 GATT might be given less weight in the interpretative process than paragraphs 2 and 4, but should not be read to redundancy. To this effect, the basic idea underlying Interpretation III is that Art. III.1 and Art. III.2 GATT must be read in conjunction, since, because of their differentiated coverage (one dealing with fiscal instruments, the other with nonfiscal instruments) none of them could on its own serve as regulation of domestic instruments: both provisions aim at expressing in operational (binding) language the principle embedded in Art. III.1 GATT (*Japan–Alcoholic Beverages II*, AB). It is Art. III.1 GATT, for example, that gives the term "like products" the meaning of referring to situations where there is no justification for treating an imported product differently from a domestic product.

The constraint imposed on fiscal instruments by Art. III GATT is thus determined *jointly* by Arts. III.1 and III.2 GATT. Unfortunately, part of the case law has relegated to quasi-redundancy the importance of Art. III.1 GATT; panels have often made their determinations within the four corners of Art. III.2 GATT, and then simply confirmed their conclusion by referring to Art. III.1 GATT as context. They have been thus led to acontextual understandings of the key terms (like products, in excess, etc.), that is, they have improperly or inadequately accounted for the context as embedded in Art. III.1 GATT which calls for a ban on protectionist-only behavior. The most common mistake that panels have made is to confuse disparate effects with discrimination, a term which is legalese for absence of protectionism. Contextual readings of the key terms help avoid (or at least reduce) the occurrence of this risk.[172]

4.4.4.2 *The Relative Facility to Find Grounds for Complaints*

An issue that is rarely discussed, but that could be of significant importance, is the advantage complainants have in picking and choosing among trading partners' fiscal instruments. Tax systems are normally highly complex, consisting of a large number of specific tax regulations, such as corporate taxation, value-added taxation, environmental taxation, income taxation, capital-gains taxation, etc. Each of these tax schemes in turn consists of intricate sets of rules. Indeed, these schemes are so complex that they represent separate fields of specialization for, e.g., tax lawyers. As a result, when comparing the components of tax schemes, it is quite likely that there will be *some* component that falls heavier on the imported product than on a like domestic product.

To illustrate, assume that an imported product requires longer transportation routes in the importing country compared to some competing domestic product. An environmentally motivated tax on gasoline would then fall more heavily on the imported product than on the locally produced good. Following Interpretation XX, such a tax could violate Art. III GATT, since the tax falls more heavily on the imported product than on the competing domestic product. At the same time, there may be no protectionist intent, and the whole set of environmental taxes (or taxes even more broadly) may actually be favorable to the imported product, and/or be internationally efficient. It would be significantly more difficult for the complainant to win such a case following Interpretation III, since the complainant would then have to show that the gasoline tax is protectionist.

The issue arises due to an incompleteness in the GATT: the agreement does not restrict the way in which a Member can pick pairs of taxes out of a tax system to complain about.[173] Of course, the DS system has not witnessed a large number of frivolous complaints, so far. But there is no assurance that Members will show such restraint also in the future. In any event, it seems desirable to reduce the potential for this problem when laying down *principles* for the interpretation of Art. III GATT. This is achieved by requesting the complaining Member to bear a significant burden of persuasion to make a plausible case that the contested measures are indeed protectionist.

---

[172] As mentioned before, it is the AB report on *Dominican Republic–Import and Sale of Cigarettes* that attempted to address this issue albeit without providing a methodology that would be appropriate to achieve this result.

[173] Ruling beyond the ambit of the claim would amount to a ruling *ultra petita*, which, standing case law suggests, is considered a cardinal sin for WTO adjudicating bodies.

4.4.4.3 *Why Not Only Policy Likeness, Why Also Market Likeness?*

Interpretation III requires that products are both market- and policy-like, in order for Art. III GATT to possibly be violated. Products are policy unlike when it would be desirable from an international efficiency point of view to treat them differently. Typically, the reason why there is a need to treat them differently is that buyers do *not* make the desirable distinction. That is, market likeness is often part of the reason why products are *not* policy-like.

But for products to be like, why not request *only* policy likeness, why include market likeness as a separate criterion? The main reason for including the market-likeness criterion is best illustrated through an example: it could by chance be the case that the joint welfare of the exporting and importing country governments would increase if the importing country government were requested to impose the same production tax on coffee cups as on diesel trucks – the products may thus be policy-like by chance. But it is obviously highly unlikely that the differential taxation would reflect protectionism. The requirement that products must also be market-like ensures that Art. III GATT will not be violated in instances where a WTO Member taxes trucks and cups differently which, as argued, are instances that protectionist behavior is highly unlikely.[174]

4.4.4.4 *The Relationship Between Like and DCS Products*

Table 1 summarizes our aforementioned claims concerning the basic ambit of the regulation of fiscal instruments under Art. III GATT, as viewed from the perspective of Interpretation III. For the tax treatment of a pair of products to come under the ambit of Art. III GATT, the products concerned have to be in a sufficiently strong competitive relationship – they have to be market-like. There is no rationale from an international efficiency point of view to treat some of these pairs of products differently – assuming of course that they are not only market- but policy-like as well; in this case no tax differential should be allowed. For other product pairs, a differential tax treatment is warranted, and thus legal; the tax differential nevertheless should correspond to whatever level is necessary to achieve the regulatory objective sought. Consequently, both like and DCS products are market-like, but they differ in the extent of policy likeness. Hence, neither set of product pairs is a subset of the other set of product pairs. Note also

---

[174] Another reason for including an explicit market-likeness criterion could perhaps be that this could be expected to enhance the quality of the adjudication process. As discussed *supra*, the case law has suffered from unclear evaluations of the market relationship between products, the *Korea–Beef* dispute being one example. The requirement of a separate demonstration of market likeness from that of policy likeness might enhance the transparency of the argumentation by the parties and the adjudication process. For instance, this would make it easier for outside evaluation of the methods employed in WTO disputes. One can here compare the interaction between research and policy in the development of principles and methods for the determination of relevant markets in antitrust.

Table 1

	Market-like	Not market-like
Policy-like	"Like"; *no* tax differential is allowed	Art. III not applicable; any tax differential is allowed
Not policy-like	"DCS"; *some* tax differential is allowed	Art. III not applicable; any tax differential is allowed

that there is no difference in the extent of market likeness that is required for like and for DCS products.

4.4.4.5 *GATT Does Not Request Full International Efficiency*

There are several reasons why a constraint on Members to tax imported and competing locally produced goods equally will not implement a fully efficient situation, and we highlighted them in Section 4.2:

- the provision has no bite in situations where the tax on the domestic product is higher than the tax on the imported product, but where the difference should be even larger;
- in cases where the tax on the imported product is higher, the provision may ensure equal treatment, but not better treatment of the imported product, even if this would be desirable from an international efficiency point of view; and
- the importing country is free to choose a common tax level it desires in case of like products, and any two tax rates that respect the permissible tax differential in the case of DCS products. Since decisions over these taxes are likely to disregard the interests of the exporting country, they are likely to be inefficient from an international perspective.

The reason why measures may deviate from what is internationally efficient in these respects is, of course, that governments will disregard the interests of trading partners when deciding on their domestic policies. This leads to the more general observation that *the GATT does not exhibit "zero tolerance" against protectionist behavior,* it only partially restricts the possibility for governments to behave in a similar fashion.

4.4.4.6 *Can a Measure That Violates Art. III GATT Be Justified Through Recourse to Art. XX GATT?*

Art. III and XX GATT are both tools to prevent protectionism. This raises the question of whether a measure that is found to be illegal protection, for the purpose of Art. III GATT, may still be granted an exception under Art. XX GATT, being found not to constitute disguised protection. According to Interpretation III, this is normally not possible, while it is fully possible according to Interpretation XX.

Interpretation III proposes that for a measure to violate Art. III GATT, it must be protectionist. Hence, as long as the meaning of protectionism in Art. III GATT is the same as, or more narrow than, the meaning of protectionism in Art. XX GATT, it would be illogical that a measure that violates the former could receive an exception under the latter, except as a result of a judicial mistake in the evaluation under Art. III GATT. In this vein, Art. XX GATT is unlikely to serve as an effective exception to Art. III GATT under Interpretation III.

Interpretation XX functions very differently in this regard, since it understands the restrictions imposed through Art. III GATT to be of a simpler form, not requesting any demonstration of protectionism. Instead, the evaluation of protection is performed under Art. XX GATT. Such a construction finds some support in the fact that Art. XX GATT is a list of "General Exceptions," with no textual support that it was not intended to play a role in disputes involving Art. III GATT.[175]

Interpretation III does not render Art. XX GATT meaningless, and therefore does not conflict with the rules concerning treaty interpretation in the *Vienna Convention on the Law of Treaties* (VCLT). Art. XX GATT may still serve as an efficient exception clause for other provisions in the GATT, such as those addressing the use of border instruments (e.g., tariffs, QRs, etc.).[176] Also, it cannot be excluded that Art. XX GATT may actually, in special cases, serve as an exception to Art. III GATT. An example might be the following situation: Country A taxes an imported product X higher than a domestically produced product that is identical in all respects, in order to punish the exporting country B for producing another product Y that pollutes the environment of country A, but that it does not import from B, and hence cannot tax directly.

4.4.4.7 *On Evaluating Market Likeness and Protection*

Interpretations III and XX both require adjudicating bodies to determine the actual extent of market likeness and the international efficiency of protection. We will here make a few reflections on how such evaluations should be done.

First, in order to determine the nature and magnitude of the effects of contested measures, it is necessary to characterize the competition between the domestic and the imported product. The current case-law approach to undertaking similar evaluation leaves much to be desired for the reasons mentioned in Section 4.3.

---

[175] Recall, however, the views of the UK negotiators that we cited supra.
[176] Indeed, there is no basis in the VCLT to argue that the GATT should be interpreted such that Art. XX GATT becomes an effective exception to each other provision in the GATT.

The evaluation of the competitive relationship between the products should primarily be based on data collected from the actual market at hand. But lacking such data, as when the differential policy treatment is sufficiently pronounced to deny market access to the exported good, one must resort to more indirect sources of information. This could, for instance, be evidence on the relationship between the same products in other (comparable) geographical markets, or between similar products in the importing country. One could also use the indicators suggested in the *Working Party report on Border Tax Adjustments* (such as end uses, physical characteristics, etc.). Another source of information is tariff classification. For the most part, if two products are in the same six-digit Harmonized System category, they are likely to be in close competition, even though such tariff classifications are not always informative about the properties of the products. With finer HS-classification, it is of course even more likely that the products are highly competitive.

Next, the data should, as far as possible, be examined through econometric analysis, using standardized techniques. Indeed, such analysis is commonplace in the antitrust-context where the relevant product market within which market power will be estimated is routinely defined in this way. In light of the similarity in the function of trade and antitrust analysis, we see no reason why econometric analysis is routinely used in the latter and sparingly so in the former. Recourse to noneconometric indicators should only be taken to complement the econometric analysis, or when econometric analysis cannot be undertaken.

Another, and more complex, task facing adjudicators is to determine whether contested measures are internationally efficient or not. But it is hard to see how this can be avoided, as long as there is to be a test for protection that allows tax differentials under some but not all circumstances, and where the guiding principle is that differential taxation should only be allowed to the extent it is in the mutual interest (a concept which is at the heart of the notion that illegal protection is essentially a beggar-thy-neighbor type of behavior). It should be emphasized, however, that the difficulty facing the adjudicator does *not* stem from the fact that the task is to evaluate challenged measures under Art. III GATT as per Interpretation III. On the contrary, in the case of DCS products, the task facing the adjudicator actually may be *simpler* when evaluating a claim under Art. III GATT than under Art. XX GATT. What is requested in the former case is, according to Interpretation III, to compare two tax pairs, the contested pair, and an Art. III.2 GATT-compatible pair. The evaluation of protection under Art. XX GATT is likely to be more onerous, since it does not constrain the evaluation to a comparison of only two tax pairs, and it may additionally require a test for whether a measure is necessary.

We believe that adjudicators actually already perform tests of this sort, albeit implicitly. When evaluating whether a measure should be accepted, an adjudicating body will naturally seek to identify both the costs that the measure

gives rise to for the complaining party, and the benefits it brings to the importing Member (even if no numbers are put on these costs and benefits). Hence,
we would argue that when an adjudicating body approaches a case like *Japan–
Alcoholic Beverages II*, it would be importantly influenced by observing that there
seem to be no noncommercial benefits to Japan that could outweigh the cost to
exporting Members. Had there been noncommercial reasons for Japan to pursue the measure, the adjudicating body would have been much more prone to
accept the measure, provided that it did not impose too large costs on the trading partners. This is how we understand the AB when it points to the revealing
"design and structure" of a contested measure. Conversely, although not a taxation case, it seems likely that in *EC–Asbestos*, adjudicating bodies felt that the
costs of the measure for Canada were dominated by the gains for France, and that
the measure for this reason preferably should pass the test; the main question
was instead *how* this could be achieved. The point of these examples is hence to
argue that adjudicating bodies already weigh the benefits of the contested regulation against the cost to the exporting country, albeit not openly. Of course, as
is often the case for judicial decisions, within the parameters described above,
the evaluation whether the contested measures constitute undesirable protection will still have to be a subjective judgment, regardless of whether done under
Art. III or XX GATT. We therefore do not believe that the protectionism test that
we envisage following both Interpretation III and XX, is significantly more onerous for adjudicating bodies than what is already being practiced. The suggested
interpretation to a considerable extent simply codifies existing practice, providing a conceptual framework within which it can be understood.[177]

4.4.4.8 *Intent Versus Effect*

As highlighted in Section 4.3, case law has repeatedly discussed the intricate
issue of whether the ASATAP notion should be seen as referring to the intent or
effect of policy measures, but without bringing much clarity to the discussion.

In our view, it is useful to distinguish between the role of intent and effect
in the *substantive obligation*, and the role of these notions from an *evidentiary*
point of view. As for the substantive obligation, the agreed general purpose of Art.
III GATT is to prevent WTO Members from circumventing their tariff concessions

---

[177] A complicating factor for any preference-based interpretation of protection in the GATT is
the fact that governments change over time. Strictly speaking, this means that a measure
that with one government is an expression of protectionism could with a change of government become legitimate, or vice versa. Allowing such changes over time is not so much a
conceptual problem. But it is a practical problem, partly since it makes the actual meaning
of tariff commitments more uncertain, and it complicates the formation of case law. The
combination of a formal lack of *stare decisis* in the WTO, with a significant focus in dispute
rulings on earlier case law, can perhaps be seen to reflect such a balancing between governments' desire for the law to be responsive to political developments, while at the same time
provide some stability to the undertakings.

through opportunistic use of domestic instruments. The main purpose of these tariff reductions is in turn to prevent negative international externalities from unilateral policies. The ultimate aim is thus to prevent measures that have the *effect* of giving rise to internationally inefficient allocations, where the effects are evaluated based on the preferences of the Members involved.[178]

As for the roles of intent and effect from an evidentiary point of view, note that the evaluation of protectionism requires knowledge concerning government preferences, which is intimately associated with determining the intent behind measures. Since preferences are not directly observable, and since the regulating state has strong incentive to behave opportunistically, the judge must rely on indirect evidence concerning intent. Examples of such indicators are:

- The consistency by which the alleged objective is pursued across products: If the same objective is disregarded in other industries, the differential treatment of the product at hand might indicate that the protection is intentional; indeed, Art. 5.5 of the SPS Agreement reflects a very similar idea.
- The use of international standards: Assume for example that an international standard exists that can appropriately take care of the legislative objective sought. Deviations from the standard, while not necessarily unwarranted, should then be viewed with suspicion: it should be normal in similar cases to request from the deviating state to explain itself on its choice to deviate, rather than allocate the burden of production of proof *à la EC–Sardines* (AB report);
- Scientific evidence: Measures based on scientific evidence are in general more likely to respond to a genuine need to intervene, at least in light of the best current knowledge about a particular issue. Of course, this does not mean that measures based on the precautionary principle are necessarily protectionist: for such measures, recourse to some or all of the criteria mentioned above might be warranted.

Indications of the intent may also be obtained from the effects of contested measures, such as the magnitude of trade effects: The larger the trade effects, the more likely that they are intended. The choice of less trade restrictive should be understood as a proxy (albeit an imperfect one) that the measure has been enacted for motives other than protectionism. This list is by no means exhaustive, but only intended to illustrate the type of indicators that could be used to evaluate whether a measure is protectionist. Hence, the effects of measures may

---

[178] The question of whether a measure should be illegal if it is intended to protect but in actuality fails to do so, seems to be of limited practical relevance, except from an enforcement perspective. Since we are not concerned with enforcement issues here, we do not take a stand on the question. Of course, unintentional protective effects characterize situations where measures are internationally efficient, but still have adverse trade effects. Such effects clearly cannot be condemned *a priori*.

signal the reason why the measures themselves have been pursued in the first place.

In sum, both effect and intent are relevant to the definition of the substantive obligation. Effect matters since the purpose is to regulate measures that cause international externalities, and intent matters since it is closely related to the question whether international externalities are present.[179] Intent and effect are also relevant from an evidentiary perspective, since both perceived intent as well as observed effects in the market could serve as evidence concerning the preferences of the regulating country.

4.4.4.9 *The Aims and Effect Test*

Interpretation III shares a certain similarity with an interpretation of Art. III GATT that has been denoted the *aims and effect* test, but also differs in important respects. This test goes back to the *US–Malt Beverages* panel report, where like is defined in the following manner (§ 5.25):

> "Consequently, in determining whether two products subject to different treatment are like products, it is necessary to consider whether such product differentiation is being made 'so as to afford protection to domestic production'. While the analysis of 'like products' in terms of Article III:2 must take into consideration this objective of Article III, the Panel wished to emphasize that such an analysis would be without prejudice to the 'like product' concepts in other provisions of the General Agreement, which might have different objectives and which might therefore also require different interpretations."

In its *US–Taxes on Automobiles* Report,[180] the Panel had the opportunity to elaborate on this proposition by providing its own legal benchmark to establish likeness, the so-called *aims and effects* test (§§ 5.7, 5.10):

> "In order to determine this issue, the Panel examined the object and purpose of paragraphs 2 and 4 of Article III in the context of the article as a whole and the General Agreement.
>
> ...
>
> The Panel then proceeded to examine more closely the meaning of the phrase 'so as to afford protection.' The Panel noted that the term 'so as to'

---

[179] Indeed, trade effects could signal intent.
[180] In this case, the European Community challenged the consistency of a U.S. tax scheme applicable to cars, according to which the total fleet of a producer would be taken into account in order to decide on the tax that would be imposed. Producers with a fleet that consisted of large cubism cars (gas guzzlers) would suffer most, as a result. Many European producers belonged to this category. The U.S. regime was apparently enacted at a time when those suffering most were U.S. producers, in an effort to dissuade consumers eager to buy such cars from buying them.

suggested both aim and effect. Thus the phrase 'so as to afford protection' called for an analysis of elements including the aim of the measure and the resulting effects. A measure could be said to have the *aim* of affording protection if an analysis of the circumstances in which it was adopted, in particular an analysis of the instruments available to the contracting party to achieve the declared domestic policy goal, demonstrated that a change in competitive opportunities in favour of domestic products was a desired outcome and not merely an incidental consequence of the pursuit of a legitimate policy goal. A measure could be said to have the *effect* of affording protection to domestic production if it accorded greater competitive opportunities to domestic products than to imported products. The effect of a measure in terms of trade flows was not relevant for the purposes of Article III, since a change in the volume or proportion of imports could be due to many factors other than government measures." (italics in the original)

According to the *aims and effect test*, likeness hence means policy likeness, in our terminology. However, contrary to what the name of the test suggests, the realized effects of contested measures are (to our understanding) explicitly irrelevant in the *aims and effect* test; in the name of the premise that Art. III GATT is about protecting competitive conditions, the *US–Taxes on Automobiles* panel held that trade effects are totally immaterial. In contrast, in our preferred approach (Interpretation III), like goods must be both market- and policy-like. We are in the dark as to the applicability of the *aims and effects* test on DCS goods, since the panel made no pronouncement in this vein.

4.4.4.10 *Taxation Based on Features of the Production Process (PPMs)*

In light of the above, it seems safe to conclude that Art. III GATT applies, in principle, to all domestic instruments (irrespective whether of fiscal or nonfiscal nature) except for the two instruments that have been explicitly exempted from its coverage. The NT provision does not, however, as already discussed above, address the question of *prescriptive jurisdiction*: can an importing country effectively impose its own regulatory choices on imports, by making adjustments at the border for taxes paid by producers of domestic goods, but not by competing imported products? The text of Art. III GATT is silent on this score.

A contentious issue involving territoriality is the legality under Art. III GATT (as well as other GATT provisions) of domestic policies that condition market access for products on the manner in which they have been produced, rather than on the physical characteristics of the products; this is what the discussion concerning the role for production and process method (PPM)-based measures address. A core issue with regard to the compatibility of such measures with Art. III GATT is whether an imported product that physically is identical to a local product can nevertheless be viewed as not being like (or DCS), because of differences in the production process and/or method.[181] According to Interpretation III, the answer is "yes."

Consider, for instance, the case where the production of an exportable causes environmental damage to the importing country, and the importing country levies a tax on the imported product to offset the damage. According to Interpretation III, the evaluation of this measure should take into consideration the environmental impact on the importing country. If the tax differential is not larger than what would be chosen if the environment objective were to be achieved in an internationally efficient manner, the measure should be allowed. Note, however, that a prerequisite for this is that the importing-country government is adversely affected by the measure other than through its impact on the competitive conditions in the domestic market – in the example there is transboundary environmental damage. If this is not the case, the only rationale for the PPM measure is protectionism.

This implication of Interpretation III is compatible with the "default rules" concerning allocation of jurisdiction in Public International Law. In short, and as briefly alluded to above, the default rules oblige states not to regulate transactions occurring outside their geographic borders except for in certain commonly agreed circumstances. However, states can exercise prescriptive jurisdiction on actions that occur outside their borders, by virtue of the so called "effects doctrine," and a reasonableness criterion will help solve conflicts in cases in which more than one state have jurisdiction through these rules. It follows that recourse to the default rules is quite helpful, but does not eliminate jurisdictional conflicts altogether; contractual solutions are hence encouraged.[182]

The default rules would thus suggest that an importing country has jurisdiction over production processes in other countries, provided that the production process has direct and foreseeable effect on the importing country, and provided that the countries in question do not have an agreement regulating the issue. Hence, the fact that the production and sales of the imported product will have effects on the competitive conditions in the importing-country market, is not a ground for the importing-country government to regulate the transaction, as long as there is an agreement concerning these effects – in this case the GATT/WTO. On the other hand, absent an international agreement between the two countries – such as might be the case in, e.g., the case of protection of the environment – the effects doctrine gives the importing country jurisdiction (assuming presence of effects in its market). When exercising jurisdiction, it will have to respect a reasonableness requirement when choosing its measures.

---

[181] PPM-based measures may take the form of border tax adjustments (BTAs); see Section 4.2 above.

[182] See Horn and Mavroidis (2008) for a discussion of jurisdictional aspects of the GATT, and the role of the default rules.

The default rules are not explicitly reflected in the GATT, nor have they been explicitly referenced in case law. However, the AB report in the *US–Shrimp* dispute can perhaps be seen as a step in this direction, in that it pointed to a "sufficient nexus" between an endangered species in the exporting country, and the importing country, absent which the regulating state would not be in position to lawfully exercise jurisdiction. The AB did not expand on this rather cryptic statement, so we still lack a legal test that will help us predict in future transactions when a nexus exists and when not.

This is not to say that recourse to the default rules is a panacea. Indeed, there is no convincing and consistent response in international adjudication regarding, for example, jurisdiction in the presence of "moral" externalities; for instance, assuming that the use of child labor causes public concern in a WTO Member, can it block the trade of a good that is produced with child labor? Or, can the importing country block trade if the exporting country uses child labor not in the imported goods, but in the production of other goods? The default rules do not provide clear answers to these questions. But they do constitute an appropriate first step to resolve a jurisdictional issue that may become of significant importance for adjudication in the WTO.

4.4.5 Revisiting the Leading Cases in Light of Our Proposals

The previous sections presented two interpretations of Art. III GATT, based on our understanding of the case law, the negotiating history, and economic theory. We will, in this section, briefly discuss whether applying our suggested interpretations would have affected the outcome in the GATT/WTO cases that have shaped the current understanding of Art. III GATT, and if so how.

As evidenced by the compilation presented in the Appendix, there are a large number of cases that have been adjudicated under Art. III GATT. Ideally, we would want to see how our suggested interpretations would fare in each of these cases, but this is not practical. Instead, we will briefly discuss how these interpretations would affect the determinations in some leading cases. To this end, we first identify the disputes that we believe represent the state-of-the-art of the existing case law. We then reexamine these disputes in light of the discussion in the study.

Although *de jure* there is no binding precedent (*stare decisis*) in WTO, it is commonplace that panels and AB have followed prior rulings. Indeed, in its report on *US–Stainless Steel (Mexico)*, the AB held that it expected panels to follow prior AB findings dealing with the same issue. It further deplored the attitude of the panel in question to disregard the AB approach on the practice of zeroing (§§ 158–162). With this in mind, it seems appropriate to try to identify the leading Art. III GATT cases where the AB has explained its overall understanding of the provision, and to which reference is customarily made in subsequent case law when issues relating to the interpretation of the provision arise.

Following this definition, the leading cases, and their main innovations, are as follows:

- *Japan–Alcoholic Beverages II* explicitly outlawed the *aims and effect* test (espoused by some GATT panels) as we saw in Section 4.3. It further incorporated the GATT leading cases (such as *Japan–Alcoholic Beverages I*, and the *Working Party report on Border Tax Adjustments*) that had opted for a test in the marketplace in order to define whether two products are like or DCS. As a result, in light of the similarity of the approach followed, we do not need to apply our approach to this class of GATT disputes as well.

- *Korea–Alcoholic Beverages* followed *Japan–Alcoholic Beverages II* in almost all aspects, but with two crucial additions: the AB established that, in order to define whether two products are *DCS/ like*, the WTO adjudicator can *interchangeably* use econometric and/or noneconometric indicators; moreover, the AB also held that for two products to be *like*, they must at the very least be *DCS* and share a detailed tariff classification as well: DCS emerges thus as a necessary but insufficient condition for likeness.

- *Chile–Alcoholic Beverages* introduced an inquiry into the objective intent of the regulator (in some, rather extreme, conditions) in order to detect whether a measure has been applied so as to afford protection to domestic production.

- *Philippines–Distilled Spirits* held that two goods are like when they are in intense competitive relationship (while DCS goods are in less intense relationship). It is unclear, nevertheless, whether this criterion in and of itself suffices to afford likeness or whether they must still share HS classification: a few pages later, in a separate finding, the AB mentions the relevance of HS classification. Because of the existing uncertainty (and the absence of a clear pronouncement overruling the relevance of HS classification as a criterion that can appropriately define likeness) we will not let this determination change our conclusions regarding the definition of likeness in case law.

    In *Philippines–Distilled Spirits*, the AB faced the following facts (§ 98): distilled spirits produced from one of the following materials, sap of the nipa, coconut, cassava, camote, etc. (predominantly produced in the Philippines), were subjected to a flat rate, whereas distilled spirits produced from other materials (predominantly imported) were subjected to a higher excise tax. The AB suggested that DCS products are those with low substitutability between them, whereas like products are those with high, almost perfect substitutability (§§ 120–122, 148). [1] In sharp contrast to its prior case law (*Japan–Alcoholic Beverages II*), the AB did not condition a finding of likeness on common tariff classification across two products: it first held that a 4-digit tariff classification was uninformative, since not sufficiently detailed, and no conclusions on likeness could be drawn (§ 182). It then noted that two of the goods did not share the same 6-digit tariff classification; it still found that they were like, overlooking thus the significance of tariff classification, satisfying itself that the goods were like since they were in intense competitive relationship (§ 164).

We will now briefly discuss how these leading cases would have been adjudicated if Interpretations III and XX were adopted.

4.4.5.1 *Japan–Alcoholic Beverages II*

Recall that in this case the AB found the Japanese measures to be in violation of Art. III.2 GATT, because Japan was taxing predominantly western drinks substantially higher than predominantly Japanese drinks. Recall further that Japan had no policy justification for this tax differential and only took recourse to *ex post facto* justifications to explain its policies; all its justifications were dismissed by the panel precisely because they were *ex post facto*. In this case, the panel found (and the AB upheld) that a class of products were DCS based on consumer surveys that were conducted in Japan, which used econometric indicators to quantify the degree of substitutability across the various products. Two products were furthermore considered like since they shared the same tariff classification. Finally, the in-excess/ASATAP-requirement was justified by the tax differential itself.

The outcome of this dispute seems desirable from both an Interpretation III and XX perspective. We are also in agreement with some of the reasoning in the report:

- DCS products should be defined by using econometric indicators, when appropriate (as was the case here);
- A substantial tax differential across two DCS products, and the absence of any policy rationale for it, suggests that the measure is protectionist.

We have two main misgivings concerning the report. First, following either of our suggested Interpretations, we would have preferred to see an explicit evaluation of whether the measure was to be considered protectionist. Second, Interpretation III is not compatible with the AB's understanding of the term like. In our view, sharing a tariff classification should not be a dispositive feature for a finding of likeness, since the products that come under the same tariff heading are not necessarily policy-like as well. In this case, however, this was immaterial since Japan was ostensibly not pursuing *any* policy goal through the differential taxation, other than providing its producers with a tax advantage.

4.4.5.2 *Korea–Alcoholic Beverages*

In this case, the AB found the Korean measures to be in violation of Art. III.2 GATT. Recall that the AB held that econometric and noneconometric indicators are equally useful methods to decide on the DCS-relationship across two products; without explaining under what circumstances recourse to either is warranted, it treated them as perfect substitutes irrespective of the facts.

As things stand, it is difficult to clearly determine whether we agree or not with the final outcome, since we lack information that is crucial for us to apply our test, irrespective whether we follow Interpretation III or XX: recall that DCS-relationship is defined in the same way under both interpretations. The evidence supporting DCS-relationship across predominantly Korean and predominantly western drinks seems at least debatable to us. As mentioned above, recourse to econometric indicators is not panacea. We do not know if this was one of those situations where recourse to econometric indicators would solve the problem (although we suspect, in light of the evidence submitted by Korea, that this is not the case). The panel in its report examined evidence from the Japanese market regarding the relationship between the products without explaining why evidence from the Korean market was inappropriate. However, as facts make it clear, western drinks did exist in the Korean market, the tax differential notwithstanding. Nevertheless, neither the panel nor the AB explained why such evidence could not have been appropriately taken into consideration. We consequently find unsatisfactory the manner in which the AB decided on the DCS-relationship across the products.

Since we are unsure about the extent of DCS-relationship, there is not much we can add with respect to *like products*, never mind the remaining parts of the test (ASATAP).

4.4.5.3 *Chile–Alcoholic Beverages*

Recall that the case concerned a Chilean progressive taxation scheme, whereby the tax rate increased with alcohol strength. The AB found the scheme to be GATT-inconsistent because the tax differential across the various tax categories was too large, without explaining, however, what would be acceptable. We are opposed to the approach used, but cannot definitely pronounce on the outcome had our preferred approach been privileged. We have reasons to believe, nonetheless, that Chile should have prevailed under either approach.

In this case, there was no dispute regarding the fact that the goods at hand were DCS. The only disputed matter was whether the tax differential was discriminatory. The AB dismissed the relevance of the claim by Chile that the majority of the products hit by the higher tax were of Chilean origin. We find this hard to accept. Under Interpretation III, just as adverse trade effects indicate (but do not prove) intent to protect, adverse effects borne primarily by domestic product should be taken to indicate lack of such a motive; the AB dismissed the relevance of this factor, invoking the no-effects test that it customarily applies in Art. III

GATT cases. To be precise, the AB accepted that it was Chileans that were burdened with paying the major proportion of the tax burden in the highest category, but explicitly dismissed its relevance arguing that this fact, in and of itself, was not enough to undo its belief that, in light of the sharp rise of the tax burden across categories and the fact that Chilean goods were predominant in the lowest tax category, the challenged tax regime was GATT-inconsistent.

As argued above, we do believe that regulatory intent is relevant for the evaluation of whether a measure is protectionist or not, and would therefore seek to understand the regulatory intent of the Chilean legislation at hand. To this effect, we would consider questions that the AB did not address, such as:

- Who is burdened by the higher tax? Chile raised this question, but it went unanswered by the plaintiffs and was considered, as mentioned, uninformative by the AB. From what we understand, however, the measure burdened Chilean producers more than it did EC producers;
- What is the alleged policy rationale for the tax differential? For instance, is it to combat alcoholism, or to raise revenue? Absent was an explanation by the respondent of what policy objectives the contested measure was meant to promote.

4.4.5.4 *Concluding Remarks on the Revisit to the Leading Cases*
It stems from this brief discussion that in these leading disputes, from the perspective of Interpretation III, we disagree more with the reasoning by the AB than with actual outcomes.

4.5 Principles
We summarize these findings in the following principles:

§ 1. The Provision Under Which a Protectionism Test Should Be Performed

The protectionism test should be performed primarily under Art. III GATT.

§ 2. The Discipline on Fiscal Instruments in Case of Like Products

Two products are like for the purpose of Art. III.2 GATT if both (i) they are in close actual or potential competition; and (ii) international efficiency requires taxation by the same amount. Like products should be taxed equally, but the level of taxation is unilaterally determined by the importing country.

§ 3. The Discipline on Fiscal Instruments in Case of DCS Products

Two products are DCS for the purpose of Art. III.2 GATT if both (i) they are in close actual or potential competition; and (ii) international efficiency requires higher taxation of the imported product. The taxation of DCS products may differ, but not by more than could be motivated from an international efficiency point of view. The level of taxation is unilaterally determined by the importing country.

REFERENCES

Bagwell, Kyle, and Robert W. Staiger. 2002. *The Economics of the World Trading System*, MIT Press: Cambridge, Mass.
Baldwin, Robert E. 1970. *Non-tariff Distortions in International Trade*, Brookings Institution: Washington, DC.
Bartels, Lorand. 2009. Trade and Human Rights, pp. 571–596 in *Daniel Bethlehem et al. (eds.), The Oxford Handbook of International Trade Law*, Oxford University Press: Oxford, UK.
Bhagwati, Jagdish, and Robert E. Hudec (eds.). 1996. *Fair Trade and Harmonization*, MIT Press: Cambridge, Mass.
Bidwell, Percy W. 1939. *The Invisible Tariff*, Council of Foreign Relations: New York.
Bronckers, Marco CEJ, and Natalie McNelis. 2000. Rethinking the Like Product Definition in GATT 1994, pp. 15–56 in *Marco CEJ Bronckers, A Cross Section of WTO Law*, Cameron May: London, UK.
Brown, Winthrop. 1950. *The United States and the Restoration of World Trade: an Analysis and Appraisal of the ITO Charter and the General Agreement on Tariffs and Trade*, Brookings Institution: Washington, DC.
Capling, Ann. 2001. *Australia and the Global Trade System: from Havana to Seattle*, Cambridge University Press: New York, NY.
Charnovitz, Steve. 1991. Exploring the Environmental Exceptions in GATT Article XX. *Journal of World Trade*, 25: 37–55.
Charnovitz, Steve. 1994. Free Trade, Fair Trade, Green Trade: Defogging the Debate. *Cornell International Law Journal*, 27: 459–525.
Charnovitz, Steve. 1996. New WTO Adjudication and its Implications for the Environment, *BNA International Environmental Reporter*, September 18, 19: 851–856.
Charnovitz, Steve. 1997. The WTO's Alcoholic Beverages Decision, Review of European Community and International Environmental Law, 6: 198–203.
Charnovitz, Steve. 1998. The Moral Exception in Trade Policy, *Virginia Journal of International Law*, 38: 689–732.
Charnovitz, Steve. 2002. The Law of Environmental PPMs in the WTO: Debunking the Myth of Illegality, *Yale Journal of International Law*, 27: 59–109.
Choi, Wong Mong. 2003. *Like Products in International Trade Law*, Oxford University Press: Oxford, UK.
Curzon, Gerard. 1965. *Multilateral Commercial Diplomacy: The General Agreement on Tariffs and Trade and Its Impact on National Commercial Policies and Techniques*, Michael Joseph: London.
Dam, Kenneth W. 1970. *The GATT: Law and International Economic Organization*, University of Chicago Press: Chicago, Illinois.
Davey, William J., and Joost Pauwelyn. 2000. MFN Unconditionality: A Legal Analysis of the Concept in View of its Evolution in the GATT/WTO Jurisprudence with Particular Reference to the Issue of 'Like Product', pp. 13–50 in *Thomas Cottier and Petros C. Mavroidis*

(eds.), *Regulatory Barriers and the Principle of Non-Discrimination in World Trade Law*, University of Michigan Press: Ann Arbor, Michigan.

DiMascio, Nicholas, and Joost Pauwelyn. 2008. Non-Discrimination in Trade and Investment Treaties: Worlds Apart or Two Sides of the Same Coin?, *American Journal of International Law*, 102: 48–89.

Dunoff, Jeff L. 2009. Linking International Markets and Global Justice, *Michigan Law Review*, 107: 1039–1058.

Ehring, Lothar. 2002. De Facto Discrimination in World Trade Law: National and Most Favoured Nation Treatment – or Equal Treatment, *Journal of World Trade*, 36: 921–977.

Feddersen, Christoph T. 1998. Focusing on Substantive Law in International Economic Relations: the Public Morals of GATT's Article XX(a) and 'Conventional' Rules of Interpretation, *Minnesota Journal of Global Trade*, 7: 75–101.

Giri, Shiva, and Michael Trebilcock. 2005. The National Treatment Principle in International Trade Law, pp. 185–238 in *E. Kwan Choi and James C. Hartigan (eds.), Handbook of International Trade*, Vol. II, Blackwell: Oxford, UK.

Hart, Michael (ed.). 1995. *Also Present at the Creation: Dana Wilgress and the United Nations Conference on Trade and Employment at Havana.* Centre for Trade Policy and Law, Carleton University and University of Ottawa: Ottawa.

Hart, Michael. 1998. Fifty Years of Canadian Statecraft: Canada in the GATT 1947–1997, Centre for Trade Policy and Law: Ottawa.

Hawkins, Harry C. 1951. *Commercial Treaties and Agreement Principles and Practice*, Rinehart & Co: New York, NY.

Horn, Henrik. 2006. National Treatment in Trade Agreements. *American Economic Review* 96(1), pp. 394–404.

Horn, Henrik. 2009. The Burden of Proof in National Treatment Disputes and the Environment. Research Institute of Industrial Economics (IFN) Working Paper No. 791.

Horn, Henrik, Giovanni Maggi, and Robert W. Staiger. 2010. Trade Agreements as Endogenously Incomplete Contracts. *American Economic Review*, 100(1), pp. 394–419.

Horn, Henrik, and Petros C. Mavroidis. 2004. Still Hazy After All These Years: the Interpretation of National Treatment in the GATT/WTO Case Law on Tax Discrimination, *European Journal of International Law*, 15: 39–69.

Horn, Henrik, and Petros C. Mavroidis. 2008. The Permissible Reach of National Environmental Policies, *Journal of World Trade*, 42: 1107–1178.

Horn, Henrik, and Petros C. Mavroidis. 2009. Non-Discrimination, pp. 833–839 in *Kenneth A. Reinert, R.S. Rajan, A.J. Glass and L.S. Davis (eds.), Princeton Encyclopedia of the World Economy*, Princeton University Press: Princeton, NJ.

Horn, Henrik, and Joseph H.H. Weiler. 2007. EC – Asbestos, pp. 27–53 in *Henrik Horn, and Petros C. Mavroidis (eds.), The American Law Institute Reporters' Studies on WTO Case Law*, Cambridge University Press: New York, NY.

Howse, Robert L., and Donald Regan. 2000. The Product/Process Distinction – An Illusory Basis for Disciplining "Unilateralism" in Trade Policy, *European Journal of International Law* 11: 249–289.

Howse, Rob, and Elisabeth Tuerk. 2001. The WTO Impact on Internal Regulations – A Case Study of the Canada – EC Asbestos Dispute, pp. 283–328 in *Grainne DeBurca and Elizabeth Scott (eds.), The EU and the WTO: Legal and Constitutional Issues*, Hart Publishing: Oxford, UK.

Hudec, Robert E. 1975. *The GATT Legal System and the World Trade Diplomacy*, Praeger: New York, NY.

Hudec, Robert E. 1988. Tiger, Tiger in the House: A Critical Evaluation of the Case against Discriminatory Trade Measures, pp. 165–210 *in Ernst-Ulrich Petersmann and Meinhard Hilf (eds.), The New GATT Round of Multilateral Trade Negotiations: Legal and Economic Problems*, Kluwer: Deventer, Holland.

Hudec, Robert E. 1993. *Enforcing International Trade Law*, Butterworth: Salem, New Hampshire.

Hudec, Robert E. 1998. GATT/WTO Constraints on National Regulation: Requiem for an 'Aims and Effect' Test, *International Lawyer*, 32: 619.

Hudec, Robert E. 2000. 'Like Product': the Differences in Meaning in GATT Articles I and III, pp. 101–123 in *Thomas Cottier and Petros C. Mavroidis (eds.), Regulatory Barriers and the Principle of Non-Discrimination in World Trade Law*, University of Michigan Press: Ann Arbor, Michigan.

Irwin, Douglas A. 1996. *Against the Tide*, Princeton University Press: Princeton, NJ.

Irwin, Douglas A., Petros C. Mavroidis, and Alan O. Sykes. 2008. *The Genesis of the GATT*, Cambridge University Press: New York, NY.

Jackson, John H. 1967. "The General Agreement on Tariffs and Trade in United States Domestic Law." *Michigan Law Review*, 66: 249–332.

Jackson, John H. 1969. *World Trade and the Law of the GATT*, Bobbs-Merril: Indianapolis, IN.

Jackson, John H. 1989. National Treatment Obligations and Non-Tariff Barriers, *Michigan Journal of International Law*, 10: 198–222.

Jackson, John H. 1998. *The World Trade Organization: Constitution and Jurisprudence.* Chatham House Papers, Royal Institute of International Affairs: London, UK.

Jackson, John H. 2006. *Sovereignty, the WTO, and Changing Fundamentals of International Law.* Cambridge University Press: Cambridge, UK.

Jackson, John H., and Grant Aldonas. 2003. The WTO: Domestic Regulation and the Challenge of Shaping Trade, *The International Lawyer*, 37: 809–813.

Johnson, Harry. 1976. Trade negotiations and the new international monetary system. In: Curzon, G., and V. Curzon (eds.), *Commercial policy issues*, A. W. Sijthoff: Leiden.

Kennedy, Matthew. 2010. When Will the Protocol Amending the TRIPs Agreement Enter into Force? *Journal of International Economic Law*, 13: 459–474.

Lydgate, Emily Barrett. 2011. Consumer Preferences and the National Treatment Principle: Emerging Environmental Regulations Prompt a New Look at an Old Problem, *The World Trade Review*, 10: 165–188.

Mattoo, Aaditya, and Arvind Subramanian. 1998. Regulatory Autonomy and Multilateral Disciplines: the Dilemma and a Possible Resolution, *Journal of International Economic Law*, 1: 303–322.

Mavroidis, Petros C. 2007. *Trade in Goods*, Oxford University Press: Oxford, UK.

Meade, James. 1990. *The Collected Papers of James Meade*, edited by Susan Howson and Donald Moggridge, vol. IV: the Cabinet Office Diary 1944–1946, Unwin Hyman: London, UK.

Meessen, Karl M. 1996. *Extraterritorial Jurisdiction in Theory and Practice*, Kluwer: London.

Melloni, Mattia. 2005. *The Principle of National Treatment in the GATT*, Bruylant: Brussels.

Miller, James N. 2000. Origins of the GATT: British Resistance to American Multilateralism, *Cambridge University, Jerome Levy Economics Institute at Bard College*, Working Paper No. 318.

Ortino, Federico. 2003. *Basic Legal Instruments for the Liberalization of Trade: a Comparison of EC and WTO Law*, Hart Publishing, Oxford, UK.

Palmeter, David N. 1993. Environment and Trade: Much Ado About Little? *Journal of World Trade*, 27: 55–65.

Palmeter, David N. 1999. National Sovereignty and the World Trade Organization, *Journal of World Intellectual Property*, 2: 77–94.

Petersmann, Ernst-Ulrich. 2002. Constitutionalism and WTO Law: from a State-Centered Approach Towards a Human Rights Approach in International Economic Law, pp. 32–67 in *Daniel L.M. Kennedy and James D. Southwick (eds.), The Political Economy of International Trade Law, Essays in Honor of Robert E. Hudec*, Cambridge University Press: Cambridge, UK.

Porges, Amelia, and Joel Trachtman. 2003. Robert Hudec and Domestic Regulation: The Resurrection of Aim and Effects, *Journal of World Trade*, 37: 783–799.

Regan, Donald H. 2002. Regulatory Purpose and 'Like Products' in Article III:4 of the GATT (With Additional Remarks on Article II:2), *Journal of World Trade*, 36: 443–478.

Regan, Donald H. 2003. The Dormant Commerce Clause and the Hormones Problem, pp. 91–117 in *Thomas Cottier and Petros C. Mavroidis (eds.), The Role of the Judge in International Trade Regulation: Experience and Lessons for the WTO*, University of Michigan Press: Ann Arbor, Michigan.

Robbins, Lionel. 1971. *Autobiography of an Economist*, Macmillan: London and New York.

Roessler, Frieder. 1996. Diverging Domestic Policies and Multilateral Trade Integration, pp. 21–56 in *Jagdish Bhagwati, and Robert E. Hudec (eds.), Fair Trade and Harmonization, vol. 2: Legal Analysis*, Cambridge University Press: Cambridge, UK.

Staiger, Robert, W. 1995. "International Rules and Institutions for Trade Policy." In *Grossman, Gene M. and Kenneth Rogoff (eds.), The Handbook of International Economics, vol. 3*. North-Holland: Amsterdam.

Staiger, Robert, W., and Alan O. Sykes. 2011. International Trade, National Treatment and Domestic Regulation, *The Journal of Legal Studies*, 40: 149–203.

Sykes, Alan O. 1999. Regulatory Protectionism and the Law of International Trade, *University of Chicago Law Review*, 66: 1–46.

Sykes, Alan O. 2003. The Least Restrictive Means, *University of Chicago Law Review*, 70: 403–419.

Trebilcock, Michael, and Michael Fishbein. 2007. International Trade: Barriers to Trade, pp. 1–61 in *Andrew T. Guzman, and Alan O. Sykes (eds.), Research Handbook International Economic Law*, Elgar Publishing: Cheltenham, UK.

Toye, Richard. 2003. The Attlee Government, the Imperial Preference System, and the Creation of the GATT. *English Historical Review* 68: 912–939.

Verhoosel, Gäetan. 2002. *National Treatment and WTO Dispute Settlement*, Hart Publishing: Oxford, UK.

Wilcox, Clair. 1949. *A Charter for World Trade*, Macmillan: New York, NY.

Wilgress, Leolyn Dana. 1967. *Memoirs*. Ryerson Press: Toronto.

Yavitz, Laura. 2002. The WTO Appellate Body Report EC – Measures Affecting Asbestos and Asbestos-Containing Products, *Minnesota Journal of Global Trade*, 11: 35–65.

Zeiler, Thomas W. 1999. *Free Trade, Free World: the Advent of the GATT*, The University of North Carolina Press: Chapel Hill, NC.

Appendix

Table 1: *NT Disputes Adjudicated Under the GATT*[1]

No.	Dispute	DS No.	Subject matter	Result	Report adopted
1)	Pakistan v. India: Tax Rebates on Exports (III.2)	2 – 24 Aug. 1948	Denial of rebates affected all of Pakistan's imports from India	India eliminated discrimination as part of broader settlement involving other trade problems.	YES
2)	France v. Brazil: Internal Taxes (III.2)	4 – 25 April 1949	Brazil's raise of taxes applied to many imports	In 1950, Brazil agreed to request corrective legislation. The tax discrimination was entirely terminated on 14 August 1957 as part of major tariffs revision.	YES
3)	Netherlands v. United Kingdom: Purchase Tax Exemptions (III.2)	12 – 26 Oct. 1950	Claim that purchase tax that provided exemptions for certain domestic products, but not for 'like' foreign products, violated III.2	Differential treatment of foreign products abolished in 1952.	YES
4)	Norway & Denmark v. Belgium: Family Allowances (III.2)	14 – 19 Sep. 1951	Claim that grants of exemptions from internal tax to products of some countries but not others were violations of Art. I and was not excused by PPA reservation for existing legislation	Entire tax abolished on 6 March 1954.	YES

(continued)

Table 1 (*continued*)

No.	Dispute	DS No.	Subject matter	Result	Report adopted
5)	France v. Greece: Special Import Taxes (III.2)	19 – 27 Sep. 1952	Claim that new tax on imports was either internal tax contrary to III.2, or a border charge contrary to II	Tax eliminated on 9 April 1953.	YES
6)	Italy v. Greece: Luxury Tax on Imports (III.2)	30 – 5 Oct. 1954	Claim that certain internal taxes applicable only to imports violated III	Discrimination in internal taxes was eliminated. Undertaking made to restore tariffs to bound rates.	YES
7)	Australia v. US: Hawaiian Regulations Affecting Imported Eggs (III.4)	36 – 28 Sep. 1955	Claim that regulation of Hawaiian territorial government requiring merchants to display 'We sell foreign eggs' sign violated III.4 and was not justified under rule-of-origin provisions of IX	Regulation invalidated, on ground that as a matter of US internal law, GATT obligations are binding upon territory of Hawaii, and that a measure violated art. III.4.	YES
8)	United Kingdom v. Italy: Turnover Tax on Pharmaceutical Products (III.2)	37 – 11 Oct. 1955	Claim that internal tax rate on imported pharmaceutical products violated III.2	Italy undertook to lower the rate on imported pharmaceuticals to 5%.	YES
9)	US v. France: Auto Taxes (III.2)	40 – 12 Sep. 1956	Claim that auto tax structure based on horsepower/weight formula ('fiscal horsepower') resulted in significantly greater tax on certain foreign autos, which constituted violation of III.2	No change in French practice. (In 1986 the ECJ ruled that the fiscal horsepower formula violated 95 EC Treaty by affording indirect protection to French producers.)	NO
10)	Netherlands v. Germany (III.2)	41 – 23 Oct. 1956	Claim that formula for computing German turn-over tax on printing work done in foreign country (Netherlands) resulted in higher tax charges that discriminated against foreign printing, in violation of III.2	Outcome not known	YES

No.	Dispute	DS No.	Subject matter	Result	Report adopted
11)	US v. Chile: Auto Taxes (III.2)	44 – 16 Nov. 1956	Claim that a new law imposing a sharply graduated tax on autos impaired value of tariffs concessions by placing significantly heavier burden on US autos	Problem rectified to US satisfaction by new legislation.	YES
12)	UK v. Italy: Discrimination Against Imported Agricultural Machinery (III.4)	46 – 29 July 1957	Claim that law granting buyers more favorable loan terms for purchase of domestic machinery violated III.4	Settled by undertaking to allow law to expire.	YES
13) 14)	Germany v. Greece: Discrimination in Credit Facilities for Imported Goods (III.4)	47 – 19– 23 Sep. 1957	Claim that Greece discriminated against imported goods in credit facilities made available to buyers, apparently claiming violation of III.4	Not reported.	CONSUL-TATIONS
15)	UK v. France: Discrimination Against Imported Agricultural Machinery (III.4)	48 – 3 Oct. 1957	Claim that subsidy to purchasers of domestic machinery violated III.4	Subsidy restored for foreign products.	YES
16)	Austria v. Italy: Measures in Favor of Domestic Productions of Ships Plates (III.4)	52 – 9 Oct. 1958	Claim that tax remission granted only to firms purchasing domestic product violated GATT	Tax remission extended in May 1961 to firms using any foreign products.	YES
17)	US v. Italy: Administrative and Statistical Fees (III.2)	60 – 1 Dec. 1969	Claim that service fee on import entries (…) violated III.2 by failing to provide National treatment to imports	A Presidential report to the US Congress for 1970 reported that the proposed law had been enacted by the Italian Senate and was expected to pass the House of Delegates and enter into force in January 1971.	YES

(continued)

Table 1 (*continued*)

No.	Dispute	DS No.	Subject matter	Result	Report adopted
18)	US v. EC: Measures on Animal Feed Proteins (III.2 and III.4)	78 – 27 April 1976	Claim that regulation requiring sellers of certain animal feed proteins, of which 85% were imports, to purchase specified quantities of domestic milk powder was an internal QR in violation of (…) III.2 and III.4	According to the panel report, the EC measures had been expressly limited to a short duration and terminated for internal reasons on 25 October 1976, before the panel had even met. They had been in force for only six months.	YES
19)	US v. Spain: Measures Concerning Domestic Sale of Soybean Oil (III.4)	91 – 1 Nov. 1979	Claim that internal restrictions on the sale of soybean oil (…) were contrary to III.4 because they failed to impose similar burdens on other vegetable oils that were 'like products' …	In seeking to overturn the panel report, the US announced that it was withdrawing its complaint against Spain – so that governments voting to reject the panel rulings would not be voting to find Spain in violation.	CONSUL-TATIONS
20)	US v. Japan: Restraints on Imports of Manufactured Tobacco (III.2 and III.4)	92 – 8 Nov. 1979	Claim that practices of state trading monopoly violated Art. III	Japan agreed, inter alia, to repel an internal tax on imported cigars, to make substantial reductions in the tariffs on cigarettes, cigars, and pipe tobacco, to expand the number of retailers allowed to sell foreign tobacco products, and to permit advertising of foreign tobacco products, in Japanese-language media.	YES

No.	Dispute	DS No.	Subject matter	Result	Report adopted
21)	US V. EC: 'Spin-Chill' Requirements on Imports of Poultry (III.4)	97 – 19 June 1980	Standards Code Complaint: Claim that standards for processing and production methods were subject to code's basic obligations via Code Section 14.25, and application of new processing standards to imports but not domestic products violated National treatment obligation of Code Section 2.1	According to US sources, the problem disappeared when US suppliers found it easy to comply with the new process, and so asked the US government to withdraw complaint.	CONSUL-TATIONS
22)	US v. Canada: Administration of the Foreign Investment Review Act (FIRA) (III.4)	108 – 26 March 1982	Claim that administrative practice of using foreign investment controls to promote undertakings by foreign investors to purchase domestic goods violates III.4 …	On 5–6 November, Canada informed the Council that it had fully complied with the ruling.	YES
23)	EC v. Finland: Internal Regulations Having an Effect on Imports of Certain Parts of Footwear (III.4)	116 – 28 Sep. 1982	Claim that III.4 violated by Finnish regulation requiring that only shoes with soles of domestic origin could be exported to USSR; regulation constituted less favorable treatment for imported soles	In July 1984, EC informed GATT Secretariat that, while bilateral consultations were still continuing, dispute could be removed from GATT agenda. Not known whether Finland's export regulation ever changed.	CONSUL-TATIONS
24)	South Africa v. Canada: Discriminatory Application of Retail Sales Tax on Gold Coins (III.2)	132 – 3 July 1984	Claim that a provincial government tax on sales of gold coins, which exempted Canadian gold coins from tax, discriminated against imported gold coins in a manner inconsistent with the requirements of II and III	Within a month of the panel ruling, the Province of Ontario announced its intention to remove the tax discrimination, and the change became effective in January 1986.	YES

(*continued*)

Table 1 (*continued*)

No.	Dispute	DS No.	Subject matter	Result	Report adopted
25)	EC v. Canada: Import, Distribution and Sale of Alcoholic Drinks by Provincial Marketing Authorities (III.2 and III.4)	139 – 12 Feb. 1985	Claim that trading practices of Canadian Provincial liquor boards were inconsistent with GATT provisions	Canada agreed to roughly the same liberalization granted to US.	YES
26)	Mexico, Canada and EC v. US: Taxes on Petroleum and Certain Imported Substances (Superfund) (III.2)	152 – 27 Oct. 1986	Claim that border tax adjustment on imported petroleum violated III.2 because it was higher than the internal tax on like domestic products. (also other claims under III.2)	In December 1989 the US Congress amended the Superfund legislation to equalize the tax on imported and domestic products.	YES
27)	EC v. Japan: Restrictions on Alcoholic Beverages (III.2)	154 – 5 Nov. 1986	Claim that tax system involving classification of alcoholic beverages into complex categories with substantially different rates for each category violated III.2	Japan abolished its ad valorem tax on the beverages affected by this ruling, its tax based on extract content, and its 'grading system' used for classification.	YES
28)	EC v. US: Tax Reform Legislation for Passenger Aircraft (III.4)	160 – 9 April 1987	Claim that tax advantage granted only to buyers of certain US-produced aircrafts violated III.4	None called for. Measure had expired.	NO
29)	EC v. US: Section 337 of the Tariff Act of 1930 ('Aramid Fibres Case') (III.4)	162 – 29 April 1987	Claim that special section '337' procedure for enforcing patent infringement claims against imported goods violated III.4 because special procedure was less favorable than procedure applicable to patent claims involving domestic goods	US indicated that compliance would be delayed until, and conditioned upon, the outcome of the Uruguay Round negotiations on intellectual property rights.	YES

No.	Dispute	DS No.	Subject matter	Result	Report adopted
30)	Canada v. US: Section 337 Action on Cellular Mobile Telephones (III.4)	167 – 15 Sep. 1987	Claim that special section 337 procedure for enforcing patent infringement claims against imported goods violated III.4 because special procedure was less favorable than court procedure applicable to domestic goods	Section 337 proceeding was terminated by consent of both parties.	YES
31)	US v. EC: Directive on Third-Country Meat Imports (III.4)	168 – 25 Sep. 1987	Claim that health requirements, which applied to imports but not to domestic products, violated III.4	In April 1988 the EC published a list of US firms found to qualify under the Directive. All or most US export firms qualified.	YES
32)	Chile v. US: Quality Standards for Grapes (III.4)	178 – 22 April 1988	Claim that law authorizing inspection of Chilean grapes at port of entry into US while Mexican suppliers were allowed inspection at point of origin in Mexico, violated I and III	No change was made in US marketing order regime.	NO
33)	US v. EC: Payments and Subsidies on Oilseeds and Animal-Feed Proteins (III.4)	179 – 22 April 1988	Claim that subsidy payments made to EC processors for processing EC oilseeds, but not foreign oilseeds, violated III.4	On 20 November 1992, the parties announced a settlement, involving both an agreement to limitations on EC soybean production and a broad agreement on the key elements of the Uruguay Round agricultural agreement then under negotiation.	CONSUL-TATIONS/ MAS

(continued)

Table 1 (*continued*)

No.	Dispute	DS No.	Subject matter	Result	Report adopted
34)	Japan v. EC: Antidumping Regulation on Imports of Parts and Components ('Screwdriver Assembly' Case) (III.4)	188 – 8 Aug. 1988	AD duties not authorized by VI or XX(d) GATT, thus violated III	In agreeing to adoption of the report, the EC undertook to comply with the report, but stated it would defer compliance until implementation of yet-to-be-determined results of Uruguay Round negotiations on the Antidumping code.	YES
35)	EC v. Chile: Internal taxes on Spirits (III.2)	207 – 8 Nov. 1989	Claim that differential in sale taxes on substitutable products violated III.1 and III.2	Not yet known. According to EC sources, the complaint was frozen for the duration of the Uruguay Round, but not abandoned.	CONSUL-TATIONS

[1] *Source:* Hudec (1993).

Table 2: *NT Disputes Adjudicated Under the WTO*[2]

No.	Dispute	DS No.	Subject matter	Report by[3]	Result
36)	EC v. Japan: Taxes on Alcoholic Beverages (Japan–Alcoholic Beverages II) (III.2)	8	Internal taxes on certain alcoholic beverages pursuant to the Liquor Tax Law	AB	Japanese Liquor Tax Law is inconsistent with GATT Article III.2.
37)	Canada v. Japan: Taxes on Alcoholic Beverages (Japan–Alcoholic Beverages II) (III.2)	10	Internal taxes on certain alcoholic beverages pursuant to the Liquor Tax Law	AB	Japanese Liquor Tax Law is inconsistent with GATT Article III.2.
38)	US v. Japan: Taxes on Alcoholic Beverages (Japan–Alcoholic Beverages II) (III.2)	11	Internal taxes on certain alcoholic beverages pursuant to the Liquor Tax Law	AB	Japanese Liquor Tax Law is inconsistent with GATT Article III.2.
39)	EC v. Japan: Measures affecting the purchase of telecommunications equipment (III.4)	15	The agreement between US and Japan regarding telecommunications	P	Although there has been no official notification, the case appears to have been settled bilaterally.
40)	Japan v. Brazil: Certain automotive investment measures (III.4)	51	Automotive investment measures incl. dom. content requirements, trade balancing requirements	P	No panel established.
41)	EC v. Indonesia: Certain measures affecting the automobile industry (Indonesia–Autos) (III.2, III.4)	54	National Car Program	P	The Panel found that Indonesia was in violation of Articles I and II.2 of GATT 1994, Article 2 of the TRIMs Agreement, Article 5(c) of the SCM Agreement, but was not in violation of Article 28.2 of the SCM Agreement.
42)	Japan v. Indonesia: Certain measures affecting the automobile industry (Indonesia–Autos) (III.2, III.4)	55	National Car Program	P	The Panel found that Indonesia was in violation of Articles I and II.2 of GATT 1994, Article 2 of the TRIMs Agreement, Article 5(c) of the SCM Agreement, but was not in violation of Article 28.2 of the SCM Agreement.

(continued)

Table 2 (*continued*)

No.	Dispute	DS No.	Subject matter	Report by[3]	Result
43)	US v. Indonesia: Certain measures affecting the automobile industry (Indonesia–Autos) (III.2, III.4)	59	National Car Program	P	The Panel found that Indonesia was in violation of Articles I and II.2 of GATT 1994, Article 2 of the TRIMs Agreement, Article 5(c) of the SCM Agreement, but was not in violation of Article 28.2 of the SCM Agreement.
44)	US v. Brazil: Certain measures affecting trade and investment in the automotive sector (III.4)	65	Discriminatory tariffs, domestic content requirements, trade balancing requirements, local content requirements	P	No panel established.
45)	EC v. Korea: taxes on Alcoholic Beverages (Korea–Alcoholic Beverages) (III.2)	75	Internal taxes imposed by Korea on certain alcoholic beverages	AB	Korea had violated Article III.2 of GATT 1994.
46)	EC v. Brazil: Certain measures affecting trade and investment in the automotive sector (III.4)	81	Discriminatory tariffs, domestic content requirements, trade balancing requirements, local content requirements		No panel established.
47)	US v. Korea: taxes on Alcoholic Beverages (Korea–Alcoholic Beverages) (III.2)	84	Internal taxes imposed by Korea on certain alcoholic beverages	AB	Korea had violated Article III.2 of GATT 1994.
48)	EC v. Chile: Taxes on Alcoholic Beverages (Chile–Alcoholic Beverages) (III.2)	87	Special Sales Tax on Spirits	AB	Chile's Transitional System and its New System for taxation of distilled alcoholic beverages was inconsistent with Article III.2 of GATT 1994.
49)	EC v. US: Tax Treatment for 'Foreign Sales Corporations' (US–FSC) (III.4)	108	Special Tax Treatment for FSCs	AB	The Appellate Body upheld the Panel's finding that the so-called "fair market value rule" under the ETI Act accorded less favourable treatment to imported products than to like US domestic products in violation of Art. III.4 by providing a "considerable impetus" to use domestic products over imported products for the tax benefit under the ETI Act.

No.	Dispute	DS No.	Subject matter	Report by[3]	Result
50)	US v. Chile: Taxes on Alcoholic Beverages (III.2)	109	Internal taxes on certain alcoholic beverages	P	The US contended that this differential treatment of imported spirits violates Article III.2 of GATT 1994.
51)	EC v. Chile Taxes on Alcoholic Beverages (Chile–Alcoholic Beverages) (III.2)	110	Additional tax on alcoholic beverages	AB	Chile's Transitional System and its New System for taxation of distilled alcoholic beverages was inconsistent with Article III.2 of GATT 1994.
52)	EC v. US: Antidumping Act 1916 (US–1916 Act) (III.4)	136	US Antidumping Act 1916	AB	Claim under conditions. Conditions not fulfilled.
53)	Japan v. Canada: Certain automotive industry measures (Canada–Autos) (III.4)	139	Automotive industry measures	AB	The Panel judged the application of the CVA requirements to be inconsistent with Article III.4 of GATT 1994.
54)	EC v. Canada: Certain measures affecting the automotive industry (Canada–Autos) (III.4)	142	Measures affecting the automotive sector	AB	The Panel judged the application of the CVA requirements to be inconsistent with Article III.4 of GATT 1994.
55)	EC v. Argentina: Measures affecting the export of bovine hides and the import of finished leather (Argentina–Hides and Leather) (III.2)	155	Export prohibition on raw and semi-tanned bovine hides, "additional VAT" on the import of products, "advance turnover tax"	P	Argentine tax inconsistent with III.2.
56)	US v. EC: Protection of trademarks and geographical indications for agricultural products and foodstuffs (EC–Trademarks and Geographical Indications) (III.4)	174	Protection of trademarks and geographical indications for agricultural products and foodstuffs	P	Regulation found to be inconsistent with III.4.

(*continued*)

Table 2 (*continued*)

No.	Dispute	DS No.	Subject matter	Report by[3]	Result
57)	US v. Philippines: Measures affecting trade and investment in the motor vehicle sector (Philippines–Motor Vehicles) (III.4)	195	Certain Measures in the Motor Vehicle Development Program		Panel established, not yet composed.
58)	Hungary v. Romania: Import Prohibition on Wheat and Wheat Flour (III.4)	240	Decree prohibiting the import of wheat and wheat flour which does not meet certain quality requirements		Withdrew request for establishment of panel.
59)	Brazil v. US: Equalizing excise tax imposed by Florida on processed orange and grapefruit Products (US–Florida Excise Tax) (III.2, III.4)	250	Equalizing Excise Tax		MAS.[4]
60)	Canada v. EC: Measures affecting the approval and marketing of biotech products (EC–Approval and Marketing of Biotech Products) (III.4)	292	Measures affecting the approval and marketing of products that contain, consist of, or are produced from, genetically modified organisms	P	Judicial Economy.
61)	Honduras v. Dominican Republic: Measures Affecting the Importation of Cigarettes (III.2, III.4)	300	Selective Consumption Tax, stamps to be affixed, bond as a prerequisite to importing		No panel established.
62)	Korea v. EC: Measures Affecting Trade in Commercial Vessels (EC–Commercial Vessels) (III.4)	301	Subsidies in favor of commercial vessels	P	Regarding the claim of Korea under Article III.4 of the GATT 1994, the Panel found that the subsidies authorized under the TDM Regulation were covered by the notion of "the payment of subsidies exclusively to domestic producers" in Article III.8(b) of the GATT 1994, and thus were not "prevented" by Article III.

No.	Dispute	DS No.	Subject matter	Report by[3]	Result
63)	Honduras v. Dominican Republic: Measures affecting the importation and internal sale of cigarettes (Dominican Republic–Import and Sale of Cigarettes) (III.2, III.4)	302	Rules, procedures, and administrative practices to determine the value of imported cigarettes for the purpose of applying the Selective Consumption Tax; stamps be affixed to cigarette packages; bond pursuant to imports	AB	Stamp requirement and bond requirement to be inconsistent with III.4; Selective consumption tax inconsistent with III.2, first sentence.
64)	US v. Mexico: Tax Measures on Soft Drinks and Other Beverages (Mexico–Taxes on Soft Drinks) (III.2, III.4)	308	Soft drinks and other beverages that use any sweetener other than cane sugar	AB	Soft drink tax and distribution tax to be inconsistent with III.2 and III.4.
65)	EC v. US: Measures Affecting Trade in Large Civil Aircraft (US–Large Civil Aircraft) (III.4)	317	US subsidies to Boeing	P	Second Complaint.
66)	EC v. Brazil: Measures Affecting Imports of Retreaded Tires (Brazil–Retreaded Tires) (III.4)	332	Import ban on retreaded and used tires	AB	The measure maintained by the Brazilian State of Rio Grande do Sul in respect of retreaded tyres, Law 12.114, as amended by Law 12.381, was inconsistent with Art. III.4.
67)	US v. Turkey: Measures affecting the importation of rice (Turkey–Rice) (III.4)	334	Import licenses for rice	P	Turkey's requirement that importers must purchase domestic rice, in order to be allowed to import rice at reduced-tariff levels under the tariff quotas, accorded less favorable treatment to imported rice than that accorded to like domestic rice, in a manner inconsistent with Article III.4 of the GATT 1994.

(continued)

Table 2 (*continued*)

No.	Dispute	DS No.	Subject matter	Report by[3]	Result
68)	EC v. China: Measures affecting import of automobile parts (China–Auto Parts) (III.2, III.4)	339	Measures affecting Imports	AB	Measures to be inconsistent with III.2 and III.4.
69)	US v. China: Measures affecting import of automobile parts (China–Auto Parts) (III.2, III.4)	340	Measures affecting Imports	AB	Measures to be inconsistent with III.2 and III.4.
70)	Canada v. China: Measures affecting import of automobile parts (China–Auto Parts) (III.2, III.4)	342	Measures affecting Imports	AB	Measures to be inconsistent with III.2 and III.4.
71)	US v. EC – Measures Affecting Trade in Large Civil Aircraft (III.4)	347	Measures affecting trade in Large Civil Aircrafts		A panel was composed, but its authority lapsed in 2006.
72)	EC v. India – Measures Affecting the Importation and Sale of Wines and Spirits from the EC (III.4)	352	Measures Affecting the Importation and Sale of Wines and Spirits		A panel was composed, but its authority lapsed in 2008.
73)	EC v. US – Measures Affecting Trade in Large Civil Aircraft (III.4)	353	Measures affecting trade in Large Civil Aircrafts	AB	Partially adopted.
74)	EC v. Canada – Tax Exemptions and Reductions for Wine and Beer (III.2, III.4)	354	Tax Exemptions and Reductions for Wine and Beer		MAS.
75)	US v. China – Certain Measures Granting Refunds, Reductions or Exemptions from Taxes and other Payments (III.4)	358	Tax Exemptions, Refunds, and other Payments to Chinese Enterprises to purchase Domestic goods instead of Imported		MAS.

No.	Dispute	DS No.	Subject matter	Report by[3]	Result
76)	Mexico v. China – Certain Measures Granting Refunds, Reductions or Exemptions from Taxes and other Payments (III.4)	359	Tax Exemptions, Refunds, and other Payments to Chinese Enterprises to purchase Domestic goods instead of Imported		MAS.
77)	US v. India – Additional and Extra – Additional Duties on Imports from the US (III.2, III.4)	360	Two border charges, consisting of the "Additional Duty" and "Extra-Additional Duty" on imports	AB	Judicial Economy.
78)	US v. China – Measures Affecting Trading Rights and Distribution Services for Certain Publications and Audiovisual Entertainment Products (III.4)	363	Restricted Trading Rights and Distribution Services for Certain Publications and Audiovisual Entertainment Products	AB	Measure to be inconsistent with XX(a) and III.4 of GATT and XVI and XVII of GATS.
79)	Canada v. EC – Certain Measures Prohibiting the Importation and Marketing of Seal Products (III.4)	369	Measures Prohibiting the Importation and Marketing of Seal Products		Panel not yet established.
80)	Philippines v. Thailand – Customs and Fiscal Measures on Cigarettes from the Philippines	371	Various Customs and Fiscal Measures on Cigarettes	AB	AB found Thailand violates its obligations by exempting only resellers of domestic cigarettes from obligation to pay VAT.
81)	EC v. India – Certain taxes and other Measures on Imported Wines and Spirits	380	Discriminatory Taxation on Imported Wines and Spirits		Panel not yet established.
82)	Canada v. US – Certain Country of Origin Labeling (COOL) Requirements	384	Certain Country of Origin Labeling (COOL) Requirements on Beef and Pork and COOL Implementation	P	Measure to be inconsistent with 2.1 and 2.2 of TBT and X.3(a) of GATT 1994 and Judicial Economy on Art. III.4 of GATT.

(*continued*)

Table 2 (*continued*)

No.	Dispute	DS No.	Subject matter	Report by[3]	Result
83)	US v. China – Grants, Loans and other incentives	387	Grants, Loans, and other incentives to Chinese Enterprises that are related to their Export Performance		Panel not yet established.
84)	Mexico v. China – Grants, Loans and other incentives	388	Grants, Loans, and other incentives to Chinese Enterprises that are related to their Export Performance		Panel not yet established.
85)	Guatemala v. China – Grants, Loans and other incentives	390	Grants, Loans, and other incentives to Chinese Enterprises that are related to their Export Performance		Panel not yet established.
86)	Philippines–Distilled Spirits	396	Discriminatory Taxation on Imported Distilled Spirits	AB	Philippines violates its obligations by taxing spirits made of cane sugar (predominantly produced in the home market) lower than spirits made of nondesignated goods (predominantly produced abroad).

[2] *Source:* Mavroidis & Horn, World Bank Database, 2011 (available at www.worldbank.org/trade/wtodisputes).
[3] AB denotes Appellate Body Report, P denotes Panel Report.
[4] MAS stands for mutually agreed solution.

Index

Printed in the United States
by Baker & Taylor Publisher Services

Printed in the United States
by Baker & Taylor Publisher Services